ADVANCES IN

# EXPERIMENTAL
# SOCIAL PSYCHOLOGY

VOLUME 15

## CONTRIBUTORS TO VOLUME 15

Leonard Berkowitz

Walter H. Crockett

Ed Donnerstein

Joseph P. Forgas

John M. Levine

Neil M. Malamuth

Richard L. Moreland

Barry R. Schlenker

ADVANCES IN

# Experimental
# Social Psychology

EDITED BY

## Leonard Berkowitz

DEPARTMENT OF PSYCHOLOGY
UNIVERSITY OF WISCONSIN—MADISON
MADISON, WISCONSIN

VOLUME 15

 1982

ACADEMIC PRESS
A Subsidiary of Harcourt Brace Jovanovich, Publishers
New York    London
Paris   San Diego   San Francisco   São Paulo   Sydney   Tokyo   Toronto

ACADEMIC PRESS, INC.
111 Fifth Avenue, New York, New York 10003

*United Kingdom Edition published by*
ACADEMIC PRESS, INC. (LONDON) LTD.
24/28 Oval Road, London NW1 7DX

LIBRARY OF CONGRESS CATALOG CARD NUMBER: 64–23452

ISBN 0–12–015215–0

PRINTED IN THE UNITED STATES OF AMERICA

82 83 84 85    9 8 7 6 5 4 3 2 1

# CONTENTS

v

## Socialization in Small Groups: Temporal Changes in Individual–Group Relations

### Richard L. Moreland and John M. Levine

## Translating Actions into Attitudes: An Identity-Analytic Approach to the Explanation of Social Conduct

### Barry R. Schlenker

## Aversive Conditions as Stimuli to Aggression

### Leonard Berkowitz

# CONTRIBUTORS

Numbers in parentheses indicate the pages on which the authors' contributions begin.

Leonard Berkowitz, *Department of Psychology, University of Wisconsin—Madison, Madison, Wisconsin 53706* (249)

Walter H. Crockett, *Department of Psychology, University of Kansas, Lawrence, Kansas 66045* (1)

Ed Donnerstein, *Department of Communication Arts, University of Wisconsin—Madison, Madison, Wisconsin* (103)

Joseph P. Forgas, *School of Psychology, University of New South Wales, Kensington 2033, Sydney, New South Wales, Australia* (59)

John M. Levine, *Department of Psychology, University of Pittsburgh, Pittsburgh, Pennsylvania 15260* (137)

Neil M. Malamuth,[1] *Psychology Department, University of Manitoba, Winnipeg, Manitoba R3T 2N2, Canada* (103)

Richard L. Moreland, *Department of Psychology, University of Pittsburgh, Pittsburgh, Pennsylvania 15260* (137)

Barry R. Schlenker, *Department of Psychology, University of Florida, Gainesville, Florida 32611* (193)

[1]Present address: Department of Communication, 232 Royce Hall, University of California, Los Angeles, Los Angeles, California 90024.

# BALANCE, AGREEMENT, AND POSITIVITY IN THE COGNITION OF SMALL SOCIAL STRUCTURES[1]

## Walter H. Crockett

DEPARTMENT OF PSYCHOLOGY
UNIVERSITY OF KANSAS
LAWRENCE, KANSAS

[1]Research for this paper was supported in part by Biomedical Sciences Support Grant #RR7037 from the University of Kansas.

ADVANCES IN EXPERIMENTAL SOCIAL
PSYCHOLOGY, VOL. 15

# I.  Introduction

## A.  BALANCE, AGREEMENT, AND POSITIVITY AS CONCEPTUAL RULES

A conceptual rule is an a priori principle that can be used to organize the relations among a set of objects. Conceptual rules serve as cognitive schemata (Neisser, 1976), which permit a perceiver to anticipate the patterns of relationship that are likely to occur among a set of objects. The term *conceptual rule* was chosen over *schema* for the present case in order to draw attention to the logical aspects of the schemata—balance, agreement, and positivity—that will be the focus of the present article. The emphasis will be on how those rules are applied in perceiving and thinking about the relations among small sets of people and impersonal entities. The logical properties of the three rules will first be sketched out, then a considerable body of research will be reviewed to discern whether and how the rules are actually employed in social cognition.

## B.  INFERENTIAL RULES COMPARED TO ORIENTING RULES

It is convenient to distinguish two types of conceptual rules, inferential rules and orienting rules. An *inferential rule* prescribes the inferences that follow from a set of information. It allows a perceiver to draw more or less extensive inferences from a limited amount of information. Balance, agreement, and positivity are all inferential rules. An *orienting rule* focuses the perceiver's attention upon one type of information or another, or states some general principle about how to deal with information. "Pay special attention to interpersonal relations" and "Make as few changes as possible" are examples of orienting rules. Our attention will be restricted largely to inferential rules.

## C.  SENTIMENTS, ATTITUDES, AND UNIT RELATIONS

The inferential rules of concern here apply to three broad classes of relations: sentiments, attitudes, and unit relations.

A *sentiment* is an orientation of attraction or repulsion held by one person toward another person. Most commonly, *like–dislike* will be used as the concrete example of a sentiment.

An *attitude* is an orientation of attraction or repulsion held by a person toward an action, a policy, a hypothetical event, a tangible object, or any other impersonal entity. As the terms are used here, the distinction between a sentiment and an attitude is that the former is directed toward another person, the latter toward an impersonal entity.

The term *unit relation* was used by Heider (1958 pp. 177–180, 200–210) to denote any condition under which two entities are perceived as belonging together. In what follows, a unit relation will usually denote such relations as ownership, kinship, common group membership, or frequent association.

Fritz Heider (1946, 1958) was the first psychologist to examine systematically the inferential properties that perceivers apply to sentiments, attitudes, and unit relations. He described the formal properties of the balance rule. Subsequently, two other inferential rules—positivity and source/target generalization—and a variety of orienting rules were identified by others, especially by Zajonc and his associates (Zajonc, 1968; Zajonc & Burnstein, 1965a; Zajonc & Sherman, 1967; Rubin & Zajonc, 1969).

## D. FOCUS OF THE PRESENT ARTICLE

The purposes of this article are (1) to describe the formal logical properties of positivity, agreement, and balance; (2) to review the literature on how the rules affect the cognition of interpersonal relations; and (3) to outline a theoretical approach that accounts for the effects of these rules upon social cognition. We shall be mainly concerned with the effects of these rules upon (1) the inferences that people draw about incomplete patterns of relations and (2) the learning and recall of relations in small social structures.

It is important, as well, to identify the topics that will not be covered systematically. First, this article will not dwell long upon how the rules are reflected in perceivers' reactions of pleasure or displeasure to patterns of relations in small social groups. As will be pointed out below, cognitive expectations about situations follow different rules from affective responses to those situations; the present concern is with cognition, not affect.

Second, the article will be only minimally concerned with research into attitude change. Balance theory, like other consistency theories, has direct implications for the development and change of attitudes. However, the present concern is with the perception and cognition of small social structures, not with long-term attitudes and beliefs of the perceivers.

Third, the article will not deal with theoretical positions—such as Abelson's (1968, 1973) concept of implicational molecules or Gollob's (1974b) S–V–O theory—which are concerned with more complex kinds of relations than the ones dealt with here. No doubt it will be essential in the long run to extend our theoretical analysis of the principles that underlie the cognition of social relations to processes which go beyond the like–dislike relations embodied in sentiments and attitudes. But the present aim is more circumscribed, namely, to examine only the perception and cognition of social patterns that are organized around sentiments, attitudes, and unit relations.

Finally, this article will not deal with applications of balance theory to the objective patterns of relations in complex organizations or in simple ones. The present concern is with relations as they are perceived, not as they occur in fact.

## II.  The Logical Properties Assumed by Balance, Agreement, and Positivity

### A.  SYMMETRY[2] AND OTHER GENERAL PROPERTIES OF SENTIMENTS, ATTITUDES, AND UNIT RELATIONS

Heider (1946, 1958) proposed that perceivers operate as if sentiments and unit relations are *symmetric*. This means that when person A likes, dislikes, or is in a unit relation with person B, then perceivers assume that person B will like, dislike, or be in a unit relation with person A.[3]

Unit relations are symmetric by definition: Whenever P is in a unit relation to O, O must be in the same unit relation to P. For sentiments, however, the actual relation between two people need not be symmetric; there are many real cases in which a person P likes but is disliked by O. For our purposes, however, the question is not whether sentiments are symmetric in fact, but whether perceivers act as if they were symmetric. A number of experiments (for example, DeSoto & Kuethe, 1959; and McNeel & Messick, 1970) have demonstrated, as Heider assumed, that sentiments are treated as symmetric. Therefore, in this introductory section, symmetry of both sentiments and unit relations will be assumed. In later sections, research that bears on this assumption will be reviewed.

In the interests of simplicity, sentiments and attitudes will be treated as if they can take just three values: *like, dislike,* and *no relation.* Degrees of liking

---

[2]This property is sometimes called *reciprocity* (e.g., Zajonc & Burnstein, 1965b). However, the term *symmetry* has long been employed in the algebra of relations to refer to relations that are characterized by this property. It is retained here because, as will be seen below, the assumption that sentiments and unit relations are reflexive, symmetric, and transitive amounts to assuming that they are equivalence relations; hence, the algebraic properties that hold for any equivalence relation ought to be found in the perception of sentiments and attitudes. It should also be mentioned that some authors make it appear that symmetry (or reciprocity) and balance are different rules. That precedent is specifically rejected here; Heider (1958, pp. 205–206) explicitly included both properties within the balance principle.

[3]Attitudes cannot properly be termed symmetric relations because the term *attitude* is defined as a person's feeling about some impersonal entity. Obviously, the entity can have no feeling in return.

and disliking will not be distinguished. It is possible to generalize the balance, agreement, and positivity rules so that they apply to degrees of a relationship (Wiest, 1965; Feather, 1965a; Wellens & Thistlewaite, 1971a,b; Tashakkori & Insko, 1979). However, restricting sentiments to three values—positive, zero, and negative—greatly simplifies the analysis of these conceptual rules. It also corresponds to the practice in all but a handful of studies. Note that the possibility of zero relations in a structure—as when a person has no feeling at all toward another person—means that not all patterns of sentiments and attitudes need to be fully connected by positive or negative relations.

Unit relations, by contrast to sentiments and attitudes, will be assumed to take only two levels, positive and zero. That is, it is assumed that a negative unit relation—an anti-unit relation—does not exist; two elements will either be in a unit relation or not. Evidence that bears on this assumption will be presented below.

## B.  INFERENCES FROM POSITIVITY

Positivity, the simplest rule, assumes only that everybody will like everything. To use this rule for inferring unknown relations, a perceiver simply ascribes a homogeneous pattern of liking relations to every pair of elements in a pattern. Obviously, a misanthropist could use the obverse rule, negativity, in the same simple-minded manner.

The positivity rule may be employed to classify the three-element structures of Table I by sorting the structures into two groups according to whether they satisfy the rule or not. Clearly, only Structure 1 fully satisfies positivity; Structure 8 fully satisfies negativity.

The rule can also be applied to the relationship between each pair of elements in turn. So applied, the rule yields three distinct classifications of the structures in Table I. Each classification sorts the structures according to whether positivity does or does not hold between one pair of elements. The three classifications are presented in the first three rows of Table I. These classifications are "one dimensional," in that a perceiver needs to know only one relation in order to decide in which category to place a structure. For example, only the relation between P and O needs to be known in order to produce the classification that is illustrated in row 1.

## C.  INFERENCES FROM AGREEMENT (SOURCE/TARGET GENERALIZATION)

Source generalization assumes that every relation *from* a person will be of the same valence, whether positive or negative. It is the same rule as Rubin and Zajonc (1969) called "friendliness–unfriendliness" but the latter term does not apply to a person's generally positive or negative attitude toward impersonal

WALTER H. CROCKETT

TABLE I
TYPES OF CLASSIFICATION OF THREE-ELEMENT SOCIAL STRUCTURES[a]

| Classification | | PLO Plx(Q) OLx(Q) | PLO Plx(Q) ODx(Q) | PLO PDx(Q) OLx(Q) | PLO PDx(Q) ODx(Q) | PDO PLX(Q) OLx(Q) | PDO PLx(Q) ODx(Q) | PDO PDx(Q) OLx(Q) | PDO PDx(Q) Odx(Q) |
|---|---|---|---|---|---|---|---|---|---|
| Type | Description | | | | | | | | |
| I | P–O Attraction | + | + | + | + | − | − | − | − |
| | P–x Attraction | + | + | − | − | + | + | − | − |
| | O–x Attraction | + | − | + | − | + | − | + | − |
| II | Source general. from P | + | + | − | − | − | − | + | + |
| | Source general. from O | + | − | + | − | − | + | − | + |
| | Agreement | + | − | − | + | + | − | − | + |
| VI | Balance | + | − | − | + | − | + | + | − |
| III | Nonsense (A) | + | + | − | − | + | − | + | − |
| IV | Nonsense (B) | + | + | + | − | + | − | − | − |
| V | Nonsense (C) | + | − | − | + | − | + | − | + |

[a]The above typology was developed by Shepard, Hovland, and Jenkins (1961). In this table, P and O denote two individuals; x is an inanimate entity; O is included to indicate that the third element in the structure might also be a third individual; L and D refer to like and dislike, respectively, between the first element of a line and the second. In the body of the table, a + indicates that the structure in that column belongs in the defining set of a classification; a − indicates that the structure in that column belongs in the contrasting set of the same classification.

objects. Agreement (or target generalization) makes the same assumption about the relations *toward* an element. What one calls this rule is largely a matter of personal taste. "Agreement" seems a more natural term when the third element is an impersonal entity, x; "popularity–unpopularity" (Rubin & Zajonc, 1969) seems appropriate when the third element is another person, Q; we shall usually employ the term *target generalization,* to parallel *source generalization.*

In order to employ either of these rules to infer unknown relations in a structure, a perceiver must be given information about at least one relation to or from an element. Thus, upon learning that P likes (or dislikes) O, a perceiver can infer from source generalization that P likes (dislikes) the other elements as well. Similarly, upon learning that O is liked by P, the perceiver can infer from target generalization (agreement) that the other people will also like O. Once those inferences have been made, the property of symmetry yields their reciprocals. Application of either of these rules leads to a homogeneous pattern of relations, as in positivity or negativity. However, the difference between these rules and positivity or negativity is that the inferences a perceiver draws will depend upon the sign of the relation that is given.

In principle, from a knowledge of just one relation between a single pair of persons a perceiver could employ source generalization and target generalization to infer all of the other relations in a very large structure. Thus, from source generalization from P, one might infer P's feelings about Q, R, . . . , N, and symmetry would yield inferences about the others' attitudes toward P. Similarly, target generalization toward O and symmetry would yield inferences about O's sentiments toward the others and theirs toward O. Once those inferences had been made from P and O to and from Q, R, . . . , N, the relations among other pairs of individuals could be filled in from the same rules. No doubt these rules are used conservatively in actual practice, however; not many perceivers can be expected to build an elaborate pyramid of higher order inferences upon a single known relation.

Source generalization makes of each element a sociometric star, radiating univalent positive or negative affect toward every other element. Target generalization, or agreement, makes of each element a sociometric magnet, attracting univalent affect from every other element. And because sentiments and unit relations are presumed to be symmetric, source generalization and target generalization yield identical patterns of inferences in the structures of Table I.

As may be seen in Table I, only Structures 1 and 8 fully satisfy these rules. Again, however, one can focus on each element, in turn, classifying the structures according to whether they satisfy the rules for that element. The three classifications so obtained are presented in rows 4, 5, and 6 of Table I. Each of these classifications is "two dimensional," to classify a structure according to these rules a perceiver needs to be given the relations between two of the three elements.

One other property of these classifications is of interest: In terms of the analysis of variance, each of the two-dimensional classifications is the interaction of two of the one-dimensional classifications in rows 1, 2, and 3. For example, the classification in row 4, based on source/target generalization from P, is the interaction of the classifications in rows 1 and 2 ("P–O attraction" and "P–Q attraction").

## D.   INFERENCES FROM BALANCE

The balance rule involves more complicated logical assumptions than the preceding ones. Let us consider each of these assumptions in turn, and then point out some of their consequences. As will be discussed at greater length below, these assumptions imply that sentiments, attitudes, and unit relations are equivalence relations. Thus, in suggesting that perceivers employ the balance rule as a schema in social cognition, one does not propose that they are reflectively aware of the logical properties that are involved, but that they apply a well-practiced schema, that of equivalence relations, to relationships in small groups of people and social objects.

## 1.  Assumptions for Balance

*a.  Transitivity.*   In advancing the balance principle, Heider (1958, pp. 205–206) proposed that perceivers treat positive sentiments, attitudes, and unit relations as if they were symmetric and transitive. The implications of symmetry are discussed above. The property of transitivity requires that when P is in the relation to O, and O is in the same relation to Q, then P will be in that relation to Q.[4]

Combined with symmetry, the assumption of transitivity makes possible an extensive set of inferences from relatively little information. To illustrate, consider the six possible like–dislike relations between three people, P, O, and Q. The assumptions of symmetry and transitivity make it possible to infer from just two of the six relations what sign the other four must take, *provided* at least one of the two known relations is positive. Thus:

1.  If one knows that P likes O and O likes Q, then it follows from transitivity that P likes Q and from symmetry that the three positive sentiments are reciprocated.
2.  Or suppose one knows that P likes O and O dislikes Q; then it follows from transivity that P dislikes Q and from symmetry that those sentiments are reciprocated.[5]

[4]Two reservations must be entered. First, there are some sentiments and some unit relations for which transitivity obviously does not hold. If P loves O and O loves Q, it is not ordinarily inferred that P will love Q. Quite the contrary. The same is true for unit relations like marriage. Relations like these can be called *singular;* they are ordinarily expected to connect pairs of elements, not triplets. Singular relations are symmetric but not transitive. In the rest of this article, our concern will be restricted to *nonsingular* sentiments, attitudes, and unit relations.

Second, transitivity only holds so long as the relations are relevant to one another. When are relations not relevant to one another? Consider the following examples: "John is in a unit relation to Phil; Phil is in a unit relation to his parents; therefore, John is in a unit relation to Phil's parents." Or, "Helen likes Ruth; Ruth likes Brussels sprouts; therefore, Helen likes Brussels sprouts." Or "I like my wife; my wife is in a unit relation to her tennis racket; therefore, I like my wife's tennis racket." How are pairs of relations in these examples not relevant to each other? In the first one, two qualitatively different unit relations are represented. In the second and third, unless the two people eat the same meals or use the same tennis racket, their relation to each other is carried out independently of the third element; consequently, the two relations in each statement can be considered irrelevant to each other. An obvious difficulty is raised by introducing so slippery a term as "relevance" of relations into the discussion. Nevertheless, most people can assess with some confidence whether two relations are relevant or irrelevant; therefore, the term will suffice for present purposes.

[5]Whenever a relation, r, is symmetric and transitive, and when the elements P, O, and Q are either in that relation or its obverse, r̄, to each other, then if PrO and Or̄Q, it follows that Pr̄Q. Proof is by contradiction. Suppose the contrary, that PrO and Or̄Q but PrQ. (1) PrO implies OrP by symmetry. (2) OrP and PrQ implies OrQ by transitivity. But this contradicts the prior assumption that Or̄Q. Therefore, if PrO and Or̄Q, it must hold that Pr̄Q.

3. A chain of reasoning similar to the second case produces the conclusion that P likes Q from knowledge that P dislikes O and O likes Q.
4. However, if one knows that P dislikes O and O dislikes Q—that is, if both of the given relations are negative—the transitivity of the liking relation provides no valid inferences about the relations between P and Q. One can use symmetry to infer that Q dislikes O and that O dislikes P, but one cannot complete the structure by inferring either a positive or a negative relation between P and Q. For that inference, another assumption is required.

*b. The Assumption of Antitransitivity for Negative Sentiments and Attitudes.* A relation will be called antitransitive if, when A is in that relation to B and B is in the same relation to C, then A is in the *opposite* of that relation to C. We propose that perceivers treat negative sentiments and attitudes as if they were antitransitive. That is, if one learns that P dislikes O and O dislikes Q, one infers that P likes Q.

The property of antisymmetry has not previously been spelled out in the literature, though it has been implicit. Heider (1958) remarked that the transitivity of positive relations does not yield a prediction when two negative relations are known. On this basis he questioned whether triplets that contain three negative relations should be considered unbalanced; he conjectured that they should be so termed. Cartwright and Harary (1956) explicitly defined a structure with three negative relations as unbalanced; subsequently, that definition has been accepted generally. Adopting the definition amounts to making the assumption that negative relations are antitransitive.[6]

It is useful to restrict this assumption to negative sentiments and attitudes, and not to extend it to nonunit relations or to zero sentiments and attitudes. Instead, these latter relations will be considered as nontransitive. This means that if one knows P is *not* in a unit relation with O and O is *not* in the same type of unit relation with Q, one can draw no valid inferences about whether P is in that unit relation with Q. The advantages of thus restricting the assumption will be discussed below.

*c. Assumed Connections between Unit Relations and Sentiments and Attitudes.* According to Heider (1958), perceivers assume the following connections between sentiments and attitudes, on the one hand, and unit relations, on the other:

1. Positive sentiments and attitudes induce unit relations (or an attempt to form unit relations) with the liked person or object.

[6]It will be noted that the preceding assumptions are very similar to those presented in Rosenberg and Abelson (1960).

2. Negative sentiments and attitudes induce the avoidance of unit relations (or an attempt to sever unit relations) with the disliked person or object.
3. Being in a unit relation with a person or object induces liking for that person or object.

The inferences that a perceiver who employs these connections can draw come close to making the properties of unit relations coincide exactly with those of patterns of sentiments and attitudes. Note, however, that nonunit relations are not assumed to induce negative sentiments. People are not expected to dislike everything with which they are not in a unit relation; consequently, from a given pattern of unit and nonunit relations, one cannot always infer a complete pattern of like–dislike relations among the elements.

### 2. Implications

*a.   Extensions to Larger Patterns.*    Transitivity and antitransivity are defined on patterns of three elements. This means that the triplet is the basic unit for inferences from the balance rule. No matter how many elements there are in a structure, inferences about relations between two elements—say P and S—cannot be made unless one is given a chain of relations from P to S via some third element, say P–O–S, P–R–S, or P–Q–S. Conversely, for sentiments and attitudes, whenever one is given a chain of relations beginning with one element in a structure and ending with another—say, for instance, P–Q–R–S–T–U–V—all of the unknown relations among the elements of that chain can be inferred. In a structure of size N, therefore, knowing a chain of N–1 sentiments and attitudes between elements would, in principle, permit a perceiver to infer the signs of all of the remaining relations.

Extended inferences for patterns of unit relations can be made in the same way but, because nonunit relations are not assumed to be antitransitive, complete inferences can only be made when successive pairs of elements are connected with positive unit relations.

*b.   The Two-Clique Restriction for Sentiments and Attitudes.*    Cartwright and Harary (1956) proved that when the assumptions of symmetry, transitivity, and antitransivity are met for relations among elements in a set, that set can have at most two mutually hostile cliques. More formally, they showed that either (a) all of the relations between pairs of elements in a structure will be positive or (b) the structure can be divided into two subsets such that only positive relations connect pairs of elements within each subset, and only negative relations connect elements from different subsets.

This two-clique restriction is not implausible for patterns that are based on sentiments and attitudes. That is, it seems reasonable that perceivers expect, as a first approximation, that friends (1) will agree with each other, (2) will like each other's friends, (3) will dislike their enemy's friends and their friend's enemies, (4) will fall out with each other—and polarize their acquaintances—when they disagree on important issues, and so on.

But the two-clique restriction has little plausibility when it is applied to patterns of unit relations. Surely most perceivers recognize that any fairly large group will usually contain more than two subsets of people united by a given unit relation. Perceivers should have little trouble conceiving of a social setting that contains more than two groups of office mates, more than two sets of coreligionists—in general, more than two subgroups of people who are associated in some unit relation. Withdrawing the assumption of antitransitivity from nonunit relations, as we have done above, removes the two-clique restriction from patterns of unit relations.

*c. Degrees of Balance.* A structure is called balanced if none of the balance assumptions is violated; otherwise it is called unbalanced. But some unbalanced structures are more nearly balanced than others. Therefore, it makes sense to define the "degree of balance" of different structures. Ways of defining degree of balance are discussed in detail, along with a number of other problems in the formalization of balance theory, by Cartwright and Harary (1956), Flament (1963), and Harary, Norman, and Cartwright (1965). For our purposes, because the triplet is the largest unit to which the balance assumptions apply, a sensible definition of the degree of balance will be given by the ratio of (a) the number of balanced pairs and triplets a structure contains to (b) the total possible number of balanced pairs and triplets in that structure.

*d. Classification of Three-Element Structures.* Return to the patterns of relations in Table I. Structures 1, 4, 6, and 7 are balanced, whereas Structures 2, 3, 5, and 8 are unbalanced. Balance is a "three-dimensional" rule for classifying these structures, because a perceiver must take into account the relations between all three pairs of elements in order to distinguish balanced structures from unbalanced ones.

In terms of the analysis of variance, the balance classification is the second-order interaction of the classifications based on the positivity rules. It is also the interaction of (1) the attraction classification between any two persons and (2) the agreement classification between those two persons and the third element. The seven classifications that are generated by positivity, target generalization, and balance define a complete set of orthogonal comparisons on these eight structures.[7]

For structures that are based on unit relations instead of sentiments and

---

[7]The conceptually neat property that the three inferential rules produce a set of orthogonal classifications does not hold for structures with more than three elements.

attitudes, the classification for Table I is not as neat. Because nonunit relations are not assumed to be antitransitive, Structure 8, with three negative relations, neither follows from nor contradicts the balance assumptions; therefore, it cannot be called either balanced or unbalanced. Thus, for structures that are based on unit relations, the balance rule yields a three-fold grouping: four balanced structures, three unbalanced structures, and one structure that is neither balanced nor unbalanced.

### 3.  Sentiments, Attitudes, and Unit Relations as Equivalence Relations

As has been shown above, the balance rule assumes that sentiments, attitudes, and unit relations are symmetric and transitive. The relations may also be shown to be *reflexive,* that is, a person likes or is in a unit relation with himself/ herself.[8] Any relation that is reflexive, symmetric, and transitive is known in the algebra of relations as an *equivalence relation.* There is a well-known theorem that an equivalence relation partitions its field into disjoint equivalence classes (Birkhoff & Maclane, 1953, pp. 155–157). Applied to the perception of relations among people, this theorem suggests that perceivers sort their acquaintances into categories according to known like–dislike or unit relations.

How many equivalence classes there will be depends upon the number of elements in the set and the type of relation. If there are infinitely many elements then a unit relation such as *belong-to-the-same-club* may yield infinitely many categories. As has been shown above, the balance rule presumes that, when all participants in a social group either like or dislike each other, for patterns of sentiments there will be only two equivalence classes.[9] For unit relations, because antitransitivity is not assumed, the balance rule permits any number of equivalence classes.

What does this mean for the proposition that balance is employed by perceivers as a cognitive schema? It means that one need not presume that perceivers are reflectively aware of the logical assumptions that underlie their use of the rule. A perceiver need not be able to make explicit the properties of reflexiveness, symmetry, transitivity, and antitransitivity in order to employ the rule, although some perceivers may be able to do so. Instead, a perceiver who sorts the people and objects under consideration into equivalence classes, based upon a knowledge of like–dislike or unit relations among them, is operating according to the assumptions of the balance rule. Thus, if a perceiver knows that O and Q know each other and learns that O supports the anti-abortion movement whereas

[8]Reflexiveness holds by definition for unit relations: P is obviously in a unit relation with P. It holds for sentiments because of the assumed connection between unit relations and sentiments: P in a unit relation with P implies P likes P.

[9]The requirement that there be just two equivalence classes for structures based on sentiments does not hold if some people neither like nor dislike each other (i.e., are in a zero relation to each other). In that case, more than two equivalence classes may be observed.

Q opposes it, the perceiver can infer that O and Q dislike each other and, at the same time, can categorize them in two disjoint groups: those who support and those who oppose the movement.

The function of sorting people and objects into equivalence classes in this way, obviously, is to permit the perceivers to keep track of, and to draw inferences about, the relationships among their acquaintances. It should be emphasized that these inferences may be tentative ones. A perceiver who later discovers that the relations among a set of people do not conform to the simple pattern that is required by the balance rule may change his/her conceptions so that the actual relations are represented in cognition. A schema serves as a guide to inferences and cognition, not as an inflexible law of thought. It should also be emphasized that the fact that like–dislike and unit relations constitute equivalence relations frees us from an overriding concern with whether the balance properties are represented in perceivers' phenomenological reports on their inferences about interpersonal relations. One can sort elements into equivalence classes without being aware explicitly of the properties of symmetry and transitivity. People may employ the properties the balance rule assumes without being able to explicate them, just as they can speak grammatically without being able to formulate the grammatical rules they are observing.

## E. SUMMARY AND COMMENTS ON THE RELATIONSHIPS AMONG THE RULES

There is a conceptually neat relationship among these rules. As one moves from one rule to the next, the complexity of the rules increases. Each more complex rule can be seen as the interaction among the rules that precede it. Further, each more complex rule provides a common-sense explanation of why the simpler rule may not hold in a particular case.

*Positivity (or negativity)* is the simplest rule, proposing only that everyone will like (or dislike) everything. The rule provides three one-dimensional classifications of structures of Table I. To make each classification, a perceiver needs to consider only one relation per structure.

*Source generalization* and *target generalization* (or *agreement*) are more complex. To use either rule for predicting unknown relations, a perceiver needs one item of information: the sign of the relation to or from an individual. For symmetric relations, source generalization and target generalization yield identical patterns of uniformly positive or negative relations. These rules provide three two-dimensional classifications of the structures of Table I. To make each classification, a perceiver needs to consider two relations per structure. In three-element structures, each classification is the interaction of two of the positivity classifications.

Common-sense aphorisms which fit these rules are: "Some people are positive thinkers, others are negative thinkers," or "Some people are generally likeable; others, nobody could like.'' These aphorisms are framed as empirical generalizations; they can be used subjectively to account for the failure of positivity (or negativity) to hold in a particular case.

*Balance* is more complex still. It assumes (a) that sentiments, attitudes, and unit relations are symmetric and transitive; (b) that negative sentiments and attitudes, but not negative unit relations, are antitransitive; and (c) that positive unit relations induce positive sentiments and attitudes; positive sentiments and attitudes induce positive unit relations; and negative sentiments and attitudes induce nonunit relations.

To infer unknown relations from the balance rule, one needs to be given one relation between each of two pairs of elements. When applied to sentiments and attitudes, balance provides one three-dimensional classification of the patterns of Table I. To make this classification, a perceiver needs to consider three relations per structure. The balance classification is the second-order interaction of the three positivity classifications; alternatively it is the interaction of attraction between two people with their agreement about the third element.

The assumptions of the balance rule define like–dislike and unit relations as equivalence relations. This means that the perceiver who employs the balance rule will sort the elements of the situation into disjoint equivalence classes.

Common-sense aphorisms that fit the balance rule include: ''Any friend of a friend of mine is a friend of mine;'' ''If my friend doesn't like it, I won't either;'' ''The enemy of my enemy is my friend;'' ''If you associate with somebody long enough you will begin to like her;'' and ''If you don't like him, don't go around with him.'' Again, these aphorisms are framed as empirical generalizations; they may be used subjectively to account for the failure of positivity, or of source/ target generalization to hold true in a particular situation.


F.  IMPLICATIONS FOR SOCIAL COGNITION

The following hypotheses may be advanced concerning the effects of these conceptual rules upon information processing in cognition.

*1. Expectations about unknown relations should follow whatever conceptual rule (if any)* a perceiver employs. If the rules are used at all in social cognition, they must affect how a person uses partial information to draw inferences about unknown relations.

*2. Learning a pattern of relations should be enhanced when the pattern matches a perceiver's inferential rule, and hindered otherwise.* When the pattern matches the rule, then all of the inferences a perceiver makes from partial information will be correct; correct inferences need not be sorted out from incorrect ones, and the pattern of relations can be learned easily. However, when the pattern violates the rule, incorrect inferences must be identified and reversed, hence learning such a pattern should take longer than learning one which matches the rule.

*3. Patterns which match an inferential rule will be recalled more accurately than those which do not.* This hypothesis can be generated from at least two different theoretical positions. The first proposes that partial information from memory will be treated in the same way as partial information from the environment; that is, that forgotten relations will be inferred according to the same principles as held when unknown relations are learned. As we shall see below, such does not seem to be the case. Instead, the balance rule, in particular, appears to serve as a cognitive schema; schema-consistent patterns are recalled more effectively than inconsistent patterns, but inconsistent patterns are not typically converted in memory into consistent ones.

## III.   Conceptual Rules and Inferences about Missing Relations

A.   INFERENCES FROM MINIMAL INFORMATION

The simplest way to test whether perceivers actually use a conceptual rule is to give them the minimum amount of information the rule requires and to ask them what inferences they can draw. For example, subjects may be asked:

*James and Ben know each other. Does James like Ben?*

*Bob knows George and Steve. Bob dislikes George. Does Bob dislike Steve?*

*Don, Phil, and Harry are all acquainted. Don likes Phil. Phil likes Harry. Does Don like Harry?*

Responses to such questions, on a scale from Definitely Likes to Definitely Dislikes, were translated by both DeSoto and Kuethe (1959) and McNeel and Messick (1970) into probability judgments. McNeel and Messick (1970) analyzed these derived probabilities by Bayesian statistics to determine which rules subjects actually employed. I have carried out a similar analysis of the probabilities obtained in the experiment by DeSoto and Kuethe (1959). The advantage of this method of analysis is that it assesses whether a subject employs a complex rule by using as a baseline the subject's application of the less complex rules to the same relations. Thus, if subjects employed positivity in their inferences about like–dislike relations, the Bayesian analysis takes that into consideration in assessing whether they also employ source generalization and target generalization with that relation. Similarly, when subjects' use of transitivity or antitransitivity is examined, the Bayesian analysis takes into account their use of source/target generalization and of positivity with that relation.

Two experiments have been reported which used these procedures effectively,[10] one by DeSoto and Kuethe (1959), the other by McNeel and Messick (1970). Thirteen different social relations were studied in one of these experiments or the other. These included three sentiments, five sentiment-like relations, and five ordered relations. We need only consider the three sentiments—*likes, dislikes,* and *hates*—and the five sentiment-like relations—*trusts, confides in, understands, avoids,* and *lies to.*

### 1.  Positivity

In both experiments, subjects used positivity with all three sentiments. The base rates were: *likes,* .54 in one experiment and .59 in the other; *hates,* .35 in one experiment and .42 in the other; and *dislikes* (which was rated in only one experiment), .42. All of these probabilities differed from .50 at the .05 level of significance or greater; obviously, however, most of the deviations from .50 were not very large.

### 2.  Source Generalization and Target Generalization

Source generalization and target generalization were applied to these sentiments somewhat less consistently than positivity. For *likes,* McNeel and Messick reported both forms of generalization, whereas DeSoto and Kuethe reported neither form. On the other hand, for the negative sentiments *dislikes* and *hates,* the two forms of generalization were consistently observed by both sets of authors.

### 3.  Balance

Subjects in both experiments employed all of the balance principles in making inferences about the three sentiments. *Likes, dislikes,* and *hates* were all treated as symmetric. *Likes* was treated as transitive; *dislikes* and *hates* were treated as antitransitive. McNeel and Messick also obtained predictions for two other higher order inferences. One of these was a "circular" pattern: *P likes O. O likes Q. Does Q like P?* The other may be called a "convergent" pattern: *P likes O. Q likes O. Does P like Q?*

For each of these patterns, if the relation is symmetric then we have a special case for the application of transitivity or antitransitivity. Inferences for *likes* actually showed these transitivity effects (McNeel & Messick, 1970), whereas those for *hates* showed antitransitivity effects.

[10]In one other study, DeSoto and Kuethe (1958) used the same procedures but permitted subjects only three responses: Yes, No, and Can't Guess. Their results were inconclusive because for almost every relation one would find interesting almost all of the subjects replied Can't Guess. Only relations such as "dominates" and "makes more money than" received a majority of Yes or No answers to questions about whether the different inferential rules would apply.

#### 4. Inferences for Sentiment-like Relations

Inferences for *avoids* and *lies to* (which are actions that might reasonably be expected to follow from dislike) showed the same pattern as those for *dislike* and *hate*. That is, for those inferences subjects employed positivity, source generalization, target generalization, symmetry, antitransitivity, and the special forms of antitransitivity. However, inferences for the other three sentiment-like relations—*trusts, confides in,* and *understands*—did not show the same patterns. All three of these relations were treated as symmetric, but none of the other inferential principles—positivity, source generalization, target generalization, transitivity, or antitransitivity—were consistently employed for these relations.[11]

#### 5. Summary Comments

In these experiments, subjects were given just enough information to employ one or another of the conceptual rules. Positivity, balance, and (to a lesser extent) source generalization and target generalization were all employed for *likes, dislikes,* and *hates.* These results are highlighted by the fact that the same rules were not all consistently applied to other sentiment-like relations.

### B. RELATIONS BETWEEN PAIRS OF PEOPLE IN SOCIAL SETTINGS

#### 1. Predictions Made for Hypothetical Situations

Feather (1966) told subjects that one person, O, either liked or disliked another person, Q. As would be expected, predictions of the return relation from Q to O established symmetry.

#### 2. Sentiments Displayed in Actual Situations

A number of studies have examined the effects of anticipated interaction with another person upon evaluations of that person. Knowing that one is going to interact with someone else implies a unit relation with that person; therefore, according to the balance rule, liking for that person should be induced. Such a result was observed for sentiments toward strangers by Darley and Berscheid (1967) and by Mirels and Mills (1964).

Insko and Wilson (1977) tested subjects in triplets. Some pairs of subjects in each triplet interacted; in other pairs, subjects listened to another's interaction but did not deal directly with that person. Subjects liked others with whom they interacted (and were, therefore, in a unit relation) better than those whom they merely overheard.

Tyler and Sears (1977) reported two experiments which varied anticipated

---

[11]A similar difference between the rules employed for likes–dislikes and those employed with other verbs of relation has also been reported by Gollob (1974a).

future interaction and the obnoxiousness or likeableness of the other person. Again, the results were consistent with the balance hypothesis. A reportedly unpleasant person was liked significantly better when interaction with the person was anticipated than when it was not; no difference in liking for a reportedly pleasant person occurred as a function of anticipated interaction.

### 3. Predicting Sentiment Relations between Oneself and Hypothetical Others

Willis and Burgess (1974) had subjects either (a) imagine that they liked or disliked another person and then predict O's feeling toward themselves or (b) imagine that another person liked or disliked them and predict their feeling toward O. The intensity of the sentiment was also varied. For both types of prediction, a strong linear relation was obtained between the strength and sign of the sentiment that was given and that of the sentiment that was predicted in return. This linearity decreased at the negative pole: Subjects tended not to predict that they would dislike someone intensely or be disliked intensely. When subjects were asked what sentiments they would *prefer* to exist, the same pattern was observed with even greater avoidance of intense dislike.

### 4. Self-Esteem and Predictions of Symmetric or Asymmetric Sentiment

Heider (1958, p. 210) remarked that if a perceiver has low self-esteem it might be expected that the *like* relation would be asymmetric, not symmetric. That is, if P dislikes P, then the discovery that O likes P should, by transitivity, result in a dislike for O. Other authors (e.g., Dittes, 1959) have made the opposite prediction, arguing that a person with low self-esteem has even greater need to be liked by others than one with high self-esteem. For a while, it appeared that a clearcut confrontation had been joined between the "consistency" prediction from the balance rule and the "self-esteem" prediction of others. However, this apparent confrontation is vitiated by a problem that the consistency hypothesis encounters within balance theory itself. To make this problem clear, it will be useful to examine the implications of the balance rule for self-esteem.

a. *Balance and Self-Esteem.* As has been shown, the balance assumptions imply that liking is a reflexive relation. Therefore, a condition of low self esteem, when P dislikes P, violates those assumptions. A loss of self-esteem is an unbalanced state; such a loss should produce efforts to revise the negative self-evaluation upward. If the efforts are successful, so that P comes to like P, the balance rule predicts that P will like a positive evaluator better than a negative one; that is, it makes the same prediction as the self-esteem hypothesis.

Beyond this, a person sometimes comes to consider that some of his/her traits or abilities are not really an important part of the self. For example, a person may accept a lack of manual dexterity, or an inability to do well in word games, or an aversion to algebra, or an inability to catch a football, as being of little or no importance; indeed, some people take a certain pride in their lack of ability in one task or another. In such a case, the perceiver has, in essence, denied being in a unit relation with those attributes. When that happens, the perceiver will expect negative evaluations from others on those qualities; an evaluator who gives the perceiver a low rating on the attributes may be liked better than one who gives a favorable rating. At the same time, on qualities that are central to the concept of self, the perceiver would be expected to like positive evaluators better than negative ones. Abelson (1959) termed this type of redefinition *differentiation,* its use in maintaining balance will be discussed in other contexts below. The point is that the balance rule predicts that P will prefer positive evaluators to negative ones so long as the qualities under evaluation are defined as part of P's self, but the reverse may hold for qualities that P dissociates from the self.

*b.    Research.*    In a typical experiment on this topic, subjects are induced to believe that they have done well or poorly on some task, they are exposed to a favorable or unfavorable evaluation from another person, and they then make an evaluation of that person. A complex pattern of results has been found. A few experiments (e.g., Deutsch & Solomon, 1959) offer at least partial support for the proposition that individuals with low self-esteem prefer negative evaluations to positive ones. Considerably more experiments (e.g., Dittes, 1959; Jacobs, Berscheid, & Walster, 1971; Jones, 1966; Jones, Knurek, & Regan, 1973) have found the opposite result: that subjects preferred favorable evaluators to unfavorable ones. Jones and Ratnor (1967) and Jones and Pines (1968) found that subjects liked favorable evaluators better than unfavorable ones if their own inferior performance would never be made public, but preferred unfavorable evaluators to favorable ones if their bad performance would be revealed in the future.

Several experiments have reported that subjects do seem to employ mechanisms such as differentiation to dissociate a poor performance from their general conception of themselves. Thus, Dutton (1972) reported that when a task reflected a trait that was unimportant to the subject, the negative evaluator was liked better than the positive one; however, when the trait was important to the subject, the same result held only if the subject was very sure about the poor self-evaluation.

Similarly, Dutton and Arrowood (1971) found that when subjects had presented a message with which they disagreed (and, hence, one with which they would not consider themselves in a unit relation), those who were told they had done poorly rated negative evaluators more highly than positive ones. However, subjects who had presented a message with which they agreed (hence, one with which they were in a unit relation) rated evaluators who agreed with them more favorably than those who disagreed with them, whatever the content of the evaluation.

Finally, Regan (1976) reported that when praise from a confederate was relevant to a task which subjects had just performed, those who had done poorly did not like the praising evaluator as much as those who had done well. However, when the praise was irrelevant to the task, subjects who had done poorly liked the praising evaluator better than did those who had done well.

In sum, liking for a person who provides the perceiver with praise or blame depends in a complex way upon the centrality of the quality to the perceiver's self-concept, upon the obviousness of the perceiver's bad performance, upon the perceiver's general level of self-esteem, and, no doubt, upon a variety of other factors as well.

### 5.  *Predicted Stability of Relations between Pairs of People*

Miller and Geller (1972) had subjects examine patterns of relations between two people and predict how each person would feel toward the other in three months' time. Subjects were presented with all combinations of liking, disliking, ambivalence, and neutrality between pairs. Symmetric relations were judged to be less likely to change: Most subjects (91%) predicted no change for like–like patterns; somewhat fewer (79%) made the same prediction for dislike–dislike patterns; and slighlty fewer still (69% and 66%, respectively) for ambivalent–ambivalent and neutral–neutral patterns. When subjects were given asymmetric relations, except for the like–dislike pattern (in which there was no consensus) subjects predicted that the pattern would change over time to a symmetric one.

### 6.  *Summary of Predictions for Pairs of Persons*

The preceding experiments give strong and consistent evidence for the balance proposition that subjects employ symmetry in predicting missing relations and also for the predicted relationship between unit relations and sentiments. The experiments also yield some evidence of positivity: Subjects seem reluctant to predict strong dislike between themselves and others. It remains unclear just when subjects who have experienced a loss of self-esteem will like others who evaluate them negatively and when the reverse will occur.

C.  INFERRING MISSING RELATIONS AMONG THREE OR MORE PEOPLE

### 1.  *Unit Relations and Sentiments Combined*

In a classic series of experiments, Morrissette (1958) asked subjects to imagine that they were about to share an apartment with several individuals their own age and sex. They were told the relations between some of these room-mates, and were asked to predict what the other relations would become in two weeks time. Patterns of relations were presented which permitted various degrees of balance in their completion, and subjects' predictions were analyzed to determine whether they tended to maximize balance. This analysis required that the degree of balance of all possible completed structures be computed. In making those computations, Morrissette defined the degree of balance of a pattern as the proportion of balanced pairs and triplets to the total number of pairs and triplets in which the subject, who took the role of P, was included. This computation is illustrated in Table II.

As may be seen, P is included in three two-person relations which involve both a unit relation and a sentiment (one of these is given in the stimulus information: the balanced pattern in which P is in a unit relation with and also likes O). In addition, P is included in three triplets of sentiments.[12]

Note first that if P predicts that he/she will dislike Q and like R, then the P–Q unit–sentiment pair will be unbalanced. However, the P–R unit–sentiment pair will be balanced, as will the three triplets of sentiments. Therefore, the degree of balance for this pair of predictions is five-sixths, or 83%.

Second, if P predicts that he/she will like both Q and R, both of the unit–sentiment pairs will be balanced. However, two of the three triplets of sentiments that include P will be unbalanced. Thus, the degree of balance for this pair of predictions is 67%.

Third, if P predicts that he/she will like Q and dislike R, one of the two unit–sentiment pairs and two of the triplets of sentiments will be unbalanced. This gives a degree of balance for this pair of predictions of .50.

Finally, if P predicts that he/she will dislike both Q and R, both of the unit–sentiment pairs and two of the three triplets of sentiments will be unbalanced. Thus, the degree of balance of this pair of predictions is 33%.

The last column of Table II presents the proportion of subjects who gave each of the four possible pairs of predictions. As may be seen, the most common pattern employed was the one that maximized balance in the completed structure.

In this case, subjects had to predict one negative and one positive relation in order to maximize balance. In many patterns, however, exclusively positive predictions were required to maximize balance, because the unit relations that are induced all require the prediction of positive sentiments if the unit–sentiment pair is to be balanced. Thus, it is impossible in Morrissette's results to disentangle completely the effects of balance from those of positivity. Still, a substantial fraction of the patterns, like the example given above, required subjects to

---

[12]Morrissette also included in his computations for the degree of balance the three triplets of unit relations that involve P, all of which are balanced. In the interests of simplicity, these are omitted from the present computations.

TABLE II

Computing the Maximum Degree of Balance for Different Completed Patterns in Morrissette's (1958) Experiment[a]

Given: P, O, Q, and R are all in unit relations
P Likes O, O Likes R, O Dislikes Q, Q Dislikes R

To Predict: P's Sentiments toward Q and R
Pairs and triplets in completed structures

| Possible predictions | Unit–sentiment pairs PUO PLO | PUQ P_Q | PUR P_R | Triplets of sentiments PLO ODQ P_Q | PLO OLR P_R | P_Q QDR P_R | Degree of balance of completed structure (%) | Percentage of subjects giving response |
|---|---|---|---|---|---|---|---|---|
| P dislikes Q<br>P likes R | Bal (Given) | Unbal | Bal | Bal | Bal | Bal | 83 | 60 |
| P likes Q<br>P likes R | Bal (Given) | Bal | Bal | Unbal | Bal | Unbal | 67 | 30 |
| P likes Q<br>P dislikes R | Bal (Given) | Bal | Unbal | Unbal | Unbal | Bal | 50 | 2 |
| P dislikes Q<br>P dislikes R | Bal (Given) | Unbal | Unbal | Bal | Unbal | Unbal | 33 | 8 |

[a]Subjects were told to assume that they were P, who is to share an apartment with three other people (O, Q, and R) of the same age and sex as P. P has met and likes O; P learns that O likes R and that both O and R dislike Q. Subject is to predict how P will feel about Q and R in two weeks' time. P, O, Q, and R are all in unit relations.

predict one or more negative relation in order to maximize degree of balance. In such cases, predictions followed the balance rule.

In three other experiments, Morrissette also tried to institute negative unit relations between the subject and others by proposing that they were competing for a job or a scholarship. He expected that subjects would dislike those with whom they were in competition, on the proposition that a negative unit relation would induce negative sentiments, but they did not. Instead, they predicted liking or disliking so as to maximize balance among the sentiments. That is, the attempted induction of a negative unit relation was not successful.

Singer (1966, 1968) referred to an unpublished experiment of his own and another by Carrier, both of which used Morrissette's methods. He reported that the tendency to institute balance diminished with increases in the amount of information subjects had to process. With two bits of information (4 relations), subjects completed structures with maximal balance; with three bits (8 relations) their predictions showed greater variability; and with four bits (16 relations) there was little or no tendency to complete structures with maximal balance.

Using Morrissette's paradigm, Shrader and Lewit (1962) varied the mean and variance of the degree of balance that could be established by subjects' predictions. The balance rule became more important in such predictions (1) as the maximum degree of balance increased and (2) as the discriminability increased between the degrees of balance of different outcomes.

## 2. Predictions for More Abstract Patterns

Ohashi (1964) asked Japanese college students to predict one missing relation in nine situations that were framed in very abstract terms: "You like O, O dislikes Q, how do you feel about Q?" Predictions revealed significant transitivity effects; however, when subjects were given two negative relations, they did not employ antitransitivity. Instead, the mean prediction was slightly, but not significantly, negative.

Vickers and Blanchard (1973) had subjects predict one relation in each of 12 structures which included themselves and same-sex others. Subjects employed both transitivity and antitransitivity to produce balanced structures.

## 3. An Experiment that Pitted Conceptual Rules Against Each Other

All of the preceding experiments were designed to test the effects of the balance rule. None of them systematically examined the effects of positivity, source/target generalization, and balance when the different rules required different predictions. Frey (1979) employed a set of incomplete patterns of relations which permitted comparing systematically the effects of the three rules against each other. Frey also varied whether the subjects were themselves involved in the situations. In their predictions of missing relations and also in the explanations they made for those predictions, subjects used the properties of transitivity and antitransitivity in preference to source/target generalization and positivity. The same basic pattern of results occurred whether subjects were to imagine themselves involved in the situations or not.

## 4. Actual Sentiments in Real Situations

In all of the previous research, subjects generated their predictions for hypothetical situations. Two experiments have tested the effects of the balance rule in real situations of this type. In the first, Festinger and Hutte (1954) induced liking between a subject and two other persons and then led subjects to believe that the other persons either liked or disliked each other. They found that changes over time in the subjects' sentiments and in their perceptions of the relations among the other two people were greater in the unbalanced condition. These changes usually involved the perception that the other people actually liked each other. Unfortunately, the experiment did not isolate the effects of balance from those of other rules; the same changes that introduced balance also instituted source/target generalization and positivity.

Aronson and Cope (1968) carried out a complete factorial design to test the same hypothesis. They established all possible combinations of like and dislike for another person, O, and of like and dislike between O and a third person Q. Subjects were then given a chance to help Q. They volunteered significantly more help to Q when (a) they liked O and O liked Q or (b) they disliked O and O disliked Q. If one assumes that helping Q indicates liking and refusal to help Q indicates disliking, then subjects' sentiments toward Q reflected the use of both transitivity and antitransitivity.

### 5.  Summary

The preceding seven papers reported 11 different experiments. All of them provided evidence for the use of transitivity in these predictions. Only one (Ohashi, 1964) did not observe the use of antitransitivity; the others, especially Frey (1979) and Aronson and Cope (1968), did observe clear evidence of the use of antitransitivity. Whenever balance was pitted against positivity or source/target generalization, the balance predictions were the ones confirmed. In one experiment (Frey, 1979) when no predictions could balance the structures, subjects used source/target generalization.

### D.  PREDICTED RELATIONS AMONG PEOPLE AND IMPERSONAL ENTITIES

### 1.  Feather's Research on Communication Settings

Feather and his associates conducted a series of experiments that was based on Newcomb's (1953, 1959) analysis of "systems of co-orientation," a theoretical framework essentially the same as Heider's. The theory behind the experiments appears in Feather (1964); much of the research is summarized in Feather (1967a). In all of these experiments, subjects were given partial information about a communication setting. For example, in one experiment (Feather, 1965a), subjects read a communication that a source had directed to a listener. In different experimental conditions, the communication either supported or opposed a general policy. The source's private attitude (favorable or unfavorable) toward the policy was also given, as was the listener's attitude toward the policy. Subjects then predicted the listener's feelings toward both the source of the communication and the communication, itself. In every case, their predictions maximized balance. In a second experiment Feather (1965b) tried to induce a negative unit relation between the source and the communication by saying that the source had been paid to make it. The induction was not effective; subjects' predictions were essentially the same as in the first experiment; that is, they introduced balance among the sentiments and attitudes as if the source were held responsible for the message.

In a third experiment, Feather (1966) examined whether symmetry or transitivity would take precedence in subjects' predictions of interpersonal senti-ments. When symmetry and transitivity yielded opposite predictions, subjects' expectations followed symmetry instead of transitivity; however, such expecta-tions were significantly less polarized than those made when the predictions from symmetry and transitivity coincided.

In two other experiments (Feather, 1967b; Feather & Jeffries, 1967), issues were selected about which subjects were known to feel strongly. Subjects rated every communicator on the favorable side of neutral, indicating a form of positivity. As would be expected from both the balance and the agreement rule, subjects rated communicators who agreed with them more positively than those who disagreed with them. (Note that target generalization and balance were confounded in these experiments. The same agreement effect that target general-ization requires would also result from the use of transitivity and antitransitivity.) Feather and Armstrong (1967) replicated these experiments except for asking subjects to predict the ratings of receivers other than themselves. The results showed balance-agreement effects and positive ratings of communicators that were essentially identical to those in the other two experiments.

### 2.  Hypothetical Settings that Did Not Include the Perceiver

Wyer and Lyon (1970) wrote brief episodes that described either (a) the relations among three people, (b) the relations between two people and an atti-tude object, or (c) the relations between one person and two attitude objects. One set of subjects then rated the probability that each level of relation among ele-ments would be expressed. Subsequently, other subjects read versions of the same episodes which included two of the relations, and predicted the third relation. Their predictions revealed a marked positivity effect and strong evi-dence of source/target generalization, but almost no evidence of use of the balance rule.

Scott (1963) asked subjects to sort nations into categories. From the balance rule, he deduced that they would place nations that were perceived to be similar and friendly in the same sets and those they perceived to be dissimilar and unfriendly in different sets. Such was the case. A measure of cognitive complex-ity was also related to this effect: Less complex subjects showed greater balance effects than did more complex ones.

In an experiment that was conducted just before the 1964 election, Burn-stein (1967) told subjects (1) whether each person in a pair of new roommates liked or disliked the other and (2) each person's attitude toward Goldwater or Johnson. Subjects then predicted how the roommates would feel toward each other and toward the candidates after they had roomed together for several weeks. Clear evidence was obtained for positivity: Negative relations were changed to positive ones more often than the reverse. (Note that this institutes balance between the sentiments and unit relations.) There were also strong balance effects: (1) For the balanced patterns, the overwhelming majority of subjects predicted that no changes would occur, either in attitudes or sentiments; (2) symmetry was introduced for unbalanced, asymmetric pairs; and, (3) for unbalanced triplets, relations were changed so as to institute balance. Little or no evidence for source/target generalization was observed. Three other tendencies were also observed in these predictions: (1) subjects made the minimum number of changes necessary to institute positivity or balance; (2) changes were predicted which would bring the roommates into agreement with the *subjects' own* attitudes; and (3) more changes were predicted in sentiments between the roommates than in attitudes toward the candidates, no doubt because the roommates were newly acquainted but their attitudes were presumed to be of long standing.

Gerbing and Hunter (1979) had subjects complete missing relations in triplets of strangers. Predictions followed the requirements of transitivity and antitransitivity, but when subjects accounted for their predictions most of them did not explicitly state the balance rule.

### 3.   Hypothetical Settings that Included the Perceiver

Rodrigues (1968) asked subjects to assume they liked or disliked a series of people and then to predict those people's attitudes toward issues or concepts with which the subjects agreed or disagreed. The predictions revealed the effects of transitivity, antitransitivity, and agreement. In a second experiment, subjects were asked to indicate the attitude they would prefer the other person to hold, both when pressure for consensus was high and when pressure for consensus was low. These preferred attitudes showed little or now effect for balance, but a marked effect for agreement, especially when pressure for consensus was high.

Fuller (1974) had subjects predict missing relations for 12 different three-element configurations. Positivity effects were found for predictions about interpersonal sentiments between the perceiver and O. In addition, in every configuration there was a significant balance effect, reflecting the use of both transitivity and antitransitivity.

Wellens and Thistlewaite (1971b) used much the same experimental structures as Fuller (1974). Positivity effects were found in predictions of interpersonal relations but not in predictions of attitudes. Evidence for the use of transitivity and antitransitivity was obtained in all conditions.

Rosenberg and Abelson (1960) asked subjects to identify with the owner of a department store who was examining the performance of one of his executives. By manipulating these relations, three experimental groups were formed. In each, the owner faced a different unbalanced situation which indicated decreased sales. Subjects rated most positively memoranda that would produce balance with minimal change, but other factors than balance also affected subjects' judgments. At the end of the experiment, when subjects were asked to reconstruct the relations among the elements of the situation, in only one group—in which changing a single relation produced a homogeneous positive pattern—did subjects produce balanced relations. In the other two groups, most subjects inferred an unbalanced final pattern which promised to yield increased sales. Thus, (1) subjects subordinated balance to a more important goal, continued high sales, and (2) subjects were constrained by the information they were given not to change relations at will in order to produce fully balanced patterns.

Stroebe, Thompson, Insko, and Riesman (1970) reasoned that reality often prevents perceivers from restoring balance to an unbalanced pattern by using simple stratagems such as misperception, denial, or selective memory. Instead, following Abelson (1959), they proposed that perceivers may differentiate two aspects of a complex situation and then treat each aspect as a distinct, conceptually balanced system which is relatively independent of the other. Subjects read material about a scientist which described both his scientific ability and his personal character. They then rated both a scientific theory that the man had supported or opposed and a woman he had recently married or divorced. As expected, subjects' ratings instituted balance within a domain (scientific theory or marital relations) but not across domains. That is, the man's scientific reputation affected ratings of the theory (reflecting use of transitivity) but not of the woman; similarly, his personal character affected ratings of the woman (again with transitivity and antitransitivity) but not of the theory. Positivity was also observed in the evaluations of both the theory and the woman.

### 4. Actual Sentiments in Real Situations

Quite a few researchers have examined the effects of these rules upon sentiments and attitudes in actual situations. Two extensive lines of research which bear on these effects are well enough known that they need only be mentioned here. One is the research paradigm initiated by Schachter (1951), which has shown that group members dislike a person who deviates from their own attitudes. This result is, of course, consistent with the balance rule. The other line of research is that carried out by Byrne and his associates (cf. Byrne, 1971) which finds that perceivers like strangers who agree with them on important issues and dislike strangers who disagree with them. Byrne ascribed these results to the presumed reinforcing quality of agreement with others; the results also confirm the balance rule.

Layton and Insko (1974) combined the Byrne paradigm with the expectation of future interaction (i.e., of an impending unit relation) with the other person. Subjects liked dissimilar others with whom they expected to interact better than they liked dissimilar others with whom they did not expect to interact. Thus they found evidence for both transitivity and antitransitivity and also for the presumed connection between unit relations and positive sentiments.

Insko, Thompson, Stroebe, Shaud, Pinner, and Layton (1973) used Byrne's procedure to induce similarity or dissimilarity of attitudes to another person, then led subjects to believe that O evaluated them either positively or negatively. Subjects' use of symmetry in their return evaluations of O served to flatten the slope of the relationship between similarity and attraction. That is, as in Feather (1966), the prediction of symmetric relations toward O reduced substantially the use of transitivity and antitransitivity in evaluations of O.

Gormly (1979) also used the Byrne paradigm to induce similarity to one confederate and dissimilarity to another. Subjects expressed greater attraction toward the similar confederate than the dissimilar one, in line with transitivity and antitransitivity. However, when they were required to choose one of the confederates for a brief discussion, most subjects picked the one with whom they disagreed and elected to discuss the items on which they differed. A plausible interpretation of these choices is that subjects hoped to change the mind of the disagreeing confederate, thereby inducing balance.

Tashakkori and Insko (1979) recently employed Byrne's method to test the relative predictiveness of three models for quantifying the balance predictions. Issues were chosen about which subjects agreed, felt neutral, or disagreed. Subjects were then presented the attitudes of bogus others who agreed with, were neutral toward, or disagreed with the same issues. Balance predictions were borne out: Subjects' sentiments were in line with the use of transitivity and antitransitivity. There was also evidence for positivity effects: Positive sentiments toward others were more polarized than negative sentiments. This effect was even more pronounced in subjects' predictions of the other persons' sentiments toward themselves.

Sampson and Insko (1964) placed subjects in the autokinetic judgment situation with confederates toward whom either liking or disliking had been induced. As would be expected from the use of transitivity and antitransitivity, when the confederate's judgment differed from their own, subjects who liked him conformed to his judgment much more than did those who disliked him. Conversely, when the confederate's judgment coincided with their own, subjects who disliked him moved their judgments *away* from his much more than did those who liked him.

Taylor (1967) caused subjects to engage with a liked or disliked confederate in half-hour discussions of a controversial issue. The confederate either agreed or disagreed with the subject's position. In conformity to transitivity and antitransitivity (1) subjects' attitudes changed toward those of the liked confederate who disagreed with them and away from those of the disliked confederate who agreed with them; and (2) in later ratings, subjects lowered their evaluation of a liked confederate who disagreed with them and raised their evaluation of a disliked confederate who agreed with them.

Sussman and Davis (1975) had subjects solve anagram problems with confederates who performed cooperatively or uncooperatively. Subjects then made oral judgments of the usefulness of the problems for personnel selection; the confederates' judgments always preceded those of the subject. When only a single confederate was employed, cooperativeness of the confederate did not affect subjects' ratings of the task. When two confederates were employed, one cooperative and the other uncooperative, there was a significant displacement of ratings away from those of the uncooperative confederate and toward those of the cooperative confederate.

Granberg and Brent (1974) studied the effects of voters' own attitudes toward the Viet Nam War upon their judgments of the stands expected from the agreement and transitivity principles. For both the Humphrey and Nixon voters there was a strong positive correlation between their own position and the one they attributed to their preferred candidate ($r = +.55$). However, contrary to the property of antitransitivity, the correlation between respondents' positions and the ones they attributed to their rejected candidates did not differ significantly from zero. The only evidence for antitransitivity was a low but significant negative correlation ($r = -.18$) between the attitudes of Humphrey voters and the attitudes these voters attributed to Wallace. This absence of dissociation from the views of disliked candidates supports Newcomb's "nonbalance" hypothesis.

## 5.   Summary

Of the 24 experiments reviewed in this section, 23 found support for the proposition that subjects' predictions conform to one or another property of the balance rule. Only 1 experiment (Wyer & Lyon, 1970) found little or no evidence of the use of transitivity; only 2 (Wyer & Lyon, 1970; Granberg & Brent, 1974) found no evidence for the use of antitransitivity. The expectation that unit relations induce positive sentiments was also supported.

Source/target generalization, by contrast, was much less commonly observed. Only Wyer and Lyon found evidence for this effect but none for the balance properties. Rodrigues (1968) found that the effects for antitransitivity were moderated considerably by an agreement effect. In half a dozen other experiments, agreement and balance were confounded, so that differential effects of the two rules could not be distinguished. Finally, Burnstein (1967) found a form of agreement in the fact that subjects predicted that the attitudes of characters in hypothetical situations would come to agree with the subjects' own.

Only Wyer and Lyon (1970) found positivity effects without balance effects as well. Burnstein's (1967) subjects predicted that roommates would come to like each other. In addition, three experiments found that subjects predicted more extreme positive sentiments between themselves and others than negative ones (Fuller, 1974; Wellens & Thistlewaite, 1971b; and Tashakkori & Insko, 1979). Finally, it appears that subjects are more likely to give positive ratings than negative ones to speakers (Feather, 1967b; Feather & Jeffrey, 1967; Feather &

Armstrong, 1967) or to a scientist's wife and the theory he supported (Stroebe *et al.*, 1970).

## E. DEVELOPMENTAL RESEARCH

All of the preceding research was conducted with adults. But these conceptual rules are most likely learned from experience, not inherent in the nature of thought; therefore it is important to study developmental differences in the way the rules are applied.

Atwood (1969) examined the use of the balance rule by children at the preoperational, concrete-operational, and formal-operational stages. Subjects were read three stories, each of which presented two of the three relations among a trio of children; their task was to predict the third relation. In scoring a subject's response as balanced, Atwood required both that the missing relation match the balance rule and that the subject's explanation of that prediction correspond to the rule. There was a clear developmental progression: Preoperational children did not employ the balance properties at all. All concrete-operational children used antitransitivity to predict a positive missing relation, but only about two-thirds used transitivity to predict a positive relation and a negative relation. Formal-operational children employed both transitivity and antitransitivity in their predictions. Those children who did use the balance rule were asked whether they could see how the predicted relation might take the opposite sign. Formal-operational children were less inflexibly bound to the balance properties than were concrete-operational ones.

Vickers and Blanchard (1973) studied subjects from the first, third, fifth, and eighth grades, as well as from high school and college. Subjects were to take the role of one person in each of 12 different three-person groups; two of the relations in each group were given and the subject predicted the third. The results revealed a developmental shift from the use of no particular rule to positivity to the use of transitivity and antitransitivity.

Pomonis (1978) suggested that the appearance of the balance rule at an earlier age among Atwood's subjects than among those of Vickers and Blanchard may have occurred because subjects were not personally involved in the situations of the former experiment but were involved in the situations of the latter. That hypothesis was tested with subjects in kindergarten, third grade, and sixth grade. Half of those in each class were presented with situations containing three unknown children; the other half had situations involving themselves and two other children. For each situation, two relations were given and the subject predicted the third. Third and sixth graders were more likely than kindergartners (1) to make predictions, employing transitivity and antitransitivity, that resulted in balanced patterns and (2) to employ some version of the balance rule to explain those balance-producing predictions. In addition, among those who did express verbally some form of the balance rule, (3) those in the two older groups held to the rule less inflexibly than the kindergartners. No extensive differences were found between subjects who were involved in the situations and those who were not, nor between third graders and fifth graders.

Two other experiments employed children from a single age group as subjects. Wiest (1965) had children in grades five, six, and seven rate their liking for all of their classmates. He then selected three classmates for each subject (the best liked, the least liked, and the one closest to neutral) and asked subjects to predict how each of those other children would rate the rest of their classmates. According to the balance rule, the correlations between a child's own ratings and those predicted for a liked person should be positive; correlations between a child's ratings and predictions for a disliked person should be negative. In fact, the results matched Newcomb's (1968) nonbalance hypothesis better than the balance rule: For the liked other, the mean correlation was significantly positive; for the neutral person, the mean correlation was lower but still significantly positive; for the disliked person, the mean correlation was approximately zero.

Ohashi (1964) reported four experiments with Japanese fifth, sixth, and seventh graders. One of these almost exactly duplicated Wiest's experiment. The results were also similar, except that a consistent agreement effect was found: Subjects predicted that most other children—liked, disliked, or neutral—would agree with their own sociometric choices, though the effect was consistently greater for those whom the subjects liked.

In three other experiments, Ohashi first required subjects to identify some classmates they liked, some they felt neutral toward, and some they disliked. Later, subjects predicted how one individual in a pair would feel about the other. These pairs were chosen so as to represent all combinations of children the subject liked, disliked, or felt neutral toward. The results of one experiment showed clear agreement effects but not positivity or balance. In a second experiment, nonbalance effects were observed: The ratings predicted for liked and neutral others agreed with the subjects' own choices, but those predicted for disliked others showed neither agreement nor disagreement. In the third experiment, subjects predicted both sentiments in a pair; that is, P's feeling for O and O's for P. Symmetry was employed for most predictions, but whenever asymmetric predictions were made, they involved pairs in which subjects liked one classmate and disliked the other; that is, the assymmetry expressed agreement with the subject's own choices.

### Summary Comments

The three truly developmental studies all found that use of the balance properties increased systematically with developmental level. However, they did not reveal a single timetable of ages at which children may be expected to employ those properties in predicting missing relations. There was some evidence of positivity in the younger children, but little or no evidence of the use of source/target generalization.

By contrast, experiments by Wiest (1965) and Ohashi (1966) with children from a single age group consistently showed either agreement effects or non-balance (agreement for liked others but neither agreement nor disagreement for disliked others). The differences between these latter experiments and the truly developmental ones probably reflected basic differences in the experimental tasks. In the three developmental studies, subjects made predictions for hypothetical situations; the predictions of children at advanced developmental levels were more likely than those of children at lower levels to employ the balance properties. In the latter two experiments, subjects predicted the sociometric choices of children they knew. Now doubt they knew how many of these acquaintances felt about the others. The agreement effects doubtless reflected such judgments as "Everybody likes Sally" or "Nobody could care for Jerry." Nonbalance effects no doubt reflected the subjects' indifference to the opinions of children they disliked.

## F.   SUMMARY AND GENERAL COMMENTS ON STUDIES OF THE PREDICTION OF MISSING RELATIONS

The preceding review covered 43 different papers, exclusive of those concerned with the self-esteem controversy. These papers reported more than fifty experiments studying the prediction of missing relations in small social groups. They showed overwhelming evidence for the use of the balance properties in drawing such inferences. Every experiment that investigated the property of symmetry observed its use. Only 1 experiment failed to report the use of transitivity; 35 others found transitivity effects. Four experiments failed to observe the use of antitransitivity, but eight times that number did observe its use. Finally, the prediction that unit relations would induce positive sentiments was consistently confirmed.

Evidence for source/target generalization was reported in no more than a dozen papers. In a third of these, the effect occurred because balance and source/target generalization were confounded experimentally, so that their separate effects could not be disentangled in the analysis. In about another third of the papers, the effect revealed a tendency for subjects to predict that others' attitudes would agree with their own. In the remaining studies, the effect depended upon the assumption that certain people are likeable and/or friendly or upon a combination of this assumption with an agreement effect. In all but one case when the predictions from the balance rule and those from source/target generalization disagreed, balance was observed, not source/target generalization.

Positivity effects were reported somewhat more often than source/target generalization but much less often than balance effects. Positivity seemed to arise from several distinct sources. One of these was the balance prediction that being in a unit relation to a person induces liking for that person; research which examines that proposition cannot, of course, disentangle the independent effects of balance and positivity. A second source of positivity effects was the apparent reluctance of subjects to express dislike, especially strong dislike, for someone else. Still a third source of positivity effects was subjects' tendency to rate favorably a person or thing that was in the public eye: speakers and their speeches, a scientist's wife and his theory, and the like. As was shown by the research of DeSoto and Kuethe (1959) and McNeel and Messick (1970), there was a consistent tendency for positivity to be employed when only one relationship was available to the subjects. However, in all but one of the experiments that varied the effects of balance and positivity independently, balance was observed, not positivity.

Other principles were also observed in one or more of these experiments. Subjects who predicted changes among relations in a pattern made the minimum number of changes necessary to satisfy the rule they were using. When the information permitted, subjects differentiated between aspects of a person's character, employing the balance rule within, but not across, different domains. Other subjects subordinated balance to a more important principle or were able to conceive of circumstances in which the predicted balance outcome would not actually occur.

In all these experiments, it seems subjects were trying to make sense of the information they had been given so as to arrive at reasonable predictions about missing relations or about probable changes in relations. In doing so, they consistently employed one or another of the conceptual rules described above, most commonly balance. But they used these rules as schemata to yield tentative predictions, not as absolute laws of social relationships.

## IV.  Conceptual Rules in Learning and Recall

### A.  LEARNING CLASSIFICATIONS OF THREE-ELEMENT STRUCTURES

We have seen that balance, source/target generalization, and positivity each yield one or more classifications of the three-element patterns in Table I. Furthermore, the eight patterns of Table I constitute one set of objects that varies along three dimensions. The classification of physical objects that vary along three dimensions was studied in detail by Shepard, Hovland, and Jenkins (1961). Shepard *et al.* defined a "classification" of eight objects varying in three dimensions as a way of sorting them into two subsets of four objects each. Those authors showed that the 70 possible classifications can be grouped into six broad categories. Category One includes classifications which can be made by attending to only one dimension (the three positivity classifications of Fig. 1 are of this type). Category Two includes classifications which require attending to two dimensions (the three source/target generalization classifications are of that type). Category Six, to skip ahead, contains one classification which requires attending to all three dimensions (the balance classification is of that type). The other Categories—Three, Four, and Five—all include classifications that are one dimensional with an exception. How these classifications are distinguished is not relevant to the present discussion. They are illustrated by the groupings in rows 8, 9, and 10 of Table I. There, they are labeled "nonsense" classifications because they do not have the conceptual simplicity of the other seven: None of them can be sorted neatly on the basis of one, or two, or three dimensions, none can be described simply in a word or phrase, none is orthogonal to the other seven classifications, and so on.

### 1. Learning Classifications of Physical Objects

Shepard et al. (1961) reported three experiments on how easily subjects can learn to use these classifications for sorting physical objects. They found that the ease of learning a classification varied with the number of dimensions it required. One-dimensional classifications were learned more easily than any of the others; two-dimensional classifications were learned more easily than those which were one dimensional with an exception; and classifications of the latter three types were learned more easily than three-dimensional ones.

### 1. Learning Classifications of POx Structures

Cottrell (1975) reasoned that if perceivers actually apply balance and the other conceptual rules to relations among people, then the results obtained by Shepard et al. would not generalize to patterns of social relations. Instead, the three-dimensional balance classification should be learned more easily than the nonsense classifications and, perhaps, just as easily as the one- and two-dimensional ones.

To test this hypothesis, Cottrell had subjects learn to sort eight patterns of social relations, each of which included the sentiments between two persons (P and O) and each person's attitude toward a social issue (x). Different groups of subjects learned to classify the structures according to *attraction between P and O,* a one-dimensional classification; *agreement between P and O about x,* a two-dimensional classification; *balance,* a three-dimensional classification; or a classification from one of the three nonsense categories. As was expected, the balance classification was learned significantly more easily than the nonsense classifications. Somewhat unexpectedly, however, the agreement classification was learned as easily as the one based on attraction between P and O; both of these were learned significantly more easily than the balance classification.

### 2. Comparative Learning of POx and POQ Structures

Crockett (1980b) observed that differences among the conceptual rules in the Cottrell experiment were confounded with the configurational properties of the stimuli that were employed. He proposed that when a pattern consists of two people and an attitude object, the two people constitute a perceptual unit. Thus, a perceiver should attend more readily to the P–O pair than to the P–x or the O–x pairs. This observation led to the hypothesis that it would be easier for subjects to learn to sort the structures according to P–O attraction than according to P–x attraction or O–x attraction. Furthermore, for two-dimensional classifications, the distinctiveness of the attitude object should make it easier for subjects to learn to sort the structures on the basis of agreement about x (i.e., P's attitude toward x and O's attitude toward x) than on the basis of source generalization from either P or O (e.g., P's sentiment for O and P's attitude toward x).

Subjects learned to sort POx structures according to one of six principles: P–O attraction and P–x attraction (both one dimensional); agreement about x and source generalization from P (both two dimensional); balance (three dimensional); or a nonsense classification. As in Cottrell's (1975) experiment, classifications based on P–O attraction and agreement were learned with equal ease and significantly more easily than the other classifications. However, P–x attraction, a one-dimensional classification, was learned at about the same rate as balance, the three-dimensional classification. Both of the latter classifications were learned significantly more easily than either source generalization from P or the nonsense classification. These last two classifications were about equally easy to learn.

By contrast to the preceding POx case, Crockett proposed that when all three elements in the pattern are people, as in the POQ structures in Table I, there are no obvious configurational properties which set one or two relations in the structures off from the others. That is, the learning of classifications based on P–O attraction and agreement between P and O would not be facilitated by configurational properties. Therefore, if subjects actually employ the balance rule in preference to positivity and source/target generalization, for POQ structures it should be as easy to learn the three-dimensional balance classification as the simpler classifications. In a second experiment, different groups of subjects learned classifications of POQ structures according to attraction between two people (one dimensional); source generalization from P and target generalization toward O (both two dimensional); balance (three dimensional); or a nonsense classification. As expected, the first four classifications, those associated with the three conceptual rules, were all learned with about equal ease and significantly more easily than the nonsense classification.

### 3. Summary Comments

In the experiment by Shepard et al. (1961) and subsequent research using physical objects, only the dimensionality of the different classifications affected the ease with which they were learned: The lower the dimensionality, the easier a classification was learned. Therefore, these experiments serve as a standard against which to assess the effects of the conceptual rules upon learning to classify patterns of social relations.

Cottrell's (1975) experiment added two other potential sources of variance to that of dimensionality: the three conceptual rules and the configural properties of the stimulus patterns. The fact that the balance classification was learned more easily than those based on nonsense rules suggests that subjects used the balance rule to learn that classification. However, as Crockett's first experiment (1980b) made clear, the relative ease of learning the positivity and agreement classifications may have resulted either from subjects' adoption of those conceptual rules or from configural properties of the stimuli. The results of Crockett's second experiment—in which, for POQ structures, the balance classification was learned as easily as the others despite its greater dimensionality—suggest a preference among subjects for employing the balance rule in representing those structures conceptually.

## B.  LEARNING PATTERNS OF RELATIONS IN SMALL SOCIAL GROUPS

In reviewing the learning of relations in small groups, it will be convenient to distinguish between two lines of experimentation. In one, subjects learned the relations in only one social structure; in experiments of this type, the priority of the balance rule has regularly been observed. In the second, subjects learned relations that were drawn from two or more social structures; such experiments often find effects for other rules than balance.

### 1.  Learning Relations from One Structure

DeSoto (1960) constructed a number of hypothetical four-person groups. Some groups represented balanced patterns of relations, others represented unbalanced patterns. DeSoto then used the paired-associates learning paradigm to examine the rate at which subjects would learn such structures. Pairs of names from one of the groups became the stimuli in the paired-associates list; the relation between the first person and the second became the correct responses. DeSoto reported that balanced structures were learned faster than unbalanced ones.[13]

### 2.  Combining Unit Relations and Sentiments

Mosher (1967), using the same paradigm, replicated the finding that balanced structures were learned more rapidly than unbalanced ones. Mosher also included a test of the assumed connections between unit relations and sentiments. This was accomplished by including some experimental conditions in which members of the structure were identified by military ranks: two as commissioned

---

[13]In the same experiment, DeSoto studied the use of the linear ordering rule for patterns with asymmetric relations. Some of the other experiments that are reviewed below also studied the linear order rule. The results for linear order will not be considered here.

officers and two as noncommissioned officers. In one condition, the two commissioned officers liked each other and both of them disliked the noncommissioned officers, who also liked each other; assuming that officers and enlisted men each have a unit relation in common, in that pattern both the pattern of sentiments and the connection between sentiments and unit relations were balanced. In a second condition, one commissioned officer and one noncommissioned officer liked each other, they both disliked the other two persons, and those two (one commissioned and one noncommissioned), liked each other; that is, the pattern of sentiments was balanced but the assumed connection between sentiments and unit relations was violated. Fewer errors were made in the first condition than the second, confirming the balance proposition that unit relations induce positive sentiments.

### 3. Individual Differences in the Use of Conceptual Rules for Learning Structures

Press, Crockett, and Rosenkrantz (1969), using a group-administered form of the paired-associates procedure, had different groups of subjects learn one of three four-person structures. One was fully balanced, a second was unbalanced but had an alternative simple rule by which it could be reproduced, and the third was both unbalanced and without an alternative simple rule. The fewest errors were made on the balanced structure; significantly more errors were made on the unbalanced structure with a simple rule; and more errors still were made on the unbalanced structure without a simple rule. Subjects below the median on a measure of cognitive complexity were especially prone to make errors when the balance rule was violated.

Delia and Crockett (1973) found the same results with a somewhat different learning procedure: Balanced structures were learned more rapidly than unbalanced ones, and the difference between balanced and unbalanced structures was greater for subjects low in cognitive complexity than for those high in complexity. In addition, a subsidiary analysis of errors in the unbalanced condition showed that significantly more errors were made on relations which, if changed, would render a structure balanced.

Yang and Yang (1973) reported an interaction between manifest anxiety and the learning of balanced and unbalanced structures. Subjects high in manifest anxiety made significantly fewer errors on balanced structures than on unbalanced ones; those low in anxiety made slightly more errors on the balanced structures than on unbalanced ones.

### 4. A Comparison of Balance to the Other Rules

Crockett (1979) compared systematically the effects of the three conceptual rules upon the learning of social structures. Fewer errors were made in learning a balanced structure than in learning any of three unbalanced ones; no evidence for either positivity or source/target generalization was observed in that balanced structure. One of the three unbalanced structures could be rendered balanced by changing just one relation; significantly more errors were made on that relation than on the others, indicating that subjects were trying to apply the balance inferences to learn that structure. For the other two unbalanced structures, which were relatively difficult to learn, there was evidence that subjects eventually employed both positivity and source/target generalization in learning individual relations.

### 5.  Testing the Two-Clique Restriction with Sentiments and Unit Relations

DeSoto, Henley, and London (1968) had subjects learn the relations in 10-person groups. For half of the subjects, like–dislike relations were learned, for the other half unit–nonunit relations were learned. Some subjects had to learn a structure containing three mutually hostile cliques, whereas other subjects learned a two-clique structure. When presented as a pattern of sentiments, the three-clique structure was unbalanced because it contained many triplets that had three negative relations; however, as a pattern of unit relations, the same structure was not unbalanced because antitransitivity is not assumed for unit relations. In confirmation of the distinction between sentiments and unit relations, the three-clique structure was learned significantly more easily with unit relations than with sentiments. By contrast, the two-clique structure was learned equally easily with sentiments as with unit relations.

### 6.  Learning Relations from More than One Structure

To study the learning of many different patterns of relations, the preceding methods are costly in experimental time. Perhaps for this reason, a good many investigators have set each subject the task of learning the relations from more than one structure. As will be seen, the results of such research vary with increases in the number of relations a subject must learn; the more complex the pattern, the less use one observes of the balance rule.

### 7.  Four Structures, Twelve Pairs of Elements

Innes (1973) required subjects to learn the three relations in each of four three-element structures. Each structure included the relation between two persons and their attitudes toward a social issue. For some subjects, the issue was one with which they agreed; for others, it was one with which they disagreed. Balanced structures were learned more rapidly than unbalanced ones. For unbalanced structures, but not for balanced ones, positive relations were learned more rapidly than negative relations. Finally, subjects who agreed with the social issue contained in the structures learned them more rapidly than those who disagreed with the issue.

In a study primarily directed at retention, Cottrell, Ingraham, and Monfort (1971) also had subjects learn relations from four three-element structures. One set of subjects learned the four balanced structures of Table I; the other half learned the four unbalanced structures. Neither balance nor any of the other rules appeared to affect the rate of learning the structures.

### 8. Six Structures, Eighteen Pairs of Elements

Zajonc and Burnstein (1965a) presented subjects with the relations from six different structures—half balanced and half unbalanced—each of which contained two persons and an attitude object. For half of the subjects the attitude issue was a socially relevant one, for the other half it was less relevant. Subjects with the relevant issue made significantly fewer errors on relations from balanced structures than on those from unbalanced structures. Subjects with the nonrelevant issue showed a slight difference in the opposite direction. In both groups, significantly fewer errors were made on positive relations than on negative ones.

### 9. Three Structures, Eighteen Pairs of Elements

In a second experiment, Zajonc and Burnstein (1965b) set out to examine separately the effects of symmetry and transitivity. Subjects learned the six relations among elements of three different structures; each structure contained two persons and two attitude objects. For some subjects, the relations between the two people were symmetric, for others they were asymmetric. Symmetric interpersonal relations were learned with fewer errors than asymmetric ones. In addition, when the interpersonal relations were symmetric, balanced structures were learned more easily than unbalanced ones. Except for the fully balanced structure, positive relations were learned with fewer errors than negative ones.

### 10. Seven Structures, Twenty-One Pairs of Elements, Three Types of Relations

Zajonc and Sherman (1967) increased the complexity of the subjects' task by having them learn three relations from each of seven three-person structures. Three types of relations could occur between persons: *likes*, *dislikes*, or *don't know*. The results showed no effects for balance. There were significant effects for positivity and for source/target generalization. In addition, when the name of one person in the structure stood out, subjects learned the relations that involved that person faster than other relations.

### 11. Eight Structures, Twenty-Four Pairs of Elements

Rubin and Zajonc (1969) had subjects learn all of the relations from the eight balanced and unbalanced structures that are illustrated in Table I. For some subjects, the structures included two persons and a social issue. For others, the structures included the names of three persons, and one of these names appeared in all eight structures. For a third group, the structures also included three persons, but the label "Me" (to be interpreted as the subject himself) appeared in all eight structures. There was no observable effect of balance upon the learning of these structures. Significant effects were observed for positivity and for source/target generalization; interpersonal relations were learned sooner than attitudes toward a social issue; and fewer errors were made on relations that involved "Me" than on relations that involved the other two persons.

## 12.   Eight Stimuli from Four Structures with Twenty-Four Pairs of Elements, Replicated Four Times

Sherman and Wolosin (1973) set their subjects the most complex task to date. Their stimuli were drawn from the 24 possible directed relations in four three-person structures. Two directed relations from each of the four structures were first presented, each for 1.8 sec, over a closed-circuit television screen. Subjects were then shown 18 ordered relations, one at a time, all drawn from the same structures; subjects were to report, for each stimulus, whether they had seen it initially. After eight trials with one set of stimuli, subjects were presented with a new set of 8 relations from four other structures for another series of study-test trials. This procedure was followed for four different sets of stimuli per subject. Nearly a third of the subjects showed no increase in accuracy at all over the eight trials; these were dropped from later analyses. The authors reported significant effects of symmetry but little evidence of transitivity or anti-transitivity. There was a strong positivity effect.

## 13.   Summary Comments

All seven of the experiments in which a subject learned the relations from a single social structure reported that balanced structures were learned more easily than unbalanced ones. Furthermore, when an unbalanced structure was balanceable by changing a single relation, the learning of that relation was markedly retarded. In such tasks, therefore, it appears that subjects do use the balance rule in preference to other rules when learning patterns of relations. In those studies, if the balance rule did not work, subjects turned to positivity, source/target generalization, and other simplifying rules as alternative schemata.

When subjects had to learn relations from many different structures, experimental results were more equivocal. When the number of relations was small and the task relatively manageable, evidence of the use of the balance rule appeared. However, when the task was more complex, little or no evidence was seen of the balance principle. Instead, positivity, source/target generalization, and other principles were employed. Crockett (1971) proposed that the absence of balance effects with these complex experimental tasks resulted from the fact that such tasks overwhelmed the subjects' cognitive resources with a mass of unorganized data. Subjects were not told initially that the stimuli fell into subgroups. To employ the balance rule they needed first to discover the fact that the stimuli fell into distinct groups, then to sort the elements into their appropriate groups, and after that to apply the principles of symmetry, transitivity, and antitransitivity to the relations within those groups. Except for the use of symmetry for relations between pairs, it appears that subjects abandoned (or did not even consider) the balance rule in attacking such complex tasks. Instead, they adopted simpler principles—positivity, source/target generalization, focusing on distinctive individuals, and the like—or they simply set out to master the material by brute force.

All of these experiments were conducted in an artificial laboratory setting, using abstract patterns of relations among people whom the subjects did not know and would never meet. Can one infer from the results of such research that subjects would employ the balance rule in sorting out the relations among people they do know? Especially when any one individual knows hundreds of other people? The question needs to be put to the test of course. Until it has been, it seems reasonable to answer it in the affirmative. That is, the preceding results make it likely that people do, in fact, use the balance rule as a schema in everyday life, especially when they are entering new social situations, so as to keep track of the pattern of relations among new acquaintances and to infer sentiments and attitudes which have not been observed directly.

## C. RETENTION OF LEARNED STRUCTURES

### 1. Short-Term Retention of Balanced and Unbalanced Structures

Gerard and Fleischer (1967) asked subjects to read six 300-word stories, each of which described a balanced or unbalanced three-element structure. Later in the same session, subjects reproduced each story as best they could. Subsequently they circled what they thought were the correct relations between the elements of each story. Scores on the second measure were virtually perfect for each story. On subjects' reconstructions, however, there was a *disagreement* effect. This was somewhat greater when P and O liked each other, but in either case, subjects remembered the stories in which P and O disagreed about the third element better than the ones in which they agreed. In the stories in which P and O liked each other, this meant that unbalanced structures were remembered better than balanced ones. The authors interpreted this outcome in terms of Heider's (1958) assumption that imbalance evokes tension. They proposed that subjects remembered unbalanced structures, or systems in tension, better than balanced ones much as Zeigarnik's (1927) subjects recalled uncompleted activities better than completed ones.

Spiro and Sherif (1975), using a similar method, had subjects read information pertaining to political candidates and issues in the 1972 presidential election. Unbalanced patterns were later recalled more accurately than balanced ones.

Sentis and Burnstein (1979) offered a parsimonious interpretation of the results of both of the above experiments, ascribing them to differential distinctiveness of the balanced and unbalanced stories. They cited an unpublished study by Sentis which found that subjects spent much more time examining unbalanced stories during the study phase of the experiment; this resulted in better recall of unbalanced structures after the study phase ended. This suggests that unbalanced stories, or those involving disagreement, being relatively unexpected, may command more of the subjects' attention than balanced ones or those involving agreement.

Instead of asking subjects to read a story and then to recall the relations among elements, Miller (1979) permitted them to view abstract P–O–X patterns for 20 sec and then gave them 4 min to write a story that embodied those patterns. Half of the subjects wrote stories about the four patterns in which P and O dislike each other. For each story, coders rated the sentiment between P and O and whether they were represented as agreeing or disagreeing. It appears that all subjects focused on the P–O relation in encoding this information: Only 4 stories out of 192 misrepresented the relation between P and O. Among subjects for whom P and O disliked each other, evidence for the balance rule was obtained: Half of the 48 stories written from unbalanced patterns misrepresented them as balanced, whereas none of the 48 stories written from balanced patterns represented them as unbalanced. Among subjects for whom P and O liked each other, the results were slightly in the opposite direction, though only 12 of 96 stories contained errors.

## 2. Longer Term Recall of Balanced and Unbalanced Structures

Feather (1969, 1970) reported a series of experiments which showed that subjects spontaneously produce more arguments with which they agree than with which they disagree, and that the magnitude of this effect increases with the strength of their attitude toward the issue in question. He interpreted this outcome in terms of selective retention of balanced information. He also suggested that the results of Gerard and Fleischer (1967) reflected short-term memory processes which would diminish over time, whereas balance effects should increase over time.

Cottrell *et al.* (1971) tested the latter hypothesis. Subjects learned to a standard criterion the 12 relations that were generated by four three-element structures. One day later they were retested. Significantly fewer errors of recall were made by subjects who learned balanced structures than by those who learned unbalanced ones. Further analysis revealed that subjects did not transform unbalanced structures into balanced ones. Instead, subjects seemed to have stored the balanced configurations more efficiently; whence, the balanced patterns were recalled accurately while inaccurate, unbalanced versions of the other structures were produced. No effects for positivity or agreement were reported.

### 3. Recall of Complete and Incomplete Structures

Using an information-processing paradigm, Picek, Sherman, and Shiffrin (1975) had subjects each read two stories which contained sentiment relations among four people. Some of these stories were complete, in that all six relations were presented; these were either balanced or unbalanced. Other stories were incomplete, in that only four of the six relationships were presented; these were either "balanceable" when completed or "unbalanceable." Later in the same session, subjects judged whether each sentiment had been presented and, if so, whether it was positive or negative. For the complete stories, balanced ones were recalled better; unbalanced stories were not converted into balanced ones, even though they were remembered less well. For incomplete-but-balanceable stories, errors in recall served to balance the triplets in which they occurred; for incomplete-and-unbalanceable stories, they did not.

### 4. A Reaction-Time Measure of Processing Balanced and Unbalanced Structures from Memory

Sentis and Burnstein (1979) had subjects read scenarios which described either balanced or unbalanced patterns between two persons and an attitude issue. Subsequently, subjects were presented with either (a) one, two, or all three of the relations from the scenario or (b) the opposite of one, two, or all three relations; in each case, subjects indicated whether or not the pattern was part of the original scenario. For unbalanced scenarios, reaction time for true patterns increased as the number of relations in the pattern increased. Conversely, for balanced scenarios, reaction time for true patterns *decreased* as the number of relations in the pattern increased.

To account for this outcome, Sentis and Burnstein proposed that balanced structures are stored in memory as complete, organized units. The entire unit is later retrieved from memory for comparison to test patterns. When the test pattern contains all three relations, it can be compared directly to the recalled unit; when the test pattern contains only one or two relations, the recalled structure must be decomposed in order to permit the proper comparison. Therefore, reaction time is shorter for identifying a complete balanced structure than for identifying part of that structure. By contrast, the authors suggested that the three relations of an unbalanced structure are stored separately. Each relation must be retrieved separately for comparison to test patterns, which accounts for the substantial increase in reaction time for unbalanced patterns as the number of relations increases.

### 5.   Long-Term Recall of Balanced and Unbalanced Structures

Crockett (1979) asked subjects to learn to a standard criterion the relations in one of four four-person structures. One of these structures was balanced, another was unbalanced but could be rendered balanced by changing only one relation, and the other two were fully unbalanced. The learned structure was then recalled after an interval of 15 min, 1 week, or 4 weeks. There were no differences between groups in recall after 15 min. After 1 week, the structure that could be balanced by changing only one relation was recalled significantly less well than the other three. After 4 weeks, the balanced structure was recalled significantly better than the other three, which were recalled about equally poorly. Again, unbalanced structures were not converted in recall to balanced ones; instead, incorrect unbalanced patterns were produced. Evidence for the use of positivity and source/target generalization was slight and restricted to the recall of initially unbalanced structures.

### 6.   Summary Comments

Four of these experiments found clear evidence of the effects of balance upon recall, and minimal evidence for the other conceptual rules. In two experiments—those of Gerard and Fleischer (1969) and Shapiro and Sherif (1975)— immediate recall of unbalanced structures, or of those involving disagreement between P and O, was better than that of balanced ones, or those with P–O agreement, probably because more time was spent studying the former.

It is important to note that balance and the other conceptual rules were not employed to reconstruct partly remembered structures. Instead, it seems that balance served as a social schema for organizing consistent patterns of relations and that schema-consistent patterns are recalled as a whole. As Picek et al. proposed, "during presentation the structures are encoded in a way that indicates them to be either 'socially balanced and logical' or 'socially imbalanced and illogical.' At testing this code is recalled" (1975, p. 767). That is, at recall the perceiver seems to access the reasonable and complete pattern of a balanced structure as a unit. Unbalanced structures, however, appear to be remembered as "unreasonable." They are not transformed into balanced ones. But when individual relations are forgotten over time, subjects have no readily available schema by which to reproduce the correct unbalanced pattern.

## V.   General Implications

A comparative tally of the use of the balance, agreement, and positivity rules in the research reviewed above shows balance winning in a landslide. In the prediction of missing relations, the learning of patterns of relations, and the recall of learned patterns, the vast majority of experiments found clear evidence of the use of balance and much less evidence for the other rules. Furthermore, most of the exceptions to the dominance of balance were easily explained, as when the amount of material subjects had to assimilate overwhelmed their cognitive resources, or when subjects who had suffered a loss of self-esteem expressed liking for others who praised them.

A similar dominance of balance over agreement and positivity has not been reported in other reviews (Zajonc, 1968; Wyer, 1974, Chapters 5 and 10; Mower White, 1979). Why the difference? One reason is that more research was available to the present article. But a more potent reason is that attention in this article has been restricted to research into the processing of information about relations in small social structures. Experiments which asked subjects to rate the pleasantness of patterns of stimuli were included in earlier reviews but not in this one. Such experiments do not reveal this dominance of balance over agreement and positivity. Crockett (1980a) has reviewed the literature on ratings of pleasantness of these situations. In order to point up the differences between that literature and the research considered above, let us summarize briefly the conclusions from that review.

## A. RESULTS OBSERVED FROM RATINGS OF BALANCED AND UNBALANCED STRUCTURES

In experiments of this sort, subjects are asked to rate stimulus patterns on one or more rating scales. Almost always, the stimulus patterns are the three-element structures in Table I. Ratings are made on scales like Pleasant–Tense or (less often) Consistent–Inconsistent or Expected–Unexpected. Ratings of consistency and expectedness yield different patterns of results from pleasantness ratings; therefore, the two types of studies must be considered separately.

### 1. Ratings of Consistency, Expectedness, and Similar Dimensions

Experiments in which subjects rate balanced and unbalanced structures on dimensions like consistent–inconsistent typically report that balanced structures are rated as more consistent or more to-be-expected than unbalanced ones. These ratings also show some evidence for positivity, in that balance effects are greater in structures in which P likes O than those in which P dislikes O. But even when P dislikes O, significant balance effects are typically found for ratings on consistency, expectedness, and similar dimensions.

### 2. Ratings of the Pleasantness of Situations

By contrast, ratings on dimensions like pleasant–tense or pleasant–unpleasant do not vary with balance but with the functional implications of those situations for P, the character with whom subjects are usually asked to identify. The pattern of the results differs according to whether the third element in the structure, along with P and O, is another person or an inanimate attitude object.

1. For structures that include P, another person O, and an issue, x:
    (a) When the other person, O, and the issue, x, are both left unspecified and ambiguous, situations in which P agrees with a liked O about x are rated as pleasant. All other situations—disagreement with a liked O about x or any involvement with a disliked O—are rated as unpleasant. That is, the satisfaction of having one's views affirmed by a friend is rated as pleasant; the dissatisfaction of one's views being challenged by a friend is rated as unpleasant; and the dissatisfaction of any association with an enemy is also rated as unpleasant.
    (b) When the issue is important to the subject, or when the subject expects to interact with O about x, agreement effects are found. As in 1(a), agreement with a friend is satisfying and pleasant whereas disagreement with a friend is dissatisfying and unpleasant. However, for important topics, to agree with an enemy is substantially more satisfying and pleasant than to disagree with an enemy, even though agreement with an enemy is by no means as pleasant as agreement with a friend.
2. For structures that include P, O, and a third person, Q:
    (a) When O and Q are unspecified, the results are the same as in 1(a), above: Situations in which P and O agree about Q are rated as pleasant; all other situations are rated as unpleasant.
    (b) When O and Q are identified as known acquaintances of P, Newcomb's nonbalance effects are found. Agreement with a liked O is satisfying and pleasant, whereas disagreement with a liked O is unsatisfying and unpleasant, as in the preceding cases. However, any situation involving a disliked O receives neutral ratings, neither pleasant nor unpleasant. Newcomb (1968) argues that in such situations, P does not have to interact with O and can, therefore, remain unconcerned about O's opinions.
    (c) When the situation is described as relatively permanent, pleasantness ratings vary with the number of positive relations in the structure and not with balance or agreement. Apparently, in a continuing situation any dislike is disturbing—especially when it involves the central character, P. The more general the dislike, the greater the disturbance and the unpleasantness. For example, the balanced situation in which P must associate with two enemies who are friends of each other is rated as very unpleasant.
    (d) When some of the relations in a structure are asymmetric, those

situations in which P has some opportunity to enter into alliances with one or more others—and hence achieve some satisfactions—are rated the most pleasant.

Crockett (1980a) accounted for these results by proposing that the amount of positive or negative affect that will be evoked by a situation—the situation's degree of pleasantness or unpleasantness for P—will depend upon whether the situation promises to yield satisfactions or dissatisfactions to P. Sometimes agreement with a disliked person will promote satisfaction and disagreement dissatisfaction; at other times the more the hostility (or the less the positivity) in the group the less the satisfaction; at still other times, agreement or disagreement with a disliked O is of no concern to P and nonbalance effects are found. In short, ratings of a situation on the pleasantness–unpleasantness dimension depend upon the situation's implications for P's satisfaction, not upon its balance.

By contrast, ratings of the consistency or expectedness of stimulus patterns reveal regular balance effects. That is, subjects anticipate that situations will be balanced even if—as when P is interacting with two enemies who like each other—those situations promise to be unpleasant.

### B. A PROCESSING ALGORITHM FOR THE USE OF INFERENTIAL RULES IN LEARNING

How does a subject employ an inferential rule to learn the relations in a structure? Figure 1 presents a processing algorithm which illustrates one possible sequence. The algorithm is written for the paired-associates paradigm, but it is easily generalized to other information-processing tasks. It is designed to apply to any inferential rule, but it will be illustrated with balance.

We begin when the subject is presented with one stimulus pair, say P and R. The subject's task is to predict whether P likes R. First, the subject retrieves from memory whatever relations, if any, he or she knows for the structure that includes P and R. A check is made of these relations to see if they include a value for P–R.

### 1. No Memory for P–R Relation

Suppose the subject can remember no value for that relation. Because some response must be made, the subject says either ''Like'' or ''Dislike'' and then checks to find the correct answer. The correct relation between P and R is then entered in memory, along with the R–P relation which is inferred by the property of symmetry. (We leave without discussion the question of whether the correct answer is more effectively stored if the subject guessed right than if he or she guessed wrong.) Memory is also checked for relations between P or R and any other members of the structure. If such relations are found, inferences are made

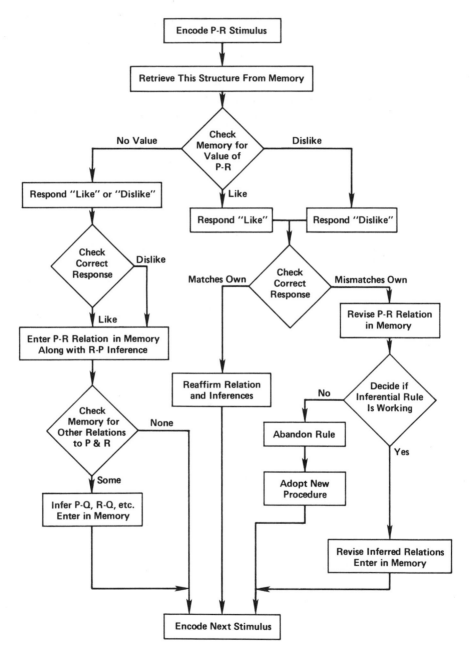

Fig. 1.   Processing algorithm for learning a pattern of relationships.

by the properties of transitivity or antitransitivity about the relations between P or R and those other persons. The subject then proceeds to the next stimulus pair.

### 2.  The Correct P–R Relation Is Recalled

On some trial, the subject will find a value in memory for the relation between P and R, will make the Like or Dislike response with some confidence, and will check its accuracy against the correct response. If the subject was right, that relation and others that it implies are reaffirmed in memory, the subject's confidence in the inferential rule is strengthened, and he or she proceeds to the next stimulus pair.

### 3.  An Incorrect P–R Relation Is Recalled

Suppose the subject's memory was wrong, either because he or she misremembered or because an inferred relation was incorrect. Then the P–R and R–P relations must first be revised and the correct values entered in memory. The subject must then make a quick decision about whether to continue using the previous inferential rule. If the error occurs early in the learning, or if there is some evidence that the rule is working, or, perhaps, if the subject can think of no alternative, then continued use of the rule will probably occur. This means that inferences from the revised P–R relation must also be drawn and entered in memory, replacing other relations that may have been there.

On the other hand, if the subject decides that the conceptual rule is not working and must be abandoned, then some new processing strategy will be adopted. This may result in a shift to some other inferential rule—say from balance to positivity—or, in the extreme case, in a determination to learn the relations by rote memory, unaided by inferential rules.

### 4.  Two Implications

We call attention to two implications of this algorithm, both of which fit the results reviewed above. The first has to do with rate of learning. If the inferential rule fully matches the structure, learning will be rapid. If it partially matches the structure, learning will be especially slow because the subject will be unlikely to abandon the rule early and its continued use will provide mistaken inferences which must be repeatedly revised. If a rule completely violates the relations in a structure, rate of learning should be intermediate to the other cases owing to a relatively early abandonment of the rule and the avoidance of continued errors that its use would produce.

The second conclusion has to do with the number of relations that can be learned by a complex rule like balance. The algorithm proposes that subjects use their experience with the stimulus pairs to make repeated revisions of relations that are stored in memory. Such revisions require that the elements of the structure and the relations among them be shifted repeatedly from long-term store to focal attention. This becomes difficult as the size of the structure increases. Consequently, use of a complex rule with the paired-associates procedure limits quite severely the size of the structure that can be learned. In fact, the research reviewed above suggests that the upper limit in size of structure for the use of the balance rule is in the range of four to six elements, or 6 to 15 symmetric relations. Note, however, that this limit holds only for paired-associates learning. Other procedures, which help subjects to visualize the elements and their relations, also enable them to use complex inferential rules with considerably larger structures. For example, DeSoto *et al.* (1968) used the following format to present subjects with all of the directed relations in 10-person groups:

> Bill is a friend of . . . Dave, John, Stan.
> Bill is an enemy of . . . Carl, Fred, Hank, Pete, Walt, Gary.
> Carl is a friend of . . . John, Fred, Hank, Pete, Walt.
> Carl is an enemy of . . . Bill, Dave, Stan, Gary.

On each trial, subjects could scan the information for a fixed time. They were able to learn the 90 directed relations (or 45 symmetric relations) of balanced structures in relatively few trials.

### 5.  Extension of the Algorithm to Other Acquisition Tasks

Suppose all of the relations are presented simultaneously, either as above or in a written paragraph. Subjects are no longer required to handle the information one item at a time and in an inflexible order. Instead, they can scan the material at will, returning to reexamine earlier relations and skipping ahead to later ones. Inferences that are made from the balance rule, say, can be checked directly. If they are confirmed—that is, if the structure is balanced—then encoding of the information is rapid and accurate. If the information describes a structure that is incomplete but balanceable, missing relations are inferred from the balance rule and remembered as if they had been part of the information (Picek *et al.*, 1975). Subjects spend more time examining unbalanced structures than balanced ones (Sentis, cited in Sentis & Burnstein, 1979), presumably checking and rechecking the inconsistencies that such structures contain. In short, the inferential processes operate in much the same way for these acquisition tasks as in paired-associates learning except that inferences can be checked more rapidly and in a sequence that is not controlled by the experimenter.

### C.  RETRIEVAL COMPARED TO ACQUISITION

It appears that the balance schema operates in a perceiver's cognitive system, probably as a predilection to treat sentiments, attitudes, and unit relations as equivalence relations. During acquisition, partial information about relations in a group invokes that schema, so that inferences may be drawn about unknown relations. The schema facilitates the acquisition of structures that are balanced or balanceable, in a manner similar to the one sketched out above.

But the balance schema is not employed in the same way in retrieval from memory as in acquisition. How and whether the schema operates depends upon whether the learned structures were balanced or unbalanced. Balanced structures are stored as a unit. They are "reasonable" or "logical" patterns. When, some time after acquisition, a balanced structure is recalled from memory, even if some of the individual relations have been forgotten, the fact that the pattern was stored as a reasonable one permits forgotten relations to be reconstructed.

By contrast, relations from unbalanced structures seem not to be recalled as a cohesive unit. If subjects are permitted to do so, they spend more time examining unbalanced structures than balanced ones.; therefore, immediate recall may be as good or better for unbalanced structures as for balanced ones. But for delayed recall, the matter is different. If some of the relations have been forgotten when the structure is recalled, the absence of a schema to accommodate the illogical pattern of relations prevents its ready reconstruction. In the research conducted to date, it does not seem that the balance schema interferes with the recall of unbalanced structures, for they are not transformed in memory into balanced ones; instead, the absence of any organizing schema prevents the perceiver from producing the correct pattern of relations for unbalanced structures. Whereas balanced structures seem to persist in memory like a good Gestalt, unbalanced ones appear to dissipate, and not to be reconstructed, for lack of coherent unity.

## D.  LOGICAL AND PHENOMENOLOGICAL STATUS OF INFERENTIAL RULES

All this makes the use of balance and other rules seem very cut and dried, altogether logical and conscious. Such can hardly be the case. No doubt, inferences are usually made quickly, intuitively, and without lengthy reflection. Few subjects, if any, would be able to explain how they had employed symmetry or transitivity or antitransitivity to arrive at one or another inferred relation. Indeed, Gerbing and Hunter (1979) asked subjects to explain their predictions of missing relations in three-person structures. Two types of explanations dominated. The more common type centered around common interests: "If O likes P who dislikes Q, then O is likely to have interests in common with P but not with Q. Therefore, O will dislike Q." The other type was based on the affective consistency of the situation: "When the people dislike other people, they stand together because of that dislike." Both explanations fit the balance rule[14] but

---

[14]Gerbing and Hunter (1979) imply that the explanations based on common interests fall outside of the framework of balance theory. However, as we have seen, the balance rule predicts that friends will agree, and enemies will disagree, about issues, which is the essence of the common-interests explanation.

neither one approaches a formulation of the properties of transitivity and antitransitivity.

But it is not necessary that perceivers be able to formulate the logical properties of rules they employ. We often use principles we cannot make explicit. Most speakers produce grammatical sentences, for example, without being able to verbalize the rules of grammar they have been using. Similarly, a perceiver can treat sentiments, attitudes, and unit relations as equivalence relations without being aware of the underlying properties that this usage presupposes. Still, it is interesting to note that a variety of common-sense aphorisms encapsulate the essence of the logical properties involved in the balance rule: symmetry, "People like those who like them"; transitivity, "Any friend of a friend of mine is a friend of mine," and "How can a nice person like you agree with a stupid thing like that?"; antitransitivity, "The enemy of my enemy is my friend," and "If she is against it, I'll probably be for it"; and unit relation–sentiment connections, "Birds of a feather flock together," and "Work with a man long enough and you'll come to like him."

Such adages do not validate an inferential rule, but they demonstrate that the principles it embodies are captured in common-sense discourse. That the same principles operate in the processing of information about small social groups is revealed in the research reviewed above.

### E.   SOME QUESTIONS AND HYPOTHESES

If it can be agreed that the balance rule operates as a schema in the acquisition and retrieval of patterns of social relations, then experimental attention can now turn from reexamining that proposition to a consideration of more complex questions. There are a good many such questions to examine.

For one thing, it is clear that balance and other rules are used as tentative hypotheses, not as hard-and-fast laws. When they do not work, they are eventually abandoned for other organizing principles. What determines whether or when balance will be abandoned for another principle? What kinds of principles are employed for what kinds of unbalanced situations? There is some evidence relevant to the latter question. Crockett (1980b) showed that configurational properties of a pattern of relations operate in conjunction with balance and other rules; Rosenberg and Abelson (1960) found that subjects subordinate the balance rule to important goals, such as the maintenance of profits in a business. Stroebe *et al.* (1970) reported that differentiation of aspects of a situation from one another permitted subjects to recognize without difficulty a potentially unbalanced pattern of relations.

We need to explore in detail the complicated connections between balance and other conceptual principles. This article has referred more than once to Sentis's observation that, if they are given the chance, subjects spend more time examining unbalanced three-element structures than balanced ones. Are they trying to find a sensible explanation for the unbalanced patterns? What kinds of explanations of unbalance make sense to perceivers? Once a sensible explanation has been found (or once the experimenter provides such an explanation) is the resulting set of cognitions, like balanced patterns, stored and recalled as a coherent unit instead of piecemeal?

And how are the balance principles acquired? It appears that their use increases with individual development, but the specific stages at which the different rules are employed remains to be determined. Which principles appear first? Symmetry? Transitivity? The inferences from unit relations to sentiments? Or are they all acquired at about the same time? Is the use of the balance principles preceded by the simpler rules—positivity and agreement—or are the three sets of rules acquired independently? These questions and others yet more complex await exploration. Let us hope that future research will turn in their direction.

## ACKNOWLEDGMENTS

Thanks are due to Professors Grace and Fritz Heider, Theodore M. Newcomb, C. Daniel Batson, Allan N. Press, and Gustav Jahoda for comments on versions of this paper and for encouragement during its writing. And special appreciation is accorded to Fritz Heider, who worked out a detailed, robust, and fruitful conceptual framework which has remained essentially intact after more than 30 years of experimental investigation.

## REFERENCES

Abelson, R. P. Modes of resolution of belief dilemmas. *Journal of Conflict Resolution,* 1959, **3,** 343–352.

Abelson, R. P. Psychological implication. In R. P. Abelson, E. Aronson, W. J. McGuire, T. M. Newcomb, M. J. Rosenberg, & P. Tannenbaum (Eds.), *Theories of cognitive consistency: A sourcebook.* Chicago: Rand McNally, 1968.

Abelson, R. P. The structure of belief systems. In K. Colby & R. Schank (Eds.), *Computer simulation of thought and language.* San Francisco: Freeman, 1973.

Aronson, E., & Cope, V. My enemy's enemy is my friend. *Journal of Personality and Social Psychology,* 1968, **8,** 8–12.

Atwood, G. A developmental study of cognitive balancing in hypothetical three-person systems. *Child Development,* 1969, **40,** 73–80.

Birkhoff, G., & MacLane, S. *A survey of modern algebra.* New York: Macmillan, 1953.

Burnstein, E. Sources of cognitive bias in the representation of simple social structures: Balance, minimal change, positivity, reciprocity, and the respondent's own attitude. *Journal of Personality and Social Psychology,* 1967, **7,** 36–48.

Byrne, D. *The attraction paradigm.* New York: Academic Press, 1971.

Cartwright, D. O., & Harary, F. Structural balance: A generalization of Heider's theory. *Psychological Review,* 1956, **63,** 277–293.

Cottrell, N. B. Heider's structural balance principle as a conceptual rule. *Journal of Personality and Social Psychology,* 1975, **31,** 713–720.

Cottrell, N. B., Ingraham, L. H., & Monfort, F. W. The retention of balanced and unbalanced structures. *Journal of Personality,* 1971, **39**, 112–131.

Crockett, W. H. *A defense of the balance principle against apparently-inconsistent evidence.* Paper presented at the meeting of the Western Psychological Association, San Francisco, April 1971.

Crockett, W. H. Inferential rules in the learning and recall of patterns of sentiments. *Journal of Personality,* 1979, **47**, 658–676.

Crockett, W. H. *Conceptual rules and ratings of balanced and unbalanced structures.* In preparation, University of Kansas, 1980. (a)

Crockett, W. H. *Inferential rules and configurational forces in learning to classify three-element structures.* In preparation, University of Kansas, 1980. (b)

Darley, J. M., & Berscheid, E. Increased liking as a result of the anticipation of personal contact. *Human Relations,* 1967, **20**, 29–39.

Delia, J. G., & Crockett, W. H. Social schemas, cognitive complexity, and the learning of social structures. *Journal of Personality,* 1973, **41**, 413–429.

DeSoto, C. B. Learning a social structure. *Journal of Abnormal and Social Psychology,* 1960, **60**, 417–421.

DeSoto, C. B., Henley, N. M., & London, M. Balance and the grouping schema. *Journal of Personality and Social Psychology,* 1968, **8**, 1–12.

DeSoto, C. B., & Kuethe, J. L. Perception of mathematical properties of interpersonal relations. *Perceptual and Motor Skills,* 1958, **8**, 1–7.

DeSoto, C. B., & Kuethe, J. L. Subjective probabilities of interpersonal relations. *Journal of Abnormal and Social Psychology,* 1959, **59**, 290–294.

Deutsch, M., & Solomon, L. Reactions to evaluations by others as influenced by self evaluation. *Sociometry,* 1959, **2**, 513–521.

Dittes, J. E. Attractiveness of group as a function of self esteem and acceptance by group. *Journal of Abnormal and Social Psychology,* 1959, **59**, 77–82.

Dutton, D. G. Effect of feedback parameters on congruency versus positivity effects in reactions to personal evaluations. *Journal of Personality and Social Psychology,* 1972, **24**, 366–372.

Dutton, D. G., & Arrowood, A. J. Situational factors in evaluation congruency and interpersonal attraction. *Journal of Personality and Social Psychology,* 1971, **18**, 222–229.

Feather, N. T. A structural balance model of communication effects. *Psychological Review,* 1964, **71**, 291–313.

Feather, N. T. A structural balance analysis of evaluative behavior. *Human Relations,* 1965, **18**, 171–185. (a)

Feather, N. T. Reactions to communications under conditions of source responsibility and source coercion. *Australian Journal of Psychology,* 1965, **17**, 179–194. (b)

Feather, N. T. The prediction of interpersonal attraction: Effects of sign and strength of relations in different structures. *Human Relations,* 1966, **19**, 213–237.

Feather, N. T. A structural balance approach to the analysis of communication acts. In L. Berkowitz (Ed.), *Advances in experimental social psychology,* Vol. 3. New York: Academic Press, 1967. (a)

Feather, N. T. Effects of institutional affiliation and attitude discrepancy on evaluation of communications and interpersonal attraction. *Human Relations,* 1967, **20**. (b)

Feather, N. T. Attitude and selective recall. *Journal of Personality and Social Psychology,* 1969, **12**, 310–319.

Feather, N. T. Balancing and positivity effects in social recall. *Journal of Personality,* 1970, **38**, 602–628.

Feather, N. T., & Armstrong, D. J. Effects of variations in source attitude, receiver attitude, and communication stand on reactions to source and content of communications. *Journal of Personality,* 1967, **35**, 435–454.

Feather, N. T., & Jeffries, J. Balancing and extremity effects in reactions of receivers to source and content of communications. *Journal of Personality*, 1967, **35**, 194–213.

Festinger, L., & Hutte, H. A. An experimental investigation of the effect of unstable interpersonal relations in a group. *Journal of Abnormal and Social Psychology*, 1954, **49**, 513–523.

Flament, C. *Applications of graph theory to group structure.* New York: Prentice-Hall, 1963.

Frey, L. R. *The differential effects of three inferential rules on predictions about unknown interpersonal relationships within simple social structures as mediated by subjects' involvement in the task activity.* Unpublished doctoral disseratation, University of Kansas, 1979.

Fuller, C. H. Comparison of two experimental paradigms on tests of Heider's balance theory. *Journal of Personality and Social Psychology*, 1974, **30**, 802–806.

Gerard, H. B., & Fleischer, L. Recall and pleasantness of balanced and unbalanced cognitive structures. *Journal of Personality and Social Psycyology*, 1967, **7**, 332–337.

Gerbing, D. W., & Hunter, J. E. Phenomenological bases for the attribution of balance to social structure. *Personality and Social Psychology Bulletin*, 1979, **5**, 299–302.

Gollob, H. F. Some tests of a social inference model. *Journal of Personality and Social Psychology*, 1974, **29**, 157–172. (a)

Gollob, H. F. The subject-verb-object approach to social cognition. *Psychological review*, 1974, **81**, 286–321. (b)

Gormly, A. V. Behavioral effects of receiving agreement or disagreement from a peer. *Personality and Social Psychology Bulletin*, 1979, **5**, 405–410.

Granberg, D., & Brent, E. E. Dove-hawk placements in the 1968 election: Application of social judgment and balance theories. *Journal of Personality and Social Psychology*, 1974, **29**, 687–695.

Harary, F., Norman, R. Z., & Cartwright, D. O. *Structural models: An introduction to the theory of directed graphs.* New York: Wiley, 1965.

Heider, F. Attitudes and cognitive organizations. *Journal of Psychology*, 1946, **21**, 107–112.

Heider, F. *The psychology of interpersonal relations.* New York: Wiley, 1958.

Innes, J. M. The influence of attitude on the learning of balanced and unbalanced social structures. *European Journal of Social Psychology*, 1973, **3**, 91–94.

Insko, C. A., Thompson, V. D., Stroebe, W., Shaud, K. F., Pinner, B. E., & Layton, B. D. Implied evaluation and the similarity-attraction effect. *Journal of Personality and Social Psychology*, 1973, **25**, 297–308.

Insko, C. A., & Wilson, M. Interpersonal attraction as a function of social interaction. *Journal of Personality and Social Psychology*, 1977, **35**, 903–911.

Jacobs, L., Berscheid, E., & Walster, E. Self esteem and attraction. *Journal of Personality and Social Psychology*, 1971, **17**, 84–91.

Jones, S. C. Some determinants of individual evaluating behavior. *Journal of Personality and Social Psychology*, 1966, **3**, 397–403.

Jones, S. C., Knurek, D. A., & Regan, D. T. Variables affecting reactions to social acceptance and rejection. *Journal of Social Psychology*, 1973, **90**, 269–284.

Jones, S. C., & Pines, H. A. Self-revealing events and interpersonal evaluations. *Journal of Personality and Social Psychology*, 1968, **8**, 277–281.

Jones S. C., & Ratnor, C. Commitment to self appraisal and interpersonal evaluations. *Journal of Personality and Social Psychology*, 1967, **6**, 442–447.

Layton, R. E., & Insko, C. A. Anticipated interaction and the similarity-attraction effect. *Sociometry*, 1974, **37**, 149–162.

McNeel, S. P., & Messick, D. M. A Bayesian analysis of subjective probabilities of interpersonal relationships. *Acta Psychologica*, 1970, **34**, 311–321.

Miller, C. E. Using hpothetical P-O-X situations in studies of balance: The problem of "misconstrual." *Personality and Social Psychology Bulletin*, 1979, **5**, 303–306.

Miller, H., & Geller, D. Structural balance in dyads. *Journal of Personality and Social Psychology*, 1972, **21**, 135–138.

Mirels, H., & Mills, J. Perception of the pleasantness and competence of a partner. *Journal of Abnormal and Social Psychology*, 1964, **68**, 456–459.

Morrisette, J. O. An experimental study of the theory of structural balance. *Human Relations*, 1958, **11**, 239–254.

Mosher, R. The learning of congruent and incongruent social structures. *Journal of Social Psychology*, 1967, **13**, 285–289.

Mower White, C. J. Factors affecting balance, agreement, and positivity biases in POQ and POX triads. *European Journal of Social Psychology*, 1979, **9**, 129–148.

Neisser, U. *Cognition and reality*. San Francisco: Freeman, 1976.

Newcomb, T. M. An approach to the study of communicative acts. *Psychological Review*, 1953, **60**, 393–404.

Newcomb, T. M. Individual systems of orientation. In S. Koch (Ed.), *Psychology: A study of a science*, Vol. 3. New York: McGraw Hill, 1959.

Newcomb, T. M. Interpersonal balance. In R. P. Abelson, E. Aronson, W. J. McGuire, T. M. Newcomb, M. J. Rosenberg, & P. H. Tannenbaum (Eds.), *Theories of cognitive consistency: A sourcebook*. Chicago: Rand, McNally, 1968.

Ohashi, M. Sociometric choice behavior and interpersonal perception in triads. *Japanese Psychological Research*, 1964, **6**, 72–87.

Picek, J. S., Sherman, S. J., & Shiffrin, R. M. Cognitive organization and coding of social structures. *Journal of Personality and Social Psychology*, 1975, **31**, 758–768.

Pomonis, B. *Developmental effects of cognitive balance in children*. Unpublished M.A. thesis, University of Kansas, 1978.

Press, A. N., Crockett, W. H., & Rosenkrantz, P. S. Cognitive complexity and the learning of balanced and unbalanced social structures. *Journal of Personality*, 1969, **37**, 541–553.

Regan, J. W. Liking for evaluators: Consistency and self-esteem theories. *Journal of Experimental Social Psychology*, 1976, **12**, 159–169.

Rodrigues, A. The biasing effect of agreement in balanced and unbalanced triads. *Journal of Personality*, 1968, **36**, 138–153.

Rosenberg, M. J., & Abelson, R. P. An analysis of cognitive balancing. In C. I. Hovland & M. J. Rosenberg (Eds.), *Attitude organization and change*. New Haven, Connecticut: Yale University Press, 1960.

Rubin, Z., & Zajonc, R. B. Structural bias and generalization in the learning of social structures. *Journal of Personality*, 1969, **37**, 310–324.

Sampson, E. E., & Insko, C. A. Cognitive consistency and performance in the autokinetic situation. *Journal of Abnormal and Social Psychology*, 1964, **65**, 184–192.

Schachter, S. Deviation, rejection, and communication. *Journal of Abnormal and Social Psychology*, 1951, **46**, 190–207.

Scott, W. A. Cognitive complexity and cognitive balance. *Sociometry*, 1963,**26**, 66–74.

Sentis, K. P., & Burnstein, E. Remembering schema-consistent information: Effects of a balance schema on recognition memory. *Journal of Personality and Social Psychology*, 1979, **37**, 2200–2211.

Shepard, R. N., Hovland, C. I., & Jenkins, H. N. Learning and memorization of classifications. *Psychological Monographs*, 1961, **75**, (Whole No. 517).

Sherman, S., & Wolosin, R. Cognitive biases in a recognition task. *Journal of Personality*, 1973, **41**, 395–412.

Shrader, E. G., & Lewit, D. W. Structural factors in cognitive balancing behavior. *Human Relations*, 1962, **15**, 265–276.

Singer, J. E. Motivation for consistency. In S. Feldman (Ed.), *Cognitive consistency*. New York: Academic Press, 1966.

Singer, J. E. Consistency as a stimulus processing mechanism. In R. P. Abelson, E. Aronson, W. J. McGuire, T. M. Newcomb, M. J. Rosenberg, & P. H. Tannenbaum (Eds.), *Theories of cognitive consistency: A sourcebook*. Chicago: Rand McNally, 1968.

Spiro, R. J., & Sherif, C. W. Consistency and relativity in selective recall with differing ego-involvement. *British Journal of Social and Clinical Psychology*, 1975, **14**, 351–361.

Stroebe, W., Thompson, V. D., Insko, C. A., & Reisman, S. R. Balance and differentiation in the evaluation of liked attitude objects. *Journal of Personality and Social Psychology*, 1970, **16**, 38–47.

Sussman, M., & Davis, H. H. Balance theory and the negative interpersonal relationship: Attraction and agreement in dyads and triads. *Journal of Personality*, 1975, **43**, 560–581.

Tashakkori, A., & Insko, C. A. Interpersonal attraction and the polarity of similar attitudes: A test of three balance models. *Journal of Personality and Social Psychology*, 1979, **37**, 2262–2277.

Taylor, H. F. Balance theory and change in the two person group. *Sociometry*, 1967, **38**, 262–279.

Tyler, T. R., & Sears, D. O. Coming to like obnoxious people when we must live with them. *Journal of Personality and Social Psychology*, 1977, **35**, 200–211.

Vickers, M., & Blanchard, E. B. The development of preference of cognitive balance. *Journal of Genetic Psychology*, 1973, **122**, 189–195.

Wellens, A. D., & Thistlewaite, D. L. An analysis of two quantitative theories of cognitive balance. *Psychological Review*, 1971, **78**, 141–150. (a)

Wellens, A. D., & Thistlewaite, D. L. Comparison of three theories of cognitive balance. *Journal of Personality and Social Psychology*, 1971, **20**, 82–92. (b)

Wiest, W. M. A quantitative extension of Heider's theory of cognitive balance applied to interpersonal perception and self esteem. *Psychological Monographs*, 1965, **79**, (Whole No. 607).

Willis, R. H., & Burgess, T. D. G. Cognitive and affective balance in sociometric dyads. *Journal of Personality and Social Psychology*, 1974, **29**, 145–152.

Wyer, R. S. *Cognitive organization and change*. New York: Wiley, 1974.

Wyer, R. S., & Lyon, J. D. A test of cognitive balance theory implications for social inference processes. *Journal of Personality and Social Psychology*, 1970, **16**, 598–615.

Yang, K. S., & Yang, P. H. L. The effects of anxiety and threat on the learning of balanced and unbalanced social structures. *Journal of Personality and Social Psychology*, 1973, **26**, 201–207.

Zajonc, R. B. Cognitive theories in social psychology. In G. Lindzey & E. Aronson (Eds.), *Handbook of Social Psychology* (2nd ed.), Vol. 1. Reading, Massachusetts: Addison-Wesley, 1968.

Zajonc, R. B., & Burnstein, E. The learning of balanced and unbalanced social structures. *Journal of Personality*, 1965, **33**, 153–163. (a)

Zajonc, R. B., & Burnstein, E. Structural balance, reciprocity, and positivity as sources of cognitive bias. *Journal of Personality*, 1965, **33**, 570–583. (b)

Zajonc, R. B., & Sherman, S. Structural balance and the induction of relations. *Journal of Personality*, 1967, **35**, 635–650.

Zeigarnik, B. Ueber das Behalten von erledigten und unerledigten. *Handlungen Psychologische Forschung*, 1927, **9**, 1–85.

# EPISODE COGNITION: INTERNAL REPRESENTATIONS OF INTERACTION ROUTINES[1]

## Joseph P. Forgas

SCHOOL OF PSYCHOLOGY
UNIVERSITY OF NEW SOUTH WALES
SYDNEY, AUSTRALIA

## I. Introduction

One of the most obvious features of everyday social life is that it largely consists of recurring, patterned activities. Most of our interactions with others occur in a limited number of situations, such as attending a colloquium, eating in a restaurant, having coffee with X, or visiting a doctor. Indeed, the very predictability of such episodes is what makes orderly interactions feasible (Mead, 1934) and what provides us with a sense of confidence in our dealings with others (Goffman, 1974). Although interest in such regular event sequences has a venerable history both in psychology (Barker, 1968; Brunswik, 1956; Murray, 1951;

[1]Financial support for many of the studies reported here was provided by the Australian Research Grants Commission.

ADVANCES IN EXPERIMENTAL SOCIAL
PSYCHOLOGY, VOL. 15

Lewin, 1951) and in sociology (Mead, 1934; Schutz, 1970; Thomas, 1928; Wolff, 1964), the study of interaction episodes is a relatively new field in social psychology. The recent advances made in our understanding of how cognitive representations about interaction routines originate, change, and affect our behavior are the topic of this article.

The Zeitgeist in social psychology in the past few years reflects a dramatic shift away from behaviorally oriented research toward the study of the internal, cognitive mechanisms and representations which govern social behavior (Bruner, 1976; Carroll & Payne, 1976; Hilgard, 1980a). One of the most important cognitive domains pertinent to social behavior is the implicit cognitive representations people have of their daily interactions. Such representations are variously called scripts (Abelson, 1976; Schank & Abelson, 1977; Bower, Black, & Turner, 1979), situations (Mischel, 1979; Pervin, 1976), action plans (Miller, Galanter, & Pribram, 1960), event schemata (Lichtenstein & Brewer, 1980), or social episodes (Forgas, 1976, 1978a, 1979b). Despite their diverse origins and objectives, these different research programs are all concerned with the cognitive and social characteristics of episode representations. For example, Abelson (1976) defined scripts as a ''coherent sequence of events expected by the individual, involving him as either a participant or an observer. Scripts are learned throughout the individual's lifetime both by participation in event sequences and by observation of event sequences'' (p. 33). And Forgas (1979b) defined social episodes as ''cognitive representations of stereotypical interaction sequences which are representative of a given cultural environment'' (p. 15). Throughout this article we shall take the term *social episode* to refer to such representations and the term *episode cognition* to refer to the field of their study.

The aim of this article is thus to provide a summary and a synthesis of the most recent research on episode cognition, to describe some of our own studies, and to outline the most promising prospects and practical implications of this work. We shall begin with a brief survey of the historical roots of interest in social episodes in psychology and sociology, followed by a review of recent research on situations and episodes in personality, social, cognitive, and clinical psychology. The major part of the article will be devoted to a discussion and integration of the two currently dominant approaches to episode cognition: the sociocultural strategy, based on modeling consensual episode spaces, and the information processing strategy, aiming to study the cognitive and affective factors in episode cognition. Finally, the practical implications of this work and the prospects of episode research in social psychology will be discussed.

## II.   The Background of Episode Cognition Research

Concern with how human beings come to codify, store, and systematize knowledge about the various interaction routines they engage in is by no means a new phenomenon. Both psychologists and sociologists have been interested in this issue for decades, with little or no interaction between the fields. However brief, this historical outline is necessary if only to show that contemporary terms such as scripts, situations, or episodes have a joint parentage in these disciplines.

## A. PSYCHOLOGICAL ANTECEDENTS

The concept of the "situation" is clearly the predecessor of the current interest in episodes, and the history of these terms in psychology is a fascinating one. By and large, it can be characterized as a gradual evolution from external, objective, physicalistic, and atomistic conceptualizations of situations, which originated with radical learning theory, to internal, cognitive, and holistic approaches as illustrated by recent work on social cognition. At the one extreme, we find behaviorist theories which would interpret behavior, for example in a restaurant, as a series of learned responses and response generalizations controlled by external reinforcers, such as food and drink. At the other extreme, cognitive and social psychologists in recent years argued that we have an internal schema, representation, or script for such routine activities as eating in a restaurant or visiting a dentist (Schank & Abelson, 1977). Such scripts not only regulate behavior (Abelson, 1980), but also influence the way we think about and remember events occurring in a restaurant (Bower et al., 1979). We shall attempt to provide a brief sketch of the way various psychological theories handled the concept of situations and episodes between these two extremes.

Radical behaviorism (Watson, 1913; Guthrie, 1952; Skinner, 1938) was perhaps the first psychological school to focus on the importance of external, environmental, and situational regularities in human behavior. However, due to the atomistic and reductionistic biases of the theory, comparative studies of situations and episodes were not undertaken. Some theorists, such as Kantor (1924) in his "interbehaviorism," proposed that more complex stimulus configurations may be thought of as "situations," and that an individual should be studied as "he interacts with all the various types of situations which constitute his behaviour circumstances" (1924, p. 92). Such "situationism" became the hallmark of modern social learning theory (Mischel, 1968; Bowers, 1973), although studies of situations and episodes were not part of orthodox behaviorism.

Gestalt psychology had an important influence on conceptualizations of social situations. Koffka (1935) differentiated between the external or "geographical" and the internal, "behavioral" situation. The perceived, behavioral environment found perhaps its most influential restatement in Lewin's field theory (1936, 1951). An actor's subjective representation of his life space is at the core of this theory: "the situation must be represented as it is 'real' for the individual in question, that is, as it affects him" (1936, p. 25). Lewin's conception of the life space as a phenomenal situation is holistic and interactionist: The actor and the situation are indivisible as a unit. Several theorists have recently argued for a similar reconceptualization of personality and social psychology (Ekehammar, 1974; Forgas, 1979b; Mischel, 1979; Pervin, 1976). Murray (1938, 1951) is another theorist who suggested that "the conduct of an individual cannot be formulated without a characterization of each confronting situation, physical and social . . . the organism and its milieu must be considered together, a single creature–environment interaction being a convenient short unit for psychology" (1938, pp. 39–40).

A particularly important contribution to the study of social situations and episodes is Brunswik's (1956) work on classifying situational events, and his arguments for a "representative" design in psychology, based on the careful sampling of the life situations relevant to the organism's everyday functioning: "the proper sampling of situations and problems may in the end be more important than proper sampling of subjects, considering the fact that individuals are probably on the whole much more alike than are situations" (p. 39). This view presaged current controversies about the role of situational variation in human behavior (Endler & Magnusson, 1975).

These early approaches selectively emphasize the external-environmental or the internal-perceived features of situations. Symbolic interactionism, perhaps still the most comprehensive theory of social cognition (Farr, 1980, 1981; Kando, 1977), allocates a pivotal place to cognitive representations about interaction routines. Mead's (1934) social behaviorism is based on the premise that a stimulus–response (S–R) theory which restricts itself to looking at simple atomistic S–R sequences excludes the uniquely human, symbolic level at which such links are endowed with representational meaning. Symbolic interactionism, as Mead's theory came to be called by Blumer (1969), emphasizes the social origins of all cognitive activity: "the internalization in our experience of the external conversation . . . which we carry on with other individuals . . . is the essence of thinking; and the gestures thus internalized are significant symbols because they have the same meaning for all individual members of a given society" (Mead, 1956, p. 159). It is the unique capacity of human beings for symbolic processes which enables them to build up expectations and internal representations about their daily interactions with each other. These representations are, in turn, the elementary building blocks of both socialized personalities and larger social systems. Social episodes are thus structural units in a culture which can be objectively established and consensually validated as social representations (Forgas, 1976; Moscovici, 1981; Triandis, 1972), and at the same time, they are also unique, ever-changing activities, which are newly reconstituted in each interaction by creative individuals (Stone & Farbermann, 1970).

[In] each episode or encounter that we engage in we find that the situation is partially structured by past definitions, it has already been defined in terms of role scripts and normative expectations. At the same time, the episode is always open, it is subject to reinterpretation, and the attendant possibility of the creation of new accounts and meanings. (Brittan, 1973, p. 84)

Mead's (1934) conception of social episodes as symbolic social objects bears some resemblance to theories that have come to be influential in cognitive psychology. Bartlett's (1932) notion of cognitive schema enjoys something of a renaissance today (Rosch & Lloyd, 1978; Rosch, 1975), and one could surmise that current work on scripts, natural categories, or prototypes (Cantor & Mischel, 1979; Hastie & Kumar, 1979; Forgas, 1982a) would have met with Mead's approval. Symbolic interactionism is a theory which, with its emphasis on social cognition and internal representations of interaction routines, is eminently social psychological. Now that the empirical tools are finally available to come to grips with these complex phenomena (Forgas, 1979a; Ginsburg, 1979; Schank & Abelson, 1977), symbolic interactionism may again be seen as a rich source of theories and hypotheses about the way social cognitive processes operate (Farr, 1980).

## B. SOCIOLOGICAL ANTECEDENTS

The symbolic interactionist perspective had its roots not only in psychology, but also in the kind of interpretive, cultural sociology mainly associated with Max Weber and his followers. Weber was unique among the nineteenth century "grand" theorists in that his conception of society was based on a theory of individual behavior and cognition. Meaningful "action is social . . . by virtue of the subjective meaning attached to it by the acting individual . . . it takes into account the behavior of others, and is thereby oriented in its course" (1968, p. 248). Even very complex and large-scale social processes, such as the advent of capitalism, may be analyzed in terms of meaningful individual actions and the subjective beliefs attached to them. This emphasis on meaningful individual action as the source of all social phenomena paved the way for an essentially cognitive approach to social behavior, which ultimately also influenced our thinking about interaction episodes.

This tradition is well represented by several twentieth century sociologists, such as W. I. Thomas, Florian Znaniecki, Willard Waller, and others. Thomas's concept of the "definition of the situation" directly anticipated current episode cognition research. He argued that "preliminary to any self-determined act . . . there is always a stage of examination or deliberation which we may call the definition of the situation" (Thomas, 1928/1966, p. 41). And later:

The individual does not find passively ready situations exactly similar to past situations; he must consciously define every situation . . . . The individual, in order to control reality for his needs must develop not a series of uniform reactions, but general schemes of situations;

his life–organization is a set of rules for definite situations, which may even be expressed in abstract formulas. (Thomas, 1928/1966, p. 29)

This approach is strikingly similar to contemporary interest in cognitive representations of social interaction episodes. Thomas was also among the first to recognize the crucial role of small-scale situations in making up the social order. Perhaps not surprisingly, the most successful method for culture training to date also relies on the critical incident or episode as its basic unit for teaching newcomers to understand the requirements of a new culture (Triandis, 1972).

Following Thomas, many sociologists continued to employ the technique of situational analysis. Waller (1961) relied on this method in his studies of family interactions and of the occupational milieus of groups such as teachers and academics. Many symbolic interactionist analyses are essentially descriptions of the subtle and often nonobvious symbols and props used in creating and staging a particular situation or episode (Stone & Farberman, 1970). The concern with situational analysis, the negotiation of the interaction episode, and the staging of social performances is central to Goffman's (1961, 1963, 1967) dramaturgical model which has become increasingly influential in social psychology over the past decade. Critics of conventional experimental social psychology drew much material from the cultural relativism (Gergen, 1973) and the situational emphasis (Harre & Secord, 1972) of this tradition.

Another sociologist who was interested in the episodic nature of social life was Alfred Schutz, who sought to combine Weber's ideas with Husserl's phenomenology to elaborate the role of individual representations, meanings, and reasons in social behavior. He emphasized the idiosyncratic nature of situation perception as based on "the sedimentation of all of man's previous experiences, organized in the habitual possession of his stock of knowledge at hand, and as such is his unique possession, given to him and to him alone" (Schutz, 1970, p. 73). This emphasis is echoed in recent calls for research on individual situation encoding strategies (cf. Mischel, 1979; Pervin, 1975c). But situations and episodes are not entirely phenomenological and subjective: There is an underlying body of cultural conventions, consensually established, which are the building blocks of subjective representations. Such "folkways" of a culture, in W. G. Sumner's use of the term, become incorporated in a person's life world: "the system of folkways establishes the standard in terms of which the in-group 'defines the situation.' Even more: originating in previous situations defined by the group, the scheme of interpretation that has stood the test so far becomes an element of the actual situation" (Schutz, 1970, p. 80). Such folkways are rules for acting in particular episodes, the equivalents to the behavioral scripts recently described by Abelson (1980), a system of "trustworthy recipes for interpreting the social world and for handling things and men in order to obtain the best results in every situation with a minimum of effort" (Schutz, 1970, p. 81).

These diverse schools of thought, Mead's (1934) symbolic interactionism,

Weber's (1947) cultural sociology, Thomas's (1928) situational analysis, and Schutz's (1970) phenomenology jointly contributed to the currently so influential microsociological movement in sociology. The study of social episodes and the symbolic processes used to represent, stage, manipulate, and enact such episodes are the central themes of Goffman's dramaturgical model, Garfinkel's ethnomethodology, and are at the heart of Harre and Secord's (1972) ethogenics, a proposed new paradigm for social psychology (Harre, 1981). This brief historical sketch can do little more than to point to the existence of long-standing interest in interaction episodes and prepare the way for a preliminary theory of episode representations.

## C. TOWARD A THEORY OF EPISODE COGNITION

Perhaps the most important theoretical insight emerging from the material reviewed above relates to the dual nature of social episodes, as both sociocultural and individual-psychological phenomena. In line with recent approaches to social cognition (cf. Krauss, 1980; Forgas, 1981a,b), any theory of episode cognition must take into account the interdependence of individual cognitive activity and consensual "collective representations" (Durkheim, 1898; Moscovici, 1981). Most existing research on social episodes has focused on either modeling collective and consensual episode representations or on studying the role of episode schemata in the cognitive activity of individuals. An integration of these two branches of research can only be achieved if the conceptual links between individual cognition and social representations are clearly recognized.

### 1. The Acquisition of Episode Representations

Cognitive representations of interaction episodes have their origin in the universal human attempt to categorize and structure the physical and social environment (Tajfel & Forgas, 1981; Rosch & Lloyd, 1978). The acquisition of prototypical representations about interaction routines is a direct consequence of social life (Mead, 1934). As we pass through social encounters, we often simplify and abstract our experiences into general schemes of classification. As Mervis and Rosch (1981) suggest, "Stimulus situations are unique, but organisms do not treat them uniquely; they respond on the basis of past learning and categorization" (p. 89). In the case of social episodes, such classifications are probably the joint result of the pre-existing pattern and structure in the interaction "types" practiced and sanctioned within any culture and the superimposition of idiosyncratic classificatory schemes on that cultural episode repertoire by individuals. The acquisition of categories such as social episodes is not a purely cognitive process of abstraction, however, and differs from cognitive explanations of schema acquisition in at least two important ways. First, the particular episode representations extracted and maintained by an individual are likely to be those which have functional significance for him (Tajfel, 1969), just as representations and scripts in childhood are formed "on the basis of function" (Nelson, Rescorla, Gruendel, & Benedict, 1978, p. 962). Several studies have shown that episode cognition is functionally related to the social status, background attitudes, and personality of the individual (Battistich & Thompson, 1980a,b; Forgas, 1978a, 1979b; Pervin, 1976). Second, the acquisition of episode representations is also influenced by the pre-existing cultural consensus about accepted patterns of interaction. Episode schemata thus do not originate in the cognitive activity of the individual, but are to a large extent passed on by members of the culture. Both the generation of such consensual episode schemata within a culture, and the cognitive internalization of such interaction prototypes by individuals is accomplished in the course of everyday social interaction. This account of the acquisition of episode representations is in many ways similar to symbolic interactionist explanations (Mead, 1934; Blumer, 1969), and to contemporary theorizing about the origins of at least some "natural" categories (cf. Rosch, Mervis, Gray, Johnson, & Boyes-Bream, 1976; Nelson *et al.*, 1978; Nelson, 1979).

## 2. The Nature of Episode Representations

Just like cognitive representations about other domains, cognitive representations about interaction episodes may be characterized in terms of structural features. Research on consensual episode representations (cf. section III) shows that culture-specific episode spaces may be characterized in terms of such quantitative indices as *complexity* (number of criterial features differentiating between episodes), *integration* (the extent to which different episodes are dispersed in the episode space), and *consensuality* (the extent to which different members of a subculture perceive episodes similarly) (Forgas, 1979b, 1981e). These structural indices of episode spaces may be empirically related to features of the social and group milieu within which the representations originated (Forgas, 1978a, 1981a).

As distinct from such structural measures of episodes as sociocultural phenomena, episodes as individual cognitive representations can also be analyzed. The *degree of prototypicality* is one such important feature: Episodes differ in the extent to which they are "good" examples of a particular category (e.g., a dinner party or a colloquium). Highly prototypical episodes represent an ideal configuration of criterial features, whereas others may be marginal members of the category (Rosch & Mervis, 1975; Rosch & Lloyd, 1978).

Episodes can also be characterized in terms of the *definitional cues* used to identify them. The validity of such cues is directly proportional to their association with members of one category, and inversely proportional to their association with other categories (Reed, 1972). This notion is similar to the idea of diagnosticity (Barsalou & Bower, 1980) developed in the context of object categorization. Thus, consuming food may be a more diagnostic feature of a restaurant episode than paying the bill, but neither are absolutely necessary for an episode to be identifiable as a restaurant episode. Existing research on the cues defining social episodes has focused on variables such as the behavior setting, the relationship between the interactants, the behavioral constraint, and the goal structure of the episode.

Another structural feature of episode schemata is their *level of abstraction*. Some episodes may be highly abstract and general (e.g., eating, fighting, traveling), whereas others may describe highly specific and concrete interactions (e.g., having dinner on a weekday at the local May Kwai chinese restaurant with my friend). But it is most likely that episodes at an intermediate-level abstraction (e.g., eating in a restaurant) achieve the optimum compromise between inclusiveness and concreteness, describing events which are very common, yet allowing the deduction of highly specific behavioral and situational details. At this level, "categories carry the most information, possess the highest cue validity, and are thus most differentiated from one another" (Rosch *et al.*, 1976, p. 383). In language, "the basic level is the one at which adults spontaneously name objects" (Mervis & Rosch, 1981, p. 93), and at which objects are most readily encoded and recalled. Most of the social episodes studied, selected from the diary entries of subjects (cf. Forgas, 1979b), are likely to have the features of basic-level cognitive categories. In terms of the rigidity of the *behavior prescriptions* implied, we may also distinguish between episodes containing exact sequential behavior prescriptions, such as "formal" episodes (Harre & Secord, 1972) or "strong" episodes (Abelson, 1980), whereas most everyday episodes allow some degree of latitude and substitution in their internal behavioral structure. Such common episodes were called "enigmatic" episodes by Harre and Secord, and "weak" episodes by Abelson (1980). It is likely that an episode's level of abstraction and the specificity of the behavior prescriptions implied are inversely related, although this may not always be the case.

Social episodes may thus on the one hand be regarded as the building blocks of social life, and in this respect they exist independently of individuals; they belong in the consensual, social domain. On the other hand, each and every individual has private, idiosyncratic cognitive representations about the stock of episodes practiced within his/her culture. As we have seen, there are numerous quantitative measures of episodes as both social and cognitive phenomena. What is relatively rare is research on how social representation features such as complexity, integration, and consensus, are related to cognitive representational features such as prototypicality, abstraction, and formality. Future research and theorizing will have to pay increasing attention to the interdependence between the social and cognitive aspects of episode representations.

## 3.  *Consequences of Episode Representations*

Episode representations have both cognitive and behavioral consequences. Considerable effort has been devoted in recent years to the study of how episode schemata influence memory, problem solving, and information processing in general (Craik, 1979; Simon, 1979). Similarly, social psychologists are paying increasing attention to the behavioral consequences of episode definitions (Barker, 1968; Triandis, 1972; Kelley, 1979) and the empirical representation of consensual episode domains (Battistich & Thompson, 1980a,b; Forgas, 1979b; Nascimento-Schulze, 1981).

The cognitive consequences of episode scripts include the tendency to better encode and recall interactions which are scripted rather than enigmatic, to fill in the gaps in incomplete or fragmented episodes by extrapolating from "standard" episode scripts, and by cognitively reordering the sequence of acts within a deviant episode to comply with the prototypical episode structure (Graesser, Gordon, & Sawyer, 1979; Bower, Black, & Turner, 1979).

The existence of episode representations also has important behavioral consequences. Having a prototypical representation about the limited number of episodes which are practiced within any social milieu (Forgas, 1979b; Pervin, 1976) enables us to act with confidence in those situations and to reduce the cognitive load that step-by-step decisions about appropriate behavior would entail (Thomas, 1966; Schutz, 1970). Episode representations give a sense of coherence and stability and a hierarchical structure to the otherwise complex and confusing ebb and flow of social life.

The hierarchical structure of interactive routines implies that the commencement of an episode usually entails a commitment to its conclusion by the actor(s) (Abelson, 1980, p. 12). Whether an actor will choose to enter an episode often depends on fairly simple policies or action rules. Abelson (1980) suggests that many studies in social psychology in areas such as conformity, helping behavior, and attitudes may be best explained in terms of such apparent action rules followed by subjects.

The acquisition, structural characteristics, and consequences of episode representations are all significantly influenced by the interplay of social representations and individual cognitive activity. The episode representations of any individual have to be constantly evaluated and reaffirmed in the course of social interaction with others (Stone & Farberman, 1970), and the consensual episode spaces thus derived become a social force of considerable prescriptive power (Durkheim, 1898; Moscovici, 1981). Unfortunately, episode cognition research to date has largely remained fragmented, with one stream of studies oriented toward the social-consensual aspects of episodes, and a second research strategy addressing the individual-cognitive features of episode scripts.

## D.  RECENT DEVELOPMENTS IN PERSONALITY, CLINICAL, SOCIAL, AND COGNITIVE PSYCHOLOGY

As distinct from the historical and theoretical considerations, recent research on episode cognition has also benefited from the contemporary shift in psychology toward a study of cognitive rather than behavioral phenomena (Hilgard, 1980a), and from a correspondent tendency to study representative rather than systematically manipulated events (Brunswik, 1956). As a result, research on various aspects of episode cognition emerged more or less simultaneously in personality, clinical, social, and cognitive psychology over the past decade.

In *personality research* many critics (Vernon, 1964; Mischel, 1968) proposed that instead of looking for personality traits, we should be studying broad environmental and situational factors which covary with behavior. For example, Mischel's (1968) "social behaviour theory seeks order and regularity in the form of general rules which relate environmental changes to behavioural changes" (p. 149–150). This "situationist" approach was the source of continued controversy (Alker, 1972; Bem, 1972; Bowers, 1973; Endler, 1973; Endler & Magnusson, 1975), which came to be resolved in the general acceptance of models based on the interaction of personal and situational factors (Ekehammar, 1974; Endler & Magnusson, 1975). In Mischel's (1973, 1979) more recent cognitive social learning model of personality, instead of personality traits, a person's cognitive situation construction competencies, encoding strategies, behavior-outcome and stimulus-outcome expectations, and the like would be the focus of analysis. For such a program to be successful, "we need a systematic way of conceptualizing the domain of situations and situational variables before we can make rapid progress in studying the role of situations in determining behavior" (Frederiksen, 1972, p. 115). Some of the earliest studies on how situations and episodes are cognitively represented were carried out by personality researchers (Magnusson, 1971; Pervin, 1975b, 1976). This idea of the person–situation as a single system is of course strongly reminiscent of the theories of Lewin (1935, 1936), Murphy (1947), Murray (1938), and Brunswik (1956). The realization of such a program hinges on our ability to empirically study cognitive representations of social episodes, a task which lies at the heart of current research on episode cognition.

*Clinical psychology* has undergone similar changes in the past decade or so. The once exclusive dominance of personological theories, locating the source of maladaptive behavior in enduring intrapsychic dysfunctions, has given way to situational models concerned with manipulating environmental and situational contingencies to bring about adaptive behavior in specific contexts (Wolpe, 1969, 1978; Bandura, 1977). Both the unit of diagnosis and the unit of therapy are often a specific episode or situation, which a patient perceives as difficult or anxiety evoking. Behavior therapies have recently given way to a more cognitive orientation, where a client's internal, cognitive representation of particular episodes and his perception of his capabilities and shortcomings in it are the focus of attention (Mahoney, 1977; Bandura, 1977). A necessary corollary to such an approach is the empirical study of exactly how such representations originate, change, and are located in psychological space relative to other representations (cf. Forgas, 1982b).

The different social skills training programs are particularly relevant here, since they specifically aim to train interactive skills in social episodes (Goldstein, Sprafkin, & Gershaw, 1976; Trower, Bryant, & Argyle, 1978). However, even in social skills training, situations and episodes are invoked intuitively, without any quantified information about their characteristics. A client's or the therapist's intuitive understanding about an episode is the only source of information. The client's perception of specific episodes and their relationship to other episodes, and more importantly, cultural representations of characteristic interaction sequences, can now be studied using objective empirical techniques, as we shall see below.

In *social psychology,* although the study of social episodes would seem to be a "natural" topic to pursue, relatively little interest in this domain has been shown until recently. In Brunswik's (1956) terms, social psychologists were more interested in the study of systematically manipulated episodes recreated in the laboratory (Gergen, 1978), than in the representative sampling of natural interactions which make up social life (Pervin, 1975a, 1976). With the realization that the laboratory episode has its own potent cultural definition (Orne, 1962; Rosenthal, 1966), and partly influenced by the growing debate about the personal consistency assumption in personality research (Argyle & Little, 1972), social psychologists have also turned to studying interaction episodes and how they are cognitively represented. One notably successful applied program has been Triandis's (1972; Triandis, Vassiliou, & Nassiakou, 1968) work on cultural differences in social interaction. His basic unit of analysis is a stereotypical interaction episode derived from Flanagan's (1954) "critical incident" technique. The assimilation of the subjective culture of the group to be approached is thought to be contingent on "learning" the requirements of typical social episodes, a process accomplished through the "culture assimilator" technique.

Another remarkable research program which was episodic in orientation is Barker's (1968; Barker & Wright, 1955) research on behavior settings, which are regarded as symbolic embodiments of cultural expectations about appropriate interaction episodes. There have also been some isolated attempts to come to terms with the range of natural interactions practiced within a culture (Watson & Potter, 1962; Bjerg, 1968) which made little impact on mainstream social psychology (Forgas, 1979b). However, many traditional concepts assuming intrapsychic consistency, such as attitudes, came to be reformulated in situationist terms in recent years (Fishbein & Ajzen, 1975; Jellison, 1980). The success of such programs once again hinges on our ability to study situations and episodes empirically.

Finally, *cognitive psychology* has also contributed to the growing interest in the study of interaction episodes. Recent thinking about cognitive categorization, and the growing popularity of fluid category concepts such as fuzzy sets (Zadeh, 1965), family resemblances (Wittgenstein, 1953; Rosch & Mervis, 1975), prototypes (Rosch & Lloyd, 1978), and scripts (Abelson, 1980) meant that complex social objects such as event sequences or episodes could for the first time be handled by cognitive models. Also, work on memory has been increasingly influenced by theories emphasizing internal representations of complex objects. As Craik (1979) in his review of memory research notes, "there is a trend to using a much broader sample of materials and situations . . . related to the current emphasis on complex materials is the growing popularity of the schema as a theoretical and exploratory device" (p. 64). Episode schemata are frequently used as illustrative examples in such studies, even though much of this work is strongly oriented toward information processing analyses, neglecting the uniquely social character of such representations (Krauss, 1980; Forgas, 1981b). Recent work on episode cognition benefited from all these various sources. We shall look at these two research domains next.

## III. Modeling Episode Spaces: The Social Consensus Approach

### A. RESEARCH ON SITUATION PERCEPTION

Attempts to empirically study cognitive representations of situations and interaction episodes can be traced to the early 1960s. The term "situation perception" was apparently first coined by Cattell (1963), and Endler and Magnusson (1975) define its scope as follows:

> Situation perception can be regarded as legitimate a research field as for example person perception. The traditional methods . . . used for data collection in person perception can also be applied in studies of situation perception. . . . In our opinion, research in this field of situation perception is one of the most urgent and also one of the most promising tasks for psychology. (pp. 16, 21)

The study of situation perception emerged from personality research, and it sought to add a situational dimension to measures of such personality constructs as, for example, anxiety. A good example is the S–R Inventory of Anxiousness (cf. Endler & Hunt, 1969), asking subjects to indicate how they would react to a series of 11 different situations (e.g., going on a date). One of the outcomes of this work was the construction of one of the first empirical taxonomies of the 11 situations included in it, in terms of subjects' anticipated reactions to them (Levin, 1965). Similar questionnaires to elicit reactions to both social and nonsocial situations were constructed by Werdelin (1975), Ekehammar and Magnusson (1973), Argyle and Little (1972), and others. These efforts were also extended into clinical research: For example, Moos (1968) asked psychiatric patients and staff to indicate their feelings and reactions to 11 situations, not all of them social, in his Setting Response Inventory (SRI). The situational dimensions emerging from this research often reflect subjects' affective, emotional reactions to the situations: Thus, evaluation, self-confidence, involvement, and perceived friendliness of the situation are typical characteristics (Moos, 1968, 1974).

One of the most significant early attempts to study social episodes taxonomically is associated with Barker's (1968; Barker & Wright, 1955; Barker & Schoggen, 1973) research program on behavior settings. Human social interaction is always situated interaction, and the environment within which it occurs is not merely a physical setting, but becomes impregnated with social norms and symbolic meaning by virtue of the behavior precedents which occurred within it. As such, behavior settings become "stable, extra-individual units with great coercive power over the behavior that occurs within them" (Barker, 1968, p. 17). Barker's taxonomic survey of the behavior settings of a small town in Kansas ("Midwest") thus provides descriptive "data on the behavior possibilities" within this town (Barker, 1968, p. 116), resulting in a classification of possible interaction episodes anchored to definite physical settings. Such an episode taxonomy is also cognitive, however, reflecting the informants' subjective perception of what is and what is not appropriate within an environment.

While in these studies perceptual dimensions of situations were only a by-product, in the early 1970s the first studies explicitly concerned with cognitive representations of situations and episodes began to appear. Magnusson (1971) suggested that

> concerning the study of situational variation, we find ourselves at the same stage as that concerning the study of individual differences at the initial developmental period of differential psychology. It is probable that the task of determining individual dimensions was at that time regarded as being as full of difficulties as we now regard the task of attacking the dimensionality of situations. (p. 852)

In his study, Magnusson argued that situations are cognitive rather than physical entities, and the task of research is to adequately represent the implicit psychological dimensions underlying their perception. His study, based on the factor analysis of similarity ratings between 36 ad hoc selected situations by small numbers of Stockholm University students did not quite achieve this objective. Similar techniques were used by Magnusson and Ekehammar (1973) and Ekehammar and Magnusson (1973) who used 20 stressful situations as stimuli. Golding (1975) used short descriptive vignettes of situations and found significant individual differences in how the situations were perceived. These attempts to come to terms with how individuals cognitively represent episodes were motivated by a desire to resolve the person–situation debate in personality research, and the studies were limited in their sampling of situations (usually ad hoc), their subject populations (small numbers of students), and in their methodologies (typically factor analysis of bipolar ratings of situations).

As distinct from these earlier fragmented attempts, several recent research programs, including our own, focused on the topic of episode representations as its main aim. These studies sought to explore problems such as the suitability of different techniques for analyzing episodes and the effects of subcultural, group, and individual differences on episode cognition.

B. STUDIES OF EPISODE DOMAINS: SUBCULTURAL, GROUP, AND INDIVIDUAL DIFFERENCES IN EPISODE COGNITION

One of the most common and salient consensual cognitive schemata that people develop in the course of their daily interactions are cognitive representations of social episodes. This is suggested by both psychological and sociological theorizing, as well as by recent research in cognitive psychology, as our foregoing discussion indicates. It should therefore be possible to reliably model the structure of such internal representations of social episodes. Several recent studies demonstrated the feasibility of this task.

A good example is a study by Forgas (1976), which aimed to (a) look at the suitability of dimensional (multidimensional scaling, MDS) and categorical (hierarchical clustering) techniques for modeling episode spaces, and (b) assess the extent to which a priori subcultural differences in episode cognition between two groups of respondents would be reflected by these methods. The MDS procedure in particular appeared promising for representing this kind of complex social stimuli, since measures of similarity alone would be sufficient as input, and the rating task could thus be made relatively meaningful and simple for the judges (Forgas, 1979a; Kruskal and Wish, 1979). Subjects came from two different subcultural milieus: They were either middle class housewives from the Oxford, England area, or undergraduate students at the University of Oxford. In the first stage of the study, a representative range of social episodes was elicited from both subcultures by means of a weekly diary kept by respondents. In the second stage of the study, the most frequently mentioned and common social episodes were identified (see Table I), and a second pool of subjects from each subculture was asked to rate these episodes for their overall similarity, using a multiple grouping task. These similarity ratings were analyzed by means of an MDS procedure, as well as by a hierarchical clustering method. Results showed that the MDS analyses resulted in stable and reliable configurations with very low stress values, and these dimensional models were both more meaningful and more sensitive to subcultural differences than the clustering solutions, although the episode domains were quite compatible as reconstructed by the two techniques.

Of more interest were the subcultural differences in episode cognition between the two samples. Housewives, moving mainly within a domestic social milieu had a simpler, two-dimensional episode domain than students, for whom work and university-related episodes were also of great importance. There was a

TABLE I

MOST FREQUENTLY MENTIONED EPISODE VIGNETTES[a,b]

Students

1. Having morning coffee with the people in the department
2. Having a drink with some friends in a pub
3. Discussing an essay during a tutorial
4. Meeting an acquaintance while checking your pigeonhole for mail in college
5. Going out for a walk with a friend
6. Shopping on Saturday morning with a friend at the supermarket
7. Acting as a subject in a psychology experiment
8. Going to the pictures with some friends
9. Having a short chat with the shop assistant while shopping
10. Getting acquainted with a new person during dinner in hall
11. Going to JCR meetings
12. Chatting with an acquaintance before a lecture begins
13. Discussing psychology topics with friends
14. Meeting new people at a sherry party in college
15. Visiting your doctor
16. Chatting with an acquaintance who unexpectedly gave you a lift
17. Visiting a friend in his college room
18. Going to see a play at the theatre with friends
19. Going to the bank
20. Having an intimate conversation with your boy/girlfriend
21. Having a short chat with an acquaintance whom you unexpectedly met on the street
22. Chatting with others while waiting for your washing in the coin laundry
23. Attending a wedding ceremony
24. Watching TV with some friends
25. Playing chess

[a]After Forgas, 1976.
[b]List elicited from student subsample.

surprising similarity between the two groups, however, in terms of the kind of implicit characteristics which were found to underlie their episode representations. It appears that affective, emotional reactions to episodes, such as self-confidence, intimacy, involvement, and pleasantness were more important than objective episode features, suggesting that subjects indeed relied on personally relevant, functional (Tajfel, 1969; Tajfel & Forgas, 1981) rather than objective, descriptive criteria in their judgments. Thus, descriptively different episodes such as a wedding party and a university tutorial occupied similar regions in the episode space, both being highly formal kinds of interactions looked at with a certain lack of self-confidence (Fig. 1). This of course substantially confirms many earlier theories suggesting the importance of subjective, affective reactions to situations (Lewin, 1951; Wolff, 1964). Furthermore, very similar episodes

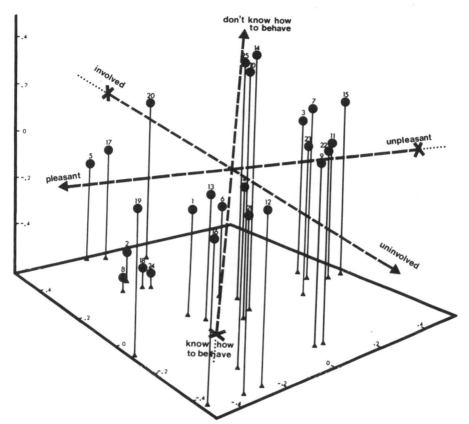

Fig. 1.  The three-dimensional model of the students' perceived episode space, with three labeling axes fitted. (After Forgas, 1976.)

(e.g., going to the pub) were perceived significantly differently by the two subcultural samples. This episode was a friendly, involved, and self-confident event for students, but apparently a social routine which was more formal and seen with much less self-confidence by housewives. This study thus established the feasibility of modeling episode domains using MDS techniques, which showed sufficient sensitivity in reflecting subtle subcultural differences in episode cognition. MDS techniques have already been shown to be reliable and powerful tools in social cognition research (Carroll & Arabie, 1980; Forgas, 1979a; Kruskal & Wish, 1979), and the applicability of this strategy to episode cognition research is promising. In the next study, this work was extended to study the effects of group differences on episode cognition, under more controlled, but still naturalistic conditions.

Subjects were members of two rugby teams, matched for most characteristics, but of course exposed to different group milieus and interaction styles (Forgas, 1981e). The question we were interested in was: To what extent would episode cognition reflect the characteristics of these two groups? One team was a competitive and successful group with some good players, but little ingroup cohesiveness and loyalty. The other team contained more average players, but was also much more motivated and cohesive, with more frequent and intense interactions as a group. It was hypothesized that the more cohesive team would have a structurally different episode domain which is (a) more complex and differentiated (larger number of cognitive dimensions used), (b) better integrated (task and social episodes are not significantly separated in the episode space), and (c) represented by team members with a greater degree of consensus. The MDS analysis of the two teams' episode spaces, followed by a series of multiple discriminant analyses of episode coordinates, confirmed these expectations. (A model of team A's episode space is shown in Fig. 2.)

These results indicate that cognitive representations of episode domains are highly sensitive to subtle group influences: Although both teams came from a highly homogenous student milieu, with a similar range of interactions and with no notable individual differences between team members, their episode spaces

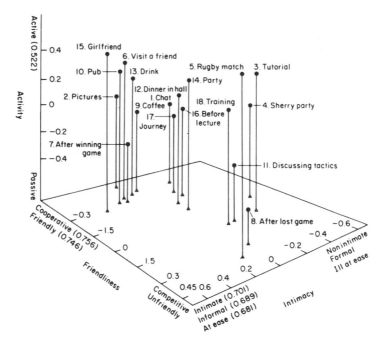

Fig. 2.    The three-dimensional episode space of the more cohesive team, showing the bipolar scales used in labeling the INDSCAL dimensions. (After Forgas, 1981e.)

nevertheless strongly reflected their differing social climates and interaction styles.

In a third study the assessment of individual differences in episode cognition was attempted, again in a naturalistic setting, using an academic group as subjects (Forgas, 1978a). The 16 members of this group were first asked to rate each other for similarity and on a number of bipolar scales, in order to get a consensual measure of the existing individual differences between members. Additionally, a priori status differences in terms of academic standing (faculty, re-

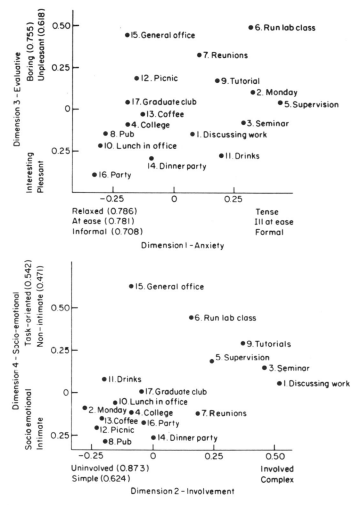

Fig. 3. The representation of an intact academic group's social episodes in four dimensions, showing the bipolar scales used to label the INDSCAL dimensions. (After Forgas, 1978a.)

search students, and staff) were also established. In the second part of the study, the commonly enacted interaction episodes of the group were elicited, and subjected to an Individual Differences Multidimensional Scaling (INDSCAL) analysis (see Fig. 3).

Finally, individual differences in episode cognition were statistically evaluated by relating measures of individual differences within the group (academic status, dominance, sociability, and conventionalism) to indices of how much each individual relied on each of the INDSCAL episode dimensions in judging the group's interactions. There was an overall significant relationship between such measures and episode cognition: For example, more dominant group members were more critical and evaluative in perceiving social episodes, and friendly and sociable members were less likely to see episodes in terms of their anxiety-evoking potential. Status subgroups, such as faculty, staff, and students also significantly differed in how they thought about social episodes (Fig. 4).

These three studies provide convergent evidence as to the feasibility of quantitatively modeling episode domains, and the relative sensitivity of such models to subcultural, group, and individual differences. They also suggest that the common interaction routines of any one subcultural group are likely to be quite limited and manageable in number. Implicit representations of such encounters are analogous to natural categories, and are reported with significant consensus by respondents (Rosch et al., 1976). A further important finding is the dominance of affective characteristics in episode representations, supporting some recent arguments emphasizing the importance of affective reactions in

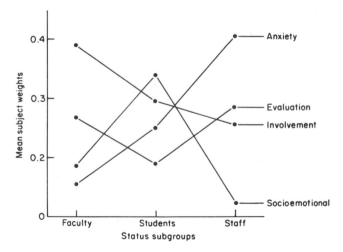

Fig. 4. Individual differences between members of formal status subgroups (faculty, staff, students) in their perception of the group's social episodes—mean dimension weights for each status subgroup on each of four episode dimensions. (After Forgas, 1978a.)

social cognition and behavior (Zajonc, 1980). Although we did not measure primary affective responses here, but subjects' recollections of particular episodes, it is significant that these recollections were dominated by subjective feelings (cf. Bower, 1980; Isen, Clark, Shalker, & Karp, 1978).

There have been several recent studies essentially confirming these conclusions. Nascimento-Schulze (1981) reports that two dimensions, constraint and involvement, underlined the perception of social situations in her British sample. Battistich and Thompson (1980a) used an MDS procedure to elicit and scale the episode cognitions of 216 American students, and found that their episodes were perceived "in terms of subjective, connotative factors" which were "highly consistent with those of the few previous studies in the area" (p. 80). In a sequel study, Battistich and Thompson (1980b) found that episode cognition was significantly related to demographic and personality differences between the subjects.

Beyond modeling existing episode domains, it is also important to come to terms with the way such representations come about and with the features of an episode which determine its location in cognitive space. It is this problem to which we shall turn next.

## C.  ELEMENTS IN EPISODE COGNITION

Given that we can reliably and quantitatively model cognitive representations of episode domains, as the previous section showed, the logical next research question becomes: What sort of influences and cues determine how a particular episode is represented? There are clearly a great many such features, ranging from the physical behavior setting through the relationship between the interactants and the goal of the interaction to the restrictiveness of the episode itself. Although there are still some gaps in current research about episode elements, much has been accomplished. In this section a brief summary of these various findings will be given.

### 1.  The Physical Setting

Following Barker's (1968) pioneering work described earlier, it is now clearly recognized that the physical setting of an episode contains strong cues as to the different kinds of interactions which are possible and approved within that environment. Whereas Barker's (1968) studies were based on extensive surveys and ratings of behavior settings, some more recent experimental studies aimed to discover the effects of setting cues on the cognitive representation of episodes. Forgas and Brown (1977) asked subjects to rate pictures of interactions superimposed on different behavior settings. Results showed that behavior setting cues interacted with the target's behavioral cues in nonobvious ways. An intimate, warm setting served to accentuate whatever behavioral cues were present, whereas a nonintimate, cold setting attenuated the same information. The definitional function of physical settings in episode cognition was also extensively researched by environmental psychologists. The physical and spatial layout of certain settings, such as courtrooms, churches, or lecture theaters, provides a congealed model of the kinds of social episodes enacted within them (Joiner, 1971). Less formal settings, such as offices, living rooms, or street corners, may also have such symbolic meanings (Laumann & House, 1970; Canter & Lee, 1974). The decoding and interpretation of such implicit cues in the physical environment is an important aspect of episode cognition, and one which readily lends itself to experimental analysis. In future studies, we plan to look at the effects of a broader range of settings on the cognitive representation of episodes, as well as the definitional roles of episodic props, such as personal items, displays, and decorations.

## 2.   The Relationship between the Partners

One of the most salient episode definition cues is the relationship between the partners. Surprisingly little work has been done in social psychology on the kind and range of interpersonal relationships which exist within a cultural milieu. Marwell and Hage (1970) factor analyzed ratings of role relationships, and more recently, Wish, Deutsch, and Kaplan (1976) used multidimensional scaling procedures to study cognitive representations of role relationships. In a similar vein, Kelley (1979), in his recent cognitive theory of relationships, pointed to the importance of internal relationship scripts and cost/payoff expectations in determining episode definitions and interactive strategies. Only the second of these studies used relationships which were sampled from and validated within a specific cultural milieu. In one of our own more recent studies, preliminary to studying the role of relationship definition cues in the perception of romantic heterosexual episodes, we sought to elicit and scale the range of heterosexual relationships known to a specific group of subjects (Forgas & Dobosz, 1980). This relationship taxonomy yielded three basic dimensions (social desirability, love and commitment, and sex). The effects of these relationship features on the definition and cogntive representation of heterosexual encounters are currently being studied.

In several studies, the weight of relationship cues as against situational cues in episode cognition was assessed. Wish (1975) created episode descriptions consisting of the factorial combination of eight situational contexts (e.g., talking at a large social gathering, attempting to work out a compromise) and 16 role relationships (e.g., husband and wife), resulting in 128 episode vignettes. These composite descriptions were rated by subjects, and the relative contributions of situational and relationship definition cues were established. Situational cues were more important in determining the perception of the encounters in terms of dimensions such as friendliness, cooperation, intensity, and task orientation, whereas relationship cues were more important in affecting ratings along the formal–informal and equal–unequal dimensions. In a similar study, Forgas (1978c) combined four situation contexts (chatting on the street, discussing a minor problem, an intimate conversation, and working on a project) with seven types of partners personally known to the subjects (family member, friend, acquaintance, neighbor, etc.) The combined episode descriptions were rated by two groups of subjects, either housewives or students. The resulting 28 episodes were cognitively differentiated by subjects in terms of three characteristics: involvement, self-confidence and task orientation. With these more salient and realistic stimuli, we found that the partner's identity accounted for most of the variance in how the subjects located the episodes along the involvement and self-confidence dimensions, but task orientation judgments were largely determined by the interaction of partner and situation cues. In another study (Forgas, 1978b) the relationship definition cues (casual acquaintance vs married couple) of intimate and nonintimate videotaped interactions were manipulated. It turned out that even with these highly realistic episodes, the relationship cues had a significant effect on judgments of the episode as well as the participants.

## 3. Behavioral Constraint in Episodes

The range of behaviors which are possible and permissible in an episode is a highly important episode definition cue, as reflected in the importance of the self-confidence and anxiety dimensions in episode representations. As Goffman (1963) suggested, "there may be one overall continuum or axis along which the social life situations vary depending on how disciplined the individual is obliged to be" (p. 199). There were several attempts to assess the constraint or restrictiveness of different kinds of situations. Price and Bouffard (1974) asked their subjects to rate the appropriateness of a range of behaviors (e.g., read, sleep, talk, eat, run) in a range of different situations (e.g., on a date, in a church, in your own room). An index of constraint for each situation may be calculated by summarizing the appropriateness ratings of all behaviors over each situation. Price and Bouffard (1974) found that situations which are private are least governed by rules and conventions, whereas in public situations there are various quantifiable degrees of rule constraint embedded in the episode. In a later study, Price (1974) sought to analyze whether "subsets or classes of behaviors can be discovered which are uniquely appropriate in certain subsets or classes of situations" (p. 569). Appropriateness ratings of a sample of behaviors across a range of situations were cluster analyzed to construct behavior and situation clusters. Next, the mean appropriateness of each behavior cluster for each situation cluster was calculated, creating something like a prototypical behavior profile for that class of episodes. Results showed distinct differences in the situational appropriateness of various behavior types. Because of the very limited range of situations and behaviors, which were selected from University of Michigan students' diaries, the generalizability of these findings is limited. Other factors, such as the relative status of the interaction partner, were also found to significantly predict the perceived constraint of an episode (Nascimento-Schulze, 1981). These studies certainly indicate that episodic constraint can be quantified, and that further work along these lines may provide useful information about the role of constraints in episode cognition.

### 4. Goals and Motives in Episodes

Much of human interaction is specifically oriented toward certain goals, and is thereby motivated in its course. Indeed, the tension states accompanying such acts were crucial to Lewin's (1951) theory of social behavior, and research on attribution processes suggests that the identification of plausible motives and intentions lies at the heart of comprehending enigmatic episodes (Heider, 1958; Kelley, 1971; Harre & Secord, 1972).

There is growing evidence suggesting that information about goals and motives profoundly affects the way we think about social episodes. Owens, Bower, and Black (1979) called this the "soap opera effect." In their study, subjects read banal episode sequences (having coffee, visiting a doctor, shopping, cocktail party, etc.) either with or without information hinting at the possible motives of the actors. Results showed that "providing the reader with a problem and a motive for the central character enabled him to remember more episodes and remember them more often in the correct order" (p. 186). In a second experiment, it was additionally found that providing a motive for the character resulted in more motive-related false recalls (intrusions), indicating that the "character's goals serve . . . to integrate the different episodes into a coherent whole" (p. 190). Motives thus appear to function as extraordinarily salient cues in episode representations, not only in the comprehension of written narratives, but also in real life: "We seem to use much the same methods . . . when we interact with people in real settings, using the same motivational schemata to interpret or explain why people act as they do" (Owens et al., 1979, p. 191). Correspondingly, the observers' goal schemata were also found to exert a significant biasing effect on the perception and interpretation of ongoing behavior in videotaped episodes (Cohen & Ebbesen, 1979).

Other studies report that even low-level goals in solitary event sequences facilitate recall. Lichtenstein and Brewer (1980) used videotaped episodes as stimuli, and found that "the recall of goal-oriented events was superior to that of non goal-oriented actions" (p. 412).

It remains to be seen whether superordinate goals, relevant to multiple episodes as in the Owen et al. study (1979), or episode-specific goals are more effective in facilitating the encoding and retrieval of representations about an event. In a study currently under way, we are attempting to evaluate the effects of goal specificity or generality on episode cognition. The evidence suggests that goals specific to a given episode are essential to the very definition of that event (Barker & Wright, 1955) and to the recall of the internal behavioral structure of the encounter, whereas superordinate goals only facilitate the recall of multiple-episode sequences. These studies suggest that motivational schemata are indeed among the most potent and salient representational strategies we possess (Liechtenstein & Brewer, 1980), which also play a crucial role in the definition of interaction episodes.

## 5. Individual Differences between Perceivers

The perceiver is, of course, perhaps the most crucial factor in episode cognition. Different individual biographies, experiences, and constructs pre-dispose a person to represent episodes in a particular way (Schutz, 1970). Idiographic studies of episode cognition could significantly contribute to realizing Brunswik's (1956) plans for applying representative designs in psychology by providing objective information about selected individuals' recurring behavior circumstances. Pervin was strongly influenced by Brunswik's (1956) arguments, and suggested that "the personality of each individual could be understood in terms of the patterns and stability or change in feelings and behaviors in relation to a defined group of situations . . . this approach might serve as the basis for the future development of a taxonomy of situations and behaviours in situations" (Pervin, 1975b, p. 1). He used an idiographic approach to study how particular individuals characterize, feel about, and behave in their typical life situations (Pervin, 1976). The resulting person-specific episode taxonomies say a lot about the particular individuals—in some sense, they are the quantified representations of a person's contemporary biography. The number of episodes Pervin's subjects listed were in all cases quite limited (23–29 per subject), and were readily rated and assigned into categories, using techniques such as factor analysis. Pervin's (1976) work could have significant implications for clinical psychology, a potential which has not yet been fully realized.

Several other studies, described earlier, also provide evidence for individual differences in episode cognition. Demographic factors (age, sex, college major, sociometric position, and social status) and personality variables (extroversion, neuroticism, social desirability, Macchiavellism) were both found to be significantly related to episode representations (Battistich & Thompson, 1980a,b; Forgas, 1978a, 1979b; Forgas, Brown, & Menyhart, 1980). Unfortunately, there is at present no conceptual metaphor which would help to systematically relate episode cognition and individual difference measures to each other, apart from the very general suggestions contained in such theories as symbolic interactionism (Stone & Farbermann, 1970; Forgas, 1978a).

## IV.  Cognitive and Affective Factors in Episode Cognition

A.  THINKING ABOUT SOCIAL EPISODES:
THE INFORMATION PROCESSING APPROACH

In the past decade or so, cognitive psychologists have increasingly become interested in how human beings think about, remember, and cognitively organize complex units of knowledge, as distinct from the very elementary kinds of stimuli studied earlier (Simon, 1979). The idea that cognitive representations of reality are organized into coherent and meaningful units is of course essentially a Gestalt theoretical concept. In cognitive psychology, Bartlett's (1932) seminal work on memory did much to establish this notion, and in developmental psychology Piaget (1952) and others (Nelson, 1979) suggested that schemata are the basic units in the child's acquisition of knowledge. The schema concept has undergone something of a revival in the past decade, and recent work on cognitive categorization (Rosch & Lloyd, 1978), as well as in cognitive science (Schank & Abelson, 1977), makes increasing use of schema-like concepts. Abelson's (1976) introduction of the notion of cognitive scripts to denote representations of common, recurring event sequences was perhaps the most influential move toward placing such complex representations into the center of interest. Nearly all of the work stimulated by this idea was carried out on scripts describing common social episodes. While the carrying power of the script concept clearly extends beyond the domain of interaction episodes, the choice of episodes as the most popular topic for study is not simply coincidental. It seems likely that one of the most common, and also the most salient kinds of complex cognitive representations we have are representations about interaction sequences (Brittan, 1963; Triandis, 1972). For example, the restaurant script described by Abelson (1976) has by now achieved considerable popularity in cognitive research on information processing. What does this research tell us about how people think about interaction episodes?

The major application of the script concept came in artificial intelligence (AI) research, where it was used in the construction of computer programs for text comprehension. The central idea is that events are interpreted in the context of relevant activated scripts rather than in isolation. Abelson (1980) distinguishes between "weak" scripts which have no strict sequential requirements about the order of the events to be performed, and "strong" scripts, such as the restaurant or the dinner party script, which involve a sequential structure and "learned associations between prior and consequent events" (p. 7). In summary, then, a script is

a hypothesized cognitive structure which when activated organises comprehension of event-based situations. In its "weak" sense, it is bundle of inferences about the potential occurrence of a set of events, and may be structurally similar to other schemas which do not deal with events. In its "strong" sense expectations are present about the order as well as occurrence of events. In the strongest sense of a totally ritualized event sequence (e.g., a Japanese tea ceremony) script predictions become infallible. (1980, p. 8)

Experimental evidence shows that people indeed use scripts in this way. In a series of studies, Bower *et al.* (1979) report that people described routine everyday activities (seeing a doctor, at the restaurant), the props, the setting, and the actions with significant consensual agreement. There was also good agreement about the order of events within a script and the hierarchical organization of such events. More important, subjects tended to recall "scrambled" script actions in the canonical order, to confuse stated actions with actions which were unstated but implied by the script, and goal-relevant deviations from a script were remembered better than script actions. There are also differences in the extent to which an event is central or peripheral to an episode. It appears that central events are more accessible and may be verified more quickly as belonging to the script than peripheral events.

Interaction episodes are also often studied by researchers interested in how complex texts or stories are processed. Various theories of story memory make use of the concept of episode, usually to refer to a constituent element of a story with a single goal at its center (Rumelhart, 1975, 1977; Kintsch, 1977; Mandler & Johnson, 1977). There is a great deal of similarity between such story episodes and our understanding of cognitive representations of social episodes. Black and Bower (1980) suggested that an episode is a single unit or chunk and therefore increased detail in other related episodes should not affect its recall; furthermore, the recall probability of superordinate actions should be facilitated by the addition of subordinate details, if episodes are indeed processed as single chunks in memory. Results showed that

goal-oriented episodes in stories are stored as separate chunks in . . . memory . . . recall of the actions in an episode was affected largely by the length of that episode but hardly at all by the length of the other episodes . . . adding related though subordinate actions to a story episode increased the recall probability of the important statements in the episodes. (p. 23)

These results together give a strong indication that our knowledge about interaction episodes constitutes effective and salient cognitive schema, with identifiable effects on memory and comprehension. We use an episode context to reconstruct the missing details of a social event and to make sense of observed instances of social behavior. Bower *et al.* (1979) also point to a number of intriguing, and as yet unresolved, issues in script theory, which also apply to our more general interest in social episodes. How does one elicit reliable lists of scripts, given that many of the things we do in social episodes are automatic and taken for granted to the extent that there is little conscious awareness of them? How do we learn to identify when a script or episode is being performed? Which are the essential or peripheral cues in episode identification? How does the knowledge represented in a script or episode representation originate and accumulate? As social behavior is a stream of continuous processes, what are the features of event boundaries which are commonly used as indicating the beginning and the end of an episode? Some of these questions are partially answered by research on modeling episode spaces described in the previous section. The remaining questions, intriguing as they are, transcend the limits of a purely information processing metaphor (Krauss, 1980). They call for a study of the cultural processes and conventions which ultimately regulate such everyday social representations as social episodes (Moscovici, 1981; Forgas, 1981b). If these questions are to be answered, there is a clear need for the various branches of episode cognition research to be more closely integrated with one another.

## B. THE EFFECTS OF MOOD AND EMOTIONAL STATES ON EPISODE COGNITION

One of the dominant characteristics of contemporary research in social psychology is the widespread use of cognitive, information processing models, and the relative neglect of affective, emotional, and motivational factors in the study of social behavior (Forgas, 1981b; Wicklund & Frey, 1981). As Hilgard (1980b) recently wrote, ''When we look at contemporary psychology from the perspective of cognition, affection and conation, it is obvious immediately that cognitive psychology is ascendant at present, with a concurrent decline in emphasis upon the affective-conative dimensions'' (p. 115). Yet when it comes to thinking about social episodes we are familiar with, affective reactions seem to be, at least intuitively, very important. As Zajonc (1980) wrote, ''When we try to recall, recognize or retrieve an episode, a person, a piece of music, a story, a name . . . the affective quality of the original input is the first element to emerge'' (p. 154). Zajonc argues that affective reactions can occur without ''extensive perceptual or cognitive encoding . . . affect and cognition are under the control of separate and partially independent systems'' (p. 151). There are already several lines of evidence from the study of social episodes which tend to confirm this assertion.

Perhaps most surprising is the fact that the overwhelming majority of taxonomic descriptive studies of social episodes resulted in classificatory systems in which affective dimensions take precedence over other objective characteristics (Forgas, 1981c). Thus, characteristics such as pleasantness, self-confidence in an episode, the perceived intimacy and friendliness of encounters, perceived anxiety and tension, competitiveness, and involvement are all episode dimensions with a clear affective component (Forgas, 1976, 1978a, 1979b, 1981c; Magnusson, 1971; Pervin, 1975b, 1976; Moos, 1968; et al.). Pervin (1976) in his study of situational dimensions notes, for example, that "what is striking is the extent to which situations are described in terms of affects (e.g. threatening, warm, interesting, dull, tense, calm, rejecting) and organized in terms of similarity of affects aroused by them" (p. 471). Similar conclusions have been reached in many other studies, supporting Zajonc's (1980) claim that affective reactions play a crucial role in social perception and behavior.

Apart from descriptive studies of social episodes, in the past few years researchers began to seriously look at the influence of affective and mood states on thinking about, remembering, and processing information about social episodes (Bower, 1980; Isen et al., 1978). Indeed, affective reactions to events are the basis for at least one comprehensive theory of social behavior (Heise, 1979). Gordon Bower at Stanford University initiated a series of studies in which subjects' mood states would be experimentally manipulated using a hypnotic mood induction procedure, and the effects of mood on remembering various sorts of information are studied.

This work has its origins in several experimental studies showing that memory is enhanced when the stimuli can be meaningfully related to either personally or socially significant events about which the subject has strong feelings. Thus, Bower and Gilligan (1979) found "superior memory from relating event descriptions to episodes from one's history" (p. 426), and pleasant episodes (not necessarily social episodes in this study) were recalled better than unpleasant ones. Keenan and Bailett (1979) also report superior recognition for self-referent information, and after an attempt to explain their findings in information processing terms, they conclude: "The crucial dimension underlying memory is not what the subject knows or the amount of knowledge used in encoding an item, but rather what the subject feels about what he knows" (p. 25). Minsky (1980) suggested a model of memory which would explicitly take into account the subject's mood or general state of mind. Affective reactions to social episodes are likely to play a particularly important role in such processes.

The effects of mood on memory were shown in a study by Bower, Monteiro, and Gilligan (1978), where highly hypnotizable subjects were asked to learn a list of words in one mood state, and then recall the list in either the same mood state or a conflicting mood state. Results showed that subjects remembered the words better when their mood state matched the mood they were in when learning the list. Isen et al. (1978) in a related study found that subjects in a good mood were more likely to give positive evaluations about their consumer goods and were more likely to recall positive rather than negative words. They interpret their results as suggesting that "mood state serves as a cue by which . . . material in memory is accessed . . . influencing a person's decision-making process, and ultimately, behavior" (p. 7). As far as remembering actual social episodes is concerned, Bower (1980) in an interesting study obtained a similar effect. Subjects were asked to record emotional events in a diary for a week, and to rate the pleasantness of each episode. A week later, they were hynotized and placed in either a pleasant or an unpleasant mood "and asked to recall every incident they could from those they'd recorded in their diary the week before . . . people in a pleasant mood recalled a greater percentage of their recorded pleasant than their unpleasant experiences, whereas people in an unpleasant mood recalled a higher proportion of their unpleasant rather than their pleasant memories" (Bower, 1980, p. 5). What is more, the emotional intensity of the episode was positively related to recall.

In a follow-up study, subjects were again induced to feel happy or sad, and they were asked this time to give free descriptions of various childhood episodes they could remember. Again, those in a pleasant mood recalled significantly more pleasant episodes than those in an unpleasant mood. Bower (1980) suggests that these findings can be readily explained within an associative network model of memory, where various mood states may be represented as nodes in memory linked to various events in the past associated with the mood. The activation of a mood node would thus facilitate the recall of events connected to it. These findings are consistent with the results of the descriptive taxonomic studies of social episodes discussed above, where affective dimensions were also found to underlie episode representations.

In a recently completed study we tried to assess the effects of a person's mood on remembering previously experimentally manipulated episodes, and on interpreting his own behavior within those episodes (Bower, Forgas, & Krantz, 1981). Subjects interacted with an experimenter in four kinds of social episodes: formal-intimate, formal-nonintimate, informal–intimate, and informal-nonintimate. The episode's formality was manipulated by changing the interaction setting, the experimenter, and her interaction style, and the episode's intimacy was manipulated in terms of the content of the topics discussed in the episode. These four interactions were videotaped. One day later, subjects were hypnotized and either an unpleasant, low self-esteem mood, or a pleasant, happy mood was induced. Subjects were then asked to recall the content of the conversations they had on the previous day, followed by a self-monitoring task, in which they were asked to rate several aspects of their own performances on the videotape. We expected that subjects in a negative mood would have more difficulty recalling formal and intimate episodes, and would be more likely to perceive negative aspects of their own behavior on the videotape. The results confirmed these hypotheses, showing significant mood effects in episode cognition even in these controlled laboratory episodes. A further implication of this research is for currently popular theories of depression: If subjects selectively remember negative episodes when in a depressed mood, and selectively identify negative aspects of their own behavior in interaction episodes (Roth & Rehm, 1980), this would strongly support cognitive theories of depressive states.

## V. Applications of Research on Episode Cognition

Since cognitive representations of episodes are a natural and inevitable outcome of social interaction (Mead, 1934), the study of such representations has numerous applied implications in areas such as clinical, personality, developmental, and environmental psychology. In this section a brief survey of some of these possibilities, and some empirical results, will be given.

In personality theory, insofar as interactionism has now come to be accepted as the dominant approach, techniques to classify and measure situations and episodes are of ever-increasing importance. Some of the procedures described in the episode cognition literature (Forgas, 1979a,b; Pervin, 1976) are directly appropriate to such a task. More importantly, episode cognition is of growing importance in clinical psychology, where cognitive therapies are gradually replacing behaviorist methods (Mahoney, 1977), and a client's internal representation of his/her significant interactions is increasingly in the focus of the therapist's attention. Behavioral difficulties may often arise because of the mistaken or inappropriate cognitive representation of particular episodes relative to other episodes, and most contemporary therapies explicitly seek to influence episode cognition by encouraging clients to change their perceptions of, and reactions to, problematic interactions. The effective modeling of a client's episode domain could be of inestimable use at the diagnostic stage, as well as a basis for therapeutic decisions. Very little research in this area has been done. The first task is clearly to show that there are significant differences in episode cognition between maladjusted and normal populations. In a study by Forgas (1982b), we compared the episode domains of a group of well-adjusted students with a group of students who scored in the lowest quartile on a battery of social skill assessment measures. The results showed that there were overall significant differences between these two groups in how they thought about social episodes. The episode domain was defined by three dimensions: social anxiety/difficulty, evaluation, and intensity. The socially unskilled group placed significantly more weight on the anxiety dimension than the highly skilled group, as might be expected. Specific differences in the locations of individual episodes in the episode space could also be meaningfully related to overall social skill. These results suggest that social skill is significantly related to episode cognition, something that has been implied by various recent cognitive and social learning conceptualizations (Mischel, 1973, 1979), but has not been empirically demonstrated.

Episode cognition research may also have applications in fields where the measurement of specific episode domains and the quantification of individual events on a consensual basis is of intrinsic interest. For example, aggressive episodes occupy a special place in our interactive repertoire. What is more, the classification of aggressive incidents is of focal interest not only for individuals, but also for various groups engaged in law definition and enforcement. In a series of studies, we attempted to model the way personally experienced aggressive incidents and criminal episodes are cognitively represented. In the first study (Forgas *et al.*, 1980), we found that aggressive episodes were differentiated by subjects in terms of four dimensions (probability of occurrence, justifiability, emotional provocation, and control), instead of the single dimension of seriousness commonly assumed (Fig. 5). Representations of these aggressive episodes were also related to such individual variables as conservatism, extroversion, and neuroticism, as established by standard measurement scales. In a sequel study (Forgas, 1980), we looked at the cognitive representation of crimes. Four dimensions—concern, violence, commonness, and intentionality—were found to define the crime space, and the subjects' sex, political affiliation, and personality were again significantly related to crime perception. As crime perception is part of the professional duties of many individuals engaged in the justice system, such as juries, judges, policemen and lawyers, the implementation of these methods in legal settings should provide important new information about implicit "images of crime" members of such groups may have, and how such cognitive representations are acquired and change over time.

Episode representations also have a direct and identifiable influence on actual social behavior, which may be of considerable applied importance when, for example, decisions about issues such as guilt or responsibility attribution are made. Certain episode definitions are more likely to result in more extreme decisions made by groups than others, as evidence from the group polarization literature suggests (Moscovici & Lecuyer, 1972; Moscovici, Doise, & Dulong, 1972; Forgas, 1977). In a recent study, we found that the definition of the interaction episode as a formal or an informal event was sufficient to selectively elicit extremity or moderate shifts in groups making responsibility attribution judgements (Forgas, 1981d). The implications of such findings for real-life decision-making groups, such as committees or interviewing panels, deserve serious attention.

Episode representations affect not only behavior, but perceptions of other social stimuli, such as people, as well. It has been implicitly assumed in social psychology that person perception is trans-situational. With a means for quantifying episode representations, it is now possible to analyze how, for example, perceptions of other people fluctuate with the episode context. Even in a cohesive and long-established group where interpersonal judgments can be based on a wealth of real-life information, person-perception judgements were found to fluctuate with the episode context (Forgas, Argyle, & Ginsburg, 1979). Characteristics which were salient in an informal, friendly episode, such as "morning coffee," or "in the pub," were quite irrelevant to describing others in a research seminar or at a dinner party. It appears as if not only individuals, but episodes

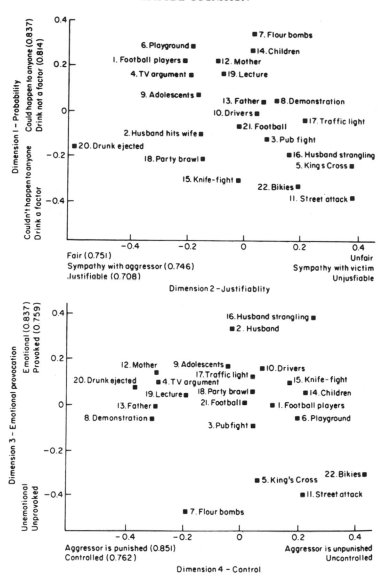

Fig. 5.   The four-dimensional representation of 22 aggressive episodes, showing the bipolar scales used in labeling the INDSCAL axes. (After Forgas *et al.*, 1979.)

also would possess their distinctive theories of personality (cf. Rosenberg & Sedlak, 1972), magnifying some traits and suppressing others.

These are just some of the many areas in which the concept of social episodes may usefully be applied. Essentially, most psychological research is situational, and as such, techniques to empirically represent how situations are cognitively represented have broad applicability. This is hardly a new insight—indeed, W. I. Thomas made much the same point over fifty years ago: "The situational method is the one in use by the experimental physiologist and psychologist who prepare situations, introduce the subject into the situation, observe the behavior reactions, change the situation, and observe changes in reactions" (Thomas, 1928/1966, p. 155). In applying episode cognition research, little more is suggested than the implementation of Thomas's situational analysis, using the most up to date empirical techniques.

## VI.  Summary and Conclusions

The aim of this article was to survey and integrate the advances made in episode cognition research, and to argue that the study of internal representations about interaction routines is one of the most important advances made in social psychology in recent years. Despite the long-standing interest in such matters both in sociology (Weber, 1968; Mead, 1934; Thomas, 1928; Schutz, 1970; Moscovici, 1981) and in psychology (Koffka, 1935; Lewin, 1951; Murray, 1938; Brunswik, 1956; Farr, 1981), the emergence of episode cognition as a distinct field of inquiry is largely attributable to recent developments in the discipline. These developments may be summarized under three headings: (1) the growing influence of cognitive formulations (Caroll & Payne, 1976; Hilgard, 1980a; Forgas, 1981a); (2) the increasing interest in "representative" designs, and in situational and episodic regularities in behavior (Brunswik, 1956; Pervin, 1976; Endler & Magnusson, 1975); and (3) the growing methodological sophistication in social psychology, particularly in areas of descriptive and taxonomic research.

Despite the relative novelty of the field, some impressive advances have been made in understanding cognitive representations about interaction routines. First, it proved both reasonable and feasible to sample naturalistic episode domains empirically, and in most milieus so far studied, the number of interaction routines reported turned out to be quite manageable. It seems that in important ways, the episodes naturally reported have the characteristics of basic cognitive categories (Rosch & Lloyd, 1978), and may be thought of as the natural building blocks of both individual life routines and cultural milieus. The second achievement of episode cognition research is the advances made in the construction of reliable empirical episode taxonomies. Such models of episode spaces have now been constructed for British, Swedish, American, and Australian students, housewives, academic groups, and sports teams. The convergent validity of the resulting episode taxonomies is quite impressive. In the majority of cases, two to four very similar episode features, based on affective reactions to the encounters, were found to define the episode domain. These findings confirm Murray's (1951) ideas of 30 years ago, that "situations are susceptible to classification in terms of the different kinds of effects which they exert (or may exert) on the subject, that is, in terms of their significance to his well-being" (p. 459). The apparent encoding and recall of episode scripts in terms of their affective, connotative meaning illustrates yet another aspect of Zajonc's (1980) theory about the primacy of affective reactions to social stimuli.

Third, the recent achievements of cognitive psychologists in studying memory and information processing about episodes resulted in a sudden expansion in our knowledge about episode cognition. There is now evidence showing that episodes function as highly salient integrative schemata in the representation of social information. Although we have taken a primarily cognitive-representational view of episode schemata here, it is essential to remember that affect and mood states have a significant complementary effect on both the structure and the processing of such representations. And fourth, the recent advances made in applying episode concepts in applied areas seem particularly promising in developing the potential of this new field.

It is perhaps too soon to make guesses about how episode cognition research is likely to develop. The field is too new and still too fragmented for detailed prognostication. Perhaps the most promising trend is the growing rapprochement between social and cognitive psychologists in dealing with episode representations, and the willingness of the latter to consider the uniquely social features, such as goals, motivations, emotions, and mood, of such events. The taxonomic-descriptive branch of episode cognition research is slowly reaching maturity, and the major task now is the application of the methods already developed to modeling episode spaces in areas with applied importance. There are also great gaps in our knowledge about how episode elements such as the setting, the relationship, the props, and the goals of the interaction affect our cognitive representations of the event.

Episode cognition research is currently in the mainstream of the cognitivist trend in social psychology. We must be careful not to forget that beside cognition, affect and conation are also part of the "trilogy of the mind," (Hilgard, 1980b), and future work may well need to focus more on these currently neglected aspects of episode representations. It would also be well to keep in mind the multiple roots of research on episodes in sociology and psychology. Hopefully this—by necessity less than complete—summary of the recent advances in episode cognition research will serve as a further impetus to explorations in this field.

## ACKNOWLEDGMENTS

Many of the ideas presented in this article benefited from discussions with Michael Argyle, Rom Harre, Gordon Bower, and Gerry Ginsburg; I am grateful to Ernest Hilgard, Robin Winkler, and Von Otto Leirer for their comments on various parts of this manuscript. Thanks are due to the Department of Psychology, Stanford University for generously extending their facilities during the period of my stay there when this paper was completed.

## REFERENCES

Abelson, R. P. Script processing in attitude formation and decision making. In J. Carroll & J. Payne (Eds.), *Cognition and social behavior*. Hillsdale, New Jersey: Erlbaum, 1976.

Abelson, R. P. *The psychological status of the script concept*. New Haven, Connecticut: Yale University, Cognitive Science Technical Report No. 2, 1980.

Alker, H. A. Is personality situation specific or intrapsychically consistent? *Journal of Personality*, 1972, **40**, 1–16.

Allport, F. H. *Social psychology*. Boston, Massachusetts: Houghton, 1924.

Allport, G. W. *The nature of prejudice*. Reading, Massachusetts: Addison-Wesley, 1954. (a)

Allport, G. W. The historical background of modern social psychology. In G. Lindzey & E. Aronson (Eds.), *The handbook of social psychology* (Vol. 1). Reading, Massachusetts: Addison-Wesley, 1954. (b)

Anderson, J. Arguments concerning representations of mental imagery. *Psychological Review*, 1978, **85**, 249–277.

Anderson, J., & Bower, G. H. *Human associative memory*. New York: Holt, 1973.

Anderson, N. Cognitive algebra: Integration theory applied to social attribution. In L. Berkowitz (Ed.), *Advances in experimental social psychology*. New York: Academic Press, 1974.

Apfelbaum, E., & Herzlich, C. La theorie de l'attribution en psychologie sociale. *Bulletin de Psychologie*, 1971, **24**, 961–976.

Argyle, M., & Little, B. R. Do personality traits apply to social behaviour? *Journal for the Theory of Social Behaviour*, 1972, **2**, 1–35.

Armistead, N. (Ed.) *Reconstructing social psychology*. Harmondsworth: Penguin, 1972.

Asch, S. E. Forming impressions of personality. *Journal of Social Psychology*, 1946, **41**, 258–290.

Asch, S. E. The data of social psychology. In E. Hollander & R. Hunt (Eds.), *Current perspectives in social psychology*. London and New York: Oxford University Press, 1972.

Bandura, A. Self-efficacy: Toward a unifying theory of behavioral change. *Psychological Review*, 1977, **84**, 191–215.

Bandura, A. Self-referent thought: The development of self-efficacy. In J. H. Flavell & L. Ross (Eds.), *Cognitive social development*. London and New York: Cambridge University Press, 1981.

Barker, R. G. *Ecological psychology*. Stanford, California: Stanford University Press, 1968.

Barker, R. G., & Schoggen, P. *Qualities of community life*. San Francisco, California: Jossey-Bass, 1973.

Barker, R. G., & Wright, H. F. *Midwest and its children*. Evanston, Illinois: Row, Peterson, 1955.

Barsalou, L., & Bower, G. H. *Diagnosticity in cognitive categorization*. Unpublished manuscript, Stanford University, 1980.

Bartlett, F. C. *Remembering*. London and New York: Cambridge University Press, 1932.

Battistich, V. A., & Thompson, E. G. Students perceptions of the college milieu. *Personality and Social Psychology Bulletin*, 1980, **6**, 74–82. (a)

Battistich, V. A., & Thompson, E. G. *Individual differences in the perception of social episodes.* Cleveland State University, Department of Psychology, 1980. (b)

Bem, D. S. Self-perception theory. In L. Berkowitz (Ed.), *Advances in experimental social psychology,* New York: Academic Press, 1972.

Bjerg, K. Interplay analysis. *Acta Psychologica,* 1968, **28,** 201–245.

Black, J., & Bower, G. H. Episodes as chunks in narrative memory. Stanford, California: Stanford University Press, 1980.

Blumer, R. *Symbolic interactionism.* New York: Prentice-Hall, 1969.

Bower, G. H. *Emotional mood and memory.* Paper presented at the APA Congress, Montreal, 1980.

Bower, G. H., Black, J. B., & Turner, T. J. Scripts in memory for text. *Cognitive Psychology,* 1979, **11,** 177–220.

Bower, G. H., Forgas, J. P., & Krantz, S. *Mood, memory and self-monitoring of social episodes.* Stanford University, 1981.

Bower, G. H., & Gilligan, S. G. Remembering information related to one's self. *Journal of Research in Personality,* 1979, **13,** 420–432.

Bower, G. H., Monteiro, K. P., & Gilligan, S. H. Emotional mood as a context for learning and recall. *Journal of Verbal Learning and Verbal Behaviour,* 1978, **17,** 573–585.

Bowers, K. S. Situationism in psychology: An analysis and a critique. *Psychological Review,* 1973, **80,** 307–336.

Brittan, A. *Meanings and situations.* Boston, Massachusetts: Routledge, Kegan & Paul, 1973.

Bruner, J. S. *Psychological theories and the image of man.* Herbert Spencer Lecture, University of Oxford, 1976.

Brunswik, E. *Perception and the representative design of psychological experiments.* Berkeley: University of California Press, 1956.

Canter, D., & Lee, T. *Psychology and the built environment.* Tonbridge: The Architectural Press, 1974.

Cantor, N., & Mischel, W. Prototypes in person perception. In L. Berkowitz (Ed.), *Advances in experimental social psychology,* New York: Academic Press, 1979.

Carroll, J. D., & Arabie, P. Multidimensional scaling. *Annual Review of Psychology,* 1980, **31,** 607–650.

Carroll, J. S., & Payne, J. W. (Eds.), *Cognition and social behavior.* Hillsdale, New Jersey: Erlbaum, 1976.

Cattell, R. B. Personality, role, mood and situation-perception: A unifying theory of modulators. *Psychological Review,* 1963, **70,** 1–18.

Cohen, C. E., & Ebbesen, E. B. Observational goals and schema activation: A theoretical framework for behavior perception. *Journal of Experimental Social Psychology,* 1979, **15,** 305–329.

Craik, F. I. M. Human memory. *Annual Review of Psychology,* 1979, **30,** 63–102.

Durkheim, E. Representations individuelles et representations collectives. *Revue de Metaphysique et de Morale,* 1898, **6,** 273–302.

Ekehammar, B. Interactionism in psychology from a psychological perspective. *Psychological Bulletin,* 1974, **81,** 1026–1043.

Ekehammar, B., & Magnusson, D. A method to study stressful situations. *Journal of Personality and Social Psychology,* 1973, **27,** 176–179.

Endler, N. S. The person vs the situation—a pseudo issue? *Journal of Personality,* 1973, **41,** 287–303.

Endler, N. S., & Hunt, J. M. The generalizability of contributions from sources of variance in the S-R Inventory of Anxiousness. *Journal of Personality,* 1969, **37,** 1–24.

Endler, N. S., & Magnusson, D. (Eds.), *Interaction: Psychology and personality.* New York: Wiley, 1975.

Farr, R. *The social psychology of mind and behaviour.* Invited address at the British Psychological Society Social Psychology Conference, Canterbury, 1980.

Farr, R. An historical look at social cognition. In J. P. Forgas (Ed.), *Social cognition: Perspectives on everyday understanding.* New York: Academic Press, 1981.

Fishbein, M., & Ajzen, A. *Belief, attitudes, intention and behavior.* Reading, Massachusetts: Addison-Wesley, 1975.

Flanagan, J. C. The critical incident technique. *Psychological Bulletin,* 1954, **51,** 327–358.

Forgas, J. P. The perception of social episodes: Categorical and dimensional representations in two social milieus. *Journal of Personality and Social Psychology,* 1976, **33,** 199–209.

Forgas, J. P. Polarization and moderation of person perception judgements as a function of group interaction style. *European Journal of Social Psychology,* 1977, **7,** 175–187.

Forgas, J. P. Social episodes and social structure in an academic setting: The social environment of an intact group. *Journal of Experimental Social Psychology,* 1978, **14,** 434–448. (a)

Forgas, J. P. The effects of behavioural and cultural expectation cues on the perception of social episodes. *European Journal of Social Psychology,* 1978, **8,** 203–213. (b)

Forgas, J. P. *The effects of the interaction partner and the situation context on episode cognition.* Unpublished, University of New South Wales, 1978. (c)

Forgas, J. P. Multidimensional scaling: A discovery method in social psychology. In G. P. Ginsburg (Ed.), *Emerging strategies in social psychology.* New York: Wiley, 1979. (a)

Forgas, J. P. *Social episodes: The study of interaction routines.* New York: Academic Press, 1979. (b)

Forgas, J. P. Images of crime: The perception of criminal incidents. *International Journal of Psychology,* 1980, **15,** 287–299.

Forgas, J. P. (Ed.), *Social cognition: Perspectives on everyday understanding.* New York: Academic Press, 1981. (a)

Forgas, J. P. What is social about social cognition? In J. P. Forgas (Ed.), *Social cognition: Perspectives on everyday understanding.* New York: Academic Press, 1981. (b)

Forgas, J. P. Affective elements in episode cognition. In J. P. Forgas (Ed.), *Social cognition: Perspectives on everyday understanding.* New York: Academic Press, 1981. (c)

Forgas, J. P. Responsibility attribution by groups and individuals: The effects of the interaction episode. *European Journal of Social Psychology,* 1981, **11,** 87–99. (d)

Forgas, J. P. Social episodes and group milieu: A study in social cognition. *British Journal of Social Psychology,* 1981, **20,** 219–230. (e)

Forgas, J. P. Person prototypes in impression formation. *British Journal of Social Psychology,* 1982, in press. (a)

Forgas, J. P. Social skills and the perception of interaction episodes. *British Journal of Clinical Psychology,* 1982, in press. (b)

Forgas, J. P., Argyle, M., & Ginsburg, G. P. The effects of social episodes on person perception: The fluctuating structure of an academic group. *Journal of Social Psychology,* 1979, **109,** 207–222.

Forgas, J. P., & Brown, L. B. Environmental and behavioral cues in the perception of social encounters. *American Journal of Psychology,* 1977, **90,** 635–644.

Forgas, J. P., Brown, L. B., & Menyhart, J. Dimensions of aggression: The perception of aggressive episodes. *British Journal of Social and Clinical Psychology,* 1980, **19,** 215–227.

Forgas, J. P., & Dobosz, B. Dimensions of romantic involvement: Towards a taxonomy of heterosexual relationships. *Social Psychology Quarterly,* 1980, **43,** 290–300.

Frederiksen, N. Toward a taxonomy of situations. *American Psychologist,* 1972, **27,** 114–123.

Gergen, K. J. Social psychology as history. *Journal of Personality and Social Psychology,* 1973, **26,** 309–326.

Gergen, K. J. Experimentation in social psychology: A reappraisal. *European Journal of Social Psychology,* 1978, **8.**

Ginsburg, G. P. (Ed.), *Emerging strategies in social psychology.* New York: Wiley, 1979.

Goffman, E. *Encounters.* Indianapolis, Indiana: Bobbs Merrill, 1961.

Goffman, E. *Behavior in public places.* Glencoe, Illinois: The Free Press, 1963.

Goffman, E. *Interaction ritual.* New York: Anchor Books, 1967.

Goffman, E. *Frame analysis.* Harmondsworth: Penguin, 1974.

Golding, L. Flies in the ointment: Methodological problems in the analysis of variance attributable to persons and situations. *Psychological Bulletin,* 1975, **82,** 278–288.

Goldstein, A., Sprafkin, R. P., & Gershaw, N. J. *Skill training for community living.* Oxford: Pergamon, 1976.

Graesser, A. C., Gordon, S. E., & Sawyer, J. D. Recognition memory for typical and atypical actions in scripted activities: Tests of a script pointer plus tag hypothesis. *Journal of Verbal Learning and Verbal Behaviour,* 1979, **18,** 319–332.

Guthrie, E. R. *The psychology of learning.* New York: Harper, 1952.

Harre, R. Rituals, rhetoric and social cognition. In J. P. Forgas (Ed.), *Social cognition: Perspectives on everyday understanding.* New York: Academic Press, 1981.

Harre, R., & Secord, P. F. *The explanation of social behaviour.* Oxford: Blackwell, 1972.

Hastie, R., & Kumar, P. A. Person memory: Personality traits as organising principles in memory for behaviours. *Journal of Personality and Social Psychology,* 1979, **37,** 25–38.

Heider, F. *The psychology of interpersonal relations.* New York: Wiley, 1958.

Heise, D. R. *Understanding events: Affect and the construction of social action.* London and New York: Cambridge University Press, 1979.

Hilgard, E. R. Consciousness in contemporary psychology. *Annual Review of Psychology,* 1980, **31,** 1–26. (a)

Hilgard, E. R. The trilogy of mind: Cognition, affection and conation. *Journal of the History of the Behavioural Sciences,* 1980, **16,** 107–117. (b)

Isen, A. M. *Positive affect, decision making strategy and risk-taking.* Unpublished, University of Maryland, 1981.

Isen, A. M., Clark, M., Shalker, T. E., & Karp, L. Affect, accessibility of material in memory and behaviour: A cognitive loop? *Journal of Personality and Social Psychology,* 1978, **36,** 1–12.

Jellison, J. M. Reconsidering the attitude concept. In J. Tedeschi (Ed.), *Impression management.* New York: Academic Press, 1980.

Joiner, D. Social ritual and architectural space. *Journal of Architectural Research and Teaching.* 1971, **3,** 11–22.

Kando, T. M. *Social interaction.* St. Louis, Missouri: Mosby, 1977.

Kantor, J. R. *Principles of psychology* (Vol. 1). Bloomington: Principia Press, 1924.

Keenan, J. M., & Bailett, S. D. Memory for personally and socially significant events. In R. S. Nickerson (Ed.), *Attention and performance.* Hillsdale, New Jersey: Erlbaum, 1979.

Kelley, H. H. *Attribution in social interaction.* Morristown, New Jersey: General Learning Press, 1971.

Kelley, H. H. *Personal relationships.* Hillsdale, New Jersey: Erlbaum, 1979.

Kintsch, W. *Memory and cognition.* New York: Wiley, 1977.

Koffka, K. *Principles of Gestalt psychology.* New York: Harcourt, 1935.

Krauss, R. M. *Cognition and communication.* Paper presented at the meeting of the Society for Experimental Social Psychology, Stanford, 1980.

Kruskal, J. B., & Wish, M. *Multidimensional scaling.* New York: Sage, 1979.

Laumann, E. D., & House, J. S. Living room styles and social attributes. *Sociological and Social Research,* 1970, **54,** 321–342.

Levin, J. Three-mode factor analysis. *Psychological Bulletin*, 1965, **64**, 442–452.

Lewin, K. *A dynamic theory of personality: Selected papers*. New York: McGraw-Hill, 1935.

Lewin, K. *Principles of topological psychology*. New York: McGraw-Hill, 1936.

Lewin, K. *Field theory in social science: Selected theoretical papers*. New York: Harper, 1951.

Lichtenstein, E. H., & Brewer, W. F. Memory for goal-directed events. *Cognitive Psychology*, 1980, **12**, 412–445.

McGuire, W. J. The ying and yang of progress in social psychology: Seven koan. *Journal of Personality and Social Psychology*, 1973, **26**, 446–456.

Magnusson, D. An analysis of situational dimensions. *Perceptual and Motor Skills, 1971*, **32**, 851–867.

Magnusson, D., & Ekehammar, B. An analysis of situational dimensions: A replication. *Multivariate Behavioural Research*, 1973, **8**, 331–339.

Mahoney, M. J. Reflections on the cognitive learning trend in psychotherapy. *American Psychologist*, 1977, **32**, 5–12.

Mandler, J. M., & Johnson, N. S. Remembrances of things parsed: Story structure and recall. *Cognitive Psychology*, 1977, **9**, 111–151.

Marwell, G., & Hage, J. The organization of relationships: Systematic description. *American Sociological Review*, 1970, **35**, 884–900.

Mead, G. H. *Mind, self and society*. Chicago, Illinois: University of Chicago Press, 1934.

Mead, G. H. In A. Strauss (Ed.), *The social psychology of George Herbert Mead*. Chicago, Illinois: University of Chicago Press, 1956.

Mervis, C. B., & Rosch, E. Categorization of natural objects. *Annual Review of Psychology*, 1981, **32**, 89–115.

Miller, G. A., Galanter, E., & Pribram, K. H. *Plans and the structure of behavior*. New York: Holt, 1960.

Minsky, M. K. Lines: A theory for memory. *Cognitive Science*, 1980, **4**, 117–133.

Mischel, W. *Personality and assessment*. New York: Wiley, 1968.

Mischel, W. Toward a cognitive social learning reconceptualization of personality. *Psychological Review*, 1973, **80**, 252–283.

Mischel, W. On the interface of cognition and personality. *American Psychologist*, 1979, **34.**

Moos, R. H. Situational analysis of a therapeutic community milieu. *Journal of Abnormal Psychology*, 1968, **73**, 49–61.

Moos, R. H. *Evaluating treatment environments: A social ecological approach*. New York: Wiley, 1974.

Moscovici, S. Social representations. In J. P. Forgas (Ed.), *Social cognition: Perspectives on everyday understanding*. New York: Academic Press, 1981.

Moscovici, S., Doise, W., & Dulong, R. Studies in group decision I. *European Journal of Social Psychology*, 1972, **2**, 385–390.

Moscovici, S., & Lecuyer, R. Studies in group decision II. *European Journal of Social Psychology*, 1972, **2**, 221–244.

Murphy, G. *Personality: A biosocial approach to origins and structure*. New York: Harper, 1947.

Murray, H. A. *Explorations in personality*. London and New York: Oxford University Press, 1938.

Murray, H. A. Toward a classification of interaction. In T. Parsons & E. A. Shils (Eds.), *Towards a general theory of action*. Cambridge, Massachusetts: Harvard University Press, 1951.

Nascimento-Schulze, C. M. Towards situational classification. *European Journal of Social Psychology*, 1981, **11**, 149–159.

Nelson, K. (Ed.) *Children's language*. New York: Gardner, 1979.

Nelson, K., Rescorla, L., Gruendel, J., & Benedict, H. Early lexicons: What do they mean? *Child Development*, 1978, **49**, 960–968.

Orne, M. T. On the social psychology of the psychological experiment. *American Psychologist,* 1962, **17,** 776–783.

Owens, J., Bower, G. H., & Black, J. B. The soap opera effect in story recall. *Memory and Cognition,* 1979, **7,** 185–191.

Pervin, L. A. Performance and satisfaction as a function of individual environment fit. *Psychological Bulletin,* 1968, **69,** 56–68.

Pervin, L. A. *The representative design in person-situation research.* Paper presented at the Symposium on Interactional Psychology, Stockholm, 1975. (a)

Pervin, L. A. *A free-response description approach to the study of person situation interaction.* (E.T.S. Bulletin No. 22). Princeton, New Jersey, 1975. (b)

Pervin, L. A. Definitions, measurements and classifications of stimuli, situations and environments. (E.T.S. Bulletin No. 23). Princeton, New Jersey, 1975. (c)

Pervin, L. A. A free response description approach to the study of person situation interaction. *Journal of Personality and Social Psychology,* 1976, **34,** 465–474.

Piaget, J. *The origins of intelligence in children.* New York: International University Press, 1952.

Popper, K. *The logic of scientific discovery.* New York: Basic Books, 1959.

Popper, K. *Conjectures and refutations.* London: Routledge, Kegan & Paul, 1963.

Price, R. H. The taxonomic classification of behaviors and situations and the problem of behavior-environment congruence. *Human Relations,* 1974, **27,** 567–585.

Price, R. H., & Bouffard, D. L. Behavioural appropriateness and situational constraint as dimensions of social behaviours. *Journal of Personality and Social Psychology,* 1974, **30,** 579–586.

Reed, S. K. Pattern recognition and categorization. *Cognitive Psychology,* 1972, **3,** 382–407.

Rosch, E. Cognitive reference points. *Cognitive Psychology,* 1975, **7,** 532–547.

Rosch, E. & Lloyd, B. B. *Cognition and categorization.* Hillsdale, New Jersey: Erlbaum, 1978.

Rosch, E., & Mervis, C. B. Family resemblances: Studies in the internal structure of categories. *Cognitive Psychology,* 1975, **7,** 573–605.

Rosch, E., Mervis, C. B., Gray, W. D., Johnson, D. M., & Boyes-Bream, P. Basic objects in natural categories. *Cognitive Psychology,* 1976, **8,** 382–439.

Rosenberg, S., & Sedlak, A. Structural representations of implicit personality theory. In L. Berkowitz (Ed.), *Advances in experimental social psychology* (Vol. 6). New York: Academic Press, 1972. Pp. 235–297.

Rosenthal, R. *Experimenter effects in behavioral research.* New York: Appleton, 1966.

Ross, B. H., & Bower, G. H. Comparisons of models of associative recall. *Memory and Cognition,* 1980 (in press).

Roth, D., & Rehm, L. P. Relationship among self-monitoring processes, memory and depression. *Cognitive Therapy and Research,* 1980, **4,** 149–157.

Rumelhart, D. E. Notes on a schema for stories. In D. G. Bobrow & A. Collins (Eds.), *Representation and understanding.* New York: Academic Press, 1975.

Rumelhart, D. E. Understanding and summarizing brief stories. In D. LaBerge & S. J. Samuels (Eds.), *Basic processes in reading.* Hillsdale, New Jersey: Erlbaum, 1977.

Schank, R., & Abelson, R. P. *Scripts, plans, goals and understanding: An inquiry into human knowledge structures.* Hillsdale, New Jersey: Erlbaum, 1977.

Schutz, A. In H. R. Wagner (Ed.), *On phenomenology and social relations.* Chicago, Illinois: University of Chicago Press, 1970.

Seligman, M. The generality of laws of learning. *Psychological Review,* 1970, **77,** 406–418.

Shantz, C. U. The development of social cognition. In E. M. Hetherington (Ed.), *Review of child development research* (Vol. 5). Chicago, Illinois: University of Chicago Press, 1975.

Simon, H. A. Information processing models of cognition. *Annual Review of Psychology,* 1979, **30,** 363–396.

Skinner, B. F. *The behavior of organisms.* New York: Appleton, 1938.

Stone, G. P., & Farbermann, H. E. (Eds.), *Social psychology through symbolic interaction.* Waltham, Massachusetts: Ginn-Blaisdell, 1970.

Tajfel, H. Social and cultural factors in perception. In G. Lindzey & E. Aronson (Eds.), *The handbook of social psychology* (Vol. 3). Reading, Massachusetts: Addison-Wesley, 1969.

Tajfel, H. Individuals and groups in social psychology. *British Journal of Social and Clinical Psychology,* 1979, **18,** 183–190.

Tajfel, H., & Forgas, J. P. Social categorization: Cognitions, values and groups. In J. P. Forgas (Ed.), *Social cognition: Perspectives on everyday understanding.* New York: Academic Press, 1981.

Thomas, W. I. *The unadjusted girl.* Boston, Massachusetts: Ginn, 1923.

Thomas, W. I. Situational analysis: The behavior pattern and the situation. Reprinted in M. Janowitz (Ed.), *W. I. Thomas on social organization and social personality.* Chicago, Illinois: Chicago University Press, 1928/1966.

Thomas, W. I., & Znaniecki, F. *The Polish peasant in Europe and America.* Chicago, Illinois: University of Chicago Press, 1928.

Titchener, E. B., Wundt, W. In W. G. Bringman & R. D. Tweney (Eds.), *Wundt studies.* Toronto: Hogrefe, 1980.

Townsend, J. T. Issues and models concerning the processing of a finite number of inputs. In B. Kantowitz (Ed.), *Human information processing.* Hillsdale, New Jersey: Erlbaum, 1974.

Triandis, H. C. *The analysis of subjective culture.* New York: Wiley, 1972.

Triandis, H. C., Vassiliou, V., & Nassiakou, M. Three cross-cultural studies of subjective culture. *Journal of Personality and Social Psychology,* 1968, **8,** 1–42.

Trower, P., Bryant, B., & Argyle, M. *Social skills and mental health.* London: Methuen, 1978.

Vernon, P. E. *Personality assessment: A critical survey.* New York: Wiley, 1964.

Waller, W. *The sociology of teaching.* New York: Wiley, 1961.

Watson, J. B. Psychology as the behaviorist views it. *Psychological Review,* 1913, **20,** 158–177.

Watson, J., & Potter, R. J. An analytic unit for the study of interaction. *Human Relations,* 1962, **15,** 245–263.

Weber, M. In T. Parsons (Ed.), *The theory of social and economic organization.* Glencoe, Illinois: Free Press, 1947.

Weber, M. *Economy and society.* New York: Bedminster, 1968.

Wegner, D., & Vallacher, R. *Implicit psychology: The study of social cognition.* London and New York: Oxford University Press, 1977.

Wegner, D. M., & Vallacher, R. R. Common sense psychology. In J. P. Forgas (Ed.), *Social cognition: Perspectives on everyday understanding.* New York: Academic Press, 1981.

Werdelin, I. *Factor analyses of an inventory of behaviour in social situations.* Stockholm University, Dept. of Psychology, 1975.

Wicklund, R., & Frey, D. Cognitive consistency: Motivation and information processing perspectives. In J. P. Forgas (Ed.), *Social cognition: Perspectives on everyday understanding.* New York: Academic Press, 1981.

Wish, M. Subjects expectations about their own interpersonal communications: A multidimensional approach. *Personality and Social Psychology Bulletin,* 1975, **1,** 11–20.

Wish, M., Deutsch, M., & Kaplan, S. J. Perceived dimensions of interpersonal relations. *Journal of Personality and Social Psychology,* 1976, **33,** 409–420.

Wittgenstein, L. *Philosophical investigations.* New York: Macmillan, 1953.

Wolff, K. H. Definition of the situation. In J. Gould & W. K. Kolb (Eds.), *A dictionary of the social sciences.* New York: Free Press, 1964.

Wolpe, J. *Psychotherapy by reciprocal inhibition.* Stanford, California: Stanford University Press, 1958.

Wolpe, J. *The practice of behaviour therapy*. Oxford: Pergamon, 1969.

Wolpe, J. Cognition and causation in human behavior and its therapy. *American Psychologist*, 1978, **33,** 437–446.

Wundt, W. *Grundriss fuer psychologie*. Leipzig: Engelmann, 1905.

Zadeh, L. A. Fuzzy sets. *Information and Control*. 1965, **8,** 338–353.

Zajonc, R. Feeling and thinking: Preferences need no inferences. *American Psychologist*, 1980, **35,** 151–175.

# THE EFFECTS OF
# AGGRESSIVE-PORNOGRAPHIC
# MASS MEDIA STIMULI[1]

## Neil M. Malamuth*

PSYCHOLOGY DEPARTMENT
UNIVERSITY OF MANITOBA
MANITOBA, CANADA

## Ed Donnerstein

DEPARTMENT OF COMMUNICATION ARTS
UNIVERSITY OF WISCONSIN—MADISON
MADISON, WISCONSIN

I. Introduction . . . . . . . . . . . . . . . . . . . . . . . . . . . . . . . . . . . . . . . . . . . . . . . . . . . . . . . . . . . . . 104
  A. Purpose . . . . . . . . . . . . . . . . . . . . . . . . . . . . . . . . . . . . . . . . . . . . . . . . . . . . . . . . . . . . . . 104
  B. Aggressive versus Nonaggressive Pornography . . . . . . . . . . . . . . . . . . . . . . . . . . . 104
  C. The Frequency of Aggressive Pornography . . . . . . . . . . . . . . . . . . . . . . . . . . . . . . 105
  D. Bases for Concern . . . . . . . . . . . . . . . . . . . . . . . . . . . . . . . . . . . . . . . . . . . . . . . . . . 106
II. Aggressive Pornography and Sexual Arousal . . . . . . . . . . . . . . . . . . . . . . . . . . . . . . 107
  A. Initial Findings . . . . . . . . . . . . . . . . . . . . . . . . . . . . . . . . . . . . . . . . . . . . . . . . . . . . . 107
  B. Victim's Responses . . . . . . . . . . . . . . . . . . . . . . . . . . . . . . . . . . . . . . . . . . . . . . . . . 108
  C. Individual Differences . . . . . . . . . . . . . . . . . . . . . . . . . . . . . . . . . . . . . . . . . . . . . . . 109
  D. Context of Assessment . . . . . . . . . . . . . . . . . . . . . . . . . . . . . . . . . . . . . . . . . . . . . . 111
  E. Conclusions . . . . . . . . . . . . . . . . . . . . . . . . . . . . . . . . . . . . . . . . . . . . . . . . . . . . . . . 111
III. The Effects of Aggressive Pornography on Responses Other than Aggression . . . . . . . 112
  A. Changes in Sexual Responsiveness . . . . . . . . . . . . . . . . . . . . . . . . . . . . . . . . . . . . 112
  B. Fantasies . . . . . . . . . . . . . . . . . . . . . . . . . . . . . . . . . . . . . . . . . . . . . . . . . . . . . . . . . 112
  C. Perceptions and Attitudes . . . . . . . . . . . . . . . . . . . . . . . . . . . . . . . . . . . . . . . . . . . 113
IV. The Effects of Aggressive Pornography on Aggression . . . . . . . . . . . . . . . . . . . . . . . 115
  A. Research Findings . . . . . . . . . . . . . . . . . . . . . . . . . . . . . . . . . . . . . . . . . . . . . . . . . . 115
  B. Summary of Effects on Aggression . . . . . . . . . . . . . . . . . . . . . . . . . . . . . . . . . . . . 121

*Present address: Department of Communication, 232 Royce Hall, University of California, Los Angeles, Los Angeles, California 90024.

[1]Research by the present authors and the writing of this chapter were facilitated in part by grants from the Social Sciences and Humanities Research Council of Canada to Malamuth and NIMH to Donnerstein.

ADVANCES IN EXPERIMENTAL SOCIAL
PSYCHOLOGY, VOL. 15
Copyright © 1982 by Academic Press, Inc.
All rights of reproduction in any form reserved.
ISBN 0-12-015215-0

# I.  Introduction

## A.  PURPOSE

Over the past 20 years there has been a great deal of debate concerning the effects of sexually explicit materials. In 1967 the U.S. Congress decided traffic in pornography was a "matter of national concern" and consequently established the Commission on Obscenity and Pornography to conduct a thorough investigation of this issue. However, on reviewing the available research, the Commission concluded that there was no evidence that pornography had antisocial effects (see *Commission on Obscenity and Pornography*, 1970). For many social scientists and members of the general community, the findings of the Commission largely settled the issue. It became widely accepted that pornography, in general, does not have any demonstrable adverse effect.

Nevertheless, a number of investigators and scientific and political groups have criticized the Commission's conclusions (e.g., Berkowitz, 1971; Liebert & Schwartzberg, 1977; Bart & Jozsa, 1980; Diamond, 1980). Several women's groups and various feminist writers have been particularly outspoken (e.g., Lederer, 1980). The purpose of this chapter is not to present a comprehensive discussion of the merits or shortcomings of the Commission's findings, but to address one aspect of the issue that was not adequately addressed in the Commission's research: the effects of stimuli that combine sexuality and aggression.

## B.  AGGRESSIVE VERSUS NONAGGRESSIVE PORNOGRAPHY

The distinction between aggressive and nonaggressive pornography is often difficult to establish both operationally and conceptually. For example, Gloria Steinem (1980), in differentiating between what she considers acceptable erotica from objectionable pornography, writes:

> Look at any photo or film of people making love; really making love. The images may be diverse, but there is usually a sensuality and touch and warmth, an acceptance of bodies

and nerve endings. There is always a spontaneous sense of people who are there because they want to be, out of shared pleasure.

Now look at any depiction of sex in which there is clear force, or an unequal power that spells coercion. It may be very blatant, with weapons of torture or bondage, wounds and bruises, some clear humiliation, or an adult's sexual power being used over a child. It may be much more subtle: a physical attitude of conqueror and victim, the use of race or class difference to imply the same thing, perhaps a very unequal nudity, with one person exposed and vulnerable while the other is clothed. In either case, there is no sense of equal choice or equal power. (p. 37)

In the series of studies reported below, *aggressive pornography* refers to portrayals of sex that would be considered "blatantly" coercive by Steinem. By and large, these are depictions in which physical force is used or threatened to coerce a woman to engage in sexual acts (e.g., rape). The conclusions and implications of the research findings concerning aggressive pornography therefore apply to such materials only, although the effects of materials that more subtly portray coercion have not been adequately researched as yet. The term *pornography* will be used throughout this chapter to refer to sexually explicit stimuli without any pejorative meaning necessarily intended.

## C.  THE FREQUENCY OF AGGRESSIVE PORNOGRAPHY

When the Commission conducted its research studies, aggressive-pornographic materials were relatively infrequent (*Commission on Obscenity and Pornography,* 1970). This may partially explain why the Commission's studies almost without exception did not include any stimuli that involved rape or other forms of coercive sexuality. The only Commission studies that paid more than passing attention to such materials were retrospective surveys comparing the reports of sexual offenders, sexual deviants, and comparison groups from the general population regarding their previous exposure to pornography. These studies unfortunately yielded highly conflicting conclusions (Goldstein, Kant, Judd, Rice, & Green, 1971; Davis & Braucht, 1971).

Although aggressive pornography was relatively rare in earlier years, a number of recent articles in the general media (e.g., *Time,* 1976; *Village Voice,* 1977) have observed that aggression has become increasingly prevalent in sexually explicit books, magazines, and films during the 1970s. More systematic content analyses of both "hard-core" materials (Smith, 1976a,b) and "soft-core" stimuli such as *Playboy* and *Penthouse* magazines (Malamuth & Spinner, 1980) generally colloborate these observations. Smith (1976a,b), for example, analyzed the content of hard-core paperback books published between 1968 and 1974. He found that in about one-third of the episodes, force is used, almost always by a male, to coerce a female to engage in an unwanted act of sex.

Furthermore, he found that the average number of acts depicting rape doubled from 1968 to 1974.

## D. BASES FOR CONCERN

There would appear to be ample reasons for concern about the effects of aggressively toned pornographic stimuli. To begin with, the antisocial effects shown to result from nonsexual depicitions of aggression in the mass media (e.g., Eron, 1980; Parke, Berkowitz, Leyens, West, & Sebastien, 1977; Thomas, Horton, Lippincott, & Drabman, 1977) would seem likely to occur also when the aggression is presented within a sexual context. However, there are theoretical reasons for being particularly concerned about the fusion of sexuality and aggression in the media (Malamuth & Spinner, 1980). First, the coupling of sex and aggression in these portrayals may result in conditioning processes whereby aggressive acts become associated with sexual arousal, a powerful unconditioned stimulus and reinforcer. In fact, current treatments for sexual offenders (e.g., Abel, Blanchard, & Becker, 1978; Brownell, Hayes, & Barlow, 1977; Hayes, Brownell, & Barlow, 1978) are based on the premise that conditioning may occur by associating fantasies of socially sanctioned arousal and behavior. It is also possible that the juxtaposition of media portrayals of aggression and sexuality could lead to conditioning and thereby increase sexual arousal to aggressive stimuli, possibly leading to concomitant changes in fantasies and behavior. Second, in many pornographic depictions the victim is frequently portrayed as secretly desiring the assault and as eventually deriving sexual pleasure from it (Malamuth, Heim, & Feshbach, 1980; Smith, 1976a,b). In other words, the victim supposedly likes being assaulted sexually. From a cognitive perspective, such information may suggest that even if a woman seems repulsed by a pursuer, she will eventually respond favorably to forceful advances, aggression, and overpowering by a male assailant (Brownmiller, 1975; Johnson & Goodchilds, 1973). While many subjects may recognize the fictional nature of this type of information, research on the availability heuristic (Tversky & Kahneman, 1973) suggests that such depictions may nonetheless have a significant impact (Hans, 1980). According to the availability heuristic concept, events that come relatively easily to mind are apt to be regarded as likely to occur. Carroll (1978) demonstrated that subjects who were asked to imagine an event that they knew was totally fictional were more likely to believe that incident would actually occur than subjects who were not instructed to imagine its occurrence. To the extent that the mass media frequently presents images of women as responding favorably to male aggression, such images may easily come to people's minds and affect their beliefs, attitudes, and behavior.

In this article, we shall describe research on the effects of aggressive-pornographic stimuli. We shall first examine the degree to which such materials stimulate sexual arousal. Next, we shall consider the effects on responses other than aggression (e.g., attitudes, perceptions). Finally, the findings of studies on the effects of aggressive pornography on behavioral aggression will be presented.

## II.  Aggressive Pornography and Sexual Arousal

### A.  INITIAL FINDINGS

Are aggressive-pornographic portrayals sexually arousing to "normals"? This question is of considerable importance because people may be more likely to seek out stimuli that are sexually arousing as contrasted with those that elicit little or no arousal.

Until recently, the limited data available seemed to suggest that aggressive sexual depictions resulted in less sexual arousal than did nonaggressive sexual stimuli (e.g., see Baron & Byrne, 1977). This conclusion was largely based on studies using sadomasochistic portrayals and relying exclusively on self-reported sexual arousal. More recently, such a conclusion appeared to have been given additional support by research comparing the sexual responsiveness of rapists and nonrapists to rape scenes, as contrasted with consenting sexual depicitions. Abel, Barlow, Blanchard, and Guild (1977) reported that while rapists in their sample evidenced high and about equal levels of penile tumescence to audio-taped portrayals of both rape and consenting sexual acts, the nonrapist comparison group showed significantly higher levels of sexual responsiveness to the consenting depictions. On the basis of such data, these investigators developed the rape index, which is a comparison of sexual arousal to rape versus arousal to consenting portrayals.

Abel and his associates argued that this index serves as an objective measure of a proclivity to rape. Using this index, an individual whose sexual arousal to rape themes was found to be similar to or greater than his arousal to consenting depictions would be considered as having an inclination to rape (see also Abel, Blanchard, & Becker, 1976, 1978). These investigators and others have been using this measure in the diagnosis and treatment of rapists and recently extended it to the identification and treatment of child molesters (Abel, Becker, Murphy, & Flanagan, 1979; Quinsey, Chaplin, & Carrigan, 1980) by comparing sexual arousal to pedophilic, as contrasted with consenting adult, sexual depictions. Quinsey *et al.* (1980) provided some support for the predictive validity of this assessment technique by showing that it predicted recidivism following discharge from a psychiatric hospital.

Both the rapist and nonrapist samples studied by Abel and his colleagues were male patients referred for evaluation of their deviant sexual arousal (e.g., pedophiles, transsexuals). The generalizability of data based on such samples is certainly suspect. However, recent studies using male graduate students and nonpatient volunteers as the nonrapist comparison groups (e.g., Barbaree, Marshall, & Lanthier, 1979; Quinsey, Chaplin, & Varney, 1981) yielded results similar to those of Abel *et al.* In contrast, there is ample recent evidence that under certain conditions rape stimuli are highly sexually arousing to individuals from the general population (Briddell, Rimm, Caddy, Krawitz, Sholis, & Wunderlin, 1978; Farkas, 1979; Malamuth, in press; Malamuth & Check, 1980a,b, in press; Schmidt, 1975). The discussion that follows presents the findings of research designed to identify the conditions that are responsible for the differing levels of nonrapists' sexual arousal to rape stimuli.

### B. VICTIM'S RESPONSES

A substantial body of data indicates that the reactions of the victim in rape scenes significantly affects the sexual arousal exhibited by both male and female members of the audience. If the victim is portrayed as becoming involuntarily sexually aroused by the assault (which might be termed "positive" outcome),[2] the subjects show levels of sexual arousal (both on self-reports and on penile tumescence measures) that are at least as high and often tend to be higher than those stimulated by mutually consenting depictions (Malamuth *et al.*, 1980b; Malamuth & Check, 1980a,b, in press; Quinsey & Chaplin, 1981). Rape portrayals that depict the victim as continuously abhorring the experience (i.e., negative outcome depictions), on the other hand, typically result in significantly less sexual arousal than mutually consenting themes (Malamuth *et al.*, 1980b; Malamuth & Check, 1980a,b), although as noted below, there is a sizeable minority of the population for whom rape portrayals in general appear to be just as sexually stimulating as consenting depictions.

These findings point to a variable (i.e., the outcome dimension) which seems to be of central importance in explaining the contradictory findings concerning sexual responsivity to aggressive pornography. Studies reporting that nonrapists showed high levels of sexual arousal to rape (e.g., Farkas, 1979) used depictions indicating victim arousal, whereas those reporting low subject arousal used rape portrayals in which the experience was abhorrent to the victim (e.g., Abel *et al.*, 1977).

These data may also account for an apparent inconsistency between the findings of Abel *et al.* (1977) and the results of content analytical studies of pornography. As noted earlier, these studies (Smith, 1976a; Malamuth & Spinner, 1980) indicate that much of hard-core pornography and an increasing percentage of soft-core pornography incorporate aggressive themes. The publishers' decision to include aggressive pornography is probably, to some degree, a reflec-

---

[2]As discussed in greater detail later in this article, research that includes depictions of victim arousal also presents, as part of the research debriefing, very explicit statements concerning the falsity of such rape myths. Recent data show that such debriefings are effective in dispelling beliefs in rape myths.

tion of buyers' interests. If very few nondeviants were sexually stimulated by any types of aggressive-pornographic portrayals, we might expect very few rape and other aggressive depictions in popular pornography. But since there is a growing number of such depictions, the type of sexual aggression found in commercially available pornography probably differs from that used in the research by Abel *et al.* (1977) and Barbaree *et al.* (1979). (Remember, their material tended to stress the rape victim's abhorrence.) Indeed, as was mentioned earlier, a good deal of pornography portrays rape victims as becoming involuntarily sexually aroused (Brownmiller, 1975; Gager & Schurr, 1976; Smith, 1976a). As we shall see later in this article, mass media portrayals that suggest victim's arousal have important effects on perceptions, attitudes, and aggressive responses.

## C. INDIVIDUAL DIFFERENCES

A series of experiments reveal that there are important individual differences in the sexual responsivity of male subjects to rape scenes as contrasted with consenting depictions. These investigations clearly show that there is a substantial percentage of subjects who tend to be equally or even more sexually stimulated by rape than by portrayals of consenting sex, whereas the majority of subjects evidence the reverse preference (see Malamuth, 1981b, for a review of these data).

The findings in this area are well illustrated in the recent data of Malamuth and Check (in press). In an initial session, male subjects were given questionnaires concerning their sexual attitudes and behavior. One of the questionnaire items inquired about the likelihood that the subject himself would rape if he could be assured of not being caught and punished (i.e., the LR item). On the basis of this item, 62 subjects were classified as low LR (a rating of 1 = "not at all likely" on the 5-point scale). Forty-two subjects were classified as high LR (a rating of 2 or higher). This distribution is similar to that of earlier studies (Malamuth, 1981a,b; Malamuth, Haber, & Feshbach, 1980; Malamuth & Check, 1980a; Tieger, 1981).

Several days later, these subjects listened to one of several tapes that included: (1) a rape depiction, wherein the victim continuously abhors the assault (i.e., negative outcome); (2) a rape portrayal, in which the rapist perceives that the victim becomes involuntarily sexually aroused (i.e., positive outcome); and (3) a mutually consenting depiction with a willing, sexually aroused partner (i.e., consenting). These depictions were otherwise equated in terms of sexual content, length, etc.

Penile tumescence and self-reported sexual arousal to each of these portrayals as a function of subjects' LR classification are presented in Fig. 1. As can be seen, low-LR subjects were more sexually stimulated by the mutually consenting than the negative-outcome depictions, whereas high-LR subjects showed the opposite tendency on the penile tumescence measure but reported the same

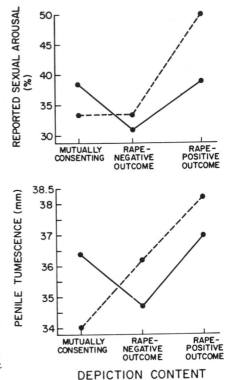

Fig. 1. Sexual arousal as a function of depiction content and subjects' Likelihood of Raping (LR) classification. (●– – –●), High LR; (●——●), low LR. (Data from Malamuth & Check, in press.)

levels of arousal to the negative-outcome and consenting depictions. The reactions of the high-LR subjects to the negative-outcome and consenting depictions parallel very closely the responses of the rapists studied by Abel *et al.* (1977), who had used only these two types of depictions. With respect to the positive-outcome portrayal (a type of depiction not used by Abel *et al.*), low-LR subjects showed about the same levels of arousal as to the consenting depictions, whereas high-LR subjects showed the highest levels of arousal to this rape portrayal.

Arousal to aggressive pornography has consistently been found to be associated with other individual difference variables in addition to LR ratings. For example, Malamuth and Check (in press) determined that arousal to rape portrayals (but not arousal to consenting-sex depictions) was positively correlated for males with power as a motive for engaging in sex (Nelson, 1979) and psychoticism as measured by the Eysenck Personality Questionnaire (Eysenck, 1978). (Note that both of these dimensions stretch through the normal non-psychiatric population.) Furthermore, Check and Malamuth (1982) showed that arousal to aggressive pornography (but not to consenting-sex depictions) was, for men, associated with higher beliefs in stereotyped sex roles. Taken as a whole, these data suggest that sexual arousal to aggressive-pornographic portrayals is not an isolated response but may reflect more general personality and belief structures. The data are consistent with the proposition that increases in aggressive themes within pornography may be partially due to the attraction of certain segments of consumers (e.g., high-LR individuals) to such portrayals (Malamuth & Spinner, 1980).

## D.  CONTEXT OF ASSESSMENT

Although no study to date has systematically examined the effect of the physical location of the research, this may be an important variable. It is now recognized that physiological measures of sexual arousal, as well as, of course, self-reports, may be voluntarily altered by subjects sufficiently motivated to do so (Abel & Blanchard, 1976; Amorso & Brown, 1973; Cerny, 1978; Henson & Rubin, 1971; Laws & Holmen, 1978; Quinsey & Carrigan, 1978). The research studies of Abel *et al.* (1977) and Quinsey *et al.* (1981) were conducted within settings designed to treat rapists. Although Barbaree *et al.* (1979) do not specifically report where their research was conducted, it appears that it was also done in a psychiatric treatment center for rapists. Awareness on the part of nonrapists of the nature of these settings may have been an important source of inhibition with respect to their arousal to rape depictions.

In keeping with this possibility are the findings of Briddell *et al.* (1977). In this experiment, undergraduate males who were led to believe that they were under the influence of alcohol (irrespective of whether they actually were) showed high sexual arousal to rape themes, comparable to their arousal to consenting depictions. Subjects who did not believe they were under the influence of alcohol, in contrast, showed differences in arousal to consenting versus rape themes similar to the differences obtained by Abel *et al.* (1977). These data clearly highlight the importance of nonrapists' cognitions as powerful influences on their sexual arousal to rape depictions. Just as the belief that one is under the influence of alcohol may serve to lessen concern about showing sexual arousal to rape depictions, the knowledge that arousal to rape is being assessed in a treatment center for rapists (which may suggest that such arousal will be interpreted as indicating aggressive tendencies) may well inhibit nonrapists' arousal to such stimuli.

## E.  CONCLUSIONS

The data from presentations that combine aggressive and sexual content reveal complex but reliable effects on sexual arousal. If the conditions of assessment resemble those employed by Abel *et al.* (1977) (e.g., a rape-abhorrence depiction, a clinical situation), then it is very likely that nonrapists in general will not be as highly aroused by rape scenes as they would by consenting depictions. Changes in the content of the rape stimuli (e.g., depicting the victim as sexually aroused) or in the nature of the assessment situation (e.g., jail vs university setting, believing one is or is not under the influence of alcohol), as well as finer distinctions among different subgroups of "normals" (e.g., low LR vs high LR), are likely to change the nature of the findings dramatically. This does not mean that the assessment of sexual reactions to rape depictions will not yield a useful measure of aggressive tendencies. As discussed below, there is some evidence that such a sexual arousal measure is predictive of aggressive behavior even among normals. However, the sexual arousal patterns of nondeviants are not clearly distinguishable from those of rapists across a wide range of conditions. Practitioners using the Abel *et al.* (1977) "rape index" should, therefore, be very careful in selecting their assessment conditions in light of a serious risk of making "false positives."

## III.   The Effects of Aggressive Pornography on Responses Other than Aggression

### A.   CHANGES IN SEXUAL RESPONSIVENESS

There is little evidence at this time to indicate that exposure to aggressive pornography increases a person's sexual responsiveness to such stimuli. A nonsignificant trend in one study (Malamuth *et al.*, 1980a) suggested that if subjects first read a sadomasochistic portrayal, their subsequent sexual arousal to a rape scene presented shortly afterward was heightened. Later research, however, has not confirmed this finding. The failure to find a sexual arousal enhancement effect of exposure to aggressive pornography has occurred both with single presentations (Malamuth, 1981a; Malamuth & Check, 1980a, in press) as well as with repeated presentations over a period of several weeks of five aggressive-pornographic feature-length movies (Ceniti & Malamuth, 1981).

### B.   FANTASIES

Only one experiment to date has examined the effects of aggressive pornography on sexual fantasies (Malamuth, 1981a). Subjects were presented with either rape or mutually consenting-sex versions of a slide–audio show. All subjects were then exposed to the same audio description of a rape incident taken from Abel *et al.* (1977). Later in the same session, they were asked to create their own sexual fantasies and then to record them. Content analyses of subjects' self-reported   fantasies indicated that those exposed to the rape version of the slide–audio show created more aggressive sexual fantasies than those exposed to the mutually consenting-sex version.

## C.  PERCEPTIONS AND ATTITUDES

There are considerable data indicating that exposure to aggressive pornography may alter observers' perceptions of rape and of rape victims. In three experiments, subjects were first presented with pornographic scenes in which aggression supposedly had positive consequences for the female victims, or with other depictions (e.g., a rape negative outcome or a mutually consenting scene). Afterward, all of these subjects were given a different depiction of rape and asked to indicate their perceptions of the experiences of the rape victim. In two of these experiments (Malamuth *et al.*, 1980a; Malamuth & Check, 1980b), those exposed to the positive-outcome version of the aggressive scene, in comparison to other subjects, thought the rape victim in the second portrayal had suffered less. The third experiment revealed effects on general perceptions of women. Malamuth and Check (1981b) found that subjects who listened to a rape depiction suggesting that the victim became sexually aroused believed that a larger percentage of women in general would derive some pleasure from being raped or from being forced to engage in various sexual acts (as compared to subjects who listened to rape scenes highlighting the victim's disgust and abhorrence or to portrayals of consenting sex showing either the woman's arousal or disgust) (see Fig. 2). These data suggest that certain types of pornography may help foster a cultural climate that is relatively tolerant of acts of aggression against women (Brownmiller, 1975; Burt, 1980).

However, in another study (Malamuth, Reisin, & Spinner, 1979) no evidence was found of changes in perceptions or in attitudes following exposure to aggressive pornography. One group of male and female subjects looked at issues of *Penthouse* and *Playboy* magazines that showed incidents of sadomasochism and rape. A second group examined issues of these magazines that contained only nonaggressive pornography and a third group was given only neutral materials. Shortly afterward, subjects watched an actual videotaped interview with a rape victim and responded to a questionnaire assessing their perceptions of the rape victim and her experience. Weeks later, in what was purported to be a general survey of public attitudes, subjects indicated their views on rape in response to a newspaper article. Exposure to the aggressive pornography did not affect perceptions of rape either in response to the videotaped interview with the rape victim or to the newspaper article.

One of the differences between this study and the three experiments that did observe significant effects on perceptions of rape concerns the content of the materials used. In the three experiments in which antisocial effects were found, the aggressive-pornographic stimuli were specifically selected because they ex-

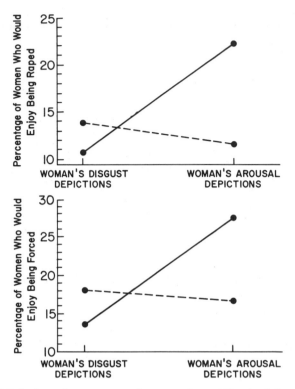

Fig. 2. Beliefs about the percentage of women who would enjoy being raped or forced sexually as a function of exposure to depictions varying along the Consent (rape vs consenting sex) and Outcome (negative vs positive) dimensions. (●———●), Nonconsenting depictions; (●‐‐‐●), consenting depictions.

plicitly depicted violence against women as having positive consequences. Malamuth *et al.* (1979), on the other hand, used materials that generally did not show such supposedly positive outcomes. At least insofar as cognitive changes, therefore, the antisocial effects of aggressive pornography may be limited to stimuli depicting positive consequences of sexual aggression.

In a recent field experiment, Malamuth and Check (1981c) obtained perhaps the strongest evidence to date to indicate that depictions of sexual aggression with positive consequences can adversely affect socially important perceptions and attitudes. Two hundred and seventy-one male and female students served as subjects in this investigation. Some had agreed to participate in a study ostensibly focusing on movie ratings. They watched on two different evenings either (1) the movies *Swept Away* and *The Getaway,* films that show women as victims of aggression within erotic as well as nonerotic incidents or (2) neutral feature-length movies. These movies were viewed in theatres on campus and two of the films (i.e., one experimental and one control movie) were being shown by the

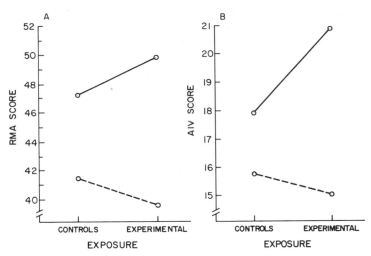

Fig. 3.    (A) Rape myth acceptance (RMA) and (B) acceptance of interpersonal violence (AIV) as a function of exposure and gender. (O– – –O), Females; (O———O), males. (From N. Malamuth & J. V. P. Check, The effects of mass media exposure on acceptance of violence against women: A field experiment, *Journal of Research in Personality*, 1981, **15**, p. 441.)

university as part of the campus film program. Members of the classes from which subjects had been recruited, but who had not signed-up for the experiment, were also used as a comparison group. The dependent measures were scales assessing acceptance of interpersonal violence (AIV) against women, rape myth acceptance (RMA), and beliefs in adversarial sexual relations (ASB). These measures were embedded within many other items in a Sexual Attitude Survey administered to all students in classes several days after some of them (i.e., those who had signed-up for the experiment) had been exposed to the movies. Subjects were not aware that there was any relationship between this survey and the movies.

Results indicated that exposure to films portraying aggressive sexuality as having positive consequences significantly increased male, but not female, subjects' acceptance of interpersonal violence against women and tended to increase males' acceptance of rape myths (see Fig. 3). These data demonstrated in a nonlaboratory setting, not vulnerable to criticisms of laboratory artificiality and "demand characteristics," that there can be relatively long-term antisocial effects of movies that portray sexual violence as having positive consequences.

## IV.    The Effects of Aggressive Pornography on Aggression

### A.    RESEARCH FINDINGS

We turn now to describe several experiments concerned with the effects of aggressive pornography on aggression. Rather than considering in detail the implications of each of these experiments, we shall first describe the studies, summarize their findings, and then consider their overall implications.

## 1. Nonaggressive- versus Aggressive-Pornographic Depictions

In a study by Malamuth (1978), male subjects were assigned to one of three exposure conditions. Subjects read pictorial stories that contained aggressive pornography, nonaggressive pornography, or neutral stimuli. Both the aggressive- and nonaggressive-pornographic stimuli were taken from issues of *Penthouse* magazine and were reported by subjects to be equally sexually arousing. The aggressive-pornographic stimuli depicted a rape of woman by a male pirate with some suggestion of a positive outcome. The nonaggressive pornography portrayed a loving interaction between a man and a woman. The neutral stimuli were taken from *National Geographic* magazine. Following exposure to these stimuli, all subjects were insulted by a female confederate and then placed in a situation where they could aggress against her via the ostensible delivery of electric shocks under one of two differing assessment conditions. Half of the subjects were assigned to read a communication that suggested that it was "okay" to behave as aggressively as they wished (disinhibitory communication); the other half were given a communication designed to make them somewhat self-conscious about aggressing (inhibitory). The experimental design thus consisted of a 3 (Exposure) × 2 (Communication) factorial design.

The results revealed no significant differences in aggression following the inhibitory communication. Following the disinhibitory communication, the highest level of aggression was found in the aggressive-pornography exposure ($M = 4.20$), which was significantly greater than that following nonaggressive-pornography exposure ($M = 2.75$). However, the neutral exposure ($M = 3.44$) was not found to differ significantly from either of the other two exposure conditions. The findings, therefore, although somewhat equivocal, pointed to the possibility that aggressive-pornographic stimuli may, under certain conditions, increase aggression against women.

In research by Donnerstein (1980a,b), male subjects were angered or treated in a neutral manner by a male or female confederate and were then given the opportunity to view one of three films. Two of the films were highly pornographic but differed in aggressive content. Whereas one film was entirely nonaggressive, the other depicted the rape of a woman by a man who breaks into her house and forces her into sexual activity at the point of a gun. Both of these films generated equal levels of physiological arousal as measured by blood pressure. The third film was a neutral film which did not contain any aggressive or pornographic content.

The results of this study, presented in Fig. 4, showed that when angered subjects were paired with a male confederate, the aggressive-pornographic film produced no more aggression than the nonaggressive-pornographic film. Both of

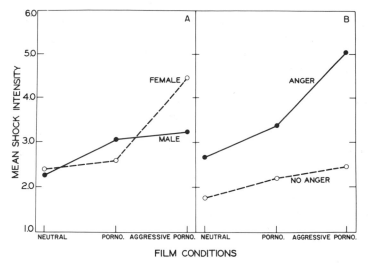

Fig. 4. Mean shock intensity as a function of (A) Sex × Film and (B) Anger × Film interactions. (From E. Donnerstein, Aggressive-Erotica and violence against women, *Journal of Personality and Social Psychology*, 1980, **39**, p. 274. Copyright 1980 by the American Psychological Association. Reprinted with permission of the publisher and author.)

these films increased aggression against the male victim in comparison with the neutral exposure. Those subjects paired with a female, however, displayed an increase in aggression *only* after viewing the aggressive-pornographic film. In fact, this increase occurred even if subjects were not angered, although the combination of anger and film exposure produced the highest level of aggressive behavior.

## 2. The Effects of Nonpornographic-Aggressive Films

Donnerstein (1983, in press) sought to examine the independent roles of pornography and aggression. Male subjects were first angered by a male or female confederate. They were then exposed to one of four films. The first was a nonaggressive highly arousing pornographic film. The second was an aggressive-pornographic film, the same as that used by Donnerstein (1980a,b). The third film was a nonpornographic, aggressive presentation in which a woman at gunpoint is "taunted" by a man. She is tied up, slapped around, and generally aggressed against. There was no nudity or even simulated sexual activity. It was chosen to be as close in content, except for aggression, as the rape film but without sexual behavior. The final film was a neutral presentation. Self-report data from subjects indicated that the aggressive film was seen as being less sexual than the two pornographic films which did not differ from each other. In addition, the aggressive film and the aggressive-pornographic films were also seen as equally aggressive. Physiological data also showed that the pornographic and aggressive-pornographic films stimulated equal arousal levels but higher than the neutral and aggressive films.

The results are presented in Fig. 5. When subjects were angered by a male, only the pornographic film increased aggression. For those subjects who were angered by a female, however, the aggressive-pornographic film produced the highest level of aggression, higher in fact, than any male target condition. The nonpornographic-aggressive film, however, also increased the level of subsequent aggression, although to a lesser degree than the aggressive-pornographic presentation.

### 3.   Victim's Reaction in Aggressive Pornography

Earlier in this article we discussed research that indicated that male subjects become sexually aroused to depictions of rape in which the victim becomes sexually aroused (i.e., positive outcome), and that such depictions increase acceptance of interpersonal violence against women and beliefs in rape myths. Two recent studies by Donnerstein and Berkowitz (1981) sought to examine the effects of the victim's reaction upon actual aggressive behavior against women.

In one of these studies, male subjects were first angered by a male or female confederate. Following this instigation, they watched one of four films. One was a neutral film which did not contain aggressive or pornographic content whereas another was a nonaggressive-pornographic film. The final two films were of an aggressive-pornographic nature. They depicted a young woman who comes to study with two men. Both men have been drinking and when she sits between

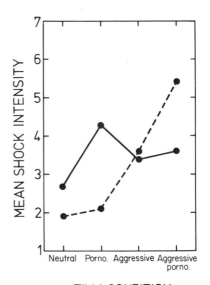

Fig. 5.   Mean shock intensity as a function of sex of target and film condition. (●– – –●), Female; (●———●), male.

them she is shoved around and forced to drink. She is then tied up, stripped, slapped around, and raped. Each film contained a different ending (30 sec out of 5 min) as well as a different narrative. In the positive-outcome aggressive-pornographic film, the ending shows the woman smiling and in no way resisting the two men. The narrative also indicates that she became a willing participant in the events at the end. In the negative-outcome version, the woman's actions are difficult to judge, and the narrative indicates that at the end she finds the experience humiliating and disgusting. Pretesting confirmed that the latter film was perceived as representing more suffering and less enjoyment on the part of the victim. After viewing one of these films, all subjects were given an opportunity to administer electric shocks to the male or female confederate. Physiological reactions were also monitored during the study.

After having viewed the films, all subjects were asked to rate them on a number of scales. These ratings are presented in Table I. As can be seen, the negative-outcome aggressive-pornographic film was seen as more aggressive than the positive-outcome version. This is interesting in light of the fact that the actual aggressive content was the same in both films. In addition, the victim in the negative-outcome film was seen as suffering more and enjoying herself less

TABLE I

MEAN SELF-REPORT AND PHYSIOLOGICAL CHANGES TO VARIOUS FILM CONDITIONS
(EXPERIMENT 1)[a]

|  | Film condition[c] | | | |
|---|---|---|---|---|
| Ratings[b] | Neutral | Pornographic | Positive ending | Negative ending |
| Film |  |  |  |  |
| Interesting | $1.6_a$ | $3.4_b$ | $3.3_b$ | $3.2_b$ |
| Sexually arousing | $1.1_a$ | $3.7_b$ | $3.7_b$ | $3.9_b$ |
| Aggressive | $1.4_a$ | $1.4_a$ | $3.5_b$ | $4.8_c$ |
| Sexual content | $1.4_a$ | $6.0_b$ | $5.9_b$ | $5.6_b$ |
| Victim |  |  |  |  |
| Suffering |  | $1.7_a$ | $2.7_b$ | $4.8_c$ |
| Enjoyment |  | $6.3_a$ | $5.1_b$ | $2.6_c$ |
| Responsible |  | $5.6_a$ | $4.1_b$ | $2.9_c$ |
| Mean blood pressure | $-0.9_a$ | $+6.1_b$ | $+8.5_b$ | $+5.5_b$ |

[a]From E. Donnerstein and L. Berkowitz, Victim reactions in aggressive-erotic films as a factor in violence against women. *Journal of Personality and Social Psychology,* 1981, **41,** p. 715. Copyright 1981 by the American Psychological Association. Reprinted by permission of the publisher and author.

[b]Film ratings are on a 7-point scale.

[c]Means with different subscripts differ from each other at the .05 level by Duncan's procedure.

than in the positive-outcome version. Furthermore, the woman in the positive-outcome version was seen as being more responsible for what had happened.

The physiological data indicated that all pornographic films, although not differing from each other, were more arousing than the neutral film. The aggression data are presented in Fig. 6. As can be seen, none of the films significantly affected aggression against a male target. However, both the positive- and negative-outcome aggressive-pornographic films increased aggression against the female. This level of aggression was significantly higher than the male target conditions except for the nonaggressive-pornographic film's male target condition.

These results show that in angered subjects, both positive- and negative-outcome rape depictions increase aggression against women. However, a critical question, for theoretical and applied purposes, concerns the effects of positive- and negative-outcome rape depictions on *nonangered* subjects. The second study by Donnerstein and Berkowitz (1981) examined this issue.

Male subjects in this experiment were first angered or treated in a neutral manner by a female confederate. Following this manipulation, subjects were exposed to one of the four films employed in the first study. After rating the films, they were given an opportunity to ostensibly administer shocks to the female confederate. Physiological reactions were monitored at various points in the experiment.

Table II presents the film ratings for subjects from this second study. As can be seen, they are identical to those in the first study, with the negative version

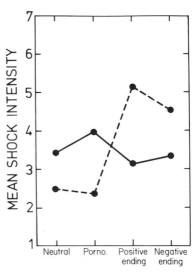

Fig. 6.   Mean shock intensity as a function of sex of target and film condition. (●‑ ‑ ‑●), Female; (●————●), male. (From E. Donnerstein & L. Berkowitz, Victim reactions in aggressive-erotic films as a factor in violence against women, *Journal of Personality and Social Psychology*, 1981, **41**, p. 716. Copyright 1981 by the American Psychological Association. Reprinted with permission of the publisher and author.)

TABLE II

MEAN SELF-REPORT AND PHYSIOLOGICAL CHANGES TO VARIOUS FILM CONDITIONS
(EXPERIMENT 2)[a]

| Ratings[b] | Film condition[c] | | | |
|---|---|---|---|---|
| | Neutral | Pornographic | Positive ending | Negative ending |
| Film | | | | |
| Interesting | $1.6_a$ | $3.8_b$ | $3.8_b$ | $3.2_b$ |
| Sexually arousing | $1.6_a$ | $4.7_b$ | $3.7_c$ | $3.7_c$ |
| Aggressive | $1.2_a$ | $1.8_a$ | $4.3_b$ | $6.2_c$ |
| Sexual content | $1.3_a$ | $6.4_b$ | $5.9_{bc}$ | $5.5_c$ |
| Victim | | | | |
| Suffering | | $1.7_a$ | $3.0_b$ | $5.7_c$ |
| Enjoyment | No anger | $5.6_{ac}$ | $5.9_{ac}$ | $1.6_b$ |
| | Anger | $6.5_a$ | $4.9_c$ | $3.2_d$ |
| Responsible | | $5.6_a$ | $4.3_b$ | $2.3_c$ |
| Mean blood pressure | $-0.5_a$ | $+8.3_b$ | $+10.7_b$ | $+8.9_b$ |

[a]From E. Donnerstein and L. Berkowitz, Victim reactions in aggressive-erotic films as a factor in violence against women. *Journal of Personality and Social Psychology,* 1981, **41**, p. 719. Copyright 1981 by the American Psychological Association. Reprinted by permission of the publisher and author.

[b]Film ratings are on a 7-point scale.

[c]Means with a different subscript differ from each other at the .05 level by Duncan's procedure.

being seen as more aggressive, the woman suffering more, enjoying less, and being less responsible than her positive-aggression counterpart. Physiological data also indicated that the three pornographic films were more arousing than the neutral presentation, although not differing from each other. Figure 7 presents the results for the aggression data. For nonangered subjects, only the positive-outcome aggressive-pornographic film significantly increased aggression against the female victim. For angered subjects, however, both the negative- and positive-outcome versions increased aggression, similar to the findings in the first study.

B.   SUMMARY OF EFFECTS ON AGGRESSION

The series of experiments described above on the effects of aggressive pornography on behavioral aggression indicate that the victim's gender is a critical mediating variable. When the male subjects were paired with a male victim, and angered, aggressive pornography was found consistently to result in levels of aggression which were not beyond that of other exposure conditions. In contrast, when the victim was female, aggressive pornography increased aggres-

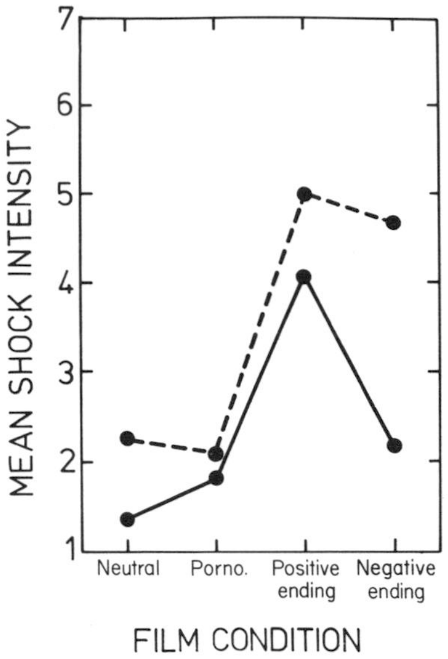

Fig. 7. Mean shock intensity as a function of anger and film condition. (●‐‐‐●), Anger; (●———●), no anger. (From E. Donnerstein & L. Berkowitz, Victim reactions in aggressive-erotic films as a factor in violence against women. *Journal of Personality and Social Psychology*, 1981, **41**, p. 716. Copyright 1981 by the American Psychological Association. Reprinted with permission of the publisher and author.)

sion well beyond that of any other exposure. In fact, nonaggressive pornography did not increase aggression against female victims in comparison with neutral exposures (see Donnerstein, 1980a,b, 1983; Donnerstein & Barrett, 1978; Donnerstein & Hallam, 1978, for a review and discussion of the effects of nonaggressive pornography on aggression against women). Aggressive-nonpornographic exposures increased aggressivity against female victims beyond the neutral or erotic exposures, but to a considerably lesser extent than the increase generated by the brigading of aggressive and sexual content.

Increased aggression against female victims following exposure to aggressive pornography was found with both nonangered and angered subjects, although the increase tended to be greater for angered subjects. Interesting differences between the effects of aggressive pornography on angered as compared with nonangered subjects emerged when the outcome of the aggression was systematically manipulated (i.e., "positive" versus negative outcome). It was found that a negative ending did not significantly increase aggression for nonangered subjects but resulted in a very clear increase in aggression for angered subjects. When the outcome of the aggressive-pornographic depictions was positive, a very clear increase in aggression was found for both angered and nonangered subjects.

## C. THEORETICAL ANALYSES

There are four theoretical analyses that are relevant to the research assessing the effects of aggressive pornography on aggressive behavior. These will be referred to as the Arousal, Hedonic Valence, Elicitation, and Disinhibition Analyses. We shall briefly describe each of these formulations and evaluate their ability to account for the empirical findings.

## 1. Arousal

Several psychological theories, such as Hull's (1943) construct of a "generalized drive" and Lindsley's (1951) "activation" concept suggest that any dominant response may be "energized" by a state of increased arousal. The concept of general arousal has been incorporated within theoretical analyses dealing with the effects of pornography both as the sole explanatory concept (Tannenbaum, 1971) and in combination with other components (e.g., Tannenbaum & Zillmann, 1975; Donnerstein, Donnerstein, & Evans, 1975). In such formulations, it is suggested that arousal stimulated by sexual materials may increase aggressive behavior in subjects predisposed to act aggressively (i.e., for whom aggression is a dominant response). Consequently, such analyses predict increased aggression only for subjects predisposed to aggress (e.g., angered subjects).

An explanation based solely on an arousal component would predict that the degree of aggression occurring following exposure to a communication would directly vary with the degree of arousal elicited by the communication. Variables such as the gender of the target of aggression or the victim's reactions within a rape portrayal would be expected to result in differing levels of aggression only if they stimulated different degrees of arousal. In the three studies on aggressive pornography by Donnerstein (1980a,b) and Donnerstein and Berkowitz (1981), all pornographic films were equal in arousal level. Yet, only the aggressive versions increased subsequent aggression against a female. Furthermore, the Donnerstein (1983) study on aggressive-nonpornographic films indicated that a film which does not increase physiological arousal can produce a level of aggression higher than a highly arousing but nonaggressive-pornographic film. These results would suggest that, at least with regard to aggressive pornography, film arousal may be a contributory factor under certain conditions, but it is not a necessary factor for the elicitation of subsequent aggression.

## 2. Hedonic Valence

Another theoretical explanation has been offered by Zillmann and his colleagues (e.g., Zillmann & Sapolsky, 1977; Zillmann, Bryant, Comisky, & Medoff, 1981). While these authors assume that arousal (excitatory potential) is an important factor in the facilitation of aggression by pornographic stimuli, the hedonic valence of the stimuli is also considered a strong contributor. Hedonic valence refers to how pleasing or displeasing are the stimuli. According to this formulation, the combined impact of the stimuli's arousal and affective potential determines its impact on aggression. Therefore, the lowest level of aggression would be predicted following exposure to nonarousing pornography that generates a positive affective state. Nonarousing negatively valenced and arousing positively valenced stimuli are expected to result in small increments in aggression. Arousing pornography that induces a negative affect would be expected to lead to the highest levels of aggression.

It should be noted that this two-component formulation was developed to account for research on the effects of nonaggressive pornography on male aggression against male targets. While there is some evidence that this analysis may also be relevant to the impact of certain types of pornographic stimuli with aggressive elements (i.e., sadomasochistic portrayals) on *intermale* aggression (Zillmann, Bryant, & Carveth, 1981; Zillmann *et al.*, 1981b), the data obtained on the effects of aggressive-pornographic stimuli (e.g., rape) on *male aggression against females* do not appear consistent with this formulation. Since this explanation focuses exclusively on the reactions of the subject to the pornographic stimuli, in direct contrast to the data, no differential effects of exposure would be predicted for male versus female targets of aggression. Furthermore, if the manipulation of the victim's reactions in rape depictions (i.e., positive vs negative outcome) alters the affective reaction of the audience, the version eliciting a more pleasing affect would be expected to result in lower aggression. The data presented by Malamuth *et al.* (1980b) suggest that aggressive pornography with a positive ending results in more positive affect than a negative-outcome version. Yet, Donnerstein and Berkowitz (1981) found that when subjects were not angered, the positive-outcome depiction resulted in more aggression; for angered subjects there were no differences in aggression following exposure to the two types of films.

## 3. Elicitation

Berkowitz (1970, 1974) proposed an explanation of the effects of media depictions that emphasizes stimulus–response (S–R) associations. According to this formulation, media stimuli elicit reactions (e.g., feelings, ideas, behavior) that are semantically associated with that particular class of stimuli. Berkowitz (1970) thus suggests that the media observer "reacts impulsively to particular stimuli in his environment, not [only] because his inhibitions have been weakened or because he anticipates the pleasures arising from his actions, but because situational stimuli have evoked the responses he is predisposed or set to make in that setting" (p. 104). Aggressive pornography that depicts male aggression against a female would be, therefore, most likely to affect responses that are most closely associated with the actions depicted in the media. It would therefore be predicted on the basis of this formulation that depictions of aggression against women would be more likely to affect female than male targets since a person's stimulus characteristics are an important component affecting the semantic associations of media depictions (Berkowitz, 1974; Berkowitz & Frodi, 1979). The striking differential effects of aggressive pornography on female as contrasted with male targets reported above are clearly compatible with this formulation.

Furthermore, as indeed was found with the negative-outcome versions, the effect of aggressive pornography on aggression would be predicted to be greatest for those viewers who are disposed to attack someone (i.e., angered). However, the increased aggression following the positive but not the negative version of the aggressive pornography in the case of *nonangered* subjects is not easily accounted for by this formulation.

### 4. Disinhibition

Inhibitory and disinhibitory effects have been discussed extensively by Bandura (1973, 1977) as major aspects of modeling influences. These effects are conceptualized as largely determined by observing the rewarding and punishing consequences accompanying models' behavior. Such vicarious learning of consequences strengthen or weaken *restraints* of similar behaviors in the observer.

The disinhibition explanation would predict that exposure to a communication such as aggressive pornography would affect the viewer's aggression only if the subject possessed some inclination to aggress that may become less restrained or if the communication suggested that aggression is expected of the viewer (Bandura, 1973). While such an inclination would be likely to result following an angering procedure, disinhibitory (and inhibitory) effects on aggression may occur in nonangered subjects as well (Bandura, 1973) if these individuals are inclined to aggress due to some other predisposing factor. Aggressive pornography may disinhibit aggression by suggesting that aggressive acts do not result in negative and may even lead to positive consequences. It is apparent, then, that this explanation would predict, as indicated by the data, that exposure to aggressive-pornographic depictions with a positive outcome would result in increased aggression.

Predictions based on this explanation vis-à-vis aggressive-pornographic depictions with a negative outcome are not very clear. Conflicting views exist regarding the effects of media presentations that depict victim suffering on the audience (Bandura, 1973). For nonangered subjects, there is a general consensus that inhibition of aggression would be expected (Bandura, 1973; Baron, 1974, 1977; Geen, 1970). However, for angered subjects, some investigators have suggested that pain cues in media presentations may increase inhibitions by sensitizing individuals to the harm they might inflict (Goranson, 1970), whereas other investigators have argued that for individuals in such a state, victim pain cues may be reinforcing (e.g., Berkowitz, 1974; Feshbach, Stiles, & Bitter, 1967; Swart & Berkowitz, 1976). Relevant to this view are the data presented earlier showing that rape portrayals with a negative outcome may be quite sexually stimulating (and therefore reinforcing) for some subjects (e.g., Malamuth & Check, in press). In summary, it is not clear whether exposure to aggressive pornography with a negative outcome would be expected, according to a disinhibition explanation, to reduce or increase viewers' aggression. The finding that such aggressive pornography increased aggression against females for angered subjects is not, therefore, readily explained by disinhibition processes.

## 5. Multiplicity of Processes

The above discussion of differing explanations of media effects in light of the current findings suggests that while the elicitation and disinhibition formulations are consistent with significant portions of the data, neither of these alone can fully account for the findings. The data point to the operation of multiple processes among which S–R associations and lowered inhibitions may play important roles (Donnerstein & Berkowitz, 1981). Clearly, elicitation and disinhibition processes (as well as others) are not incompatible but may operate simultaneously. Furthermore, different processes may be more relevant to differing experimental conditions.

### D. THE CONSTRUCT VALIDITY OF ASSESSING AGGRESSION

In light of the research findings indicating that aggressive pornography affects aggression against women within the laboratory (as well as fantasies, attitudes, and perceptions), there would appear to be reasons for social concern about the prevalence of such mass media stimuli. In drawing implications from these data to social behavior outside of the experimental settings, however, it is important to examine the construct validity (Cronbach & Meehl, 1955) of the measures used. This is particularly relevant to the assessment of aggressive behavior, since it is not feasible to experimentally assess the type of nonlaboratory aggression against women (e.g., rape) that may be affected by exposure to aggressive pornography. While there is considerable support for the construct validity of the "Buss paradigm" as a measure of aggression in general (Baron, 1977; Berkowitz & Donnerstein, 1982), in drawing implications from the research presented herein, it is desirable to assess the validity of the measures used as they relate to real-world aggression against women that involves emotions and attitudes linked with sexuality.

The logic of construct validity as discussed by Cronbach and Meehl (1955) suggests that to assess the validity of a measure it is necessary to determine whether it relates to other responses or measures in a theoretically predicted pattern. Using this approach, Malamuth (in press) designed an experiment to determine whether measures developed to assess factors that cause rape and related acts of aggression against women would predict "normal" males' aggressive behavior against a woman within a laboratory setting. While it was not suggested that such laboratory aggression constitutes an actual analog to the crime of rape, there exists considerable theorizing to suggest that rape is an act of aggression against women (Brownmiller, 1975; Burt, 1980; Clark & Lewis, 1977). Moreover, recent data suggest that within the general population there are many men who, although they may never actually commit acts of violence such as rape, have a relatively high proclivity to aggress against women (Malamuth, 1981b). If measures designed to assess factors contributing to rape and related acts of aggression against women were found to successfully predict aggression within a laboratory setting, this would provide support for the construct validity of the nomological network composed of: (1) the theory underlying the development of the predictive measures, (2) the measures designed to predict rape and other acts of aggression against women, and (3) the methodology of assessing such aggression within an experimental context as a basis for testing theory in the area, further refining the predictive measures and for drawing implications to nonexperimental settings.

The research by Malamuth (in press) was conducted in two phases. In the first phase, two factors theorized to cause rape and related acts of aggression against women were assessed. The subjects were 42 males from the general population, mostly college students. The first factor assessed was labeled Sexual Arousal to Rape, which was measured by the rape index developed by Abel *et al.* (1977) and described earlier in this chapter. Two separate measurements of this index (i.e., sexual arousal to rape relative to arousal to consenting depictions) were taken several weeks apart using different rape and consenting depictions. As noted earlier, Abel *et al.* contend that this measure assesses a "proclivity to rape."

The second factor assessed in the first phase of the research was labeled Attitudes Facilitating Violence. This was measured by the Rape Myth Acceptance (RMA) and Acceptance of Interpersonal Violence (AIV) scales developed by Burt (1980). These scales were embedded within many other items so that the subjects would not be aware of their specific focus. As discussed earlier, Burt (1978, 1980) theorizes that such attitudes about rape and violence contribute to rape acts.

The second phase of the research was held several days after each subject completed the first phase. In this phase, aggression was assessed. However, subjects were completely unaware of the relationship between the two phases of the research, but they believed that they were participating in two completely unrelated experiments. This procedure eliminated the possible role of "demand characteristics." In this second phase, subjects were angered by a woman (a confederate) and given the opportunity of ostensibly punishing her with aversive noise. Also, subjects were later asked about their desire to hurt the woman with the aversive noise (Baron & Eggleston, 1972).

The results showed that the measures assessed in the first phase successfully predicted aggressive behavior in the second phase of the research. This was apparent both in correlational data and in the results of an analysis using "causal" modeling with latent and manifest variables (Bentler, 1978, 1980; Bentler & Bonnett, 1980; Joreskog & Sorbom, 1977). Using the causal modeling approach (See Fig. 8), a latent variable named Sexual Arousal to Rape was operationally defined by the two assessments of the rape index. A second latent factor, named Attitudes Facilitating Violence, was operationally defined by the RMA and AIV scales. A latent factor labeled Aggression Against Women was operationally defined by the levels of aversive noise and levels of the reported desire to hurt the woman. The model appearing in Fig. 8, which has causal paths from the Sexual Arousal to Rape and from the Attitudes Facilitating Violence factors to the Aggression Against Women factor was tested by the LISREL IV program (Joreskog & Sorbom, 1978). This model was found to successfully represent the data, and both of the causal paths to aggression were found to be significant. Together, the Arousal to Rape and the Attitudes Facilitating Violence factors accounted for 43% of the variance of the Aggression Against Women factor.

Malamuth and Check (1982) recently attempted to replicate and extend one aspect of the above findings—the prediction of aggression on the basis of scales measuring attitudes about aggression. In addition to the RMA and AIV scales, they administered to 76 male undergraduates a scale, specifically developed for this research, which assessed General Acceptance of Violence (GAV). The

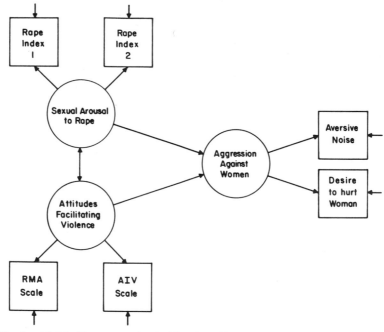

Fig. 8.   Model of factors associated with real-world aggression against women as predictors of laboratory aggression. (From N. Malamuth, Factors associated with rape as predictors of laboratory aggression against women, *Journal of Personality and Social Psychology,* in press. Copyright by the American Psychological Association. Reprinted with permission of the publisher and author.)

results indicated that the RMA and AIV, but not the GAV scales successfully predicted aggression against women. These data are in keeping with the findings reported above regarding the effects of aggressive pornography in suggesting that male aggression against women may be affected by processes that differ from those that may affect male–male aggression.

## V. Ethical Concerns

Some concerns have been recently raised regarding the ethics of research that exposes subjects to aggressive pornography, particularly those depictions that portray rape myths (e.g., positive outcome) (Sherif, 1980). These concerns have prompted investigators to attempt to assess the effectiveness of debriefing procedures presented following research participation (Check & Malamuth, 1981; Donnerstein & Berkowitz, 1981; Malamuth & Check, 1981a). Such debriefings have been designed to dispel rape myths by presenting more accurate information. Assessment of the effectiveness of such debriefings have been conducted as long as 4 months following research participation (Donnerstein & Berkowitz, 1981), as well as without subjects' awareness that the assessment is at all related to their earlier research participation (Check & Malamuth, 1981; Malamuth & Check, 1981a).

The findings of these studies consistently show that the overall impact of research participation (including the debriefings) is to *reduce* subjects' acceptance of rape myths. While the data indicate that the information contained within the debriefings may be sufficient for some attitude change, the combination of exposure to violent pornography that portrays rape myths and the presentation of a debriefing that specifically addresses these myths appears to be most effective in reducing rape myth acceptance (Check & Malamuth, 1981).

These data have important implications for researchers focusing on the possible detrimental effects of violence in pornography because the possibility of adversely affecting research participants could be a serious inhibitor to future research. Knowledge that a debriefing may result in the total research experience having a beneficial impact is likely to encourage future work in this area. These data, however, should not be taken as a carte blanche to justify any pornography exposure–debriefing procedures. It is important that researchers in this area design debriefing procedures that are appropriate for their specific materials and assess their effectiveness whenever possible (Sherif, 1980).

## VI. Conclusions and Future Research

The data across the laboratory and field experiments discussed in this article support the proposition that exposure to mass media stimuli that have violent and sexual content increases the audience's aggressive-sexual fantasies, acceptance of aggression, beliefs in rape myths, and aggressive behavior. These findings were obtained both with unedited, commercially available stimuli (e.g., feature-length films) and with edited stimuli in which systematic manipulations enabled the assessment of the impact of specific content dimensions. Effects were found directly following exposure as well as several days later. Moreover, the data indicate that individuals with relatively higher aggressive inclinations are more sexually aroused by aggressive pornography than those with lower aggressive tendencies. A bidirectional causal relationship is therefore suggested by the findings, with aggressive inclinations resulting in greater attraction to aggressive-sexual stimuli and exposure to such depictions increasing aggressive tendencies.

These data raise a variety of theoretical and empirical issues that should be addressed in future research. Particularly noteworthy are questions concerning stimuli, subject, and setting characteristics.

## A.  STIMULI CHARACTERISTICS

The aggressive-pornographic stimuli used in the research described in this article fall, as noted earlier, into the "blatantly" coercive category according to the distinctions suggested by Steinem (1980). Are the effects found limited to such materials or might similar effects be obtained with stimuli that more subtly or indirectly portray unequal power relations between males and females? In other words, is there a clear distinction to be made between aggressive and nonaggressive pornography or is it more accurate to distinguish sexually explicit stimuli that place emphasis on "shared pleasure" (Steinem, 1980) from aggressive pornography that varies on a continuum of blatancy? Future research should also assess the impact of sexual materials that portray unequal power relations between males and females without the explicit depiction of aggression.

A related question concerns the type of aggressive-sexual stimuli that are most likely to cause antisocial effects. The increased acceptance of aggression against women found by Malamuth and Check (1981c) occurred following exposure to movies that have been shown on national television and were clearly not X-rated pornographic films. Moreover, the primary theme of the films was not aggressive sexuality. It may be that a film that is explicitly pornographic is perceived as highly unrealistic and stimulates subjects' defenses against uncritically accepting the information conveyed. In contrast, the type of film used by these investigators may communicate more subtly false information about women's reactions to sexual aggression and thus may have more potent effects since the viewers are not "forewarned" (Freedman & Sears, 1965) by the label "X-rated" or "pornographic." Similarly, the portrayal of sexual aggression within such "legitimate" magazines as *Playboy* or *Penthouse* may have a greater impact than similar portrayals in hard-core pornography. Research is needed that specifically examines the impact of the context within which aggressive pornography appears.

### B. SUBJECT CHARACTERISTICS

While the data described herein mostly assessed the impact of aggressive pornography on subjects generally, it is important in future research to more systematically determine the relationship between subject characteristics and the impact of aggressive pornography. While, as described earlier, some work has been done on the relationship between individual differences and sexual arousal to aggressive pornography, little research has been directed at establishing the mediating effects of subject variables in relation to the impact of aggressive pornography on fantasies, attitudes, beliefs, and aggressive responses. Initial efforts in this area (Malamuth & Check, 1981b) suggest that those individuals who, from the outset, are more inclined to believe in rape myths show the greatest increase in acceptance of such myths following the presentation of aggressive pornography. Much more work is needed that systematically assesses the effects of aggressive pornography on individuals differing in such factors as aggressive tendencies, familial experiences with violence and male–female power relations, hostility toward women, previous pornographic exposure, sex-role stereotyping, and sexual experiences. The selection of particular variables should be guided by theoretical formulations such as the elicitation and disinhibition analyses discussed earlier.

### C. SETTING CHARACTERISTICS

In concluding their discussion of research on the effects of mass media violence on children's aggression, Parke et al. (1977) stress the need to address the question, "How does this influence occur in naturalistic settings?" A similar emphasis is needed in research on aggressive pornography. While laboratory experiments provide a useful framework for determining whether aggressive pornography *can* affect aggressive tendencies (Berkowitz & Donnerstein, 1982), there is a need at this point to proceed to examine the extent to which such mass media stimuli actually exert an impact in naturalistic settings. To accomplish this goal it will be necessary to employ a multimethod approach including correlational analyses using statistical controls (e.g., causal modeling, Bentler, 1980), as well as laboratory and field experiments.

We need to obtain survey data regarding the use of aggressive and other types of pornography by differing subject populations. These data should be gathered in the context of developing theoretical models concerning the motivations for seeking such media stimuli (i.e., uses and gratifications), as well as concerning the effects of exposure. The development of models will require information not only about pornography consumption, but about other aspects of the person. The testing of these models may require experimental research to move beyond single exposures in order to measure impact over long time periods of differing "dosages" of aggressive pornography in the context of other media stimuli. Causal modeling may prove particularly useful in testing aspects of theoretical models not amenable to experimental manipulations (e.g., the hypothesis that childhood experiences mediate the impact of pornography). Such a multiplicity of research strategies is clearly necessary if we are to fully assess the hypothesis that aggressive pornography and related mass media stimuli play a significant role in creating a cultural climate conducive to the commission of aggressive acts against women.

## REFERENCES

Abel, G. G., Barlow, D. H., Blanchard, E., & Guild D. The components of rapists' sexual arousal. *Archives of General Psychiatry,* 1977, **34,** 895–903.

Abel, G. G., Becker, J., Murphy, W., & Flanagan, B. *Identifying dangerous child molesters.* Paper presented at the 11th Banff International Conference on Behaviour Modification, Banff, Canada, 1979.

Abel, G. G., & Blanchard, E. B. The measurement and generation of sexual arousal in male deviates. In M. Hersen, R. M. Eisler, & P. M. Miller (Eds.), *Progress in behavior modification* (Vol. 2). New York: Academic Press, 1976.

Abel, G. G., Blanchard, E. B., & Becker, J. V. Psychological treatment of rapists. In M. Walker & S. Brodsky (Eds.), *Sexual assault: The victim and the rapist.* Lexington, Massachusetts: Lexington Books, 1976.

Abel, G. G., Blanchard, E. B., & Becker, J. V. An integrated program for rapists. In R. Rada (Ed.), *Clinical aspects of the rapist.* New York: Grune & Strutton, 1978.

Amorso, D. M., & Brown, M. Problems in studying the effects of erotic material. *The Journal of Sex Research,* 1973, **9,** 187–195.

Bandura, A. *Aggression: A social learning analysis.* New York: Prentice-Hall, 1973.

Bandura, A. *Social learning theory.* New York: Prentice-Hall, 1977.

Barbaree, H. E., Marshall, W. L., & Lanthier, R. D. Deviant sexual arousal in rapists. *Behaviour Research and Therapy,* 1979, **17,** 215–222.

Baron, R. A. The aggression-inhibiting influence of heightened sexual arousal. *Journal of Personality and Social Psychology,* 1974, **30,** 318–322.

Baron, R. A. *Human aggression.* New York: Plenum, 1977.

Baron, R. A., & Byrne, D. *Social psychology: Understanding human interaction,* Boston, Massachusetts: Allyn & Bacon, 1977.

Baron, R. A., & Eggleston, R. J. Performance on the "Aggression Machine": Motivation to help or harm? *Psychonomic Science,* 1972, **26,** 321–322.

Bart, P., & Jozsa, M. Dirty books, dirty films and dirty data. In L. Lederer (Ed.), *Take back the night: Women on pornography.* New York: Morrow, 1980.

Bentler, P. M. The interdependence of theory, methodology and empirical data: Causal modeling as an approach to construct validation. In D. B. Kendel (Ed.), *Longitudinal research on drug use.* New York: Wiley, 1978.

Bentler, P. M. Multivariate analysis with latent variables: Causal modeling. *Annual Review of Psychology,* 1980, **31,** 419–456.

Bentler, P. M., & Bonnett, D. G. Significance tests and goodness of fit in the analysis of covariance structures. *Psychological Bulletin*, 1980, **88**, 588–606.

Berkowitz, L. The contagion of violence: An S-R mediational analysis of some effects of observed aggression. In W. J. Arnold & M. M. Page (Eds.), *Nebraska symposium on motivation* (Vol. 18). Lincoln, Nebraska: Univ. of Nebraska Press, 1970.

Berkowitz, L. Sex and violence: We can't have it both ways. *Psychology Today*, May 1971, pp. 14–23.

Berkowitz, L. Some determinants of impulsive aggression: Role of mediated associations with reinforcements for aggression. *Psychological Review*, 1974, **81**, 165–176.

Berkowitz, L., & Donnerstein, E. External validity is more than skin deep: Some answers to criticisms of laboratory experiments (with special reference to research on aggression). *American Psychologist*, 1982, **37**, 245–257.

Berkowitz, L., & Frodi, A. Reactions to a child's mistakes as affected by her/his look and speech. *Social Psychology Quarterly*, 1979, **42**, 420–425.

Briddell, D., Rimm, D., Caddy, G., Krawitz, G., Sholis, D., & Wunderlin, R. Effects of alcohol and cognitive set on sexual arousal to deviant stimuli. *Journal of Abnormal Psychology*, 1978, **87**, 418–430.

Brownell, K. D., Hayes, S. C., & Barlow, D. H. Patterns of appropriate and deviant sexual arousal: The behavioral treatment of multiple sexual deviations. *Journal of Consulting and Clinical Psychology*, 1977, **45**, 1144–1155.

Brownmiller, S. *Against our will: Men, women and rape*. New York: Simon & Schuster, 1975.

Burt, M. R. Attitudes supportive of rape in American culture. *House Committee on Science and Technology, Subcommittee Domestic and International Scientific Planning Analysis and Cooperation: Research into violent behavior: Sexual assaults*, Hearing, 95th Congress, 2nd session, January 10–12, 1978. Washington, D.C.: Government Printing Office, 1978. Pp. 277–322.

Burt, M. R. Cultural myths and supports for rape. *Journal of Personality and Social Psychology*, 1980, **38**, 217–230.

Carroll, J. S. The effect of imagining an event on expectations for the event: An interpretation in terms of the availability heuristic. *Journal of Experimental Social Psychology*, 1978, **14**, 88–96.

Ceniti, J., & Malamuth, N. *Self-assessed rape proclivity: Attitudinal and sexual correlates*. In preparation, 1981.

Cerny, J. A. Biofeedback and the voluntary control of sexual arousal in women. *Behavior Therapy*, 1978, **19**, 847–855.

Check, J. V. P., & Malamuth, N. *Can participation in pornography experiments have positive effects?* Paper presented at the annual meeting of the American Psychological Association, Los Angeles, August, 1981.

Check, J. V. P., & Malamuth, N. *Sex-role stereotyping attitudes and reactions to stranger and acquaintance rape*. Submitted for publication, 1982.

Clark, L., & Lewis, D. *Rape: The price of coercive sexuality*. Toronto: Women's Press, 1977.

Commission on Obscenity and Pornography. *The report of the commission on obscenity and pornography*, New York: Bantam, 1970.

Cronbach, L. J., & Meehl, P. Construct validity in in psychological tests. *Psychological Bulletin*, 1955, **52**, 281–302.

Davis, K. E., & Braucht, G. N. Exposure to pornography, character and sexual deviance: A retrospective survey. *Technical reports of the Commission on Obscenity and Pornography* (Vol. 7). Washington, D.C.: U.S. Government Printing Office, 1971.

Diamond, I. Pornography and repression: A reconsideration. *Signs: Journal of Women in Culture and Society*, 1980, **5**, 686–701.

Donnerstein, E. Pornography and violence against women. *Annals of the New York Academy of Sciences,* 1980, 347, 277–288. (a)

Donnerstein, E. Aggressive-Erotica and violence against women. *Journal of Personality and Social Psychology,* 1980, **39,** 269–277. (b)

Donnerstein, E. Erotica and human aggression. In R. Geen & E. Donnerstein (Eds.), *Aggression: Theoretical and empirical reviews.* New York: Academic Press, 1983.

Donnerstein, E. Aggressive pornography: Can it influence aggression against women. In G. Albee & J. Joffe (Eds.), *Primary prevention of psychopathology* (Vol. 7). Hanover, New Hampshire: University of New England Press, in press.

Donnerstein, E., & Barrett, G. The effects of erotic stimuli on male aggression towards females. *Journal of Personality and Social Psychology,* 1978, **36,** 180–188.

Donnerstein, E., & Berkowitz, L. Victim reactions in aggressive-erotic films as a factor in violence against women. *Journal of Personality and Social Psychology,* 1981, **41,** 710–724.

Donnerstein, E., Donnerstein, M., & Evans, R. Erotic stimuli and aggression: Facilitation or inhibition. *Journal of Personality and Social Psychology,* 1975, **32,** 237–244.

Donnerstein, E., & Hallam, J. The facilitating effects of erotica on aggression toward females. *Journal of Personality and Social Psychology,* 1978, **36,** 1270–1277.

Eron, L. D. Prescription for reduction of aggression. *American Psychologist,* 1980, **35,** 244–261.

Eysenck, H. J. *Sex and personality.* London: Sphere Books, 1978.

Farkas, G. M. *Trait and state determinants of male sexual arousal to description of coercive sexuality.* Doctoral dissertation, University of Hawaii, 1979.

Feshbach, S., Stiles, W. B., & Bitter, E. The reinforcing effect of witnessing aggression. *Journal of Experimental Research in Personality,* 1967, **2,** 133–139.

Freedman, J., & Sears, D. Warning, distraction and resistance to influence. *Journal of Personality and Social Psychology,* 1965, **1,** 262–266.

Gager, N., & Schurr, C. *Sexual assault: Confronting rape in America.* New York: Grosset & Dunlap, 1976.

Geen, R. G. Perceived suffering of the victim as an inhibitor of attack induced aggression. *Journal of Social Psychology,* 1970, **81,** 209–215.

Goldstein, M. J., Kant, H. S., Judd, L. L., Rice, C. J., & Geen, R. Exposure to pornography and sexual behavior in deviant and normal groups. *Technical reports of the Commission on Obscenity and Pornography* (Vol. 7). Washington, D.C.: U.S. Government Printing Office, 1971.

Goranson, R. E. Media violence and aggressive behavior: A review of experimental research. In L. Berkowitz (Ed.), *Advances in experimental social psychology* (Vol. 5). New York: Academic Press, 1970.

Hans, V. P. *Pornography and feminism: Empirical evidence and directions for research.* Paper presented at the meeting of the American Psychological Association, Montreal, September 1980.

Hayes, S. C., Brownell, K. D., & Barlow, D. H. The use of self-administered covert sensitization in the treatment of exhibitionism and sadism. *Behavior Therapy,* 1978, **9,** 283–289.

Henson, D., & Rubin, H. Voluntary control of eroticism. *Journal of Applied Behavior Analysis,* 1971, **4,** 37–44.

Hull, C. L. *Principles of behavior.* New York: Appleton, 1943.

Johnson, P., & Goodchilds, J. Pornography, sexuality, and social psychology. *Journal of Social Issues,* 1973, **29,** 231–238.

Joreskog, K. G., & Sorbom, D. G. Structural equation models in the social sciences: Specification, estimation and testing. In P. R. Krishnaiah (Ed.), *Application of statistics.* Amsterdam: North Holland Publ., 1977.

Joreskog, K. G., & Sorbom, D. G. *LISREL IV: Estimation of linear structural equation systems by maximum likelihoods methods.* Chicago, Illinois: National Educational Resources, 1978.

Laws, D. R., & Holmen, M. L. Sexual response faking by pedophiles. *Criminal Justice and Behavior,* 1978, **5,** 343–356.

Lederer, L. (Ed.). *Take back the night: Women on pornography.* New York: Morrow, 1980.

Liebert, R. M., & Schwartzberg, N. S. Effects of mass media. *Annual Review of Psychology.* 1977, **28,** 141–173.

Lindsley, D. B. Emotion. In S. S. Stevens (Ed.), *Handbook of experimental psychology.* New York: Wiley, 1951.

Malamuth, N. *Erotica, aggression and perceived appropriateness.* Paper presented at the 86th annual convention of the American Psychological Association, Toronto, September 1978.

Malamuth, N. Rape fantasies as a function of exposure to violent sexual stimuli. *Archives of Sexual Behavior,* 1981, **10,** 33–47. (a)

Malamuth, N. Rape proclivity among males. *Journal of Social Issues,* 1981, **37,** 138–157. (b)

Malamuth, N. Factors associated with rape as predictors of laboratory aggression against women. *Journal of Personality and Social Psychology,* in press.

Malamuth, N., & Check, J. V. P. Penile tumescence and perceptual responses to rape as a function of victim's perceived reactions. *Journal of Applied Social Psychology,* 1980, **10,** 528–547. (a)

Malamuth, N., & Check, J. V. P. Sexual arousal to rape and consenting depictions: The importance of the woman's arousal. *Journal of Abnormal Psychology,* 1980, **89,** 763–766. (b)

Malamuth, N., & Check, J. V. P. *Debriefing effectiveness following exposure to pornographic rape depictions.* Paper presented at the annual convention of the Canadian Psychological Association, Toronto, June 1981. (a)

Malamuth, N., & Check, J. V. P. *The effects of exposure to aggressive-pornography: Rape proclivity, sexual arousal and beliefs in rape myths.* Paper presented at the annual convention of the American Psychological Association, Los Angeles, August 1981. (b)

Malamuth, N., & Check, J. V. P. The effects of mass media exposure on acceptance of violence against women: A field experiment. *Journal of Research in Personality,* 1981, **15,** 436–446. (c)

Malamuth, N., & Check, J. V. P. *Factors related to aggression against women.* Paper presented at the annual convention of the Canadian Psychological Association, Montreal, June 1982.

Malamuth, N., & Check, J. V. P. Sexual arousal to rape depictions: Individual differences. *Journal of Abnormal Psychology,* in press.

Malamuth, N., Haber, S., & Feshbach, S. Testing hypotheses regarding rape: Exposure to sexual violence, sex differences, and the "normality" of rapists. *Journal of Research in Personality,* 1980, **14,** 121–137. (a)

Malamuth, N., Heim, M., & Feshbach, S. Sexual responsiveness of college students to rape depictions: Inhibitory and disinhibitory effects. *Journal of Personality and Social Psychology,* 1980, **38,** 399–408. (b)

Malamuth, N., Reisin, I., & Spinner, B. *Exposure to pornography and reactions to rape.* Paper presented at the 87th annual convention of the American Psychological Association, New York, August 1979.

Malamuth, N., & Spinner, B. A longitudinal content analysis of sexual violence in the best-selling erotic magazines. *The Journal of Sex Research,* 1980, **16,** 226–237.

Nelson, P. A. *A sexual functions inventory.* Doctoral dissertation, University of Florida, 1979.

Parke, R. D., Berkowitz, L., Leyens, J. P., West, S. G., & Sebastian, R. J. Some effects of violent and non-violent movies on the behavior of juvenile delinquents. In L. Berkowitz (Ed.), *Advances in experimental social psychology* (Vol. 10). New York: Academic Press, 1977.

Quinsey, V. L., & Carrigan, W. F. Penile responses to visual stimuli. *Criminal Justice and Behavior,* 1978, **5,** 333–341.

Quinsey, V. L., & Chaplin, T. C. *Stimulus control of rapists' and non-sex offenders' sexual arousal.* Unpublished manuscript, 1981.

Quinsey, V. L., Chaplin, T. C., & Carrigan, W. F. Biofeedback and signaled punishment in the modification of inappropriate sexual age preferences. *Behavior Therapy,* 1980, **11,** 567–576.

Quinsey, V. L., Chaplin, T. C., & Varney, G. A comparison of rapists' and non-sex offenders' sexual preferences for mutually consenting sex, rape, and physical abuse of women. *Behavioral Assessment,* 1981, **3,** 127–135.

Schmidt, G. Male-female differences in sexual arousal and behavior. *Archives of Sexual Behavior,* 1975, **4,** 353–364.

Sherif, C. W. Comment on ethical issues in Malamuth, Heim, and Feshbach's "Sexual responsiveness of college students to rape depictions: Inhibitory and disinhibitory effects." *Journal of Personality and Social Psychology,* 1980, **38,** 409–412.

Smith, D. G. The social content of pornography. *Journal of Communication,* 1976, **26,** 16–33. (a)

Smith, D. G. *Sexual aggression in American pornography: The stereotype of rape.* Paper presented at the annual meeting of the American Sociological Association, New York City, 1976. (b)

Steinem, G. Erotica and pornography: A clear and present difference. In L. Lederer (Ed.), *Take back the night: Women on pornography.* New York: Morrow, 1980.

Swart, C., & Berkowitz, L. The effect of a stimulus associated with a victim's pain on later aggression. *Journal of Personality and Social Psychology,* 1976, **33,** 623–631.

Tannenbaum, P. H. Emotional arousal as a mediator of erotic communication effects. *Technical Report of the Commission on Obscenity and Pornography* (Vol. 8). Washington, D.C.: U.S. Government Printing Office, 1971.

Tannenbaum, P. H., & Zillmann, D. Emotional arousal in the facilitation of aggression through communication. In L. Berkowitz (Ed.), *Advances in experimental social psychology* (Vol. 8). New York: Academic Press, 1975.

Thomas, M. H., Horton, R. W., Lippencott, E. C., & Drabman, R. S. Desensitization to portrayals of real-life aggression as a function of exposure to television violence. *Journal of Personality and Social Psychology,* 1977, **35,** 450–458.

Tieger, T. Self-rated likelihood of raping and the social perception of rape. *Journal of Research in Personality,* 1981, **15,** 147–158.

Time Magazine. *The porno plague,* April 5, 1976, 58–63.

Tversky, A., & Kahneman, D. Availability: A heuristic for judging frequency and probability. *Cognitive Psychology,* 1973, **5,** 207–232.

Village Voice. *Pretty poison: The selling of sexual warfare.* May 9, 1977, 18–23.

Zillmann, D., Bryant, J., & Carveth, R. The effect of erotica featuring sadomasochism and bestiality on motivated intermale aggression. *Personality and Social Psychology Bulletin,* 1981, **7,** 153–159. (a)

Zillmann, D., Bryant, J., Comisky, P. W., & Medoff, N. J. Excitation and hedonic valence in the effect of erotica on motivated intermale aggression. *European Journal of Social Psychology,* 1981, **11,** 233–252. (b)

Zillmann, D., & Sapolsky, B. S. What mediates the effect of mild erotica on annoyance and hostile behavior in males? *Journal of Personality and Social Psychology,* 1977, **35,** 587–596.

# SOCIALIZATION IN SMALL GROUPS: TEMPORAL CHANGES IN INDIVIDUAL-GROUP RELATIONS[1]

## Richard L. Moreland
## John M. Levine

DEPARTMENT OF PSYCHOLOGY
UNIVERSITY OF PITTSBURGH
PITTSBURGH, PENNSYLVANIA

## I. Introduction

After languishing for many years, research on small groups has recently become a more active area of social psychological inquiry. In accordance with Steiner's (1974) predictions, an increasing number of investigators have begun to explore the interpersonal dynamics of small groups, expanding and refining our

[1]Preparation of this article was supported by Grant BNS-8104961 from the National Science Foundation. Because we contributed equally to the article the order of authorship was determined arbitrarily.

137

ADVANCES IN EXPERIMENTAL SOCIAL
PSYCHOLOGY, VOL. 15

knowledge about traditional topics such as group decision making (e.g., Brandstätter, Davis, & Schuler, 1978) and leadership (e.g., Hollander, 1978), and applying that knowledge to real-world groups, such as juries (e.g., Davis, Bray, & Holt, 1977), youth gangs (e.g., Cartwright, Tomson, & Schwartz, 1975), and religious cults (e.g., Robbins, Anthony, & Richardson, 1978). This renewed interest in small groups has led some observers (e.g., Back, 1979; Borgatta & Baker, 1981; McGrath & Kravitz, 1982; Zander, 1979a,b) to evaluate the current status of research in the field, noting those problem areas that have been widely studied and suggesting directions for future research. Although there is not total consensus about the type of group-dynamics research that ought to be done, there appears to be some agreement that social psychologists need to learn more about the process of *socialization* in small groups.

As Zander (1977) has pointed out, many interesting questions relating to group socialization remain unanswered. Why do groups recruit one person rather than another, and what criteria are employed in the recruitment process? How do groups instill commitment in a member, and what implications does that commitment have for his or her subsequent behavior? Why is it so difficult for many groups to expel an individual, and when does expulsion become necessary? These and related questions are important for both theoretical and practical reasons and thus deserve to be investigated more fully.

Although research on group socialization has been relatively sparse, some information has been acquired about nearly every aspect of the socialization process. Unfortunately, this information has not yet been integrated in a satisfactory manner, perhaps because of certain conceptual limitations in how research on group socialization has been conducted. At least two of these limitations can be readily identified. First, most researchers have adopted a fairly narrow *temporal perspective,* focusing on only one phase of the socialization process. Although there has been work on such topics as entry into groups (e.g., Aronson & Mills, 1959; Gerard & Mathewson, 1966; Jacoby, 1965; Putallaz & Gottman, 1981; Trice, 1957), the experiences of new group members (e.g., Feldbaum, Christenson, & O'Neal, 1980; Lofland & Lejeune, 1960; Nash & Heiss, 1967; Zander & Cohen, 1955; Ziller & Behringer, 1960), conformity and deviance within groups (e.g., Allen, 1965; Levine, 1980; Moscovici, 1976), and exit from groups (e.g., Sagi, Olmsted, & Atelsek, 1955; White & Butts, 1963; Zander, 1976; Zurcher, 1970), very few researchers have studied how the socialization process develops. Consequently, social psychologists know almost nothing about how the relationship between a group and its members might change over time. As several observers have noted (e.g., McGrath & Kravitz, 1982; Shaw, 1981; Ziller, 1977), research that is essentially static in form cannot adequately capture the dynamic nature of social interaction in small groups.

A second major conceptual limitation in research on group socialization has been a restricted *social perspective* on the part of most researchers. In nearly every topic area, socialization research has reflected the viewpoint of the group rather than that of the individual. For example, many studies of newcomers have focused on changes in individual attitudes and behaviors that groups produce in their new members (e.g., Feldbaum *et al.*, 1980; Gauron & Rawlings, 1975; Nash & Wolfe, 1957; Snyder, 1958; Vaught & Smith, 1980; Zander & Cohen, 1955). In contrast, only a few studies have examined changes in group structure and dynamics that newcomers produce in the groups that they join (e.g., Fine, 1976; Merei, 1949; Ziller & Behringer, 1960). As social psychologists, our understanding of group socialization is thus incomplete, because the reciprocal perspectives of groups and individuals have not been adequately considered. As Moscovici (1976, 1980) has pointed out, individual members can have a powerful influence on the groups to which they belong, and this influence deserves more research attention.

An awareness of these and other problems has led us to construct a general model of group socialization. Our primary goal has been to describe and explain the passage of individuals through groups. Unlike other analyses of group socialization, which tend to be relatively static in form, our model offers a *dynamic* look at the nature of group membership. Our model also adopts a *reciprocal* approach to major socialization phenomena, conceptualizing them in terms of basic psychological processes that characterize both groups and individuals. The model is meant to apply primarily (but not exclusively) to small, autonomous, voluntary groups whose members interact on a regular basis, have affective ties with one another, share a common frame of reference, and are behaviorally interdependent.

In formulating the model, we have sampled broadly from many different research literatures. These include not only the available work on socialization in small groups, but also work on political participation, social movements, and voluntary associations; religious affiliation and disaffiliation; migration, acculturation, and assimilation; college choice, student socialization, and dropout; socialization in total institutions, such as prisons, mental hospitals, and military units; occupational choice, career development, and job turnover; professional socialization; organizational socialization; and the development of dyadic relationships. The latter two areas of research proved to be especially relevant, because psychologists working in these areas have recently begun to conceptualize social influence processes as both dynamic and reciprocal (cf. Altman, Vinsel, & Brown, 1981; Burgess & Huston, 1979; Duck & Gilmour, 1981; Levinger, 1974; Levinger & Huesmann, 1980; Van Maanen & Schein, 1979; Wanous, 1980).

## II.  A Model of Group Socialization

Three basic psychological processes underlie the model: evaluation, commitment, and role transition. Each process is considered from the perspectives of both the group and the individual. *Evaluation,* which reflects efforts by groups and individuals to assess and alter one another's rewardingness, involves developing normative expectations, monitoring discrepancies between expected and actual behavior, and attempting to reduce such discrepancies. *Commitment,* which depends on the outcome of the evaluation process, is based on the group's and the individual's assessment of the past, present, and (anticipated) future rewardingness of their own and alternative relationships. Finally, *role transition,* which occurs when commitment rises or falls to a decision criterion, involves relabeling the individual's relationship with the group and changing how the group and the individual subsequently evaluate one another.

Before we discuss each of these processes in more detail, it may be useful to comment briefly on our use of the term *group.* When we say that a group evaluates its members, is highly committed to a particular person, or has a decision criterion regarding a role transition, we do not mean to reify the group as a social entity with its own thoughts, feelings, and behaviors. Like most social psychologists, we acknowledge the fact that a group is a collection of individuals, each of whom differs in certain ways from the others. A group's evaluation of a person, therefore, is actually a combination of various members' evaluations of that person. Some members may contribute more to the group evaluation than do others, because of their relative "visibility" (cf. Marwell, 1963) within the group, but most members probably have at least some influence. Similarly, a group's commitment to a particular person, or its decision criterion regarding a specific role transition, involves some weighted combination of the commitment levels or decision criteria of group members. Although definitional problems also arise when we talk about an individual evaluating a group and feeling some commitment to it as a result, they are not as serious. Research has shown that individuals, unlike social psychologists, are quite comfortable thinking about groups as social entities (cf. Wilder, 1981).

## A. EVALUATION

Every group has goals or objectives that the majority of group members would like to accomplish (cf. Shaw, 1981). Because groups value these goals, they evaluate the degree to which individuals contribute to goal attainment. For each person it evaluates, the group decides which goals the individual is expected to contribute to; determines the behavioral, cognitive, and affective dimensions on which those contributions will be assessed; and develops normative expectations for each dimension. Conformity to behavioral expectations can be observed directly, whereas conformity to cognitive and affective expectations must be inferred from observed behavior, so we will restrict our subsequent discussion of evaluative processes to behavioral expectations alone.[2]

---

[2]Clearly, cognitive and affective expectations are often important to the group. Many groups

Behavioral expectations can be conceptualized in terms of Jackson's (1965, 1966) return-potential model of norms. Jackson suggests that for each relevant behavioral dimension, a return-potential curve can be drawn specifying the amount of potential approval or disapproval (''return'') that an individual will receive from the group for each behavior along the dimension. As a means of conceptualizing the evaluation process, Jackson's model offers two important advantages. First, it is applicable to any norm, regardless of the shape of the overall relationship between the amount of behavior exhibited by the individual and the level of approval–disapproval expressed by the group. Second, Jackson's model specifies several important properties of norms, including ideal behavior, the range of tolerable behavior, the intensity of the group's feelings about the behavior, and the degree of norm crystallization. Ideal behavior represents the group's expectation about how the individual *ought* to behave. Ideal behavior on the part of the individual elicits the most positive evaluation from the group. The range of tolerable behavior includes all of the different behaviors that the group responds to with approval. Whenever the behavior of the individual falls within this range, the person will receive some degree of positive evaluation from the group. The intensity of the group's feelings about the individual's behavior provides a rough index of how important the norm is to the group. Intensity can be determined by averaging the absolute values of the approval–disapproval levels associated with all of the possible behaviors that the individual might exhibit. Insofar as a norm is important to the group, the individual will receive more positive evaluations for meeting the group's expectations and/or more negative evaluations for violating those expectations. Finally, norm crystallization refers to the degree of agreement among group members about how the individual ought to behave. One useful measure of norm crystallization is the within-group variance of behavioral expectations.

Although Jackson's (1965, 1966) model was originally developed to describe the properties of stable norms, it seems applicable to changing norms as well. Clearly, group expectations can vary in systematic ways over time, such that an individual is expected to show specific temporal changes in behavior (cf. Glaser & Strauss, 1971; Roth, 1963). On any particular behavioral dimension, therefore, the ideal behavior, range of tolerable behavior, intensity of group feeling, and degree of norm crystallization may all shift over time. Figure 1 illustrates temporal changes in a hypothetical group's norm regarding talkativeness at meetings. The relationship between talkativeness and group approval remains curvilinear over time. When the individual is moderately talkative, he or she is evaluated positively, but negative evaluations are made when the person

---

have cognitive expectations about members' knowledge and beliefs and affective expectations about their feelings toward people within and outside of the group. Groups may also have expectations about individuals' characteristics (e.g., physical attractiveness, external status) that exist prior to or independent of membership in the group.

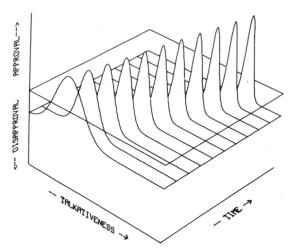

Fig. 1.    Temporal changes in a hypothetical group's norm regarding talkativeness at meetings.

talks either very little or very much. As time passes, however, the return-potential curve changes in several ways. First, the point of ideal behavior increases: In order to obtain the maximum level of approval from the group, the individual must become more talkative. Second, the range of tolerable behavior decreases: The group grants approval for a narrower set of behaviors. Finally, the intensity of the group's feelings increases: The individual receives more positive evaluations for meeting the group's expectations. Given these changes, the degree of norm crystallization (which is not illustrated) probably also rises over time.

The group may have the same set of expectations for all of the persons it evaluates, or expectations may be tailored to fit particular individuals. In general, however, those who occupy the same role within the group will tend to be evaluated in terms of the same expectations. The group's expectations for an individual are based on (a) the group's own characteristics (e.g., role and status structure, need for particular skills, degree of "mannedness"), (b) the environment in which the group operates (e.g., hostility of outgroups, availability of essential resources), and (c) the characteristics of the person under evaluation (e.g., status, aptitudes and abilities, perceived loyalty).

In order to determine the degree to which an individual fulfills normative expectations, the group must monitor the person's behavior on relevant dimensions. This monitoring involves first assessing the individual's behavior on each dimension and then comparing the observed behavior with the group's expectation for that individual on that dimension at that point in time. Monitoring may vary in frequency and regularity, depending on such factors as the nature and importance of the specific dimension under consideration and the length of time that the individual has been a group member. It should be noted that the group's monitoring of an individual's behavior actually involves a complex sequence of cognitive tasks, including attention and recognition, information organization and storage, search and recall, and integration and judgment processes (cf. J. M. Feldman, 1981; Naylor, Pritchard, & Ilgen, 1980).

Insofar as the individual fails to meet the group's expectations, the group may take some form of corrective action to reduce the discrepancy. Such action can involve efforts to change the individual's behavior, alterations in the group's expectations, or rejection of the individual. The probability that a group will take corrective action, and the type of action that it undertakes, may depend on the perceived importance of the behavioral dimension(s) under consideration, as well as other factors. Several analyses of social power shed light on the techniques that groups can use to shape members' behavior (e.g., Etzioni, 1961; Hackman, 1976; Raven & Kruglanski, 1970), and Levine (1980) has provided a detailed discussion of group reactions to deviating members.

As a result of all of its evaluations, the group has a general sense of the rewardingness of its relationship with the individual at any time. Rewardingness is based on the rewards and costs associated with the individual's behavior on all relevant dimensions. Rewards are acts that fall within the range of tolerable behavior on a given dimension, and costs are acts that fall outside this range. The magnitude of a particular reward or cost is determined by the relevant return-potential curve. Rewardingness, then, can be defined as the algebraic sum of all the perceived rewards and costs that the individual generates for the group.

Because the relationship between groups and individuals is reciprocal, it is important to consider how individuals develop normative expectations for groups and then monitor, evaluate, and attempt to influence those groups. Individuals join groups in order to satisfy personal needs (cf. Shaw, 1981). As a result, individuals evaluate the degree to which different groups can contribute toward need satisfaction. In evaluating a group, the individual decides which needs the group is expected to satisfy, determines the behavioral, cognitive, and affective dimensions on which need satisfaction will be assessed, and develops normative expectations for each dimension. Once again we will focus on behavioral expectations, which can be conceptualized in terms of Jackson's (1965, 1966) return potential model of norms, except that here the individual evaluates the group's behavior rather than vice versa. As with group expectations, an individual's expectations for a group can vary in systematic ways over time, such that the group is expected to show specific temporal changes in behavior. The individual may have the same set of expectations for all of the groups under evaluation, or expectations may be tailored to fit particular groups. Again, expectations are derived from the characteristics of the group, the environment in which the group operates, and the individual's own characteristics.

To determine if a group is fulfilling his or her normative expectations, the individual first monitors the group's behavior on each relevant dimension and then compares the behavior with expectations for that group on that dimension at that point in time. When the group fails to meet the individual's expectations, he or she may undertake some form of corrective action to reduce the discrepancy. Such action might involve efforts to change the group's behavior, alterations in the individual's expectations for the group, or rejection of the group (cf. Argyris, 1964; Moscovici, 1976). Finally, it should be noted that the individual's efforts to monitor the group's behavior and elicit conformity to his or her expectations will vary positively with the perceived importance of those expectations.

Individuals also have a general sense of the rewardingness of their relationship with the group at any particular time. In this case, rewardingness is based on the rewards and costs associated with the group's behavior. Once again, the classification of an act as a reward or cost and the assessed magnitude of that reward or cost are determined by the relevant return-potential curve. Rewardingness can again be defined as the algebraic sum of all the perceived rewards and costs that the group generates for the individual.

So far we have focused on how the group and the individual determine the present rewardingness of their relationship with one another. Two other important aspects of evaluation should also be noted. First, it seems likely that evaluations of the past and anticipated future are also important to both the group and the individual. In other words, groups and individuals probably think back occasionally to how rewarding their relationship was in the past and think ahead occasionally to how rewarding their relationship will be in the future (cf. Altman & Taylor, 1973; Huesmann & Levinger, 1976). Evaluations of past rewardingness are similar to evaluations of present rewardingness in the sense that the relevant rewards and costs have already been experienced. Evaluations of future rewardingness are different, however, because they require predictions about rewards and costs that have not yet been experienced. In determining rewardingness, therefore, both the group and the individual probably weight future rewards and costs by their perceived probability of occurrence.

A second important aspect of evaluation is that it need not be restricted to the relationship that the group and the individual have with one another. Groups and individuals also evaluate the past, present, and future rewardingness of their available alternative relationships.[3] These alternative relationships may be either actual or potential. Rewards and costs associated with actual past and present relationships have already been experienced and therefore will combine to pro-

[3]Some theorists have restricted their discussion of alternative relationships to the best single alternative relationship (e.g., Thibaut & Kelley, 1959). We believe, however, that both groups and individuals compare their own relationship with many or all of the alternative relationships that are available to them. We propose that the rewardingness of each alternative is weighted by its perceived probability of occurrence and that these weighted values are then averaged to produce an overall estimate of the rewardingness of alternative relationships.

duce evaluations of rewardingness in the usual way. However, rewards and costs associated with potential past and present relationships and all future alternative relationships will again be weighted by their perceived probability of occurrence when rewardingness is assessed.

## B.  COMMITMENT

According to the model, evaluation leads to feelings of commitment on the part of both groups and individuals. At an intuitive level, commitment involves a motivational link between groups and individuals—a link that may grow stronger or weaker with the passage of time. A more precise definition of commitment might involve the concept of instrumentality (cf. Mitchell & Biglan, 1971). Groups are more committed to individuals who help them attain group goals, and individuals are more committed to groups that help them satisfy personal needs.

In previous work, the term "commitment" has been used to describe a wide variety of cognitive, affective, and behavioral responses. Nearly all of this work has taken the perspective of the individual rather than that of the group. Thus, individuals have been viewed as more or less committed to other persons (e.g., friends, romantic partners) or to large groups (e.g., work organizations, religious congregations, unions, fraternities). Rarely have investigators discussed the commitment of groups to individuals. Many theoretical perspectives have been offered regarding the determinants and consequences of individual commitment (e.g., Angle & Perry, 1981; Becker, 1960; Farrell & Rusbult, 1981; Gordon, Philpot, Burt, Thompson, & Spiller, 1980; Hinde, 1979; Kanter, 1968, 1972; Levinger, 1980; Mowday, Steers, & Porter, 1979; Rosenblatt, 1977; Rusbult, 1980; Scanzoni, 1979). Rather than presenting an exhaustive review of these perspectives, we have used selected aspects of prior formulations in constructing a definition of commitment suited to our current needs. In so doing, we have considered the basic psychological factors that influence commitment, the manner in which these factors are combined to produce a given level of commitment in a particular situation, and the consequences of commitment for both groups and individuals.

Previous theories of commitment have emphasized the rewardingness of relationships. In general, it has been suggested that the more rewarding a relationship becomes, the more committed the participants will feel. Our analysis of commitment is also based on the concept of rewardingness. As mentioned in the previous section, both the group and the individual evaluate their present relationship on a variety of behavioral dimensions and thereby determine its rewardingness. Groups and individuals also evaluate the rewardingness of their past and future relationship with one another. As the past, present, and future rewardingness of a relationship increase, the group and the individual become more committed to one another. Commitment also involves the rewardingness of other actual and potential relationships. Evaluations of these relationships are not only carried out in the present, but may also be extended to the past and the future. As the past, present, and future rewardingness of alternative relationships increase, the group and the individual become less committed to one another.

This analysis suggests that six basic factors can affect both group and individual commitment. Each of these factors, which are summarized in Table I, involves some form of rewardingness. Together, the six factors are hypothesized to produce commitment in the following way:

$$\text{Commitment} = (PR - PRa) + (R - Ra) + (FR - FRa).$$

As the formula indicates, commitment is the sum of three important comparisons. First, the group and the individual compare the rewardingness of their past relationship with the rewardingness of other previous relationships in which they were or could have been involved $(PR - PRa)$. Second, the group and the individual compare the rewardingness of their present relationship with the rewardingness of other relationships in which they currently are or could be involved $(R - Ra)$. Finally, the group and the individual compare the expected rewardingness of their future relationship with the expected rewardingness of other future relationships in which they will or might become involved $(FR - FRa)$. Commitment between the group and the individual will be high insofar as (a) their past relationship is remembered as more rewarding than other previous alternative relationships, (b) their present relationship is regarded as more rewarding than other current alternative relationships, and (c) their future relationship is expected to be more rewarding than other future alternative relationships.

The commitment formula raises several issues that deserve to be discussed briefly. One such issue involves the degree to which each of the three comparisons $(PR - PRa; R - Ra; FR - FRa)$ contributes to the overall level of commitment between the group and the individual. Because present relationships are generally more salient than either past or future relationships, the $(R - Ra)$ comparison is probably the most important determinant of commitment. Similarly, the $(PR - PRa)$ comparison may often be more important than the $(FR -$

TABLE I

PERCEIVED REWARDINGNESS OF CURRENT AND ALTERNATIVE RELATIONSHIPS
IN PAST, PRESENT, AND FUTURE

| Past | Present | Future |
| --- | --- | --- |
| Past rewardingness of current relationship $(PR)$ | Present rewardingness of current relationship $(R)$ | Future rewardingness of current relationship $(FR)$ |
| Past rewardingness of alternative relationships $(PRa)$ | Present rewardingness of alternative relationships $(Ra)$ | Future rewardingness of alternative relationships $(FRa)$ |

$FRa$) comparison, because evaluations of past relationships are based on more concrete information than are evaluations of future relationships. The relative importance of the three comparisons may also be affected by the nature of the current relationship between the group and the individual. In the case of newcomers, for example, neither the group nor the individual has engaged in much past evaluation, and therefore the $(PR - PRa)$ comparison is unlikely to be very important. Similarly, the $(FR - FRa)$ comparison will probably be relatively unimportant to the group and the individual when their relationship is expected to end soon.

Another issue raised by the commitment formula concerns the independence of the three comparisons. One factor that probably influences independence is the relative importance of these comparisons. As the importance of a particular comparison increases, distortions may occur in the perceived outcomes of other comparisons. These distortions usually involve ''assimilation,'' in the sense that the outcomes of less important comparisons are distorted to seem more similar to the outcomes of more important comparisons. For example, if the $(R - Ra)$ comparison is important and positive, then the outcomes of the $(PR - PRa)$ and/or $(FR - FRa)$ comparisons may be distorted in a positive direction. Similarly, if the $(PR - PRa)$ and/or $(FR - FRa)$ comparisons are important and negative, then the outcome of the $(R - Ra)$ comparison may be distorted in a negative direction.[4]

Under certain circumstances, the interdependence of the three comparisons in the commitment formula can also be influenced by specific rewards and costs that the group and the individual have experienced in their own and alternative relationships. For example, some costs that the group and the individual have incurred in their past or present relationship with one another, and some rewards that they have foregone in past or present alternative relationships, may be perceived as ''investments'' (Becker, 1960; Farrell & Rusbult, 1981; Hinde, 1979; Johnson, 1973; Kanter, 1968, 1972; Levinger, 1980; Rosenblatt, 1977; Rusbult, 1980). Costs incurred and rewards foregone are only perceived as investments, however, when they are viewed as necessary for the attainment of future rewards or the avoidance of future costs. As a result, investments increase the expected outcome of the $(FR - FRa)$ comparison, rather than decrease the outcome of the $(PR - PRa)$ or $(R - Ra)$ comparison. Another special way in which costs incurred and rewards foregone may influence the perceived outcomes of comparisons involves cognitive dissonance. Dissonance should only occur, however, insofar as the group and the individual perceive these costs and

[4]Contrast effects could conceivably occur as well, although they are probably much less common. When contrast effects do occur, the outcomes of less important comparisons are distorted to seem more *different* from the outcomes of more important comparisons. This probably only occurs when the outcome of one comparison is extremely positive or negative relative to the outcomes of other comparisons.

rewards as explicit, irrevocable, volitional, and public (cf. Kiesler, 1971; Salancik, 1977). When dissonance is aroused, it may be reduced by increasing the perceived outcome of one or more of the three comparisons in the commitment formula (e.g., Aronson & Mills, 1959; Gerard & Mathewson, 1966).

There are also circumstances under which rewards that the group and the individual have obtained in their past or present relationship with one another actually decrease the perceived outcome of particular comparisons. This may occur in at least two ways. First, the group or the individual may feel a sense of indebtedness due to a felt obligation to repay the rewards that have been obtained (cf. Greenberg, 1980). Feelings of indebtedness are most likely to arise when the recipient of the rewards (a) believes that the donor was concerned about the recipient's welfare, (b) perceives the rewards as large and costly to the donor, and (c) caused the rewards to be given. When indebtedness occurs, rewards decrease the expected outcome of the $(FR - FRa)$ comparison, rather than increase the outcome of the $(PR - PRa)$ or $(R - Ra)$ comparison. Second, rewards obtained in a relationship may produce "overjustification" effects (Deci, 1975; Lepper & Greene, 1978). These effects are most likely to occur when the relationship is already rewarding and the rewards in question are made to seem essential for the maintenance of the relationship. When overjustification occurs, rewards decrease rather than increase the outcome of the $(PR - PRa)$ or $(R - Ra)$ comparison (e.g., O'Reilly & Caldwell, 1981).

Having defined the psychological factors that determine commitment and the relationships among them, it is important to discuss some of the consequences of commitment. Previous analyses of individual commitment to a group have suggested that there are four major consequences of commitment: acceptance of the group's goals and values; positive affective ties to group members; willingness to exert effort on behalf of the group and to fulfill group expectations; and desire to gain or maintain membership in the group (Buchanan, 1974; Gordon et al., 1980; Kanter, 1968, 1972; Mowday et al., 1979). These four consequences of commitment can be labeled, respectively, consensus, cohesion, control, and continuance (cf. Kanter, 1968, 1972). It has been suggested that the type of commitment that group members feel is determined by their experiences within the group. For example, Kanter proposes that renunciation and communion experiences produce cohesion commitment, mortification and surrender (transcendence) experiences produce control commitment, and sacrifice and investment experiences produce continuance commitment (see also Etzioni, 1961). Although interesting, these distinctions will not be highlighted in the subsequent discussion. Instead, we shall treat commitment as a unitary construct that embodies all four of the consequences mentioned above. Moreover, although commitment has generally been conceptualized in terms of an individual's cognitive, affective, and behavioral responses to a group, we shall also use the term to refer to a group's responses to an individual. Thus, the consequences of group commitment include acceptance of the individual's needs and values, positive affective ties to the individual, willingness to exert effort on behalf of the individual and to fulfill his or her expectations, and desire to gain or retain the individual as a group member.

At any given time, the levels of commitment that the group feels toward an individual and that the individual feels toward the group may or may not be highly correlated (cf. Altman *et al.*, 1981; Duck, 1982; Edwards & Saunders, 1981; Levinger, 1980; Rosenblatt, 1977). When commitment disequilibrium occurs, the "principle of least interest" probably applies. That is, the party that feels less committed has greater power in the relationship. If the group's level of commitment greatly exceeds that of the individual, then he or she may come to occupy a position of status and authority within the group. In contrast, if an individual's level of commitment is greater than that of the group, then he or she will tend to have low power and may be derogated and devalued by other group members. Presumably, the greater the commitment disequilibrium in a relationship, the less stable the relationship is. Therefore, we assume a general pressure toward commitment equilibrium between groups and individuals.

## C.  ROLE TRANSITION

Commitment, on the part of both the group and the individual, can change over time. Both groups and individuals formulate *decision criteria* to indicate important changes in their relationship to one another, and these criteria can be conceptualized in terms of commitment. Decision criteria are based on (a) general beliefs about the evolution of typical relationships between individuals and groups and (b) specific beliefs about the evolution of the particular relationship under consideration. When commitment rises or falls to a decision criterion, the individual is perceived as ready to undergo a role transition. Thus, group membership is not an all-or-none phenomenon. Instead, there is an ingroup–outgroup dimension along which all persons associated with the group can be placed (Moreland, 1978). This dimension can be thought of in terms of three role regions: nonmember, quasi-member, and full member. Nonmembers include *prospective members* who have not yet joined the group and *ex members* who have left the group. Quasi-members include *new members* who have not yet attained full member status and *marginal members* who have lost this status. Finally, *full members* are those who are most closely identified with the group and who have all of the privileges and responsibilities associated with group membership.

The relationships among commitment, decision criteria, and role transitions for both the group and the individual can be elaborated as follows. Changes in the group's commitment to an individual alter the extent to which that person is regarded as an important part of the group. If commitment rises or falls to a decision criterion, then the group will perceive the role of the person differently and will attempt to relabel him or her accordingly. Thus, the group will try to impose a role transition on the individual, reflecting the group's view of his or her new position on the ingroup–outgroup dimension. Similarly, as the individual's commitment to the group changes, group membership will seem more or less valuable. If commitment rises or falls to a personal decision criterion, then the individual will seek to make a role transition, on the grounds that his or her personal involvement in the group has undergone a significant change.

To the extent that the group and the individual feel equally committed to one another during all phases of their relationship and share the same decision criteria, role transitions would be expected to proceed smoothly. However, this state of affairs may not always prevail. As mentioned earlier, group commitment to the individual and individual commitment to the group may not be equal. The group and the individual may also hold different decision criteria for a given role transition. These possibilities can complicate the process of role transition. For example, consider the case in which the group and the individual hold the same decision criterion for a role transition, but one party's commitment exceeds that criterion while the other party's does not. In this situation, the more committed party may attempt to force the transition before the less committed party feels ready for it (Glaser & Strauss, 1971). If the more committed party is powerful enough, then a role transition may in fact occur, but it is likely to anger the less committed party and thereby cause future problems for the relationship. Similar problems can arise if the group and the individual hold different decision criteria for a given role transition but feel equal commitment to one another, or if they differ in both decision criteria and commitment. If neither party wishes or is able to force a role transition on the other, then the group and the individual may negotiate regarding the appropriateness of a role transition (Glaser & Strauss, 1971; Roth, 1963; Van Maanen, 1977).

Even when there is agreement that a role transition *should* occur, the group and the individual may disagree about whether the role transition *did* occur. In some situations (e.g., when commitment disequilibrium is very large or when decision criteria have varied substantially over time), one party may perceive that a role transition has occurred, but the other party may not agree. Because role transitions are important for both the group and the individual, it is functional if both parties engage in *reciprocal* relabeling of their relationship, so that changes in the evaluation process can be mutually perceived and adhered to. In order to reduce disagreements about when a role transition *should* occur, many groups formalize their decision criteria and attempt to convince members to adopt these criteria as their own. Similarly, individuals may sometimes publicize their personal decision criteria in the hope that the group will adopt these criteria as its own. In order to reduce disagreements about whether a transition *did* occur, many groups evolve formal rites of passage to provide a public demonstration that a transition has in fact taken place (e.g., Garfinkel, 1956; Glaser & Strauss, 1971; Roth, 1963; Sarbin & Allen, 1968; Schwartz, 1979; Van Gennep, 1908/1960). Individuals may also try to prove that a role transition has occurred by conducting their own personal rite of passage, such as throwing a party, getting drunk, or buying themselves a present (cf. Hinde, 1979). Rites of passage enable both groups and individuals to minimize errors regarding their reciprocal rights and obligations.

It should be noted that role transitions can differ from one another on several dimensions. Some efforts to conceptualize role transitions have used dichotomous or trichotomous categorization schemes. For example, Schwartz (1979) distinguishes between degradation and accreditation ceremonies, and Van Gennep (1908/1960) discusses separation, transition, and incorporation rites. A more complex analysis of the dimensions underlying role transitions and other aspects of passage through groups has been offered by Glaser and Strauss (1971). These authors organize their discussion of "status passages" around several major themes, including reversibility, temporality, shape, desirability, and circumstantiality. From the perspectives of both the group and individual, however, one of the most important dimensions of a role transition is its difficulty. Some role transitions are made relatively easily, with little effort or stress, whereas others are much more difficult to accomplish. Nearly all of the dimensions described by Glaser and Strauss (1971) can affect the difficulty of a role transition. For example, role transitions that have an unclear schedule, take a long time to complete, seem undesirable, and can only be accomplished by a single person are probably rather difficult. Burr (1972) has also described several factors that can influence the difficulty of a role transition, including the clarity of the new role, the degree to which the individual is capable of fulfilling the expectations of that role, and differences in expectations associated with the new and old roles.

## D. PASSAGE THROUGH THE GROUP

The passage of an individual through a group can be viewed in terms of an ordered set of phases, each representing a qualitatively different relationship between the person and the group. These phases are demarcated from one another by role transitions. Each role transition represents a significant alteration in group and individual commitment levels, which are themselves determined by changes in evaluation. The model thus involves a temporal process that is basically recursive in nature. Within each phase, evaluations produce changes in commitment, which in turn lead to a role transition when a decision criterion has been reached. Once a role transition has taken place, a new phase is entered and evaluations begin anew, often on different behavioral dimensions than before.

These new evaluations lead to further changes in commitment, which may later produce yet another role transition, and so on. In this way, the individual moves through different phases of group membership.

Figure 2 provides a more detailed description of how the relationship between a group and an individual might change over time. The diagram, which relates changes in commitment to specific kinds of role transitions, could potentially be interpreted from the viewpoint of either the group or the individual, because the same basic factors (evaluation, commitment, role transition) are assumed to operate in each case.[5]

Initially, both the group and the individual go through an *investigation* phase, in which they assess the potential value of forming a relationship with one another. During this period, in which the individual is perceived as a prospective member, the group engages in *recruitment,* looking for persons who seem likely to make a substantial contribution to the attainment of group goals. At the same time, the individual undertakes a *reconnaissance* of the different groups to which he or she might belong, assessing the degree to which each is likely to satisfy personal needs. As time passes and the group and the individual come to view one another as increasingly attractive, commitment on both sides increases. When the group's commitment to the individual rises to its *entry criterion* (EC), an offer of membership is made. Similarly, the individual makes an effort to join the group when his or her commitment to it has risen to a personal entry criterion. Once the group and the individual agree to become affiliated, *entry* occurs, marking the first major role transition. Entry into the group involves a joint relabeling of the individual as a new member.

When a new member enters the group, both the individual and the group undergo a period of *socialization.* During socialization, the group attempts to teach the individual "appropriate" behaviors, thoughts, and feelings, and evaluates how much he or she contributes to the attainment of group goals. To the extent that the group is successful in altering the individual, the individual shows *assimilation.* At the same time, the individual tries to alter the group's expectations to fit his or her own abilities and interests, and evaluates how much the group satisfies personal needs. To the extent that the individual is successful in altering the group, the group shows *accommodation.* If the group's and the individual's commitment to one another rise to their respective *acceptance criteria* (AC), then the individual will be jointly relabeled as a full member.

During the *maintenance* phase, the group and the individual engage in *role negotiation.* The group attempts to define a specialized role for each full member that maximizes his or her contributions to the attainment of group goals and

---

[5]In this section we focus on changes in the present rewardingness of the relationship between the group and the individual (R), because that relationship is generally most salient and hence has the greatest impact on commitment.

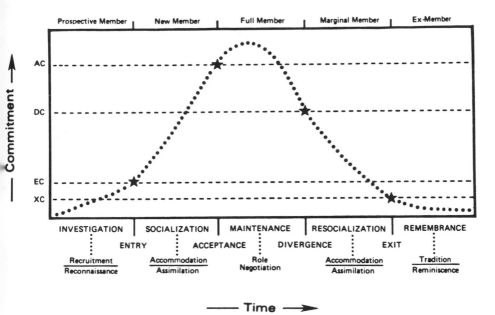

Fig. 2. A model of group socialization.

minimizes the group's obligations to the person. In contrast, each full member attempts to define his or her own role so as to maximize the satisfaction of personal needs and minimize obligations to the group. If the group feels that a particular person is not meeting its expectations, then pressure will be exerted on the individual. Similarly, a person who feels that the group is not meeting his or her expectations will exert pressure on the group. Insofar as these tactics fail and the group and the individual regard their relationships as unrewarding, both will feel reduced commitment to one another. If the group's and the individual's levels of commitment fall to their respective *divergence criteria* (DC), then the person will be jointly relabeled as a marginal member.

Marginality causes the group and the individual to attempt to resocialize one another. During the *resocialization* phase, the group tries to change the individual in ways that will facilitate his or her *assimilation* and evaluates the probability that the individual will once again meet the group's expectations for a full member. At the same time, the individual tries to increase the group's *accommodation* and assesses the probability that the group will once again satisfy personal needs. Resocialization can end in one of two ways. First, if the group's and the individual's commitment to one another rise to their respective divergence criteria, then the marginal member will undergo a special role transition (convergence) and will be relabeled again as a full member of the group.

Second, if the group's and the individual's commitment fall to their respective *exit criteria* (XC), then a joint relabeling of the individual as an ex-member will take place. The second outcome of resocialization is depicted in Fig. 2.

Finally, after the individual has left the group, there is a period of *remembrance* regarding their relationship with one another. The group arrives at a consensus concerning the person's past behavior in the group and his or her prior contribution to group goals, and this consensus becomes part of group *tradition*. The individual engages in *reminiscence* about the group's behavior and the degree to which the group satisfied personal needs. Groups and individuals may also engage in an ongoing evaluation of one another, insofar as they continue to provide mutual rewards and costs. Commitment between the group and the individual eventually stabilizes at some level.

Of course, the sequence of events shown in Fig. 2 is really an idealized version of how a "typical" individual might pass through a "typical" group. The diagram masks many complex aspects of passage through groups, some of which deserve to be mentioned briefly. First, commitment appears to change smoothly over time in the diagram, suggesting that the feelings of a group and an individual toward one another are modified gradually and continuously as the relationship develops. Although this may be true in most instances, changes in commitment might also occur in a more abrupt manner, reflecting the impact of particular events that seem important to the people involved. For example, group commitment to a newcomer might increase sharply because of some heroic act on his or her part, or a marginal member might experience a marked decrease in commitment to a group because of an insult by other members. It is also possible, of course, for commitment to remain stationary for long periods of time.

A second complex aspect of passage through the group involves the stability of group and individual decision criteria. As noted earlier, these decision criteria are not necessarily generalizable across relationships, since groups may have different decision criteria for different members and individuals may have different decision criteria for different groups to which they belong. What may not be clear from Fig. 2 is that decision criteria within a particular relationship are not necessarily stable either. As time passes, decision criteria may be altered in response to changing circumstances (cf. Roth, 1963). For example, a group's acceptance criterion for a new member might be affected by his or her rate of assimilation or that of other newcomers, and a marginal member's exit criterion might change because he or she acquires new information about what it would be like to be an ex-member of the group.

As decision criteria are altered, the amount of time an individual spends in related membership phases may also change. Although the duration of a membership phase depends on several factors, the most important of these is probably the "distance" (on the commitment dimension) between the decision criteria marking its beginning and end. Since commitment generally changes rather slowly over time, there is a strong tendency for membership phases to increase in length as their demarcating decision criteria grow further apart. Socialization thus takes longer as the distance between the entry and acceptance criteria increases, whereas resocialization passes more quickly as the distance between the divergence and exit criteria decreases. When, as sometime happens, two adjacent decision criteria become equivalent to one another, the membership phase that they demarcate will disappear altogether. If the entry and acceptance criteria are identical, for example, then new members of the group will be regarded as full members, and neither the group nor the individual will undergo socialization. At the other extreme are membership phases that persist for long periods because their demarcating decision criteria are very far apart. Investigation and remembrance are special examples in this regard, because each of these phases is bounded by only one decision criterion. As a result, both investigation and remembrance may last almost indefinitely, so long as the group and the individual continue evaluating one another.

Decision criteria may also vary in their positions relative to one another. Fig. 2 indicates that $AC > DC > EC > XC$, but this is only one of several possible orderings of the four decision criteria. Clearly, the commitment level for the acceptance criterion must be as high as or higher than that for the entrance criterion and higher than the commitment levels for the divergence and exit criteria. Moreover, the divergence criterion must fall at or above the commitment level associated with the exit criterion. The location of the divergence and exit criteria in relation to the entry criterion, however, cannot be specified in general terms because their relative positions can vary across groups and individuals. For example, the group may have higher (or lower) standards for persons it admits than for those it retains. Similarly, the individual may be more (or less) willing to join a group than to leave it. Many relationships among decision criteria can occur, and each has different implications for an individual's experiences within the group. In spite of these potential variations, the decision criteria shown in Fig. 2 probably represent a rather typical pattern.

A related aspect of passage through the group involves the number of role transitions that an individual experiences and the order in which these transitions occur. According to Fig. 2, group membership involves four separate role transitions. Each transition marks the beginning of a particular membership phase, and no membership phase (except investigation) can be entered unless the person has passed through the preceding role transition. As suggested earlier, however, some of these role transitions will be combined if their decision criteria are based on the same level of commitment. For example, if the entry and acceptance criteria are equal and the divergence and exit criteria are equal, then an individual will undergo only two role transitions: entry/acceptance and divergence/exit. The ordering of role transitions may also differ from that shown in Fig. 2. It seems clear that the first three role transitions have a logical order that cannot be violated. That is, entry must precede (or accompany) acceptance, and acceptance must precede divergence. Divergence, however, is not a necessary prerequisite for exit. Not only can divergence and exit occur simultaneously (thereby causing the individual to leave during the maintenance phase and skip resocialization), but exit can also occur in the investigation and socialization phases if the group's and the individual's commitment to one another fall below their respective exit criteria.

Finally, it is important to realize that Fig. 2 accurately represents the perspectives of both the group and the individual *only* if we assume that both parties share the same set of decision criteria and are equally committed to one another throughout their relationship. Although these assumptions are probably correct in most cases, they may not always be valid. As mentioned earlier, groups and their members sometimes have different decision criteria and experience commitment disequilibrium. As a result, the group and the individual may perceive the same sequence of events differently and therefore may have different views of the individual's passage through the group. In general, the more the group and the individual differ in this regard, the more problematic their relationship will be.

## III.  Temporal Changes in Individual–Group Relations

The five phases of group membership are similar to one another in many ways, as are the four role transitions. Nevertheless, there are certain aspects of each membership phase and role transition that make it distinctive. It is worthwhile, therefore, to discuss each phase and transition in greater detail, focusing on its special features.

### A.  INVESTIGATION

The group and the individual begin their relationship with a period of mutual investigation. During this period, the group is involved in the recruitment of new members. Groups differ, of course, in how often they engage in recruitment and how skillful they are at it. As Ziller (1965) has noted, some groups are relatively "open," in the sense that they are accustomed to and often interested in recruiting new members. In contrast, other groups rarely recruit new members and therefore are relatively "closed." Many factors can influence a group's tendency to be open or closed to new members. Perhaps the most important factor is the group's current level of success. Groups that are unsuccessful tend to be open and look for new members who can help attain group goals (Festinger, Riecken, & Schachter, 1956; Wicker & Mehler, 1971). Successful groups, however, often tend to be closed and view new members as potentially disruptive.

Once a group has decided to recruit new members, it must first identify prospective candidates. This task, which is often assigned to recruitment specialists, may be more or less difficult, depending on the exclusiveness of the group's selection criteria and its attractiveness to potential recruits. The group may advertise its recruitment effort, so that any interested individuals can apply for membership, or the group may proceed more covertly, searching for prospective candidates in a more unobtrusive manner (Snow, Zurcher, & Ekland-Olson, 1980). The latter strategy attracts fewer prospective members, but more of those individuals are likely to be acceptable to the group.

Individuals identified as candidates for group membership must next be evaluated in terms of their potential contributions to group goals. This evaluation process may be more or less formal, depending on such factors as (a) the level of consensus among group members about what they desire in a newcomer, (b) the extent to which those characteristics can be readily assessed, and (c) the perceived costliness of evaluative errors. Information about candidates may be obtained from a number of sources, including formal records or applications, contacts with people who are familiar with the individuals under consideration, or actual meetings with the candidates themselves. Naturally, groups vary in what they look for in prospective members. Task-oriented groups tend to focus their evaluations on the perceived skills and abilities of prospective members (e.g., Gilchrist, 1952; Kipper, Bizman, & Einat, 1981), whereas social groups tend to evaluate prospective members in terms of their probable compatibility with the current membership (e.g., Cleveland, 1980; Longino & Kart, 1973; Scott, 1965). Most groups, however, probably evaluate both the ability and the sociability of prospective members (Wanous, 1980; Zander, 1976).

As recruitment proceeds and the group obtains more information about its prospective members, commitment to those individuals will change. In some cases, prospective members will seem unacceptable, and so the group's commitment to them will never rise above its entry criterion. Offers of membership will not be extended to such persons, and attempts may even be made to discourage their interest in the group. In other cases, however, prospective members will become increasingly attractive to the group over time. When the group's commitment to such persons reaches its entry criterion, offers of membership will be made, and prospective members who are ready to join will enter the group and become new members.

Of course, some prospective members may be reluctant to make this role transition if their own commitment to the group has not yet reached their personal entry criteria. This reluctance may stem from the group's recruitment activities (Rynes, Heneman, & Schwab, 1980) and/or from prospective members' beliefs about the probable costs of group membership. Many groups try to persuade reluctant persons to join by (a) engaging in anticipatory accommodation to make the group seem more rewarding, (b) convincing prospective members that belonging to the group will serve their own best interests, or (c) offering prospective members direct inducements, such as money or status, for joining. If these tactics are impractical or prove to be ineffective, then the group may have to resort to subtler methods. One such method, which reflects the dependence of attitudes on behaviors (Bem, 1967; Festinger, 1957), involves efforts to increase prospective members' voluntary participation in group activities (Lofland, 1977; Zander, 1976). As their level of behavioral involvement gradually increases, prospective members are likely to develop positive attitudes toward joining the group (cf. Hackman, 1976; Salancik, 1977).

From the perspective of the individual, the investigation phase involves a reconnaissance of the groups to which he or she might belong. Reconnaissance is often prompted by transitory needs (e.g., Lindt & Pennal, 1962; Schachter, 1959). However, people may also vary in their dispositional tendencies to be "open" or "closed" to the general notion of group membership itself. Depending upon their need for affiliation, some individuals may often search for new groups to join, whereas others may tend to be "loners," preferring to avoid group membership altogether (cf. Latané & Bidwell, 1977; Heshka & Lang, 1978). By and large, though, most people will probably consider joining new groups if they believe that group membership might be beneficial to them.

Successful reconnaissance for a prospective member involves first identifying potentially desirable groups, then evaluating the degree to which membership in those groups might satisfy personal needs, and finally persuading chosen groups to accept one as a member. Locating appropriate groups may be more or less difficult, depending on the particular selection criteria that the individual uses and his or her attractiveness as a prospective group member. Some individuals openly approach groups that they might like to join, whereas others prefer a more indirect approach that masks their possible interest in becoming a group member. The former strategy has the advantage of communicating clearly the prospective member's interest in the group, but may also make him or her seem too supplicatory. The latter approach preserves the prospective member's (apparently) disinterested stance, but can lead to subsequent misunderstandings regarding his or her intentions toward the group.

In order to evaluate groups, the individual must obtain accurate information about them. This task is not always easy, especially if the group is not actively recruiting new members. A prospective member may request or search out information about a group and its members, or try to arrange some personal contact with the group. Many individuals become interested in groups because they know people who are or once were members, and these acquaintances may also serve as valuable sources of information (e.g., Jacoby, 1965; Richardson & Stewart, 1977; Snow et al., 1980; Trice, 1957).

A variety of factors can influence a prospective member's evaluations of a group. Some individuals become attracted to a group because they like the people in it (Galanter, 1980; Good & Good, 1974; Good & Nelson, 1971; Snow *et al.*, 1980), whereas others enjoy the group's activities (Henshel, 1973; Sherif & Sherif, 1953; Warriner & Prather, 1965) or approve of its goals (Gouldner, 1960; Hoge & Polk, 1980). A group may also become attractive not so much because of its intrinsic desirability, but rather because it mediates extrinsic rewards (Chisholm, Gauntner, & Munzenrider, 1980; Gordon & Babchuk, 1959; Willerman & Swanson, 1953). Whatever rewards they provide, however, groups generally attract prospective members insofar as they promise to satisfy personal needs (Shaw, 1981; Strand, Levine, & Montgomery, 1981; Wanous, 1980).

As reconnaissance progresses, a prospective member may decide that some groups are unsatisfactory, and so his or her commitment to those groups will never surpass the entry criterion. No efforts will be made to join such groups, and some individuals may even try to remove themselves from consideration as prospective group members. Other groups, however, may become increasingly desirable as a prospective member learns more about them. Once commitment to a group reaches his or her entry criterion, the individual will make an effort to join the group and will become a new member if the group is willing. Of course, the group will be reluctant to allow this role transition to occur if its commitment to that person has not yet reached the group's entry criterion. In that case, a prospective member may (a) engage in anticipatory assimilation in order to become more rewarding to the group, (b) try to persuade the group that it would be in its best interests to admit him or her as a member, or (c) offer the group direct inducements, such as service or information, if it will allow entry to occur.

## B. ENTRY

Entry occurs when the group's commitment to the individual and his or her commitment to the group reach their respective entry criteria. At entry, the individual passes from the role of prospective member to that of new member. Entry thus marks the first major role transition in the relationship between the group and the individual.

Groups vary widely in their attitudes and behavior regarding the entry of new members. Many informal groups have relatively permeable boundaries (Scott & Scott, 1981) and make few distinctions between members and nonmembers (cf. Yablonsky, 1959). These groups often have low entry criteria and encourage the *continuous entry* of new members. Prospective members are allowed to join the group as soon as they elicit sufficient commitment from it, and therefore all newcomers elicit the same initial level of group commitment (the entry criterion) regardless of when they actually join. The entry of newcomers into such groups is generally uneventful and attracts little attention from other group members.

In contrast, many formal groups have boundaries that are relatively impermeable and members who regard themselves as special or distinctive in some way. These groups typically have high entry criteria and prefer the *periodic entry* of new members. Prospective members are only admitted to the group in batches and/or at certain specified times, and therefore newcomers often differ in how much initial commitment they elicit from the group, although that commitment must always exceed the group's entry criterion. The entry of new members into groups of this sort is nearly always accompanied by some ceremony, which involves acknowledging the newly established relationship between the group and the individual and/or renouncing the person's prior relationships with other groups.

The major purpose of entry ceremonies is to increase new members' commitment to the group. Whatever positive qualities they may possess, newcomers inevitably pose some threat to group integrity (Ziller, 1965). For example, newcomers often have a fresh and relatively objective view of the group, which causes them to ask questions or express opinions that are unsettling to older members. Newcomers may also destabilize the group by producing changes in intragroup relations (cf. Snyder, 1958). These changes often seem undesirable to other group members, and if the group changes too extensively or rapidly, then it may become less successful at attaining its goals or may fail altogether (Chapin, 1957; Darley, Gross, & Martin, 1951; White & Butts, 1963). In order to minimize these and other potential problems, many groups devise entry ceremonies to generate commitment in new members and thereby facilitate their assimilation.

Entry ceremonies can take many forms. Some groups treat newcomers positively, welcoming them with parties, gifts, offers of advice or aid, and other special benefits (Lewicki, 1981). These tactics are designed to make newcomers feel grateful to the group and perhaps guilty about the (as yet) undeserved rewards that they have received. Other groups treat newcomers in a more neutral manner, behaving cordially but making it clear that membership is provisional and subject to revocation if the group's expectations are not met (Hazer & Alvares, 1981; Kanter, 1972). Finally, some groups treat newcomers negatively, forcing them to undergo unpleasant and even dangerous initiations (Kanter, 1968; Schein, 1964). These tactics are designed to create commitment through dissonance reduction; newcomers who have voluntarily endured unpleasant initiations often justify their behavior by evaluating the group positively (e.g., Aronson & Mills, 1959; Gerard & Mathewson, 1966).

Individuals also differ from one another in their attitudes and behaviors regarding entry. Of course, there may be relatively little room for such individual differences in groups that have formal entry ceremonies. Newcomers in such groups are expected to exhibit the proper reactions at the appropriate times; they should gratefully accept the benefits they receive at entry and be "good sports" about unpleasant initiation experiences. Above all, new members should participate whole-heartedly in entry ceremonies, thereby displaying a proper appreciation for the provisional nature of their membership. In groups that treat entry more informally, however, the behavioral expectations for a newcomer are less well specified, and individuals must devise their own tactics for becoming group members.

Although there are several ways for individuals to gain entry into such groups, the most successful tactic is to progressively increase one's level of involvement in the group's activities (Merei, 1949; Phillips, Shenker, & Revitz, 1951; Putallaz & Gottman, 1981). As the group becomes accustomed to seeing and interacting with a prospective member, the individual is gradually relabelled as a new member. Interestingly, the success of this tactic appears to derive in part from its unobtrusive nature: Behaviors that make salient the individual's attempted entry often disrupt the progress of the role transition. Another successful tactic for achieving entry is to attach oneself to someone who already belongs to the group (e.g., Richardson & Stewart, 1977; Warriner & Prather, 1965). Prospective members typically select a friend or relative for this purpose, since those persons are relatively easy to approach. Aspiring newcomers who do not have close relationships with anyone in the group may attach themselves to marginal members for the same reason (cf. Merei, 1949; Ziller & Behringer, 1961). Insofar as the group identifies the individual with one of its current members, he or she also may begin to be viewed as a member of the group.

Even if these and other tactics prove to be successful, entry still can be a stressful experience. Entry is usually an iconoclastic experience, in the sense that the "real" nature of the group is revealed to the individual for the first time. Prospective members often have unrealistic and overly optimistic expectations about the groups that they intend to join (Wanous, 1980). As a result, they may have difficulty understanding and/or accepting what life within the group is like (Louis, 1980; Van Maanen, 1977). Entry also can be a demeaning experience, in the sense that the individual generally has low status in the group and therefore is subject to the demands of other group members. Newcomers are often ignored, devalued, or actively rejected by the groups that they join (e.g. Feshbach & Sones, 1971; Ziller, 1965) and therefore become withdrawn, anxious, and dependent (Feldbaum et al., 1980; Heiss & Nash, 1967; Nash & Wolfe, 1957; Snyder, 1958; Walker, 1973; Ziller, 1964, 1965). Entry can be less unpleasant when the group is cohesive (Heiss, 1963) and the newcomers (a) are similar or attractive to the rest of the group (Blau, 1960; Ziller, Behringer, & Goodchilds, 1960; Putallaz & Gottman, 1981), (b) have a high level of ascribed status in the group (Zander & Cohen, 1955), or (c) possess skills that the group needs in order to attain its goals (Fromkin, Klimoski, & Flanagan, 1972; Ziller & Behringer, 1960; Ziller, Behringer, & Jansen, 1961).

Entry is more stressful when a person is the only newcomer in the group—a situation that often arises in groups that permit continuous entry. A "solo" newcomer is highly salient to the rest of the group. This salience may evoke relatively high levels of interest and attention from other group members and may cause the newcomer to be perceived and/or treated in stereotypic ways (cf. Heilman, 1980; Taylor & Fiske, 1978; Taylor, Fiske, Close, Anderson, & Ruderman, 1977). Concomitant changes in the newcomer's self-perceptions may also occur. The fact that other group members focus their attention on the newcomer may increase his or her level of objective self-awareness (Wicklund, 1975), and self-evaluations arising from that increased awareness are likely to be based on the group's behavioral standards (Wicklund & Frey, 1980). In addition, the idea of being "new" may become an important part of the newcomer's spontaneous self-concept (cf. McGuire & McGuire, 1981). When that occurs, the individual's attitudes and behaviors may grow increasingly stereotypic, reflecting his or her conception of the typical new group member.

Entry is generally less stressful when newcomers join a group together, as they do in groups that encourage periodic entry. In such groups, social categorization processes (cf. Brewer, 1979; Tajfel, 1979; Wilder, 1981) can have an important impact on newcomers. Any set of entering newcomers can, of course, be regarded as a "group" in and of themselves. Newcomers are more likely to categorize themselves as an ingroup, whose outgroup consists of the oldtimers, insofar as seniority is a salient factor in intragroup relations. Seniority is likely to be salient to newcomers when they (a) constitute a relatively small proportion of the total membership of the group, (b) feel that they are systematically different from oldtimers, or (c) possess little or no prior information about the group and are unacquainted with its members. Feelings of camaraderie among newcomers can ameliorate the usual stresses associated with entry in at least two ways. First, newcomers can engage in social comparison with one another in order to evaluate their experiences within the group. These comparisons reduce the uncertainty and may ease some of the disappointments that accompany entry. Second, newcomers can rely on one another for emotional support during stressful periods and for defense against harassment by other group members. In some cases, newcomers may grow strong enough to violate the group's norms with impunity or even to take over the group entirely. Moreland (1978) has investigated some of the ways in which social categorization by newcomers can affect their relationships with one another and with oldtimers.

C.  SOCIALIZATION

Once entry has occurred, the group and the individual begin a period of mutual socialization. During this phase, the group accommodates itself to the individual, who in turn is assimilated into the group. Socialization may be more or less difficult, depending on the amount and type of adjustments that are needed to make the group and the individual compatible with one another. Thus, socialization can vary in length (the amount of time that passes between entry and acceptance), breadth (the number of different dimensions along which accommodation and assimilation take place), and depth (the degree to which affective and cognitive as well as behavioral changes are produced within the group and the individual). In general, the more selective the group and the individual are during investigation, the less assimilation and accommodation are needed during socialization (Etzioni, 1961; Wanous, 1980).

During socialization, the group attempts to provide the newcomer with the knowledge, ability, and motivation that he or she will need to play the role of a full group member (Brim, 1966; Feldman, 1976, 1980, 1981; Schein, 1968, 1971; Van Maanen, 1976, 1978; Van Maanen & Schein, 1979; Wanous, 1980). First, the group must decide what it requires from a full member and communicate these expectations to the newcomer in a clear and consistent manner. Although some newcomers already possess such knowledge because of an earlier reconnaissance of the group or previous experience in similar groups, most newcomers feel a strong need to obtain information about what is expected of them (Louis, 1980; Van Maanen, 1977; Wanous, 1980). Groups communicate this knowledge through formal and informal indoctrination sessions (e.g., Gauron & Rawlings, 1975; Jacobs & Campbell, 1961; Zurcher, 1965, 1970) and through "coaches" who serve as role models (Bartell, 1971; Shuval & Adler, 1980; Strauss, 1959; Weiss, 1977). In addition to accurate information about role requirements, the newcomer also may need to acquire particular skills. These skills may be obtained through a formal training program, apprenticeship to a more experienced group member, or simulation and role-playing experiences. Finally, assimilation cannot proceed unless the newcomer is motivated to behave in the "appropriate" manner. One technique used to increase the newcomer's motivation to fulfill group expectations is debasement, in which the newcomer is forced to give up his or her prior self-image and seek a new one within the context of the group (Van Maanen, 1976; Vaught & Smith, 1980). The group can also use a variety of more conventional social influence techniques to motivate its new members (cf. Etzioni, 1961; Hackman, 1976; Raven & Kruglanski, 1970; Schein, 1980).

The goal of the group during socialization is to make the new member progressively more similar to a full member. Insofar as the new member consistently meets the group's expectations, he or she will elicit higher commitment. If the group's commitment to an individual rises to its acceptance criterion, then it will attempt to make that person a full member. Conversely, the group will become less committed to a new member who fails to meet its expectations. If commitment falls to the group's exit criterion, then the newcomer will be asked to leave, without even having been a full member.

Although individual assimilation occurs during socialization, newcomers should not be viewed as passive recipients of influence. Newcomers also exert pressure on the group to accommodate to their personal needs. In order to produce accommodation, the newcomer must first provide the group with information about his or her needs. In some cases, the group already possesses such information because of earlier recruitment of the newcomer or previous experience with similar individuals. If the group is uninformed about the newcomer's needs and the person feels inhibited about expressing these needs, then he or she may confide in a mentor in the hope that the relevant information will be disseminated throughout the group. In addition to possessing information about the newcomer's needs, the group must also have the requisite skills to fulfill those needs if accommodation is to take place. If these skills are lacking in the group, then the newcomer may try to "train" group members to behave in desirable ways or attempt to bring into the group other newcomers who possess the necessary skills. Finally, accommodation cannot proceed unless the group is motivated to adjust itself to the newcomer's needs. The individual, like the group, can utilize one or more social influence techniques to produce such motivation. Evidence indicates that newcomers can indeed change the groups that they enter (e.g., Fine, 1976; Merei, 1949; Phillips *et al.*, 1951; Ziller & Behringer, 1960).

The goal of the new member during socialization is to induce the group to satisfy his or her personal needs. Insofar as the group meets those needs, it will elicit higher commitment. If the individual's commitment to the group rises to his or her acceptance criterion, then the person will seek to become a full member. Conversely, the new member will become less committed to a group that fails to meet his or her expectations. If commitment falls to the individual's exit criterion, then he or she will leave the group, without ever having been a full member.

Several dimensions of socialization can influence assimilation and accommodation (Van Maanen, 1978; Van Maanen & Schein, 1979). These dimensions include the degree to which socialization is (a) individual versus collective, (b) formal versus informal, (c) sequential versus random, (d) fixed versus variable, (e) serial versus disjunctive, (f) an investiture versus a divestiture, and (g) a tournament versus a contest. As an example, we shall discuss some of the consequences of individual versus collective socialization. Individual socialization is more likely to be used when the skills to be acquired are complex, when there are few opportunities for full membership compared to the number of newcomers, and when collective identity among newcomers is viewed as unimportant (Van Maanen & Schein, 1979).

In general, groups that engage in individual socialization may find the assimilation process somewhat easier than do groups that engage in collective socialization, because the former groups deal with new members one at a time and therefore can exert more control over how they are treated. Newcomers who are socialized by themselves may also be relatively malleable, because they are alone and therefore feel especially vulnerable to group pressure (Heiss & Nash, 1967; Walker, 1973). However, groups that use individual socialization may have particular problems assimilating new members in a consistent manner. Since newcomers in such groups are dealt with one at a time, and often at different points in time, the assimilation process may vary a good deal from one newcomer to another. Over time, this can result in a heterogeneous group whose members differ in important ways. Groups that use collective socialization are less likely to suffer from this problem. Because they deal with several newcomers at any given time, such groups are better able to standardize their assimilation process. Moreover, when newcomers are assimilated together, they sometimes can be used to socialize one another, thereby easing the group's task. The corresponding danger, from the group's perspective, is that a batch of newcomers may coalesce into a subgroup whose structure and dynamics are antithetical to the assimilation process (Becker, 1964; Schein, 1968; Wheeler, 1966). This can make the group's task more difficult and can sometimes lead to drastic changes in the group itself.

Accommodation is generally more difficult for the new member to achieve in groups that use individual rather than collective socialization, because in the former groups newcomers are alone in the socialization struggle. However forceful he or she becomes, a lone newcomer probably will find it difficult to produce much accommodation in the group. In collective socialization groups, accommodation is more easily accomplished. By banding together, newcomers in such groups often can circumvent or openly resist pressure toward assimilation. Moreover, by forcefully and consistently expressing their shared needs, they sometimes can produce sudden and dramatic accommodation within a group (cf. Moscovici, 1976).

### D. ACCEPTANCE

Acceptance, which occurs when the group's and the individual's commitment to one another reach their respective acceptance criteria, marks the passage of the individual from the role of newcomer to that of full member. Groups that utilize a system of continuous entry may also tend to favor continuous acceptance. In these groups, newcomers are allowed to become full members as soon as they reach the group's acceptance criterion. Periodic-entry groups, in contrast, may utilize a system of periodic acceptance, allowing newcomers to become full members only in batches and/or at certain times. These different systems can, as described earlier, affect the degree to which individuals begin their new role occupancy on an equal basis. In continuous-acceptance groups, each full member elicits the same initial level of commitment, regardless of when he or she actually is accepted into the group. Under a system of periodic acceptance, however, some individuals may be ready for their role transition before it is scheduled to occur or before their fellow newcomers have reached the group's acceptance criterion. The former individuals, once they are accepted into the group, will elicit more commitment and perhaps have higher status than their peers who became full members at the same time.

Once an individual has been accepted into the group, he or she no longer is regarded as someone who requires the special attention usually accorded to new members. Many groups, especially those that view newcomers as qualitatively different from oldtimers, mark this role transition by conducting special rites of passage (Feldman, 1977; Louis, 1980; Nuwer, 1978; Schein, 1978; Vaught & Smith, 1980). These rites may be more or less formal and may involve a variety of behaviors on the part of the group. Thus, the group may share valuable material resources with the individual, provide the individual with access to special information that was previously hidden, include the individual in informal cliques, relax its vigilance of the individual's behavior, and bestow increased responsibilities on the individual.

Occasionally, the group may try to accept an individual as a full member before he or she feels ready to undergo the role transition. For example, newcomers are sometimes fearful about their ability to function effectively as full members, especially if they feel that they entered the group under false pretenses (cf. Breakwell, 1979). In these cases, the group may adopt a variety of tactics to reassure newcomers about their readiness, such as downplaying the importance of the role transition and stressing the newcomers' similarity to other full members (and/or dissimilarity to other newcomers). These tactics assume, of course, that the newcomers are already highly committed to the group and want to become full members. If someone has serious doubts about the ability of the group to satisfy his or her personal needs, then acceptance will be delayed until the group can somehow manage to elicit greater commitment from the individual.

Acceptance cannot occur unless newcomers also relabel themselves as full members. Once the individual's commitment to the group reaches his or her acceptance criterion, the newcomer will want to become an "insider" and be treated like other oldtimers in the group. If the group is amenable to this role transition, then acceptance will take place. Individuals often mark acceptance by conducting a personal rite of passage. Such an event involves affective, cognitive, or behavioral changes that bring the individual closer to other oldtimers and more distant from other newcomers (Friendly & Glucksberg, 1970; Tannenbaum & McCleod, 1967; Ziller, 1965; Zurcher, 1965). Affective changes include feelings of solidarity with oldtimers, pride about the group's past accomplishments, and concern regarding the group's future welfare. Cognitive changes include increased ingroup–outgroup discrimination, self-perception as a group member, and adoption of the group's frame of reference. Finally, behavioral changes include expressions of enthusiasm for the group's activities, willingness to undertake unpleasant tasks on behalf of the group, and active efforts to promote the group among outsiders.

It is quite common, especially in highly attractive groups that admit few people to full membership, for newcomers to seek acceptance before the group is ready for this transition. The individual may try to persuade the group that he or she should become a full member or offer the group special inducements for acceptance. Sometimes, newcomers gain acceptance by engaging in extreme forms of behavior that serve to dramatize their commitment to the group (cf. Van Maanen, 1976). Such tactics probably only work if the group is relatively committed to the individual and is at least open to the idea of accepting him or her as a full member. If the group is very uncertain about the ability of the individual to make appropriate contributions to the attainment of group goals, then the newcomer is unlikely to be able to force acceptance, regardless of the tactics he or she employs.

E. MAINTENANCE

Once acceptance has occurred, a period of maintenance begins. During maintenance, feelings of commitment between the group and the individual are at their highest levels. The individual is regarded as an important member of the group, and the group is regarded as a central part of the individual's life. Both parties, therefore, are motivated to maintain their relationship and to make it more rewarding if possible (cf. Huesmann & Levinger, 1976; Levinger & Huesmann, 1980).

The major way in which the group and the individual increase the rewardingness of their relationship during maintenance is by redefining the full member's role within the group. As a result, there tends to be more role differentiation during maintenance than during other phases of group membership. Roles are redefined through a process of role negotiation between the group and the individual. The group tries to define a special role for each full member that maximizes his or her contributions to group goal attainment and minimizes the group's obligations to the individual. In contrast, each full member tries to define his or her role so as to maximize the satisfaction of personal needs and minimize obligations to the group

The process of role negotiation has often been discussed in the context of group leadership (cf. Caine, 1976; Graen & Cashman, 1975; Hollander, 1978, 1980). For example, Hollander's "transactional" theory assumes that leadership involves an exchange relationship between the group and the individual. The group awards a leader the perquisites associated with high status, treats him or her with respect, and allows the leader to exert power within the group. In exchange, the leader helps to set realistic goals for the group, facilitates goal attainment, and arbitrates conflicts among group members. The transactional approach also assumes that the leader's role is constantly being redefined by both the group and the individual. As circumstances change, the perceived fairness of the social exchange between the group and its leader may be altered. Insofar as either party regards their relationship as unfair, negotiation will occur to redefine the leader's role.

Although leadership roles are obviously important, the group and the individual can negotiate about other roles as well. From the group's perspective, role negotiation begins with a general assessment of the kinds of roles that would maximize the attainment of group goals. These roles, which can vary widely along such dimensions as importance, formality, and status, typically center around task and social–emotional issues (e.g., Bales, 1958; Benne & Sheats, 1948; Cloyd, 1964). Some particularly interesting roles involve socialization activities (Wallace, 1964). Thus, groups often have special "recruiters" who identify, evaluate, and attract desirable prospective members; "trainers" who socialize new members; "retrainers" who resocialize marginal members; and "trackers" who keep in touch with ex-members and solicit their continued support.

Once the group has decided that a particular role needs to be filled, it must select one of its full members to occupy that role. This selection requires a consideration of several factors, including (a) how well each person would perform the role, (b) what rewards each person would demand in exchange for role performance, and (c) the extent to which each person's contributions to group goal attainment would be greater in the new role than in his or her current role. In general, the group will view a full member as an attractive candidate for role occupancy insofar as that person is expected to perform the role well, ask little from the group in return, and increase his or her contribution to the attainment of group goals.

Finally, the group must somehow move its favorite candidate into the selected role. If the individual sees that role as instrumental to the satisfaction of his or her personal needs, then this task can be relatively easy. However, the individual may balk at accepting a new role if the role that he or she currently occupies (or wishes to occupy) seems more rewarding than the new one. When this happens, the group can try one or more of the usual social influence techniques to get the person to perform the new role. If these tactics fail, then the group may be forced to use more subtle methods. For example, the group may try to make the individual's preferred role seem less rewarding, so that he or she will regard the selected role as more rewarding. If the person desires to remain in his or her current role, then the group can criticize the individual's role performance or make the role more demanding than it was in the past. If the individual wishes to shift to a role other than the selected one, then the group can increase the obligations and/or decrease the benefits of the individual's preferred role. In some cases, the group may hurriedly fill that role with another occupant, so that the individual cannot shift to it. Finally, the group can subtly shape the individual's behavior so that it becomes increasingly congruent with the selected role and incongruent with other roles. As the person behaves more like an occupant of the selected role, he or she will come to internalize that role and "freely" accept it (cf. Haney, Banks, & Zimbardo, 1973).

The amount of pressure that the group exerts on a person to perform a role probably depends on the relative importance of the role for the group and the number of other full members who are attractive candidates for role occupancy. If its attempts to move the individual into the new role are unsuccessful, then the group may redefine the role so that it is more desirable to the person, find another candidate for the role, or abandon the role altogether.

The group's commitment to a full member depends primarily on the rewardingness of his or her current role performance. To the extent that a person fails to fulfill role expectations, he or she will elicit less commitment. When commitment falls to the group's decision criterion for the individual's current role, the group will search for another and less demanding role for the person that is still commensurate with full membership. If such a role is found, then the group will try to move the individual into it. If the individual is recalcitrant, or no suitable new role can be found, then commitment will fall to the group's general divergence criterion and the person will be relabelled as a marginal member.

From the perspective of the individual, role negotiation begins with a general assessment of the roles that would maximize the satisfaction of personal needs. The individual may consider roles that already are occupied by other full members, roles that traditionally have existed in the group but are currently unoccupied, or new roles (cf. Benne & Sheats, 1948). Once the individual has identified alternative roles, he or she must next decide which role to try to occupy. This decision requires a consideration of such factors as (a) how well the individual could perform the various roles, (b) what demands the group would make regarding each role, and (c) the extent to which the group's contributions to personal need satisfaction would be greater in the new role than in the person's current role. When the person considers a role that is already occupied, he or she will also have to take into account the probability of evicting the current occupant and the costs associated with that eviction. The individual will generally regard a new role as attractive insofar as he or she seems likely to perform it well, the role involves minimal demands, and the role is likely to increase the satisfaction of personal needs.

Finally, the individual must find a way to move into his or her preferred role. If the group views the role as instrumental to the attainment of its goals and the individual as a promising role occupant, then this task can be relatively easy. However, the group may not want the individual to occupy the role for a variety of reasons, including a desire for the person to continue performing his or her current role and a hesitancy to evict the present occupant of the individual's preferred role. When that happens, the individual can employ a variety of conventional social influence techniques to convince the group to allow occupancy of the preferred role. If these tactics fail, then the person may have to resort to other methods. For example, the individual may make his or her current role performance less rewarding by performing poorly or by demanding increased resources in exchange for role performance. The individual can also create or participate in cliques that allow the person to perform a variant of his or her preferred role. In some cases, these cliques may be powerful enough to thrust the individual into the role that he or she prefers in the larger group.

In seeking to occupy a new role, the amount of pressure that the individual exerts on the group probably depends on the relative importance of that role for the person and the extent to which the same or similar roles are available in other groups that the individual currently belongs to or might easily join. If the individual's attempts to move into the new role are unsuccessful, then he or she may redefine the role in ways that make it seem more desirable to the group, seek another group in which the same or a similar role could be performed, or abandon the role altogether.

A full member's commitment to the group depends primarily on the rewardingness of his or her special role. To the extent that the role is unrewarding, the individual will become less committed to the group. When commitment falls to the individual's decision criterion for his or her current role, the person will search for another and less demanding role that is still commensurate with full membership. If such a role is found, then the individual will try to move into it. If the group resists, or no suitable new role can be found, then commitment will fall to the individual's general divergence criterion and the person will relabel himself or herself as a marginal member.

F.  DIVERGENCE

The third role transition in the relationship between the group and the individual is divergence, which marks the passage of the individual from the role of full member to that of marginal member. Divergence occurs when the group's and the individual's commitment to one another reach their respective divergence criteria. Depending on the circumstances under which it occurs, divergence may be either expected or unexpected by the group and the individual. In some groups (e.g., Boy/Girl Scouts), the maintenance phase has a predetermined, or normative, length. Since no one is expected to remain a full member of such a group indefinitely, divergence is generally regarded as the beginning of a natural separation between the group and the individual. In other groups, however, the maintenance phase has no established length and is expected (or hoped) to last indefinitely. Divergence in these kinds of groups is generally regarded as a troubling development in the relationship between the group and the individual. (For discussions of divergence in intimate dyadic relationships, see Duck [1982] and Edwards & Saunders [1981].)

*Expected divergence* is a common phenomenon, at least in open groups, but relatively little research has been done on it. Instead, the attention of most investigators has been captured by *unexpected divergence* and the group's labeling of diverging individuals as deviates. Although labeling theory represents an important development in the sociology of deviance, it can be criticized on several grounds (see Birenbaum & Sagarin, 1976; and Gibbs & Erickson, 1975). One of the most important criticisms is that labeling theorists have not clearly specified the psychological processes that underlie the labeling decision (Orcutt, 1973). Therefore, although the labeling perspective may shed light on selected aspects of unexpected divergence (Brinkerhoff & Burke, 1980), it does not provide an adequate explanation of this role transition.

A more promising approach can be found in attribution theory. As suggested in Levine's (1980) model of reactions to deviance, the group uses information about a deviating individual's past and current behavior, and the social context in which that behavior occurs, to make inferences about his or her internal dispositions. These attributed dispositions, in turn, are used to assess the individual's probable present and future impact on the attainment of group goals (Zander, 1976). Finally, the individual's presumed impact on goal attainment determines the group's level of commitment. Following this line of reasoning, we would suggest that the probability of a dispositional attribution for deviance will vary positively with such factors as the extremity and consistency of the deviance and the presence of external inhibiting causes for the deviant act. Holding constant the importance of the dimension(s) on which the deviance occurs, the more the group believes that deviance is internally caused, the more likely the group is to view such behavior as a threat to goal attainment, and the lower will be the group's commitment to the individual. When the group's commitment to the person falls below its divergence criterion, the person will be relabeled as a marginal member. Thus, a crucial factor affecting divergence may be whether the perceived locus of causality for deviance is external, and hence relatively easy to change, or internal, and hence difficult or impossible to alter (cf. Orcutt, 1973).

Several other variables may also influence the group's tendency to label an individual as a marginal member. One of the most important of these is the person's status within the group (see Levine, 1980; Ridgeway, 1978, 1981). According to Wahrman (1970), the higher a person's status, the less likely he or she is to be labeled as a deviate. This resistance to defining a high-status person as a deviate stems from group members' desire to maintain cognitive consistency about high-status individuals and to believe that the group bestows status wisely (cf. Hollander & Willis, 1967). Another important variable is the degree to which full members resist pressures to conformity. The group is unlikely to label an individual as a marginal member until it has tried and failed to maintain its commitment to the person at a level above the divergence criterion. Attempts to influence a person to conform more closely to group expectations can involve one or more of the social influence processes discussed in previous sections. The more full members resist group pressures to conform, the more likely they are to be relabeled as marginal members, because their behavior will be attributed more strongly to dispositional factors.

After relabeling has occurred, the group typically communicates its decision to the individual in some way. This communication may be more or less explicit, depending on such factors as the type of expectation (behavioral, cognitive, or affective) that has been violated, the availability of effective resocialization techniques to deal with the individual, the ease with which he or she can be replaced as a group member, and so on. Groups may be more likely to emphasize their dissatisfaction with a marginal member when (a) deviance occurs on role-specific dimensions, (b) effective resocialization techniques are readily available, and (c) the deviate can be replaced relatively easily. In general, the techniques that the group uses to mark divergence are mirror images of those used to mark acceptance. Thus, the group may refuse to share valuable material resources with the individual, withhold special information, exclude the person from informal cliques, and so on.

Divergence also involves the individual relabeling himself or herself as a marginal member of the group. From the viewpoint of the individual, divergence is often an expected event that signifies a growing maturity and freedom from the group. Once again, however, most research has focused on unexpected divergence. There are several reasons why people might decide to relabel themselves as deviates. From an attributional perspective, full members use information about a group's past and current behavior, as well as the social context in which that behavior occurs, to make inferences about group members' internal dispositions. These attributed dispositions, in turn, are used to assess the group's probable present and future impact on the satisfaction of personal needs. Finally, the group's presumed impact on need satisfaction determines the individual's level of commitment to it. If the group's failure to satisfy personal needs is extreme and consistent and occurs in the presence of external inhibiting causes, the individual will view this behavior as internally caused and as a serious threat to need satisfaction. Such a perception will decrease the individual's commitment to the group. When the person's commitment to the group falls below his or her divergence criterion, the person will relabel himself or herself as a marginal member.

People might also relabel themselves as marginal members because they feel rejected by other group members or lack the ability or motivation to fulfill the group's expectations. Individual divergence that stems from feelings of rejection has been described by labeling theorists as "secondary deviation": People who are labeled as deviates internalize this label and then modify their behavior accordingly (Brinkerhoff & Burke, 1980). Of course, it is also possible that rejected individuals will not internalize the deviant label, but will nevertheless feel alientated from their rejectors, if only because they have been ''misperceived.'' The lack of ability or motivation to fulfill group expectations might lead to two different types of individual divergence. The individual may accept the legitimacy of group expectations but seek to avoid them, or may feel that group expectations are illegitimate and should be altered.

People are unlikely to label themselves as marginal members until they have tried and failed to maintain their commitment to the group at a level above their divergence criterion. If divergence stems from the perception that the group ought to be changed, then the individual can use one or more of the usual social influence techniques to try to alter the group. After self-relabeling has occurred, the individual may or may not communicate the new self-image to the group, depending on several variables. The individual may be inhibited, for example, by a fear that the group will attempt to coerce him or her back into the fold, or by a concern that group members will be hurt by the individual's rejection of them. Also, the dimension(s) along which the group has deviated from the individual's expectations, the availability of resocialization techniques that might be used to alter the group, and the ease with which alternate group memberships could be obtained may influence the probability that the individual will communicate his or her marginality to the group. As in the case of the group, the techniques that the individual uses to mark divergence are often mirror images of those used to mark acceptance.

## G. RESOCIALIZATION

Following divergence, the group and the individual undergo a period of resocialization. The nature of resocialization depends partly on the type of divergence that preceded it. In cases of expected divergence, the individual typically cannot reoccupy the role of a full group member. Instead, both the group and the individual use the resocialization phase to prepare for the person's anticipated exit from the group and subsequent role as an ex-member. In cases of unexpected divergence, however, resocialization involves attempts to return to maintenance. Both the group and the individual try to provide one another with the knowledge, ability, and motivation necessary to make their relationship satisfactory once again. As with socialization, this kind of resocialization may be more or less difficult, depending on the amount and type of readjustment necessary to raise the group's and the individual's commitment above their respective divergence criteria.[6]

One important determinant of resocialization efforts on the part of the group is whether the group is open or closed (Ziller, 1965). As mentioned earlier, open

---

[6]Some groups, such as prisons or mental institutions, are devoted entirely to resocializing individuals who have been expelled from other groups (e.g., Goffman, 1961; Wheeler, 1966). Specialized groups also exist for recruitment (e.g., employment agencies), socialization (e.g., schools), and remembrance (e.g., alumni associations).

groups have relatively frequent membership changes, whereas closed groups have a more stable composition. It seems likely that resocialization is less often necessary in closed than in open groups, because members' perceived external options are lower in closed groups. Moreover, should resocialization become necessary, it probably will be easier and more effective in closed than in open groups. Ziller points out that social power in closed groups depends primarily on interpersonal relationships among members, whereas power in open groups is usually based on relationships between individuals and the group as a whole. In most instances, interpersonal relationships among group members probably will prove to be more effective in reassimilating an errant individual than will the relationship between the individual and the group as a whole. This notion is consistent with Ziller's suggestion that members of closed groups have more power over one another than do members of open groups because of their higher probability of future interaction.

Several additional variables can also influence the group's attempts to resocialize a marginal member. For example, the individual's apparent reason for behaving inappropriately may be important. A person who fails to meet the group's expectations because of lack of motivation probably will be subjected to more intensive resocialization efforts than one who fails to meet those expectations because he or she lacks the necessary ability or knowledge (Brim, 1966; Kipnis, 1976). Other variables that may influence the group's efforts to reassimilate a marginal member include the perceived difficulty of replacing the individual, the person's prior status within the group, and the sanctions and countersanctions available to the group and the individual, respectively.

The group's commitment to a marginal member can either rise or fall during resocialization, depending on whether the individual is seen as facilitating or inhibiting the attainment of group goals. In the former case, commitment may rise above the group's divergence criterion once again. When that happens, the marginal member will undergo a special role transition, which can be termed *convergence,* and will be relabeled again as a full member of the group. It is interesting that, of all the decision criteria identified in our model, only the divergence criterion produces a change in membership status when it is crossed from either above (maintenance) or below (resocialization).

Although an individual can move from full to marginal membership in the group and vice versa, these two role transitions may differ in important ways. One difference involves the publicity given to each event by the group. In many groups, the rite of passage that signals a loss of full membership is more public and dramatic than the one that marks its recovery. Thus, even though a person has been allowed back into the fold, the stigma associated with his or her former marginality may not be completely erased. A second difference between divergence and convergence involves the effect of previous role transitions on the probability of future role occupancy. The more frequently an individual has moved between maintenance and resocialization, the more likely the group is to lose commitment when that person is in the maintenance phase and the less likely it is to gain commitment when he or she is in the resocialization phase. Of course, the group's commitment to an individual can consistently fall rather than rise during resocialization. If commitment falls to the group's exit criterion, then the individual will be relabeled as an ex-member.

During resocialization, the individual exerts pressure on the group to reaccommodate itself to his or her needs. The effectiveness of the individual's efforts can be influenced by whether the group is open or closed. As Ziller (1965) has suggested, the role of potential egressor occurs only in open groups, and the power of such individuals is contingent upon such factors as how much longer they will be group members, the likelihood that they will eventually be replaced by others, and the attractiveness of the group that they are expected to join. This power may be manifested in many ways, such as flouting group expectations with impunity, denying the group the benefit of personal skills and knowledge, threatening the group's image by signaling that group membership is no longer valued, and revealing negative aspects of the group to outsiders. If an individual has enough power, then he or she may be able to force the group to reaccommodate.

An individual's efforts to resocialize the group can also be influenced by other factors. One such factor is the group's apparent reason for behaving inappropriately. A group that fails to meet individual expectations because of a lack of motivation will usually be subjected to more intensive resocialization efforts than one that fails to meet expectations because it lacks the necessary ability or knowledge. Additional variables that may affect the individual's efforts to reaccommodate the group include the person's behavioral style, prior status within the group, chances of joining another group, and the sanctions available to the person and the group.

An individual's commitment to the group can either rise or fall during resocialization, depending on whether the group is able to satisfy personal needs. If commitment rises to the individual's divergence criterion, then he or she will attempt to become a full member once again. However, because of the asymmetrical rites of passage that mark divergence and convergence, the individual may feel somewhat estranged from other members even after a return to full membership. Also, the more frequently an individual has undergone divergence and convergence, the more likely that person is to seek divergence when in the maintenance phase and the less likely he or she is to seek convergence when in the resocialization phase. If commitment to the group falls to the exit criterion, then the individual will relabel himself or herself as an ex-member.

## H.  EXIT

Exit is more complicated than other role transitions, because it can occur in several phases of group membership. During resocialization, exit involves a transition from marginal member to ex-member that occurs when the group's commitment to the individual and the individual's commitment to the group fall below their respective exit criteria. Exit can also occur during the investigation or socialization phase of group membership if the group's and the individual's commitment to one another fall too low. In these cases, the individual will make a special role transition from prospective or new member directly to ex-member, without ever having become a full member or passing through the resocialization phase. Obviously, the exit process may differ for prospective, new, and marginal members. Our discussion of exit will focus on the departure of marginal members from the group, since this form of exit has received the most research attention.[7]

Exit for the group is preceded by a period of declining commitment to the individual. Zander (1976) has discussed several factors that can influence a group's decision to remove a marginal member. These include the quality of the person's most recent contributions to the attainment of group goals and the likelihood that he or she will make valuable contributions in the future. If the group is doing poorly, then it will be more likely to expel the individual, especially if group cohesiveness is relatively high. Finally, the group must consider the potential harm that both it and the individual might suffer if exit occurs.

Once the group has decided to remove a marginal member, it must next determine how to terminate the individual's membership. Several rites of passage may be used to mark this role transition, ranging from covert techniques that save face for the individual and reduce the probability that he or she will retaliate against the group to more overt techniques that are designed to humiliate the marginal member publicly. Covert rites of passage include making secret arrangements for the individual to be recruited by another group, eliminating the individual's duties within the group, allowing the individual to resign quietly from the group, and giving the individual a "grace period" before he or she must depart. Overt rites of passage often involve the use of informal social pressure to force a person out of the group (cf. Brinkerhoff & Burke, 1980). The group may also stage a public demonstration of its lack of regard for the marginal member and its desire for his or her exit. For example, Garfinkel (1956) has discussed "status degradation ceremonies," in which the identities of marginal members

---

[7]It is important to note that exit can occur during any of the first four membership phases even though the group's and the individual's commitment levels are above their respective exit criteria. The group may be subjected to various economic and social pressures that make it less capable of retaining a particular member. Similarly, illness, relocation, or membership in other groups can force an individual to leave the group. When external factors force someone to depart before exit would normally occur, the person and the group will experience sadness in direct proportion to their mutual commitment. This sadness is often expressed through positive rites of passage, such as going-away parties, that give the group and the individual a chance to express their positive regard for one another.

are ritually destroyed and those members are placed symbolically (and often physically) outside of the group.

There are often cases in which a group would like someone to leave but he or she would prefer to stay. Initially, the group may feel flattered about the person's continued commitment and perhaps a little chagrined that exit has become necessary. These feelings will lead the group to begin with relatively gentle and covert exit techniques. Continued resistance on the part of the individual, however, will force the group to use progressively stronger measures. In extreme cases, the individual may have to be physically ejected from the group.

Exit can have a variety of consequences for the group. These depend in part on whether the role transition is initiated by the group or the individual. In the former case, exit may create feelings of solidarity among group members, because they have reaffirmed group norms and have worked together to expel the marginal member (cf. Coser, 1956). The group may also gain respect from outsiders, because of its proved intolerance of deviance. In contrast, when exit is initiated by the individual, group morale may suffer and the group may acquire an unfavorable public image because of its apparent inability to retain members. Other consequences of exit arise from the simple fact that the group has lost one of its members. These consequences can involve either negative or positive changes in the group (cf. Price, 1977; Staw, 1980; Steers & Mowday, 1981; Ziller, 1965). Negative changes include costs associated with selecting, recruiting, and training replacements for the marginal member and disruptions in the group's activities. Positive changes include higher average levels of group performance, reductions in intragroup conflicts associated with the presence of the marginal member, expectations of increased upward mobility within the group, and improved adaptation of the group to its environment.

Exit for the individual is preceded by a period of declining commitment to the group (e.g., Levinger, 1976; Porter, Steers, Mowday, & Boulian, 1974; Tinto, 1975) caused by the inability of the group to meet the person's expectations (cf. Albrecht & Kunz, 1980; Hom & Hulin, 1981; Porter & Steers, 1973; Ross & Zander, 1957; Sagi et al., 1955; Wanous, 1980). Specific factors that can prompt an individual to leave a group include the person's recent experiences in the group, relationships with other group members, likelihood of obtaining more satisfactory membership in some other group, and level of self-esteem and personal confidence (Bouma, 1980; Galanter, 1980; Knoke, 1981; Martin & Hunt, 1980; Mobley, Hand, Meglino, & Griffeth, 1979; Pascarella & Terenzini, 1979; Roozen, 1980; Weiss, 1963). Like the group, the individual must also consider the potential costs associated with the loss of membership.

Once a marginal member has decided to terminate his or her membership in a group, the person must next determine how to accomplish this role transition (cf. Duck, 1982). The person may gradually disengage from the group by failing to participate in its activities and telling no one about the intended departure.

Such tactics are often chosen because the individual either does not want to deal with the strong emotions that can accompany exit or cares very little about the group. Sometimes, a marginal member will tell a few close friends in the group that he or she is leaving, or simply notify the group leader of the impending departure. Finally, an individual who is angry at the group may conduct a public rite of passage by denouncing the group, repudiating his or her prior membership, and discouraging other people from joining. In extreme cases, the individual may band together with other apostates to try to destroy the group (Birenbaum & Sagarin, 1976).

There are, of course, instances in which an individual wants to leave the group, but it would like him or her to stay. At first, the individual may feel flattered about the group's interest and perhaps embarrassed about wanting to leave. If the group persists in its efforts to retain the individual, then he or she may grow angry and arrange to leave in a more dramatic fashion.

Exit can be very stressful for the individual, especially when he or she had a long and relatively rewarding relationship with the group and did not want to leave it (cf. Little, 1976; Weiss, 1976). Negative consequences associated with this type of exit include a loss of self-esteem and/or change in personal identity, feelings of powerlessness, a sense of alienation, and possible disruptions of other relationships and activities. In trying to cope with these and related problems, the individual may distort his or her attributions for the exit (Newman & Langer, 1981; Steers & Mowday, 1981), rely on the emotional support of family and friends (Schlossberg & Leibowitz, 1980), join new groups (Roozen, 1980; Weiss, 1963), or focus on the positive aspects of being an ex-member of the group. Indeed, exit can sometimes benefit the individual, especially if he or she initiated the role transition (cf. Little, 1976; Muchinsky & Morrow, 1980). Some of the possible positive consequences of exit include a decrease in the tension associated with being a marginal group member and the prospect of new and more rewarding memberships in other groups.

## I.  REMEMBRANCE

The relationship between the group and the individual ends with a period of remembrance. Remembrance begins with exit and ends when the individual and the group pass completely out of each other's awareness and thereby lose all feelings of commitment to one another. Remembrance may be relatively brief, or it may last almost indefinitely, depending on such factors as the amount of time that the individual spent within the group, the maximum level of commitment that the group and the individual elicited from one another during their relationship, and the degree to which the group and the individual regarded one another as unique.

During remembrance, the group arrives at some consensus about how much the individual contributed to the group's goals while he or she was a member.

This *retrospective evaluation* is often the major determinant of the group's commitment to the ex-member. Insofar as the group believes that the individual made valuable contributions, it will feel relatively committed to him or her. In gratitude for past services, the group may reward the individual with material (e.g., goods, money) and/or psychological (e.g., love, respect) benefits.

If the group's commitment to the individual is high enough, then it may even try to bring that person back into the group. Although an ex-member usually cannot re-enter a group, this can happen under special conditions. A more common tactic is to increase the individual's informal involvement in group activities. For example, an ex-member may be asked to train new members, rehabilitate marginal members, advise the group regarding how to attain its goals, or aid in acquiring new resources for the group. If ex-members are unable or unwilling to become actively involved with the group, then such persons may simply be used (with or without their permission) as models for appropriate behavior.

Of course, groups do not always want to strengthen their associations with ex-members. If the individual made few contributions to the group's goals while he or she was a member, then the group will not feel committed to the person and may try to prevent his or her active involvement in group activities. In addition, the group may refuse to provide benefits to which the person would otherwise be entitled and may use the person as a role model for inappropriate behavior.

The group's commitment to the individual during remembrance is determined not only by that person's previous contributions, but also by his or her current activities outside the group. Insofar as an ex-member is identified by other people as having been in the group, he or she can give the group pride and prestige through later personal success (cf. Richardson & Cialdini, 1981). Conversely, an ex-member who later suffers personal failure can cause the group shame and disgrace. Thus, even though ex-members are no longer actively involved with the group, they can still contribute indirectly to the attainment of its goals.

Because individuals can indirectly affect a group through their prior association with it, many groups conduct an *ongoing evaluation,* as well as a retrospective evaluation, of their ex-members. In making an ongoing evaluation, groups take into account at least three factors. The first factor concerns the circumstances surrounding the individual's exit. Thus, an individual can officially "graduate" from the group (in the sense that exit is expected and marks the conclusion of a successful relationship), or the person can leave prematurely. In the latter case, the decision to exit can be made primarily by the group, or by the individual, or can be shared equally by both parties (Ziller, 1965). A second factor that can affect a group's ongoing evaluation of an ex-member is the person's success subsequent to exit. Finally, the group's appraisal of its own success since exit also may be important.

The outcome of an ongoing evaluation of an ex-member has implications for the group's commitment to that person. For example, if an individual graduated from the group and has been successful since exit, while the group has been unsuccessful, then the group will feel highly committed to the person and will publicize the fact that he or she once was a member. In contrast, if an individual graduated from the group and has been unsuccessful since exit, while the group has been successful, then the group will feel little commitment to the person and will try to suppress the knowledge of his or her prior membership.

As time passes and the individual becomes less salient to the group, he or she will pass into the group's tradition. At first, the group may tell stories or jokes that provide didactic examples of the person's appropriate/inappropriate behavior and its outcomes (cf. Glaser & Strauss, 1971). Eventually, the details of these stories will be leveled and sharpened, and the true identity of the main character may be forgotten. The most important long-term impact of the individual on the group usually involves changes in the group's expectations for other members. If an individual exhibited exemplary behavior when he or she was in the group, then that person's departure may cause the group to raise its expectations for current and future members. Conversely, individuals who consistently failed to please the group during their (presumably short) period of membership may cause the group to lower its expectations for other members.

For the individual, remembrance is a time to reflect on the degree to which group membership satisfied personal needs. This retrospective evaluation is often the major determinant of the ex-member's commitment to the group. Insofar as the individual believes that the group made valuable contributions to need satisfaction, he or she will feel relatively committed to it. To repay the group, an ex-member may offer material (e.g., goods, money) and/or psychological (e.g., friendship, advocacy) support. If commitment to the group is high, then the individual may try to renew his or her involvement in it. This can involve efforts to re-enter the group, informal participation in the group's current activities, enrollment in some type of alumni association (Wheeler, 1966; Ziller, 1965), vicarious membership in the group through friends or relatives, or membership in a similar type of group (Bouma, 1980; Weiss, 1963).

Naturally, people do not always want to strengthen their associations with groups to which they formerly belonged. If the individual feels that the group did not contribute adequately to the satisfaction of personal needs, then commitment to the group will be relatively low. This lack of commitment can cause an ex-member to curtail support to the group. Ex-members who are expelled from a group may also band together in a new group, in which they seek either (a) to rehabilitate themselves so that they will be allowed to rejoin the original group or (b) to alter the norms of the original group, and in extreme cases to destroy it, so that they will no longer be defined as deviates (Birenbaum & Sagarin, 1976). The latter goal, which involves confronting and altering group norms, can also be adopted by groups of ex-members who resigned, rather than were expelled, from the original group (Shupe, Spielmann, & Stigall, 1977).

During remembrance, the individual may also engage in an ongoing evaluation of the former group, periodically monitoring its successes and failures. Insofar as other people identify an individual as having once been in the group, he or she can derive reflected glory or shame from the public image that the group projects (cf. Richardson & Cialdini, 1981). Prior membership in a successful group, for example, can sometimes help an individual to acquire a new job, additional friends, or entrance into other more exclusive groups. In contrast, an ex-member of a failing group may suffer reduced chances for happiness and success. Identification with the group can thus affect the degree to which an individual is able to satisfy his or her needs, even though that person is no longer a group member (Wheeler, 1966).

Once again, the circumstances associated with the individual's departure from the group, as well as the person's and the group's subsequent success, can affect the individual's commitment to the group. For example, individual commitment is likely to be high when the person graduated from the group and has been unsuccessful since exit, while the group has been successful. In contrast, individual commitment is likely to be low when the person graduated from the group and since has been successful, while the group has been unsuccessful.

As time passes and the group becomes less salient to the individual, the group is gradually incorporated into personal reminiscences. Initially, the individual will recall particular characteristics of other members and specific experiences within the group. Eventually, such memories will become less clear cut and may be distorted in various ways (cf. Duck, 1982; Howard & Rothbart, 1980; Messé, Buldain, & Watts, 1981; Ross, McFarland, & Fletcher, 1981; Steers & Mowday, 1981). General changes in an ex-member's self-concept may also occur as a function of his or her prior group membership (Jackson, 1981; Ziller, 1964). Probably the most important long-term effect of the group on the individual is the alteration of his or her expectations for other groups. If the group was extremely satisfying to the individual, then expectations will increase for other groups that he or she currently belongs to or might join. Conversely, a group that consistently failed to satisfy the individual's needs may cause that person to lower his or her expectations for other groups.

## IV. Conclusions

In this article we have described a model of socialization in small groups. The model assumes that groups and individuals exert reciprocal influence on one another and experience important temporal changes during their relationship together. Three major psychological processes, each of which can be viewed from the perspectives of both the group and the individual, operate within the model. First, the group and the individual engage in an ongoing *evaluation* of the rewardingness of their own and alternative relationships. On the basis of these evaluations, feelings of *commitment* develop between the group and the individual. Levels of commitment change in systematic ways over time, rising or falling to previously established decision criteria. When a decision criterion is reached, a *role transition* takes place. The individual enters a new phase of group membership, and the relationship between the group and the individual changes. Evaluation proceeds, often along different dimensions, producing further changes in commitment and subsequent role transitions. In this way, the individual passes through five consecutive phases of group membership (investigation, socialization, maintenance, resocialization, remembrance), separated by four role transitions (entry, acceptance, divergence, exit).

The model has several advantages as a means of conceptualizing group processes. First, it provides a useful framework for organizing and integrating research from different fields, including social, developmental, and organizational psychology; sociology; and anthropology. Second, the model raises a number of interesting questions that have been neglected by researchers interested in small groups. For example, our approach suggests that role transitions in small groups are quite important, but these transitions have received virtually no research attention. Commitment disequilibrium and its effects also have been neglected, despite their potential importance. Finally, the model offers a fresh perspective on several issues of current interest to group researchers. One such issue is minority influence, or innovation. We have recently used the model to analyze how changes in the relationship between a group and its members can influence various aspects of innovation, including the factors that motivate individuals to produce change, the kinds of influence techniques that they use, and the circumstances under which innovation efforts are successful (Levine & Moreland, 1982). Clearly, the model also would be useful in analyzing majority influence, or social control.

In formulating the model, we have focused on small, autonomous, voluntary groups, because these groups are quite common and have been studied extensively by social psychologists. We believe, however, that the socialization processes we have identified are also relevant in other contexts. Socialization occurs in large organizations and dyadic relationships, as well as in small groups. In addition, socialization also takes place in non-autonomous groups and affects individuals whose group membership is involuntary. In all of these cases, there is reason to believe that people evaluate one another, experience feelings of commitment as a result, and undergo role transitions when commitment reaches a decision criterion. Moreover, temporal changes in these relationships may follow a sequence similar to that described in our model. If so, the five phases and four role transitions that we have posited may be applicable to a broad range of social relationships.

In discussing socialization in small groups, we have offered a number of general and specific hypotheses. Clearly, these hypotheses need to be empirically tested. Longitudinal studies of natural groups are essential for evaluating many of our ideas. In addition, valuable information can be obtained from cross-sectional studies of natural groups and from laboratory experiments. Laboratory experiments, for example, may involve observations of ad hoc groups that meet several times or natural groups whose members interact under controlled conditions. Finally, retrospective reports and computer simulations may also provide useful information about group socialization (cf. Levinger, 1980).

We are currently conducting both field and laboratory studies designed to test some of the hypotheses presented in this article. Data obtained in these investigations will no doubt suggest modifications of our model. In an important sense, however, the validity of specific aspects of the model is less important than the general issues raised by the group socialization perspective. Most of the research on small groups has ignored the fact that real groups often exist for long periods of time and that important temporal changes occur in the relationship between groups and their members. Unless these changes and the psychological processes that give rise to them receive explicit theoretical and empirical attention, social psychologists are unlikely to achieve an adequate understanding of group dynamics.

## ACKNOWLEDGMENT

We would like to thank the following colleagues for their helpful comments on an earlier draft of this article: William Francis, Mark Pavelchak, Janet Schofield, Paul Sweeney, Richard Willis, Robert Zajonc, and Alvin Zander. Also, thanks are extended to Deborah Connell for help in preparing the manuscript.

## REFERENCES

Albrecht, S. L., & Kunz, P. R. The decision to divorce: A social exchange perspective. *Journal of Divorce*, 1980, **3**, 319–337.

Allen, V. L. Situational factors in conformity. In L. Berkowitz (Ed.), *Advances in experimental social psychology* (Vol. 2). New York: Academic Press, 1965. Pp. 133–175.

Altman, I., & Taylor, D. A. *Social penetration: The development of interpersonal relationships.* New York: Holt, 1973.

Altman, I., Vinsel, A., & Brown, B. B. Dialectic conceptions in social psychology: An application to social penetration and privacy regulation. In L. Berkowitz (Ed.), *Advances in experimental social psychology* (Vol. 14). New York: Academic Press, 1981. Pp. 107–160.

Angle, H. L., & Perry, J. L. An empirical assessment of organizational commitment and organizational effectiveness. *Administrative Science Quarterly*, 1981, **26**, 1–14.

Argyris, C. *Integrating the individual and the organization.* New York: Wiley, 1964.

Aronson, E., & Mills, J. The effect of severity of initiation on liking for a group. *Journal of Abnormal and Social Psychology*, 1959, **59**, 177–181.

Back, K. The small group: Tightrope between sociology and personality. *Journal of Applied Behavioral Science*, 1979, **15**, 283–294.

Bales, R. F. Task roles and social roles in problem-solving groups. In E. E. Maccoby, T. M.

Newcomb, & E. L. Hartley (Eds.), *Readings in social psychology* (3rd ed.). New York: Holt, 1958. Pp. 437–447.

Bartell, G. *Group sex*. New York: Wyden, 1971.

Becker, H. S. Notes on the concept of commitment. *American Journal of Sociology*, 1960, **66**, 32–40.

Becker, H. S. Personal changes in adult life. *Sociometry*, 1964, **27**, 40–53.

Bem, D. J. Self-perception: An alternative interpretation of cognitive dissonance phenomena. *Psychological Review*, 1967, **74**, 183–200.

Benne, K. D., & Sheats, P. Functional roles of group members. *Journal of Social Issues*, 1948, **4**, 41–49.

Birenbaum, A., & Sagarin, E. *Norms and human behavior*. New York: Praeger, 1976.

Blau, P. M. A theory of social integration. *American Journal of Sociology*, 1960, **65**, 545–556.

Borgatta, E. F., & Baker, P. M. (Eds.), Small groups: An agenda for research and theory. *American Behavioral Scientist*, 1981, **24**, 601–717.

Bouma, G. D. Keeping the faithful: Patterns of membership retention in the Christian Reformed Church. *Sociological Analysis*, 1980, **41**, 259–264.

Brandstätter, H., Davis, J. H., & Schuler, H. *Dynamics of group decisions*. Beverly Hills, California: Sage, 1978.

Breakwell, G. M. Illegitimate group membership and inter-group differentiation. *British Journal of Social and Clinical Psychology*, 1979, **18**, 141–149.

Brewer, M. B. In-group bias in the minimal intergroup situation: A cognitive-motivational analysis. *Psychological Bulletin*, 1979, **86**, 307–324.

Brim, O. G. Socialization through the life cycle. In O. G. Brim & S. Wheeler (Eds.), *Socialization after childhood: Two essays*. New York: Wiley, 1966. Pp. 1–49.

Brinkerhoff, M. B., & Burke, K. L. Disaffiliation: Some notes on "falling from the faith." *Sociological Analysis*, 1980, **41**, 41–54.

Buchanan, B. Building organizational commitment: The socialization of managers in work organizations. *Administrative Science Quarterly*, 1974, **19**, 533–546.

Burgess, R. L., & Huston, T. L. (Eds.), *Social exchange in developing relationships*. New York: Academic Press, 1979.

Burr, W. R. Role transitions: A reformulation of theory. *Journal of Marriage and the Family*, 1972, **34**, 407–416.

Caine, B. T. Role making and the assumption of leadership. In Associates, Office of Military Leadership (Eds.), *A study of organizational leadership*. Harrisburg, Pennsylvania: Stackpole, 1976, Pp. 362–372.

Cartwright, D. S., Tomson, B., & Schwartz, H. (Eds.), *Gang delinquency*. Monterey, California: Brooks-Cole, 1975.

Chapin, F. S. The optimum size of institutions: A theory of the large group. *American Journal of Sociology*, 1957, **62**, 449–460.

Chisholm, R. F., Gauntner, D. E., & Munzenrider, R. F. Pre-enlistment expectations/perceptions of Army life, satisfaction, and re-enlistment of volunteers. *Journal of Political and Military Sociology*, 1980, **8**, 31–42.

Cleveland, J. N. *The relationship between in-group stereotype and applicant suitability evaluations*. Paper presented at the meeting of the American Psychological Association, Montreal, August 1980.

Cloyd, J. S. Functional differentiation and the structure of informal groups. *Sociological Quarterly*, 1964, **5**, 243–250.

Coser, L. A. *The functions of social conflict*. Glencoe, Illinois: Free Press, 1956.

Darley, J. G., Gross, N., & Martin, W. E. Studies of group behavior: Stability, change, and interrelations of psychometric and sociometric variables. *Journal of Abnormal and Social Psychology*, 1951, **46**, 565–576.

Davis, J. H., Bray, R., & Holt, R. The empirical study of decision processes in juries: A critical review. In J. L. Tapp & F. J. Levine (Eds.), *Law, justice, and the individual in society: Psychological and legal issues.* New York: Holt, 1977. Pp. 326–361.

Deci, E. L. *Intrinsic motivation.* New York: Plenum, 1975.

Duck, S. W. A topography of relationship disengagement and dissolution. In S. W. Duck (Ed.), *Personal relationships 4: Dissolving personal relationships.* New York: Academic Press, 1982, in press.

Duck, S. W., & Gilmour, R. (Eds.). *Personal relationships 2: Developing relationships.* New York: Academic Press, 1981.

Edwards, J. N., & Saunders, J. M. Coming apart: A model of the marital dissolution decision. *Journal of Marriage and the Family,* 1981, **43**, 379–389.

Etzioni, A. *A comparative analysis of complex organizations.* New York: Free Press, 1961.

Farrell, D., & Rusbult, C. E. Exchange variables as predictors of job satisfaction, job commitment, and turnover: The impact of rewards, costs, alternatives, and investments. *Organizational Behavior and Human Performance,* 1981, **27**, 78–95.

Feldbaum, C. L., Christenson, T. E., & O'Neal, E. C. An observational study of the assimilation of the newcomer to the preschool. *Child Development,* 1980, **51**, 497–507.

Feldman, D. C. A contingency theory of socialization. *Administrative Science Quarterly,* 1976, **21**, 433–452.

Feldman, D. C. The role of initiation activities in socilization. *Human Relations,* 1977, **30**, 977–990.

Feldman, D. C. A socialization process that helps new recruits succeed. *Personnel,* 1980, **57**, 11–23.

Feldman, D. C. The multiple socialization of organization members. *Academy of Management Review,* 1981, **6**, 309–318.

Feldman, J. M. Beyond attribution theory: Cognitive processes in performance appraisal. *Journal of Applied Psychology,* 1981, **66**, 127–148.

Feshbach, N., & Sones, G. Sex differences in adolescent reactions toward newcomers. *Developmental Psychology,* 1971, **4**, 381–386.

Festinger, L. *A theory of cognitive dissonance.* Stanford, California: Stanford University Press, 1957.

Festinger, L., Riecken, H. W., & Schachter, S. *When prophecy fails.* Minneapolis, Minnesota: University of Minnesota Press, 1956.

Fine, G. A. *The effect of a salient newcomer on a small group: A force field analysis.* Paper presented at the meeting of the American Psychological Association, Washington, D.C., September 1976.

Friendly, M. L., & Glucksberg, S. On the description of subcultural lexicons: A multidimensional approach. *Journal of Personality and Social Psychology,* 1970, **14**, 55–65.

Fromkin, H. L., Klimoski, R. J., & Flanagan, M. F. Race and competence as determinants of acceptance of newcomers in success and failure work groups. *Organizational Behavior and Human Performance,* 1972, **7**, 25–42.

Galanter, M. Psychological induction into the large-group: Findings from a modern religious sect. *American Journal of Psychiatry,* 1980, **137**, 1574–1579.

Garfinkel, H. Conditions of successful degradation ceremonies. *American Journal of Sociology,* 1956, **61**, 420–424.

Gauron, E. F., & Rawlings, E. I. A procedure for orienting new members to group psychotherapy. *Small Group Behavior,* 1975, **6**, 293–307.

Gerard, H. B., & Mathewson, G. C. The effects of severity of initiation on liking for a group: A replication. *Journal of Experimental Social Psychology,* 1966, **2**, 278–287.

Gibbs, J. P., & Erickson, M. I. Major developments in the sociological study of deviance. In A. Inkeles, J. Coleman, & N. Smelser (Eds.), *Annual review of sociology* (Vol. 1). Palo Alto, California: Annual Reviews, 1975. Pp. 21–42.

Gilchrist, J. C. The formation of social groups under conditions of success and failure. *Journal of Abnormal and Social Psychology,* 1952, **47,** 174–187.

Glaser, B. G., & Strauss, A. L. *Status passage.* Chicago, Illinois: Aldine, 1971.

Goffman, E. *Asylums: Essays on the social situation of mental patients and other inmates.* Garden City, New York: Doubleday, 1961.

Good, L. R., & Good, K. C. Similarity of attitudes and attraction to a social organization. *Psychological Reports,* 1974, **34,** 1071–1073.

Good, L. R., & Nelson, D. A. Effects of person-group and intra-group attitude similarity on perceived group attractiveness and cohesiveness. *Psychonomic Science,* 1971, **25,** 215–217.

Gordon, C. W., & Babchuk, N. A typology of voluntary associations. *American Sociological Review,* 1959, **24,** 22–29.

Gordon, M. E., Philpot, J. W., Burt, R. E., Thompson, C. A., & Spiller, W. E. Commitment to the union: Development of a measure and an examination of its correlates. *Journal of Applied Psychology Monograph,* 1980, **65,** 479–499.

Gouldner, H. P. Dimensions of organizational commitment. *Administrative Science Quarterly,* 1960, **4,** 468–490.

Graen, E., & Cashman, J. F. A role-making model of leadership in formal organizations: A developmental approach. In J. G. Hunt & L. L. Larsen (Eds.), *Leadership frontiers.* Kent, Ohio: Kent State University Press, 1975. Pp. 143–165.

Greenberg, M. S. A theory of indebtedness. In K. J. Gergen, M. S. Greenberg, & R. H. Willis (Eds.), *Social exchange: Advances in theory and research.* New York: Plenum, 1980. Pp. 3–26.

Hackman, J. R. Group influences on individuals. In M. Dunnette (Ed.), *Handbook of industrial and organizational psychology.* Chicago, Illinois: Rand-McNally, 1976. Pp. 1455–1525.

Haney, C., Banks, W., & Zimbardo, P. Interpersonal dynamics in a simulated prison. *International Journal of Criminology,* 1973, **1,** 69–97.

Hazer, J. T., & Alvares, K. M. Police work values during organizational entry and assimilation. *Journal of Applied Psychology,* 1981, **66,** 12–18.

Heilman, M. E. The impact of situational factors on personnel decisions concerning women: Varying the sex composition of the applicant pool. *Organizational Behavior and Human Performance,* 1980, **26,** 386–395.

Heiss, J. The dyad views the newcomer: A study of perception. *Human Relations,* 1963, **16,** 241–248.

Heiss, J., & Nash, D. The stranger in laboratory culture revisited. *Human Organization,* 1967, **26,** 47–51.

Henshel, A. Swinging: A study of decision making in marriage. *American Journal of Sociology,* 1973, **78,** 885–891.

Heshka, S., & Lang, D. Predicting student participation in voluntary associations from attitudes and personality: A preliminary report. *Journal of Voluntary Action Research,* 1978, **7,** 28–33.

Hinde, R. A. *Toward understanding relationships.* New York: Academic Press, 1979.

Hoge, D. R., & Polk, D. T. A test of theories of Protestant church participation and commitment. *Review of Religious Research,* 1980, **21,** 315–329.

Hollander, E. P. *Leadership dynamics: A practical guide to effective relationships.* New York: Free Press, 1978.

Hollander, E. P. Leadership and social exchange processes. In K. J. Gergen. M. S. Greenberg, & R. H. Willis (Eds.), *Social exchange: Advances in theory and research.* New York: Plenum, 1980. Pp. 103–118.

Hollander, E. P., & Willis, R. H. Some current issues in the psychology of conformity and nonconformity. *Psycholoical Bulletin,* 1967, **68,** 62–76.

Hom, P. W., & Hulin, C. L. A competitive test of the prediction of re-enlistment by several models. *Journal of Applied Psychology,* 1981, **66,** 23–39.

Howard, J. W., & Rothbart, M. Social categorization and memory for in-group and out-group behavior. *Journal of Personality and Social Psychology,* 1980, **38,** 301–310.

Huesmann, L. R., & Levinger, G. Incremental exchange theory: A formal model for progression in dyadic social interaction. In L. Berkowitz (Ed.), *Advances in experimental social psychology* (Vol. 9). New York: Academic Press, 1976. Pp. 192–230.

Jackson, J. Structural characteristics of norms. In I. D. Steiner & M. Fishbein (Eds.), *Current studies in social psychology.* New York: Holt, 1965. Pp. 301–309.

Jackson, J. A conceptual and measurement model for norms and roles. *Pacific Sociological Review,* 1966, **9,** 35–47.

Jackson, S. E. Measurement of commitment to role identities. *Journal of Personality and Social Psychology,* 1981, **40,** 138–146.

Jacobs, R. C., & Campbell, D. T. The perpetuation of an arbitrary tradition through several generations of a laboratory microculture. *Journal of Abnormal and Social Psychology,* 1961, **62,** 649–658.

Jacoby, A. P. Some correlates of instrumental and expressive orientations to associational membership. *Sociological Inquiry,* 1965, **35,** 163–175.

Johnson, M. P. Commitment: A conceptual structure and empirical application. *Sociological Quarterly,* 1973, **14,** 395–406.

Kanter, R. M. Commitment and social organization: A study of commitment mechanisms in utopian communities. *American Sociological Review,* 1968, **33,** 499–517.

Kanter, R. M. *Commitment and community: Communes and utopias in sociological perspective.* Cambridge, Massachusetts: Harvard University Press, 1972.

Kiesler, C. A. *The psychology of commitment: Experiments linking behavior to belief.* New York: Academic Press, 1971.

Kipnis, D. *The powerholders.* Chicago, Illinois: University of Chicago Press, 1976.

Kipper, D. A., Bizman, A., & Einat, Y. Selecting group members: Effects of the content of the feedback and the characteristics of the problem. *Small Group Behavior,* 1981, **12,** 443–457.

Knoke, D. Commitment and detachment in voluntary associations. *American Sociological Review,* 1981, **46,** 141–158.

Latané, B., & Bidwell, L. D. Sex and affiliation in college cafeterias. *Personality and Social Psychology Bulletin,* 1977, **3,** 571–574.

Lepper, M. R., & Greene, D. (Eds.), *The hidden costs of reward.* Hillsdale, New Jersey: Erlbaum, 1978.

Levine, J. M. Reaction to opinion deviance in small groups. In P. Paulus (Ed.), *Psychology of group influence.* Hillsdale, New Jersey: Erlbaum, 1980. Pp. 375–429.

Levine, J. M., & Moreland, R. L. Innovation and socialization in small groups. In S. Moscovici, G. Mugny, & E. Van Avermaet (Eds.), *Perspectives on minority influence.* Cambridge, England: Cambridge University Press, 1982, in press.

Levinger, G. A three-level approach to attraction: Toward an understanding of pair relatedness. In T. L. Huston (Ed.), *Foundations of interpersonal attraction.* New York: Academic Press, 1974. Pp. 99–120.

Levinger, G. A social psychological perspective on marital dissolution. *Journal of Social Issues,* 1976, **32,** 21–47.

Levinger, G. Toward the analysis of close relationships. *Journal of Experimental Social Psychology,* 1980, **16,** 510–544.

Levinger, G., & Huesmann, R. L. An "incremental exchange" perspective on the pair relationship: Interpersonal reward and level of involvement. In K. J. Gergen, M. S. Greenberg, & R. H. Willis (Eds.), *Social exchange: Advances in theory and research.* New York: Plenum, 1980. Pp. 165–196.

Lewicki, R. J. Organizational seduction: Building commitment to organizations. *Organizational Dynamics,* 1981, **10,** 5–21.

Lindt, H., & Pennal, H. A. On the defensive quality of groups: A commentary on the use of the group as a tool to control reality. *International Journal of Group Psychotherapy*, 1962, **12**, 171–179.

Little, C. Technical-professional unemployment: Middleclass adaptability to personal crisis. *Sociological Quarterly*, 1976, **17**, 262–274.

Lofland, J. "Becoming a world-saver" revisited. *American Behavioral Scientist*, 1977, **20**, 805–819.

Lofland, J. F., & Lejeune, R. A. Initial interaction of newcomers in Alcoholics Anonymous: A field experiment in class symbols and socialization. *Social Problems*, 1960, **8**, 102–111.

Longino, C. F., Jr., & Kart, C. S. The college fraternity: An assessment of theory and research. *Journal of College Student Personnel*, 1973, **14**, 118–125.

Louis, M. R. Surprise and sense making: What newcomers experience in entering unfamiliar organizational settings. *Administrative Science Quarterly*, 1980, **25**, 226–251.

Martin, T. N., & Hunt, J. G. Social influence and intent to leave: A path-analytic process model. *Personnel Psychology*, 1980, **33**, 505–528.

Marwell, G. Visibility in small groups. *Journal of Social Psychology*, 1963, **61**, 311–325.

McGrath, J. E., & Kravitz, D. A. Group research. In M. R. Rosenzweig & L. W. Porter (Eds.), *Annual review of psychology* (Vol. 33). Palo Alto, California: Annual Reviews, 1982. Pp. 195–230.

McGuire, W. J., & McGuire, C. V. The spontaneous self-concept as affected by personal distinctiveness. In M. D. Lynch, A. A. Norem-Hebeisen, & K. J. Gergen (Eds.), *Self-concept: Advances in theory and research*. Cambridge, Massachusetts: Ballinger, 1981. Pp. 147–172.

Merei, F. Group leadership and institutionalization. *Human Relations*, 1949, **2**, 23–39.

Messé, L. A., Buldain, R. W., & Watts, B. Recall of social events with the passage of time. *Personality and Social Psychology Bulletin*, 1981, **7**, 33–38.

Mitchell, T. R., & Biglan, A. H. Instrumentality theories: Current uses in psychology. *Psychological Bulletin*, 1971, **76**, 432–454.

Mobley, W. H., Hand, H. H., Meglino, B. M., & Griffeth, R. W. Review and conceptual analysis of the employee turnover process. *Psychological Bulletin*, 1979, **86**, 493–522.

Moreland, R. L. Social categorization and the assimilation of "new" group members. (Doctoral dissertation, University of Michigan, 1978). *Dissertation Abstracts International*, 1978, **39**, 5145-B. (University Microfilm No. 7907141).

Moscovici, S. *Social influence and social change*. New York: Academic Press, 1976.

Moscovici, S. Toward a theory of conversion behavior. In L. Berkowitz (Ed.), *Advances in experimental social psychology* (Vol. 13). New York: Academic Press, 1980. Pp. 209–239.

Mowday, R. T., Steers, R. M., & Porter, L. W. The measurement of organizational commitment. *Journal of Vocational Behavior*, 1979, **14**, 224–247.

Muchinsky, P. M., & Morrow, P. C. A multidisciplinary model of voluntary employee turnover. *Journal of Vocational Behavior*, 1980, **17**, 263–290.

Nash, D., & Heiss, J. Sources of anxiety in laboratory strangers. *Sociological Quarterly*, 1967, **8**, 215–221.

Nash, D., & Wolfe, A. W. The stranger in laboratory culture. *American Sociological Review*, 1957, **22**, 400–405.

Naylor, J. C., Pritchard, R. D., & Ilgen, D. R. *A theory of behavior in organizations*. New York: Academic Press, 1980.

Newman, H. M., & Langer, E. J. Post-divorce adaptation and the attribution of responsibility. *Sex Roles*, 1981, **7**, 223–232.

Nuwer, H. Dead souls of hell week. *Human Behavior*, October 1978, 53–56.

O'Reilly, C. A., & Caldwell, D. F. The commitment and job tenure of new employees: Some evidence of postdecisional justification. *Administrative Science Quarterly*, 1981, **26**, 597–616.

Orcutt, J. D. Societal reaction and the response to deviation in small groups. *Social Forces*, 1973, **52**, 259–267.

Pascarella, E. T., & Terenzini, P. T. Interaction effects in Spady's and Tinto's conceptual models of college dropout. *Sociology of Education*, 1979, **52**, 197–210.

Phillips, E. L., Shenker, S., & Revitz, P. The assimilation of the new child into the group. *Psychiatry*, 1951, **14**, 319–325.

Porter, L. W., & Steers, R. M. Organizational, work, and personal factors in employee turnover and absenteeism. *Psychological Bulletin*, 1973, **80**, 151–176.

Porter, L. W., Steers, R. M., Mowday, R. T., & Boulian, P. V. Organizational commitment, job satisfaction, and turnover among psychiatric technicians. *Journal of Applied Psychology*, 1974, **59**, 603–609.

Price, J. L. *The study of turnover*. Ames, Iowa: Iowa State University Press, 1977.

Putallaz, M., & Gottman, J. M. An interactional model of children's entry into peer groups. *Child Development*, 1981, **52**, 986–994.

Raven, H. H., & Kruglanski, A. Conflict and power. In P. Swingle (Ed.), *The structure of conflict*. New York: Academic Press, 1970. Pp. 69–109.

Richardson, K. D., & Cialdini, R. B. Basking and blasting: Tactics of indirect self-presentation. In J. T. Tedeschi (Ed.), *Impression management theory and social psychological research*. New York: Academic Press, 1981. Pp. 41–53.

Richardson, J. T., & Stewart, M. Conversion process models and the Jesus movement. *American Behavioral Scientist*, 1977, **20**, 819–838.

Ridgeway, C. L. Conformity, group-oriented motivation, and status attainment in small groups. *Social Psychology*, 1978, **41**, 175–188.

Ridgeway, C. L. Nonconformity, competence, and influence in groups: A test of two theories. *American Sociological Review*, 1981, **46**, 333–347.

Robbins, T., Anthony, D., & Richardson, J. T. Theory and research on today's "new religions." *Sociological Analysis*, 1978, **39**, 95–122.

Roozen, D. A. Church dropouts: Changing patterns of disengagment and re-entry. *Review of Religious Research*, 1980, **21**, 427–450.

Rosenblatt, P. C. Needed research on commitment in marriage. In G. Levinger & H. L. Rausch (Eds.), *Close relationships: Perspectives on the meaning of intimacy*. Amherst, Massachusetts: University of Massachusetts Press, 1977. Pp. 73–86.

Ross, I. C., & Zander, A. Need satisfaction and employee turnover. *Personnel Psychology*, 1957, **10**, 327–338.

Ross, M., McFarland, C., & Fletcher, G. J. O. The effect of attitude on recall of personal histories. *Journal of Personality and Social Psychology*, 1981, **40**, 627–634.

Roth, J. A. *Timetables: Structuring the passage of time in hospital treatment and other careers*. Indianapolis, Indiana: Bobbs-Merrill, 1963.

Rusbult, C. E. Commitment and satisfaction in romantic associations: A test of the investment model. *Journal of Experimental Social Psychology*, 1980, **16**, 172–186.

Rynes, S. L., Heneman, H. G., & Schwab, D. P. Individual reactions to organizational recruiting: A review. *Personnel Psychology*, 1980, **33**, 529–542.

Sagi, P. C., Olmsted, D. W., & Atelsek, F. Predicting maintenance of membership in small groups. *Journal of Abnormal and Social Psychology*, 1955, **51**, 308–311.

Salancik, G. R. Commitment and the control of organizational behavior and belief. In B. M. Staw, & G. R. Salancik (Eds.), *New directions in organizational behavior*. Chicago, Illinois: St. Clair Press, 1977. Pp. 1–54.

Sarbin, T. R., & Allen, V. L. Role theory. In G. Lindzey & E. Aronson (Eds.), *The handbook of social psychology* (Vol. 1, 2nd ed.). Reading, Massachusetts: Addison-Wesley, 1968, Pp. 488–567.

Scanzoni, J. Social exchange and behavioral interdependence. In R. L. Burgess & T. L. Huston (Eds.), *Social exchange in developing relationships*. New York: Academic Press, 1979. Pp. 61–98.

Schachter, S. *The psychology of affiliation: Experimental studies of the sources of gregariousness*. Stanford, California: Stanford University Press, 1959.

Schein, E. H. How to break in the college graduate. *Harvard Business Review*, 1964, **42**, 93–101.

Schein, E. H. Organizational socialization and the profession of management. *Industrial Management Review*, 1968, **9**, 1–16.

Schein, E. H. The individual, the organization, and the career: A conceptual scheme. *Journal of Applied Behavioral Science*, 1971, **7**, 401–426.

Schein, E. H. *Career dynamics: Matching individual and organizational needs*. Reading, Massachusetts: Addison-Wesley, 1978.

Schein, E. H. *Organizational psychology* (3rd ed.). New York: Prentice-Hall, 1980.

Schlossberg, N. K., & Leibowitz, Z. Organizational support systems as buffers to job loss. *Journal of Vocational Behavior*, 1980, **17**, 204–217.

Schwartz, W. Degradation, accreditation, and rites of passage. *Psychiatry*, 1979, **42**, 138–146.

Scott, W. A. *Values and organizations: A study of fraternities and sororities*. Chicago, Illinois: Rand McNally, 1965.

Scott, W. A., & Scott, R. Intercorrelations among structural properties of primary groups. *Journal of Personality and Social Psychology*, 1981, **41**, 279–292.

Shaw, M. E. *Group dynamics: The psychology of small group behavior* (3rd ed.). New York: McGraw-Hill, 1981.

Sherif, M., & Sherif, C. W. *Groups in harmony and tension*. New York: Harper, 1953.

Shupe, A. D., Spielmann, R., & Stigall, S. Deprogramming: The new exorcism. *American Behavioral Scientist*, 1977, **20**, 941–956.

Shuval, J. T., & Adler, I. The role of models in professional socialization. *Social Science & Medicine*, 1980, **14**, 5–14.

Snow, D. A., Zurcher, L. A., & Ekland-Olson, S. Social networks and social movements: A microstructural approach to differential recruitment. *American Sociological Review*, 1980, **45**, 787–801.

Snyder, E. C. The Supreme Court as a small group. *Social Forces*, 1958, **36**, 232–238.

Staw, B. M. The consequences of turnover. *Journal of Occupational Behaviour*, 1980, **1**, 253–273.

Steers, R. M., & Mowday, R. T. Employee turnover and post-decision accommodation processes. In B. M. Staw & L. L. Cummings (Eds.), *Research in organizational behavior* (Vol. 3). Greenwich, Connecticut: JAI Press, 1981. Pp. 235–281.

Steiner, I. D. Whatever happened to the group in social psychology? *Journal of Experimental Social Psychology*, 1974, **10**, 94–108.

Strand, R., Levine, R., & Montgomery, D. Organizational entry preferences based upon social and personnel policies: An information integration perspective. *Organizational Behavior and Human Performance*, 1981, **27**, 50–68.

Strauss, A. L. *Mirrors and masks: The search for identity*. Glencoe, Illinois: Free Press, 1959.

Tajfel, H. (Ed.), *Differentiation between social groups: Studies in the social psychology of intergroup relations*. New York: Academic Press, 1979.

Tannenbaum, P. H., & McLeod, M. On the measurement of socialization. *Public Opinion Quarterly*, 1967, **31**, 27–37.

Taylor, S. E., & Fiske, S. T. Salience, attention, and attribution: Top of the head phenomena. In L. Berkowitz (Ed.), *Advances in experimental social psychology* (Vol. 11). New York: Academic Press, 1978. Pp. 249–288.

Taylor, S. E., Fiske, S. T., Close, M., Anderson, C. E., & Ruderman, A. J. *Solo status as a psychological variable: The power of being distinctive*. Unpublished manuscript, Harvard University, 1977.

Thibaut, J. W., & Kelley, H. H. *The social psychology of groups.* New York: Wiley, 1959.

Tinto, V. Dropout from higher education: A theoretical synthesis of recent research. *Review of Educational Research,* 1975, **45**, 89–125.

Trice, H. M. A study of the process of affiliation with Alcoholics Anonymous. *Quarterly Journal of Studies on Alcohol,* 1957, **18**, 39–54.

Van Gennep, A. *The rites of passage* (M. B. Vizedom & G. L. Caffee, trans.). Chicago, Illinois: University of Chicago Press, 1960. (Originally published, 1908.)

Van Maanen, J. Breaking in: Socialization to work. In R. Dubin (Ed.), *Handbook of work, organization, and society.* Chicago, Illinois: Rand-McNally, 1976. Pp. 67–130.

Van Maanen, J. Experiencing organization: Notes on the meaning of careers and socialization. In J. Van Maanen (Ed.), *Organizational careers: Some new perspectives.* New York: Wiley, 1977. Pp. 15–45.

Van Maanen, J. People processing: Strategies of organizational socialization. *Organizational Dynamics,* 1978, **7**, 18–36.

Van Maanen, J., & Schein, E. H. Toward a theory of organizational socialization. In B. M. Staw (Ed.), *Research in organizational behavior: An annual series of analytical essays and critical reviews* (Vol. 1). Greenwich, Connecticut: JAI Press, 1979. Pp. 209–264.

Vaught, C., & Smith, D. L. Incorporation and mechanical solidarity in an underground coal mine. *Sociology of Work and Occupations,* 1980, **7**, 159–187.

Wahrman, R. Status, deviance, and sanctions. *Pacific Sociological Review,* 1970, **13**, 229–240.

Walker, T. C. Behavior of temporary members in small groups. *Journal of Applied Psychology,* 1973, **58**, 144–146.

Wallace, W. L. Institutional and life-cycle socialization of college freshmen. *American Journal of Sociology,* 1964, **70**, 303–318.

Wanous, J. P. *Organizational entry: Recruitment, selection, and socialization of newcomers.* Reading, Massachusetts: Addison-Wesley, 1980.

Warriner, C. K., & Prather, J. E. Four types of voluntary associations. *Sociological Inquiry,* 1965, **35**, 138–148.

Weiss, H. M. Subordinate imitation of supervisor behavior: The role of modeling in organizational socialization. *Organizational Behavior and Human Performance,* 1977, **19**, 89–105.

Weiss, R. F. Defection from social movements and subsequent recruitment to new movements. *Sociometry,* 1963, **26**, 1–20.

Weiss, R. S. The emotional impact of marital separation. *Journal of Social Issues,* 1976, **32**, 135–145.

Wheeler, S. The structure of formally organized socialization settings. In O. G. Brim & S. Wheeler (Eds.), *Socialization after childhood: Two essays.* New York: Wiley, 1966. Pp. 53–116.

White, R. E., & Butts, W. M. Near-sociometric investigations of group membership survival. *Group Psychotherapy,* 1963, **16**, 182–188.

Wicker, A. W., & Mehler, A. Assimilation of new members in a large and a small church. *Journal of Applied Psychology,* 1971, **55**, 151–156.

Wicklund, R. A. Objective self-awareness. In L. Berkowitz (Ed.), *Advances in experimental social psychology* (Vol. 8). New York: Academic Press, 1975. Pp. 233–275.

Wicklund, R. A., & Frey, D. Self-awareness theory: When the self makes a difference. In D. M. Wegner & R. R. Vallacher (Eds.), *The self in social psychology.* London and New York: Oxford University Press, 1980. Pp. 31–54.

Wilder, D. A. Perceiving persons as a group: Categorization and intergroup relations. In D. L. Hamilton (Ed.), *Cognitive processes in stereotyping and intergroup behavior.* Hillsdale, New Jersey: Erlbaum, 1981. Pp. 213–257.

Willerman, B., & Swanson, L. Group prestige in voluntary organizations. *Human Behavior,* 1953, **6**, 57–77.

Yablonsky, L. The delinquent gang as a near-group. *Social Problems,* 1959, **7**, 108–117.

Zander, A. The psychology of removing group members and recruiting new ones. *Human Relations,* 1976, **29,** 969–987.

Zander, A. *Groups at work.* San Francisco, California: Jossey-Bass, 1977.

Zander, A. The psychology of group processes. In M. R. Rosenzweig & L. W. Porter (Eds.), *Annual review of psychology* (Vol. 30). Palo Alto, California: Annual Reviews, 1979. Pp. 417–451. (a)

Zander, A. The study of group behavior during four decades. *Journal of Applied Behavioral Science,* 1979, **15,** 272–282. (b)

Zander, A., & Cohen, A. R. Attributed social power and group acceptance: A classroom experimental demonstration. *Journal of Abnormal and Social Psychology,* 1955, **51,** 490–492.

Ziller, R. C. Individuation and socialization: A theory of assimilation in large organizations. *Human Relations,* 1964, **17,** 341–360.

Ziller, R. C. Toward a theory of open and closed groups. *Psychological Bulletin,* 1965, **64,** 164–182.

Ziller, R. C. Group dialectics: The dynamics of groups over time. *Human Development,* 1977, **20,** 293–308.

Ziller, R. C., & Behringer, R. D. Assimilation of the knowledgeable newcomer under conditions of group success and failure. *Journal of Abnormal and Social Psychology,* 1960, **60,** 288–291.

Ziller, R. C., & Behringer, R. D. A longitudinal study of the assimilation of the new child in the group. *Human Relations,* 1961, **14,** 121–133.

Ziller, R. C., Behringer, R. D., & Goodchilds, J. D. The minority newcomer in open and closed groups. *Journal of Psychology,* 1960, **50,** 75–84.

Ziller, R. C., Behringer, R. D., & Jansen, M. J. The newcomer in open and closed groups. *Journal of Applied Psychology,* 1961, **45,** 55–58.

Zurcher, L. A. The sailor aboard ship: A study of role behavior in a total institution. *Social Forces,* 1965, **43,** 389–400.

Zurcher, L. A. The "friendly" poker game: A study of an ephemeral role. *Social Forces,* 1970, **49,** 173–186.

# TRANSLATING ACTIONS INTO ATTITUDES: AN IDENTITY-ANALYTIC APPROACH TO THE EXPLANATION OF SOCIAL CONDUCT[1]

## Barry R. Schlenker

DEPARTMENT OF PSYCHOLOGY
UNIVERSITY OF FLORIDA
GAINESVILLE, FLORIDA

.

[1]The present article and/or several of the studies reported herein were supported by a Research Scientist Development Award (K02-MH00183) from the National Institute of Mental Health, which provided the time necessary to complete the article, and grants from the National Science Foundation (BNS 77-08182) and the graduate school at the University of Florida from NIH Biomedical Research Support Program funds.

ADVANCES IN EXPERIMENTAL SOCIAL
PSYCHOLOGY, VOL. 15

# I.  Introduction

People's explanations of their social conduct can reverberate through their personal and public identities. For example, people who can convince others and themselves that their apparent misbehaviors are justified escape the onerous implications of being a transgressor; those who convincingly explain why meritorious conduct resulted from their own talents and insights are entitled to approbations. The present article examines the social character and functions of explanations of conduct. The identity-analytic theory that is presented provides a basis for understanding when and why people's attributions and self-presentations sometimes appear personally biased, if not downright distorted, to the outside observer. We shall concentrate especially, although not exclusively, on changes or shifts in attitudes that occur following counterattitudinal behaviors. As has been frequently noted, attitude expressions can be employed to create, enhance, and defend desired identities (e.g., Alexander & Rudd, 1981; Cialdini, Petty, & Cacioppo, 1981; Hass, 1981; Jellison, 1981; Jones & Wortman, 1973; Pepitone, 1966; Schlenker, 1973, 1978, 1980; Secord, 1968; Tedeschi & Rosenfeld, 1981). When conduct occurs that (a) violates personal or public standards in ways that threaten one's identity, or (b) meets commendable standards but ambiquity exists about the relevance of the event for one's identity, explanations are proffered. These explanations often rely on attitude expressions that are discrepant from one's preexisting attitudes.

# II.  Theoretical Background

## A.  THE NATURE OF IDENTITY

### 1.  Delineating Identity

Identity is a theory (or schema) that is constructed about how one is and should be perceived, regarded, and treated in social life (Schlenker, 1980).[2] As

---

[2]Identity is sometimes defined solely by an individual's roles in social interaction. From the present perspective, however, roles constitute only a portion of what is meant by identity. Aspects of people's appearance (e.g., type of dress, observable features such as fat–thin, tall–short, blond–brunette), background (e.g., schools attended, ancestors), apparent goals and motives (e.g., accommodativeness), apparent personal characteristics (e.g., intelligence), and behavior in general (e.g., test performance) also serve to define people in social life and affect how they are perceived, regarded, and treated (Schlenker, 1980). Thus identity is viewed as an organization of knowledge about a person that is relevant to social life.

This definition of identity is similar in many respects to Erikson's (1963) use of the term. Erikson defined a sense of identity as "the accrued confidence that the inner sameness and continuity

such, it is an organization of knowledge about the self in actual and imagined social situations and relationships. It includes relevant facts, constructs, beliefs, values, standards for conduct, and iconic components that provide a portrait of the individual as a social entity, aggregated over a variety of experiences. Immediate audiences have or develop such a theory of the actor, and actors possess such a theory of themselves.

More than being one general schema, identity comprises numerous less inclusive schemata that pertain to specific situations, audiences, and behaviors. These will be termed identity images and are organized, at least to some degree, under the rubric of the larger theory of identity.[3] Although people may recognize that they project somewhat different images in one situation than another, these discrepancies can usually be explained through reference to the larger theoretical structure (e.g., "I am an assertive individual normally but will, of course, show deference to elders, employers, and people who deserve respect"). In this sense, people may display as many "social selves" as there are audiences to be encountered (James, 1890/1952), yet still possess a composite identity that is pertinent to generalizations and person–situation interactions.

Epstein (1973) similarly defined the self-concept as a "theory the individual has unwittingly constructed about himself as an experiencing, functioning individual" (p. 407). The self-concept is a broader, more inclusive term than identity, since it includes aspects of experience that people regard as nonsocial in nature. One's perceived identity is thus a theory about oneself embedded within the larger theory called the self-concept.

## 2. Identity Images as Prototypes

Like other schemata, identity images usually contain behavioral prototype or response-specifying information that can act as a guide or script to direct behavior (e.g., Abelson, 1976; Carver, 1979; Langer, 1978; Schlenker, 1980).

---

prepared in the past are matched by the sameness and continuity of one's meaning for others" (p. 261). It is the feeling that one is unique yet integrated within a social framework in which one has a purposeful role, and can act accordingly. If one's place in society seems meaningless or one's roles conflict, identity confusion results. Like the present view, Erikson stresses the social influences on identity. He also considers as part of the concept perceptions of characteristics that go beyond roles per se but have social implications, such as "aptitudes developed out of endowment" (p. 261), and discusses the reconciliation of personal goals and social requirements. Unlike the present view, he roots the concept in post-Freudian dynamics, for example, suggesting that identity arises from "the ego's ability to integrate all identifications with the vicissitudes of the libido" (p. 261).

[3]No attempt is made to distinguish between structures that are almost exclusively iconic, which are occasionally called images in the literature on social cognition, and those that are almost exclusively verbal or propositional, which are occasionally called schemas (e.g., Lord, 1980). Most images, as the term is used here, probably contain both iconic and linguistic aspects (Abelson, 1976). When referring to more specific self or identity schema, the term image will be employed, since it appears to capture the everyday meaning of conveying images or making impressions in social life.

For example, people can describe an "honest" person by designating the sorts of conduct that fit the prototype. Although people may disagree when it comes to details, the image itself has clear implications for what an honest person should do and how others should respond. Given that a particular identity image is engaged, either because it is triggered by situational cues without the actor's full awareness or consciously selected after consideration of the situational context, it provides the direction for subsequent acts (cf. Child, 1968; Langer, 1978; Schlenker, 1980).

In addition, identity images affect how information is processed and retained. Given a salient schema, people are more likely to:

1. Notice and attend to schema-relevant information in the setting, especially to the degree that the information is highly consistent or highly inconsistent with it (e.g., Judd & Kulik, 1980; Neisser, 1976)
2. Process schema-relevant information more easily and quickly (Markus, 1977)
3. Organize and interpret supporting or ambiguous information, from both the present situation and from memory, in ways that are consistent with the schema (e.g., Cantor & Mischel, 1977, 1979; Carson, 1969; Judd & Kulik, 1980; Neisser, 1976; Swann & Read, 1981)
4. Polarize attitudes to make them more supportive of the schema. (Tesser, 1978)

Identity images (or self-schemata) normally are excellent guides for processing information (e.g., Greenwald, 1980; Kuiper & Rogers, 1979; Markus, 1977).

Given that our eventual focus will be on how people explain counterattitudinal behavior, it is worth noting in this context that I am *not* suggesting that people have needs for cognitive consistency that operate as a master motive to control behavior. Instead, cognitive consistency is a by-product of the way people process information (cf. Judd & Kulik, 1980; Kelman & Baron, 1974; Schlenker & Schlenker, 1975). Reality must be construed before people can get about the business of behaving. To the extent that inconsistencies are noticed, they serve as signals that there may be trouble ahead; more or better information may have to be acquired and greater assessment of the situation is needed. There is no reason to assume, and there is even evidence against the assumption (e.g., Judd & Kulik, 1980; Schlenker & Schlenker, 1975), that inconsistencies per se activate all manner of distorting mechanisms to force cognitions to be consistent.

As prototypes, images also provide *standards* for the evaluation of relevant behaviors. Take the case of actors who view themselves as honest, prefer to present that image to others, and therefore try to behave in ways that project the image. If their behavior fails to meet important standards (e.g., they cheat; they perceive or anticipate that others view them as dishonest), it will be evaluated negatively and generate negative affect, anxiety, and feelings of incompetence or unworthiness (Carver, 1979; Schlenker & Leary, 1982a).[4] If their behavior meets or exceeds important standards (e.g., they resist temptation; they perceive that others view them as honest), it will be evaluated positively and generate positive affect and feelings of accomplishment, pride, etc. (Carver, 1979; Schlenker & Leary, 1982a).

## 3. Controlling Identity Images

Identity-relevant information has an inherently evaluative quality, since it can have implications for how actors should behave and how they are or should be defined, regarded, and treated in social life. Whenever people are in the presence of others, it is usually in their best interests to convey particular types of identity images (Goffman, 1959, 1971; Jones & Pittman, 1982; Jones & Wortman, 1973; Schlenker, 1980; Tedeschi, 1981). Some projected images will be appropriate to the situation, make a desired impression on others, result in desired reactions from others, and produce self-satisfaction; other images will be inappropriate, make undesired impressions, generate undesired reactions, and produce self-dissatisfaction. Maximizing one's reward:cost ratio (both tangible and intangible outcomes) in social life involves, in large part, control of the identity images that are presented to others.

Self-presentation is the attempt to control identity-relevant information before real or imagined audiences (Schlenker, 1980, 1981). It is an intentional (i.e., goal directed) act whose immediate goal is to construct and maintain desired images of oneself. As such, it is a form of social influence. Through self-presentation people can attempt to control how others will perceive, evaluate, and treat them, and they might ultimately influence their personal perceptions of their own identities. The information that is conveyed can cut across a variety of dimensions, including its relevance to particular types of identities (e.g., a businessman vs a physician), its categorization under different types of personal constructs (e.g., competence vs likeableness), and its evaluation (e.g., good vs bad).

The concept of self-presentation has a "bad image" in the minds of many people, since it is often regarded as a cynical and deceitful form of behavior. It is therefore worth noting that self-presentation can be conscious or nonconscious, may or may not involve deception or the flagrant distortion of personal values, beliefs, and so on, and need not involve projecting only "approved" images of

[4]As explored more fully shortly, not all standards are important to the actor or others. Failure to conform to trivial standards should generate few or no negative repercussions. Some deviations may even generate humorous reactions, as when a minor flub is passed off as a joke, and some individuals delight in gaining a reputation as an eccentric who will do the unexpected. To the degree that deviations threaten the desired identity of the actor, however, negative repercussions should be produced.

self that curry the favor of immediate others (Schlenker, 1980). Of course, people sometimes try to project images of themselves that are self-aggrandizingly inaccurate, as when they lie in order to impress a specific other person. In many cases, however, self-presentation involves bringing one's perceived attributes, beliefs, conduct, or accomplishments to the attention of others, including by performing meritorious deeds in their presence. In addition, self-presentation can comprise habitual action patterns that are elicited by relevant social cues without conscious attention, as when cues trigger a particular identity image (and its prototypical behavior patterns) because of the image's established effectiveness in impressing others.

Finally, the types of impressions people prefer to create must be defined in terms of their idiosyncratic preferences in the situation. People may, for example, attempt to show that they will not conform to others' beliefs or that they have high personal standards that will not be sacrificed on the altar of expediency (e.g., Braver, Linder, Corwin, & Cialdini, 1977). In a similar vein, although people frequently prefer to present themselves in "socially approved" ways, such as by appearing reasonably competent, attractive, honest, there are a variety of other self-presentations and accompanying audience reactions that can best serve people's interests in specific situations (Jones & Pittman, 1982; Schlenker, 1980). For example, there are occasions when people might try to appear powerless or incompetent in order to receive the protection and nurturance of others, or when they might attempt to appear hostile and unattractive in order to maximize their "toughness" in the eyes of opponents during a negotiation or other conflict. Thus, the types of impressions people desire to create on others depends in part on their other goals in the situation.

### 4.   For Which Audience?

The process of categorizing and evaluating social conduct is intrinsically social in nature, but it may or may not take into account the perceived views and inclinations of a particular *immediate* audience of others.[5] Symbolic interactionists (e.g., Cooley, 1902/1922; Mead, 1934) proposed that (a) self-reflection, the process of viewing oneself as an object, (b) the concept of self, (c) the perceived relationship between self and others, and (d) standards for conduct, arise from the nature of the social interaction process.[6] Without social experi-

---

[5]Throughout the article, the phrase "views and inclinations" will be used as a shorthand to designate the values, standards, preferences, views, images, beliefs, attitudes, and other information that may be pertinent in a particular situation.

[6]Symbolic interactionists have hardly stood alone in tracing the development of the self and personality in general to the social interaction process. Neo-Freudian thought, especially that of Sullivan (1953) but also that of Adler and Horney, similarly traces the development of personality to social antecedents. Carson (1969) persuasively argued that personality develops from and is inseparable from real or imagined relationships with others. Hogan (e.g., Hogan & Cheek, 1982) proposed a

ence, people could not evaluate their own characteristics and conduct in the fashion we associate with mature human judgment (e.g., Carson, 1969; Hogan & Cheek, 1982; Meddin, 1979). Social experience, in conjunction with inherent mental capacities, allows people to view themselves as either specific others or others in general might, to anticipate and apply the appropriate evidence, views, and inclinations in such judgments, and to regulate their conduct in ways that permit them to fit into the social matrix of relationships between members of society. Indeed, Mead (1934) argued that the process of thought itself is *interactive* in nature, as when people privately talk to themselves; this private interactive process may be especially evident in the context of explaining and evaluating one's own conduct.

Over time, *personal* views and inclinations develop that exist and can be manifested irrespective of the presence of specific others. People typically seem to assume, though, that truly significant others—those real or imagined persons who are meaningful because they are admired, respected, loved, and so on— would agree with the majority of these personal assessments. To feel good about oneself usually implies that one expects significant others, though not necessarily all of them, to approve and applaud the characteristics or conduct in question. Personal feelings of self-satisfaction/dissatisfaction, worthiness/unworthiness, and so forth, following the personal evaluation of one's own conduct are the internalized residue of a socialization process that once focused on the reactions of significant immediate others. The self-evaluation process arose in social experience and the implications of the process for identity and social relationships provide the usual raison d'être for it. Maintaining personal (self) esteem and public esteem usually go hand in hand.

There are, of course, occasions when people perceive discrepancies between their own personal views and inclinations and those of specific others with whom they are interacting. For example, a person may value autonomy, view herself as independent, and have beliefs about how business concerns should function; she also knows many people who would concur with her self-assessments and value her opinions highly. Her employer, unfortunately, is not one of them; the employer values conformity, teamwork, and going by the company's rules rather than innovating. Depending on the strength of her motivation to be regarded positively by her employer, her self-presentations to the employer and her evaluations of her conduct will be guided by (a) her personal views and inclinations, (b) her perceptions of her employer's views and inclinations, or (c)

---

socioanalytic theory of personality that roots the concept in the nature of people's identities and examines individual differences from the perspective of identities vis-à-vis others. Snyder *et al.* (in press) considered the process of rationalization from the perspective of projecting desired selves to real or imagined audiences, and suggested that attention ''revolves'' between the self as audience and others as audience.

some weighted combination of each. Her focus of attention—on her personal views and inclinations, her employer's views and inclinations, or neither (e.g., she may be concentrating on a job-related problem and directing attention away from self)—should similarly influence her conduct and its evaluation, and may both affect and be affected by her motivation to impress the employer (see Scheier & Carver, 1981; Schlenker & Leary, 1982a).

In this sense, the desire to please one's self and the desire to please or impress specific others are both important (see also Hogan & Cheek, 1982; Snyder and Smith, 1982). Often they generate the same demands on the actor. However, one or the other can predominate in certain people or in most people under certain conditions. In such cases, it is assumed that the actor's behavior will be guided by the concerns that are pertinent vis-à-vis the salient audience (oneself or specific others). With this in mind, it should be noted that we shall be concentrating in this article on circumstances where the desire to please or impress specific others either converges with or is dominant over the desire to please oneself. The "average" subject in most experiments, for example, is usually quite concerned about creating a desirable impression on the researcher and others in the situation.

## B.   EXPLANATIONS OF CONDUCT

People are confronted daily by events that have implications for their identities. Some events might appear to support or enhance desired identities; others might appear to discredit or tarnish them. The explanations that people provide for such events constitute an integral part of the construction and maintenance of identities. As such, we shall now turn to a consideration of the nature of explanations of conduct and their social implications.

### 1.   When Do Explanations Occur?

According to proper English usage, an explanation gives an interpretation or meaning to something that is *not known or clearly understood*. The term is used here in the same way. *An explanation of conduct gives an interpretation or meaning to the event when such meaning appears to be unclear or might be "misinterpreted" or "misconstrued" by audiences.* Typical day-to-day events do not require explanations. Their meaning is clear to anyone who has been properly socialized in the particular culture. People's existing schemata about themselves and the world permit them to orient and respond to such events almost automatically, without conscious assessment of and attention to them (Langer, 1978; Schlenker, 1980). This economy of cognitive effort frees people to devote their attentions to more significant goals and problems. In everyday life questions arise or are anticipated about events for a reason, and only when reasons exist will explanations be consciously considered and proffered (cf. Goffman, 1971; Mills, 1940; Peters, 1960).

It is proposed that *explanations of conduct are proffered, to oneself and/or others, when behavior appears to: (a) violate standards in ways that threaten one's identity, or (b) meet commendable standards but ambiguity exists about the relevance of the event for one's identity* (e.g., one's responsibility is unclear). The standards may be one's own or those believed to be held by others in the situation. Such circumstances prompt attention and action by the actor and others in the situation and, while I would not contend they are the only conditions under which explanations occur, they describe a major, highly inclusive set of conditions. Such conduct usually (a) raises the issue of whether negative sanctions should be inflicted for untoward or unfortunate conduct (e.g., transgressions, failures) or positive sanctions should be awarded for meritorious conduct (e.g., heroism, successes), (b) raises the possibility that existing images of the actor might have to be modified (e.g., a college student in a premedical program receives several failing grades and may have to change his images of himself and modify his goals; friends and family may also have to change their views of him), and/or (c) may have been unanticipated by audiences, thereby disrupting on-going personal and social activities. Given these potential implications, an assessment process should be evoked in which relevant knowledge and evidence is scrutinized to construct an explanation for the conduct.

Actors may construct explanations in advance if they anticipate their conduct to be commendable or condemnable (Hewitt & Stokes, 1975; Schlenker, 1980; Snyder & Smith, 1982; Snyder, Stucky, & Higgins, in press). Such explanations can attempt to place the conduct in the desired light when it occurs. The process of constructing anticipatory explanations may also have a controlling or regulating effect on conduct itself. "Often anticipations of acceptable justifications will control conduct. ('If I did this, what could I say? What would they say?') Decisions may be, wholly or in part, delimited by answers to such queries . . . . Acts often will be abandoned if no reason can be found that others will accept" (Mills, 1940, p. 907).

## 2. Chronicling the Event

Explanations of conduct do not exist in a vacuum, but represent a more or less integrated conceptual/linguistic construal of an event (i.e., an act and its consequences) that takes into consideration a variety of relevant knowledge and evidence. Generalizing Burke's (1969) analysis of motives, it can be said that a complete explanation of conduct describes, implicitly or explicitly (a) what occurred (the event in question), (b) when and where it occurred (the scene), (c) who did it (the actor or agent), (d) how it was done (agency), and (e) why (the allocation of responsibility and, if the act is perceived as intentional, an ascription of motives). In short, explanations of conduct relate an actor to an event in a way that, given the particular context and circumstances, permits the behavior to be judged in accord with relevant principles and standards (e.g., laws, rules, norms, preferences, identity prototypes). Depending on the outcome of such judgments, appropriate sanctions may have to be applied to the actor and the actor's identity may be altered (in either a positive or negative direction).

From the actor's perspective, a *desirable explanation* is one that is *believable,* that is, is a reasonably accurate construal of the event given the relevant knowledge and evidence possessed or assumed to be possessed by audiences (oneself included), and is *personally beneficial,* that is, interprets the event in a way that facilitates the actor's goals in the situation (Schlenker, 1980, 1981; cf. Greenwald, 1980). Believability is shaped by the constraints of reality; personal benefaction is shaped by one's desires. As Heider (1958) put it, "Since one's idea includes what 'ought to be' and 'what one would like to be' as well as 'what is,' attributions and cognitions are influenced by the mere subjective forces of needs and wishes as well as by the more objective evidence presented in the raw material" of experience (pp. 120–121). The relative weighting of believability and personal benefaction will be considered after a further look at factors that influence both.

### 3. Believability

Explanations interpret conduct by relating it to the relevant views, values, information, and evidence held by people (oneself included) to whom the conduct must be explained (Carson, 1969; Foote, 1951; Lindesmith & Strauss, 1956; Mills, 1940; Peters, 1960; Schlenker, 1980; Snyder et al., in press; Scott & Lyman, 1968). Explanations that contradict existing knowledge or evidence will be rejected as being unbelievable or unacceptable (i.e., not a valid reason for violating the standards). Explanations must be fitted to:

1. General and societal knowledge, often represented by laws, norms, rules, and mores of a social, legal, and scientific sort (e.g., mental illness is a potentially believable explanation for aberrant behavior in this society, whereas demonic possession is not; self-defense is an acceptable explanation for killing another person, whereas doing so because he had annoying personal habits is not)
2. The identity of the actor (e.g., it is more believable to attribute malicious motives to a convicted felon than to someone who has the reputation of a kind, philanthropic individual)
3. The identities of others who are involved in the incident, as co-actors, beneficiaries, or victims (e.g., it is more acceptable to deceive self-centered, nasty, cruel individuals than kind, trusting ones)
4. The "facts" and evidence about the scene, the act, how the act was performed, and why (e.g., one cannot make a believable public case that one was pressured to deceive others if the person who purportedly applied the pressure emphasized one's decision freedom).

In short, reality provides constraints on people's personal perceptions of events (e.g., Heider, 1958) and their self-presentations to others (e.g., Baumeister & Jones, 1978; Schlenker, 1975, 1980).

### 4. Personal Benefaction

Explanations specify or imply how the conduct should be categorized (e.g., was the act a lie or did the actor express his honest opinions?), the polarity of the categorization (e.g., was the lie "good" or "bad," and how good or bad?), and the amount of responsibility, if any, that should be assigned to the actor (e.g., was the actor pressured into lying or did she do it on her own volition?).[7] Depending on these specifications, the event may have considerable implications for the actor's identity and relationships with others.

Alternative constructions of reality are not only possible, they are seemingly inevitable. Evidence can be amassed to reduce the believability of some constructions and increase that of others, but it virtually never leaves people with only one possible way an object or event can be construed (e.g., Einstein & Infeld, 1963; Kelly, 1955). To make the point, simply contemplate asking a radical behaviorist, psychoanalyst, personal construct theorist, symbolic interactionist, social worker, and lawyer to explain a particular case of rule-breaking.

Was a bombing a terrorist act or an act of freedom? Was Robin Hood a criminal or a paladin? Was the delivery of electric shock to another experimental subject an act of aggression or a helpful means of assisting him with his learning task? Such categorizations are based in part on evidence, and in part on the existing views and inclinations of the person making the judgment. In many, perhaps most, situations such categorizations are made almost automatically, as situational cues trigger the relevance of one rather than another schema (e.g., Taylor & Crocker, 1980; Wyer, 1980). However, as the importance of the conduct increases (see below), people should engage in a more active assessment that generates a more detailed examination and alternative ways of explaining the event (e.g., from the perspective of alternative identity images). The choice between them often is a matter of personal preference.

When people are responsible for an event, they are answerable or accountable for it in the sense that they can be condemned or praised (Fincham & Jaspars, 1980; Hamilton, 1980; Hart, 1968; Heider, 1958; Schlenker, 1980; Turner, 1968). Responsibility is the adhesive that links an actor to an event and attaches the deserved sanctions to the actor. People who are responsible for

---

[7]D'Arcy (1963) proposed a framework for classifying explanations of conduct based on three factors: (a) qualifying circumstances, which are the conditions that must exist before responsibility can be assigned to an actor, (b) specifying circumstances, which are the conditions that permit an action to be labeled one way rather than another, and (c) quantifying circumstances, which are the conditions that determine the amount of commendation or condemnation that should occur. Although not identical to the present framework, his analysis bears some similarities.

actions that meet or exceed important standards, such as helping others, doing an exceptional job on a test, or supporting worthy causes become entitled to reap benefits. Benefits can include approval, respect, esteem, and so on from others who are aware of the conduct; an enhanced or solidified reputation that can be carried into future dealings with others; tangible rewards such as prizes, trophies, awards; and personal feelings of pride, self-worth, accomplishment, and self-satisfaction. In contrast, people who are responsible for actions that fail to meet relevant standards, such as transgressing against laws, rules, or norms, committing embarrassing breaches of conduct, failing important tests, being rejected by others they had wanted to impress, and so forth, become liable for the appropriate punitive measures. These can include disapproval, disrespect, dislike, and so on from others who are aware of the conduct; a damaged reputation that must be carried into future dealings with others; tangible punishments such as fines or loss of privileges; and personal feelings of shame, guilt, loss of self-worth, and anxiety.

Responsibility is not an all-or-none matter of course. Heider (1958) described five levels of responsibility that can be assigned to actors:

1. Global association, a tenuous, noncausal connection between actor and outcomes based on such factors as group membership or category association
2. Simple commission, where the actor's behavior generated the outcomes but these were accidental or unforeseeable
3. Foreseeability, where the actor's behavior generated the outcomes and these were either foreseen or foreseeable, but not intended
4. Intentionality, where the actor intended to produce the outcomes that occurred
5. Mitigating circumstances, where intended outcomes may be partially attributed to situational pressures or coercive influences.

Attributions of responsibility appear to increase through the first four levels and decrease with the addition of mitigating circumstances (e.g., Fincham & Jaspars, 1980; Shaw & Sulzer, 1964). The amount of commendation or condemnation due actors is adjusted to the amount of responsibility assigned (Heider, 1958; Schlenker, 1980).

From the actor's perspective, the most personally beneficial explanation is usually one that characterizes the event positively (the more positively, the better it is) and ascribes high responsibility. The most personally detrimental explanation is usually one that characterizes the event negatively (the more negatively, the worse it is) and ascribes high responsibility. Because of the implications, people should be motivated to construct explanations that favor the former state and avoid the latter one, at least to the degree that the constraints of reality permit (Schlenker, 1980).[8] For example, if it appears that audiences view the conduct negatively,

---

[8]As noted earlier, a personally beneficial explanation is one that interprets the event in a way that facilitates the actor's goals. In most situations it would be beneficial (though not necessarily

people may attempt to reduce their responsibility by citing mitigating circumstances or unforeseeability. Or, if it appears that audiences perceive high responsibility, people may attempt to reduce the apparent negativity of the consequences. Such efforts may involve the choice of merely the least undesirable of several undesirable alternatives. As Austin (1970) put it, "Few excuses get us out of it completely: the average excuse, in a poor situation, gets us only out of the fire into the frying pan—but still, of course, any frying pan in a fire" (p. 177).

### 5. Explanatory Bias

A bias in the interpretation and explanation of events is a subjective tendency to prefer one interpretation over another; such an interpretation may or may not be an error according to some "objective" criterion for assessing the event (Harvey, Town, & Yarkin, 1981). Since we rarely have precise objective criteria for assessing (say) responsibility, or how much "harm" was done, it takes a rather severe distortion of the evidence before an explanation can be termed an error. However, the personal implications of explanations provide people with an impetus for bias. If several alternative explanations of an event are viewed as roughly comparable in believability, personal benefaction provides the grounds for selection. Bias may occur in actors' personal (private) explanations of the event, and may be even more pronounced, perhaps to the point of distorting personal views, in public explanations that are employed for self-presentational purposes (Bradley, 1978; Schlenker, 1980; Weary & Arkin, 1981).

The amount of bias that occurs is proposed to be a function of (a) the ambiguity of the relevant information, (b) the importance of the conduct, (c) the importance of the relevant identity images and other standards (e.g., laws,

---

believable) to describe the event more rather than less positively (or less rather than more negatively), while taking higher responsibility for increasingly positive events and lower responsibility for increasingly negative events. However, there appear to be some situations where a simple evaluation of the standard, conduct, or consequences on a positive–negative continuum would be misleading, because the most positive characterization would not facilitate the actor's goals in the particular situation. For example, conduct that surpasses some commendable standards might create obligations that the actor would prefer to avoid. He may do so well in an achievement setting, say, that he creates expectations on the part of others that he does not want to fulfill, either because he lacks the ability to continue such a high level of performance or merely does not want to put in the requisite effort. While he might evaluate such a performance positively when it is presented in the abstract, he would not evaluate it positively for him in that context. Thus, he may try to minimize personal responsibility for the achievement. As another example, there are occasions when people try to appear responsible for violating the standards of certain others, for example, a member of a street gang who wants to build an image of toughness and unpredictability. In such cases, there may be a large differences between what the actor and certain groups regard positively and what other groups regard positively. For the sake of simplicity, the terms positive and negative will be used in this paper, since there is usually considerable agreement on such evaluative judgments. However, keep in mind that the evaluation of the standards, conduct, and consequences must be considered in the context of the actor's situational goals. See Schlenker (1980) for a more complete discussion.

norms), and (d) the motivation to create a favorable impression on real or imagined audiences. As evidence becomes more ambiguous, that is, capable of being interpreted in a wider variety of ways (both qualitatively and quantitatively), a greater number of alternative schemata and possible explanations become viable; subjective preferences therefore have more latitude. The importance of the conduct refers to its implications for the actor in terms of the benefits or punishments (described earlier) that might be associated. The importance of the relevant identity images and other standards refers to their subjective value or centrality (i.e., the ability to subsume other images and standards). The motivation to create a desired impression on others refers to the subjective value of doing so either intrinsically or because of the implications for the satisfaction of other goals (see Schlenker & Leary, 1982a). The last three factors are usually interrelated (e.g., the importance of the relevant identity image may affect both the importance of the conduct and the motivation to create a desired impression on onlookers). The size of the potential discrepancy between the conduct and the relevant standards can also influence the importance of the conduct to the extent that it affects the implications for the actor. As each of these factors increases, so should the amount of the bias that occurs.

This analysis of bias—what it is and when it occurs—does not assume that people recognize one state of affairs to be true, either consciously or unconsciously, and then attempt to distort or deny this "truth" to themselves. Rather, a self-assessment process takes place in which explanations are considered in terms of their believability and personal benefaction (Schlenker, 1980). Benefaction will tip the scales in favor of one reasonably believable explanation over another or weight them in terms of their contribution to the event. Pertinent schemata may then play a role in further organizing and polarizing information around the more beneficial explanation(s) (cf. Tesser, 1978), perhaps making it (them) appear to be even more believable. Of course, people may perceive that others will condemn their conduct and proffer a public explanation that disagrees sharply with their personal views: They may privately recognize one "truth" but publicly advance the most believable lie they can muster to escape the public repercussions of the event. This is not the same, however, as assuming that some sort of cognitive homunculus censors and distorts that which it will allow the person to believe.

## III.  Predicaments

### A.  ACCOUNTING

When situational cues permit the inference that people may be responsible for events that can be characterized negatively, they confront a predicament that threatens their identities and might expose them to punitive responses (Schlenker, 1980). The greater the possible responsibility for and negativity of the conduct and its consequences, the more threatening are the implications for the actor. Actors should then construct public and/or personal explanations that are maximally desirable (or minimally undesirable), thereby eliminating or reducing the threat. Such explanations have been termed *accounts;* they present an interpretation that attempts to reconcile the event with relevant standards (Austin, 1970; Backman, 1976; Goffman, 1971; Harré, 1977; Schlenker, 1978, 1980; Tedeschi, 1981). Accounts are a particular type of explanation. Explanations in general may or may not provide an interpretation that reconciles the event with the relevant standards, and hence they may or may not be in the actor's best interests. For example, a transgression can be explained by noting that the actor had malicious motives and is a bad person who should be punished. In this case, the event is not brought into greater harmony with the standards, rather it is recognized as being seriously discrepant from these standards and worthy of negative sanctions. Accounts are explanations that attempt to achieve greater reconciliation with standards than might otherwise be apparent. They can be offered by the actor or by others. Furthermore, they need not be explicit or even verbal. People often communicate an account through the implications of their speech or actions, for example, a self-professed "good" tennis player who misses an easy shot might mention that he is using a new racquet or might adjust the wrapping on the handle of the racquet in a way that makes it clear the instrument is being blamed for the failure.

Two major classes of accounts are excuses and justifications, and they can be used separately or in combination. *Excuses* are explanations that minimize the actor's responsibility for the event. They include such tactics as denying one did it, denying foreseeability or intent (e.g., "It was an accident"; "How could I have known he would have been harmed?"), citing mitigating external circumstances (e.g., "He made me do it"; "I am the product of an impoverished childhood"), or citing mitigating internal circumstances (e.g., "I couldn't help it, I was drunk, or on drugs, or emotionally overwrought, or exhausted").

A large quantity of research suggests that people do attempt to minimize their responsibility for producing negative consequences, thereby excusing their actions (see Bradley, 1978; Schlenker, 1980; Snyder & Smith, 1982; Snyder *et al.,* in press). For example, the extensive literature on self-serving biases in attribution indicates that people tend to attribute their successes to factors that increase their personal responsibility while attributing failures to factors that decrease it (Bradley, 1978; Snyder et al., 1978; Weary & Arkin, 1981). This tendency appears to occur privately (Riess, Rosenfeld, Melburg, & Tedeschi, 1981), and is sometimes even more pronounced under public evaluation conditions (e.g., Weary, 1980). There are, of course, factors that minimize such biases, but these have been interpreted in terms of the presence of (a) reality constraints that block the believability of self-flattering attributions, or (b) conditions that favor modesty over braggadocio (Bradley, 1978; Schlenker, 1980; Tetlock, 1980).

*Justifications,* in contrast, implicitly or explicitly admit some responsibility, but minimize the negativity of the act and its consequences. For example, the act may be described as one not deserving condemnation (e.g., "I did it for your own good"; "It was a 'white' lie") or the consequences may be minimized (e.g., "Little harm was done"). A variety of research suggests that people will attempt to justify transgressions and personal failures (e.g., Brock & Buss, 1962; Davis & Jones, 1960; Modigliani, 1971; Mynatt & Sherman, 1975; Schlenker, 1980). For example, subjects who were given high rather than low choice about administering electric shocks to a confederate during a "learning task" later rated the shocks as less painful (Brock & Buss, 1962). The subjects in the low-choice condition already had an excuse; subjects in the high-choice condition needed a justification. Similarly, subjects who change their attitudes following counterattitudinal behavior are usually said to be *justifying* the behavior.

## B.  ATTITUDE CHANGE FOLLOWING COUNTERATTITUDINAL BEHAVIOR

### 1.  Variations on Responsibility and Consequences

What happens if inconsistencies are forced into people's cognitive structures like a monkey wrench calculatedly tossed into a well-oiled machine? Theoretical responses to that question proliferated about 20 years ago, providing the impetus for volumes of work and some of the more fascinating research social psychologists have produced (see Abelson, Aronson, McGuire, Newcomb, Rosenberg, & Tannenbaum, 1968; McGuire, 1969; Wicklund & Brehm, 1976). One of the most heuristic notions that emerged was that people will, under certain conditions, change their attitudes to make them consistent with behaviors that were previously counterattitudinal. The notion has numerous implications for the effectiveness of socialization practices, psychotherapy procedures, token economies, and tactics of social influence, to name but a few applied topics (Abelson *et al.,* 1968; Collins & Hoyt, 1972; Wicklund & Brehm, 1976).

As research accumulated, however, the focus shifted away from cognitive inconsistencies and converged on the conclusion that people must appear to be responsible for generating undesired consequences before they will change their attitudes to bring them more in line with counterattitudinal behaviors (e.g., Aronson, 1968; Bramel, 1968; Calder, Ross, & Insko, 1973; Collins & Hoyt, 1972; Cooper & Goethals, 1974; Cooper & Worchel, 1970; Cooper, Zanna, & Goethals, 1974; Greenwald & Ronis, 1978; Hoyt, Henley, & Collins, 1972; Insko, Worchel, Folger, & Kutkus, 1975; Nel, Helmreich, & Aronson, 1969; Schlenker, 1973, 1980; Verhaeghe, 1976). (The amount of consensus on this point is almost surprising given the nature of our field.) Responsibility has usually been operationally defined by giving subjects high rather than low choice about performing the behavior or high choice plus a small rather than large payment. Undesired consequences have been defined as ones subjects would prefer not to occur, such as causing harm or unpleasantness to others or creating an unpleasant experience for themselves.

To illustrate, Hoyt *et al.* (1972) gave college students high or low choice about writing essays arguing that toothbrushing is a danger to one's health. These essays supposedly would be used by the researchers in a project being conducted in surrounding junior high schools. The anticipated consequences of the essays were manipulated by leading some of the subjects to believe that their essays would be used to "effectuate the abandonment of preventative dental hygiene" by the students (high consequences), whereas other subjects merely believed the essays would be part of a classroom demonstration and have no impact on the students' dental habits (low consequences). After completing the essays, subjects' attitudes toward toothbrushing were assessed as part of a survey of medical, health-related opinions. As in many similar studies, the results indicated that subjects moderated their attitudes toward toothbrushing, contending that toothbrushing is less healthy and toothpastes more harmful, only when both high choice and high consequences co-existed.

From the perspective of identity analysis, the results fall into line. The counterattitudinal behavior paradigms employed by social psychologists usually induce subjects to lie, cheat, harm others, refrain from doing what they obviously prefer to do, do something they obviously would prefer to avoid doing, and otherwise make themselves appear to be immoral, unattractive, incompetent, inconsistent, or irrational. In short, the paradigms place subjects in situations where they might appear to have *violated personal or public standards for conduct and threatened their identities.* Their behavior requires an explanation. If they had low personal responsibility (e.g., low choice), the mitigating circumstances provide a salient, believable, and personally beneficial excuse. If, however, they had high personal responsibility (e.g., high choice), believable excuses become less obvious and one of the major alternatives becomes a justification. By shifting their attitudes about the topic or object of the behavior, their conduct does not appear as harmful or discrepant from relevant standards as it otherwise might. Subjects who have been assigned to low-consequences conditions, in contrast, do not experience much if any of a threat: They have not done anything especially untoward or in violation of standards, and their desired identities are intact.

Producing aversive consequences for others is not always in violation of standards. Self-defense is an exonerating reason for harming others, and virtually all societies recognize the norm of reciprocity in its negative form—harm for harm (Tedeschi & Lindskold, 1976). Depending on the circumstances, harming a harm-doer may even be commendable. Furthermore, certain types of people can be "justifiably" accorded less than normal civility and concern because they are evil, unworthy, potentially dangerous, obnoxious, and so on. Failure to maintain norms of propriety with such people is not a breach of conduct. Unless the conduct toward them is especially flagrant and aversive, it can be readily justified by describing the victim in a way that warrants the conduct (Schlenker, 1980; Scott & Lyman, 1968).

Given such social standards, it should be expected that misleading others who are clearly obnoxious and rude would not lead to attitude change toward the topic of the behavior. Indeed, Cooper *et al.* (1974) found that subjects who successfully misled a polite, sincere, and generally attractive person subsequently changed their attitudes toward the topic. But those who misled an impolite, cynical, generally unattractive person did not. Verhaeghe (1976) found similar results.

People whose identities are damaged by their transgressions often engage in helpful, prosocial behaviors as an identity-repairing tactic (Tedeschi & Riordan, 1981). Similarly, compensating victims of one's transgression is a remedial behavior that admits wrong-doing and attempts to make amends by redressing the damage that was done; the actor is then likely to be restored to grace and his or her identity is mended (Goffman, 1971; Schlenker, 1980). If subjects could adequately compensate those they misled in the forced-compliance situation, they would have less reason to engage in the alternative remedial behavior of justifying their conduct through attitude change. Verhaeghe (1976) found support for this hypothesis. The setting was arranged for some subjects to compensate a pair of confederates—whom they had misled into working on a boring task for a longer period of time—by allowing them to receive free movie tickets; in so doing, the subjects did not receive a ticket. The self-sacrifice and compensation even appeared exemplary: One of the confederates expressed his delight, saying that for the tickets he would be willing to work on the task for an even longer time than was suggested. As expected, subjects in this condition did not show attitude change toward the task.

Verhaeghe (1976) also included a condition where attitude change toward the task was made to be an unbelievable justification. After misleading confederates into working for a longer time on a boring task, subjects were given a questionnaire and told by the experimenter to respond "honestly and sincerely," since "I know very well that the task is *very* boring and monotonous." These subjects did not change their attitudes toward the task, but accounted instead by saying they were under greater obligation (an excuse) *and* by evaluating the confederates less favorably (an alternative justification).

In sum, attitude change toward a counterattitudinal topic is a means, though not the only means, of accounting for conduct that appears to violate personal or social standards and threaten subjects' identities. From this perspective, the inconsistency between (say) subjects' attitudes toward the topic of a speech and the speech itself is irrelevant as a motivating factor behind attitude change. If anything, such an inconsistency may merely serve as an additional signal that the conduct may be in violation of standards (Schlenker & Schlenker, 1975).

## 2. Foreseeability of the Consequences

Courts of law recognize unforeseeable consequences as an exonerating condition for harm-doing (Hart, 1968). When the consequences of one's conduct could not have been foreseen by a reasonable person who exercised appropriate judgment, one's responsibility for those consequences is low (Austin, 1970; Heider, 1958; Schlenker, 1980). If, however, wrongful consequences are either foreseen or should have been foreseen, one is responsible.

Numerous studies have explored the question of whether the consequences of counterattitudinal behavior must be foreseen in order for attitude change to occur (e.g., Cooper & Goethals, 1974; Cooper & Worchel, 1970; Goethals & Cooper, 1975; Goethals, Cooper, & Naficy, 1979; Pallak, Sogin, & Van Zante, 1974; Sogin & Pallak, 1976; Wicklund & Brehm, 1976). Initial results seemed mixed, with some suggesting that consequences must be foreseen and others suggesting they need not be. Goethals et al. (1979) appear to have integrated the literature by distinguishing among consequences that are unforeseeable, those that should have been foreseeable, and those that are foreseen. Subjects were given high choice to write essays arguing for the counterattitudinal position that the size of the student body at their university should be doubled. Those in an unforeseeable consequences condition were not led to expect, nor could they reasonably anticipate, that anyone who was not connected with the experiment would have access to their essays. In contrast, subjects in a foreseeable consequences condition were told that another group on campus would get to see their essays, but no specific mention was made of what group it might be. Finally, subjects in a foreseen consequences condition were also told that another group on campus would see the essays, and it was added that the group might be the university's board of admissions, which was currently studying the issue and might be influenced by the essays. After writing the essays, subjects in each group were either told that a random drawing had determined that their essays would be delivered to the admissions board or no mention was made of what group, if any, might receive the essays.

When wrongful consequences are clearly unforeseeable, people are not accountable for those consequences even if they occur; if their conduct is questioned, they merely explain the exonerating circumstances. Hence, we should expect no justificatory attitude change in the unforeseeable consequences condition even when subjects learn the admissions board will see their essays. When wrongful consequences are foreseeable, though not clearly foreseen, people are accountable for them if they occur. Hence, we should expect subjects in the foreseeable consequences condition to display justificatory attitude change if they learn that the admissions board will receive their essays, but no attitude change if they do not. Finally, when wrongful consequences are clearly foreseen, it should not matter whether subjects learn that their essays will definitely go to the admissions board or they are simply left in the dark; they are accountable for those consequences, and should attempt to justify the conduct. The results supported each of these hypotheses.

What would occur if subjects were told, after writing their essays, that the essays would *not* be used for any wrongfully persuasive purpose? The results of a study by Goethals and Cooper (1975) provide the answer. Attitude change still occurred for subjects who initially believed either that persuasive consequences would definitely occur or that they would not discover whether it would occur. Attitude change did not occur if subjects had been previously informed that their essays might not be used to persuade, and they would later play a role in determining this. Thus, the *actual* consequences of the behavior are less crucial than is the appearance that one clearly foresees wrongful consequences being produced by the conduct. Given such an appearance, justificatory attitude change is unnecessary only when wrongful consequences do not occur and the actor can explain the conduct by pointing to conditions that suggested that negative consequences might not occur.

### 3.   Audience Feedback about Responsibility

Audiences often wittingly or unwittingly provide actors with accounts for misbehaviors, as when a defense lawyer or psychiatrist suggests a possible exonerating reason for a client's law-breaking, or a friend provides comfort after an embarrassing incident by remarking, "Oh, it wasn't so bad" or "You really couldn't help it" (Goffman, 1959; Schlenker, 1980; Scott & Lyman, 1968). People often look to others for indications of how they viewed the conduct, and can willingly embrace interpretations that provide desirable accounts.

Riess and Schlenker (1977) examined the effect of receiving exonerating feedback from an audience on attitude change. Subjects were given either high or low choice by the experimenter about writing and videotaping a counterattitudinal speech against toothbrushing; as in the Hoyt *et al.* (1972) high-consequences condition, the speeches supposedly would be used to persuade junior high school students. After the speech, they received feedback from three observers indicating that either all, two, one, or none of them believed the subjects had very little choice about making the speech; in cases where not all observers ascribed little choice, the other observer(s) attributed considerable choice. The results showed that subjects significantly moderated their attitudes toward toothpastes, viewing them as less beneficial than subjects in a control group who did not make a counterattitudinal speech, only when they initially had been given high choice by the experimenter *and* all or a majority of the observers also attributed high choice

to them ($ps < .05$). If excusing information existed in the form of the experimenter's initial low-choice induction or if feedback from a majority of the
observers indicated low choice, no significant attitude change occurred. In both
cases, subjects could point to ''evidence'' that excused their conduct and accounted for their behavior.

The readiness with which subjects accepted the excusing feedback, even
when it may have conflicted with their initial ''reading'' of the situation, suggests the possibility that people may actively solicit and attempt to shape opinions from others to provide acceptable explanations of suspect conduct. Swann
and Read (1981) found that subjects will actively seek, elicit, and recall social
feedback from others that confirms their self-conceptions. A comparable process
may take place following suspect conduct. Although no data has been gathered
on this question in the forced compliance area, it seems a reasonable possibility.
If attitude change is a justification that is employed only when alternative accounts are not salient, the real-world prevalence of attitude change following
counterattitudinal behavior may be much less than earlier theorizing led us to
believe.

## C. ACCLAMATIONS

### 1. Commendable Conduct

Conduct that appears to meet or exceed commendable standards can generate a variety of benefits for actors (e.g., self-satisfaction, esteem from others,
tangible rewards). Of course, meeting just any standard does not imply that the
conduct is noteworthy or praiseworthy. Many standards are relevant to behaviors
that are expected of the typical person. Meeting them merely reveals that one is
''normal,'' although violating them generates attention and requires an explanation. Commendable standards, in contrast, are ones that are sufficiently distinctive that their achievement is regarded positively rather than neutrally. The more
positive the achievement, the greater are the potential implications for the actor.
Such accomplishments could include helping others, supporting worthy causes,
doing kind deeds, succeeding on important tests, and achieving important goals
in general.

As we have seen, explanations of events that violate standards can be called
accounts when they focus on excuses that minimize personal responsibility,
justifications that provide less-negative characterizations of the conduct and its
consequences, or both. In a complementary fashion, explanations of events that
meet commendable standards can be called *acclamations* when they focus on
entitling the actor to responsibility, enhancing the characterization of the conduct
and its consequences, or both (Schlenker, 1978, 1980).

*Entitlements* are explanations that maximize the actor's responsibility for the event. They include techniques such as attributing an achievement to factors that enhance personal responsibility (e.g., ability and effort) and/or discounting factors that detract from personal responsibility (e.g., luck, external forces), or indicating that the act was freely intended and the beneficial consequences were foreseen, as opposed to the event arising due to external pressure, fortuitous circumstances, accident, or mistake (e.g., "I gave the money to charity because I believed in the cause, and was not pressured into it by the canvasser for the charity"). *Enhancements* are explanations that categorize and evaluate the event in as personally beneficial a way as possible. Typically (but see footnote 7), this involves endorsing the most positive possible interpretation of the conduct and its consequences (e.g., "Her contribution put the charity drive over the top," should be preferred to "She only gave $10"; or "He *really* needed my help, since without it he would have had problems"). Entitlements and enhancements often go hand in hand, since many explanations accomplish both objective simultaneously (e.g., "I helped her because I knew the help would be valuable," highlights both the benefits of the conduct and its intentional nature). Acclamations need not be explicit or even verbal. Indeed, more subtle approaches that lead the audience to draw the desired conclusion probably create a better impression than explicit verbal claims that might appear egotistical or braggartly.

Much of the research that is relevant to acclamations has concerned the attribution of responsibility in achievement or test situations. As noted earlier, the self-serving bias literature indicates that people accentuate their personal responsibility for successes, and prefer feedback from others that ascribes greater rather than less responsibility to them (e.g., Bradley, 1978; Greenwald, 1980; Riess *et al.*, 1981; Schlenker, 1980; Sicoly & Ross, 1977; Weary & Arkin, 1981). Such findings are not confined to the domain of task achievement, however. Schlenker, Hallam, and McCown (in press) reasoned that people can gain maximal acclaim for an intended, beneficial act (e.g., helping others) only when their motives or reasons appear to be "good" (e.g., "I helped because the other needed assistance"). Since good acts are sometimes performed for "bad" reasons (e.g., to make a favorable impression; because the experimenter expected it), actors' descriptions of their conduct should accentuate positive motives and discount negative ones. Indeed, Schlenker *et al.* found that actors ascribed their own helpful act largely to positive motives and denied negative ones, while observers showed little differentiation on the basis of the attractiveness of the motives. Also as anticipated, the effect occurred under both private- and public-response conditions, and was more pronounced when the consequences of the help were large rather than small.

### 2.   *Attitude Change as an Acclamation*

When conduct violates standards, the predicament is alleviated by salient evidence that provides a ready excuse or justification (e.g., "I was given no choice"). But actors must go beyond the evidence at hand and construct their own excuses and justifications when exonerating information is not obvious (e.g., by moderating their attitudes toward the topic). In a complementary fashion, when conduct meets commendable standards, acclaim is obviously due if salient evidence or feedback entitles the actor to responsibility and indicates the event is laudatory (e.g., "I was given high choice about agreeing to help this worthy cause"). But actors must go beyond the evidence at hand and construct their own entitlements and enhancements when salient evidence that might provide acclaim is ambiguous or contradictory.

Modesty typically arises when salient evidence already provides actors with credit for superior accomplishments or attributes and audiences are aware of the evidence. Actors can then underplay the event, thereby avoiding the risk of appearing eogtistical and gaining credit for both their accomplishment and humility. In contrast, self-enhancement typically arises when actors may have reason to believe their conduct or attributes are commendable but (a) the evidence is ambiguous or contradictory, or (b) audiences are believed to be uncertain about how positively they should regard the actor. Indeed, subjects' public self-descriptions are more self-enhancing when audiences are believed to be unaware rather than aware of their meritorious attributes (Baumeister & Jones, 1978; Schlenker, 1980). Furthermore, subject-observers express more favorable attitudes toward actors who are modest rather than pompously accurate in their descriptions of a known superior accomplishment; but when subjects are unaware of the actors' levels of performance, they prefer actors who appear self-positive over those who do not (Schlenker & Leary, 1982b).

Such reasoning can be applied to the forced-compliance situation irrespective of whether the relevant behavior is attitude consistent or inconsistent. Suppose situational cues suggest low rather than high decision freedom for producing positive consequences, such as doing a speech that should benefit others. Actors are then less entitled to the appropriate credit, feelings of self-satisfaction, approval, and other benefits that might otherwise be associated. To the extent that these benefits are important, subjects should attempt to entitle themselves to credit. One means of doing so without contradicting the salient information about low choice is to express a strongly favorable attitude toward the topic/object of the behavior. Subjects who deliver strong, extreme essays are viewed by observers as having essay-consistent personal beliefs even when the actors clearly had no choice in selecting their essay topics (Jones, Worchel, Goethals, & Grumet, 1971). Similarly, by expressing strongly favorable attitudes toward the topic, actors should be indirectly discounting the pressures (e.g., "I strongly believed this all along and did not do it simply because of the pressure") and making the consequences of the speech appear even more commendable (e.g., "This is an extremely positive cause to advocate"). In contrast, when there seems to be high choice, subjects appear to be responsible. Their explanations can merely describe the circumstances and credit follows. There is relatively little reason to modify prior attitudes.

An identity analysis thus leads to the hypothesis that people are more likely to express highly favorable attitudes toward the topic/object of their conduct when they are given low rather than high choice to perform an act that produces important, positive consequences. Schlenker and Schlenker (1975) tested this hypothesis in a situation where subjects performed a *counterattitudinal* act that produced *positive* consequences. Under the guise of an investigation of how people form and react to interpersonal evaluations, subjects were given high or low choice to deliver an extremely favorable interpersonal evaluation to another participant. The other had been previously portrayed during an interview as a rather dull to average individual, so the favorable evaluation, which had been prepared by the researchers, was inconsistent with subjects' initial beliefs about the other. However, the evaluation should be expected to make the other person feel good and be appreciative. The importance of obtaining credit for the evaluation was manipulated by telling subjects either that they would never meet and that the other would never learn the evaluation might not represent their true opinions (low importance), or that they would be introduced to the other at the end of the session, at which time the other would learn they chose or were told to deliver a standardized evaluation (high importance). After delivering the evaluation, subjects were asked to indicate their actual attitudes toward the other on 12 bipolar evaluative adjectives (e.g., good–bad, intelligent–unintelligent) and an item asking how attractive the other is as a person. Since both types of measures produced comparable patterns, only the average ratings on the evaluative adjectives will be described in detail.

As shown in Table I, the interaction of choice and importance ($p < .02$) revealed that subjects expressed an extremely favorable evaluation of the other only when importance was high and they had been given low choice about delivering the evaluation. This was the only condition that differed significantly from a control group who merely listened to the interview and rated the other ($p < .01$). It also differed from the other orthogonal experimental conditions ($ps < .02$). As hypothesized, attitude change appears to be inversely related to choice when the conduct generates positive consequences and the importance of obtaining credit is high.

It is difficult to reconcile these results with predictions derived from self-perception theory (Bem, 1972). The latter suggests that people infer their attitudes from their behaviors when prior attitudes are not salient and cues suggest that the behavior was not compelled by situational pressures. Thus, more attitude change should have been expected in the high- than low-choice conditions, not the reverse. There was no reason to assume that subjects' prior attitudes were any more or less salient in this situation than in any other situation to which self-

TABLE I
Evaluative Ratings of the Other Person

| Condition | Condition[a] | |
|---|---|---|
| | High importance | Low importance |
| High choice | 9.6 | 10.6 |
| Low choice | 12.2 | 10.0 |
| Control | | 9.3 |

[a]Higher ratings indicate more favorable evaluations on 15-point scales.

perception theory has been applied, but even so, the best the theory would then do is predict no attitude change, not an apparent reversal of the inference process that is at the core of the theory.

The results also suggest that straightforward inconsistencies between beliefs and behaviors take a back seat to the positive or negative character of the behavior. The findings lend no support to the idea that subjects were motivated to reduce the cognitive inconsistency between holding one belief ("The other is dull") and saying the opposite ("I praised the other"). If they were, attitude change should have occurred under the high-choice conditions (Festinger, 1957). The "evolved" form of dissonance theory would most likely suggest that no attitude change should occur, since no negative consequences took place and "white lies" are usually justified by the positive consequences they entail (cf. Aronson, 1968). It thus would stand mute about the findings that were obtained. Of course, still another evolution of dissonance theory could take place to handle such results. One could assume that dissonance was created by the cognitions "I am a good person who should be responsible for doing good deeds," and "I do not appear to be responsible for doing this good deed." Thus, a no-responsibility-for-positive-consequences proposition could be added to the responsibility-for-negative-consequences proposition. The degree to which doing so strains the credulity of dissonance theory must be left up to the reader.

It is worth noting that the identity hypotheses can also be applied to situations where people behave in an attitude-consistent fashion and the act and its consequences are commendable. Although space does not permit a thorough review of that literature, it has been found that people increase the polarity of their prior attitudes when they are given low rather than high choice, the consequences are important and positive, and self-presentational concerns are high (Schlenker & Goldman, 1982; Schlenker & Riess, 1979).

D.  SELF-ATTENTION, IDENTITY IMAGES, AND COUNTERATTITUDINAL BEHAVIOR

### 1.  Self-Attention

Self-attention appears to play an important role in the activation of concerns about identity. Self-attention refers to directing conscious attention inward, toward rather than away from the self (Buss, 1980; Carver, 1979; Duval & Wicklund, 1972; Fenigstein, 1979; Fenigstein, Scheier, & Buss, 1975; Scheier & Carver, 1981). According to Mead (1934), it reflects the capacity to look at oneself from a social perspective, the way specific (significant or nonsignificant) others or others in general might. Such a state can be situationally induced (e.g., by the presence of a mirror or camera), and some people are chronically more likely to focus attention on themselves.[9]

Self-attention appears to activate the self/identity system. It (a) prompts people to attend to and interpret information from the perspective of its relevance to self/identity schemata (e.g., Hull & Levy, 1979; Fenigstein, 1979), (b) increases the salience of and adherence to personal or public/social standards for conduct (e.g., Carver, 1979; Carver & Scheier, 1982; Diener & Srull, 1979), (c) intensifies the processes of self-assessment and self-evaluation (e.g., Carver, 1979; Fenigstein, 1979), and (d) enhances self-reinforcement and positive affect when standards are met or self-punishment and negative affect when standards are not met (e.g., Carver, 1979; Diener & Srull, 1979). Deindividuation, a state in which people lose a sense of identity and fail to adhere to relevant standards for conduct, appears to involve an extended absence of self-attention (Diener, 1980).

Distinctions have been drawn between private self-attention, which is an increased awareness of personal thoughts, feelings, standards, and so on and public self-attention, which is an increased awareness of the views, inclinations, standards, and information believed to be held or known by other people or groups (Buss, 1980; Carver & Scheier, 1982; Fenigstein et al., 1975; Scheier & Carver, 1981). Dispositional tendencies seem to exist for each (Fenigstein et al., 1975), and each also can be situationally induced. Public self-awareness has been induced by making the presence of a specific audience salient or placing subjects in front of a camera and other videotaping equipment; private self-awareness has been induced by directing subjects' attentions away from specific others and on themselves, such as by placing them before a mirror that reflects their faces (Scheier & Carver, 1981). Each state appears to create somewhat different concerns about one's identity.

People who are publicly self-attentive appear to be motivated to impress specific immediate others. Public self-consciousness (but not private self-con-

---

[9]The situationally induced state will be called self-awareness, the chronic disposition will be called self-consciousness, and self-attention will be used to refer to the concept as a whole.

sciousness) is highly correlated ($r = +.67, p < .001$) with the Fear of Negative Evaluation (Leavy, 1980); the latter scale assesses concerns with gaining approval and avoiding disapproval. People who are publicly self-conscious also are more likely to report being socially anxious (Fenigstein *et al.*, 1975; Leary & Schlenker, 1981). People who are publicly self-attentive report that they feel like they are being observed when in the company of others, have a high awareness of how others regard them, view others' behaviors as having high personal relevance, and demonstrate an increased responsiveness to evaluations, especially negative ones (Fenigstein, 1979). When interacting with others, their actions seem to be influenced more by what they think others believe and value than what they believe and value (Scheier & Carver, 1981).

People who are privately self-attentive, in contrast, appear to be more concerned with presenting an identity that is consistent with their personal views and inclinations. They are not especially hungry for approval from specific, immediate others, many of whom may be relatively insignificant in the long run. Instead, they are concerned about how they look to themselves. When interacting with others, their actions seem to be influenced more by what they personally believe and value than what others believe and value (Scheier & Carver, 1981).

Consistent with the above, privately self-conscious subjects display increased reactance when pressured by others, whereas publicly self-conscious subjects display decreased reactance (Carver & Scheier, 1981). It could be that (a) personal opinions are more salient for the privately self-conscious subjects, thus making the contradictory pressures more salient, and/or (b) the concern with being viewed as autonomous and self-reliant, especially to themselves, was greater for the privately self-conscious subjects. Reactance has been associated with self-presentational efforts to demonstrate autonomy in social situations (Baer, Hinkle, Smith, & Fenton, 1980; Grabitz-Gniech, 1971). It has also been found that privately self-conscious subjects resist conformity pressures whereas publicly self-conscious subjects go along with an incorrect majority (Froming & Carver, 1981); and that publicly self-conscious subjects moderate their attitudes prior to discussions with others, suggesting a desire to maintain a flexible, middle-of-the-road position that can be easily defended, whereas privately self-conscious subjects do not display such anticipatory attitude moderation (Scheier, 1980).

Public self-attention also appears to facilitate the construction of personally beneficial public explanations of conduct. Federoff and Harvey (1976) found that subjects attributed their outcomes to personal factors more following success than failure, and this effect was enhanced for subjects who were made publicly self-aware by videotaping their performances. Arkin, Gabrenya, Appelman, and Cochrance (1979) found a similar effect, but only for subjects who were also high self-monitors.

Scheier and Carver (1980) examined the relationship between self-attention and attitude change in the forced-compliance setting. Three studies were conducted in which subjects were given high or low choice about writing counterattitudinal essays arguing that students should have little or no control over the kinds of courses offered by the university. In one study (Experiment 2), self-awareness was situationally manipulated by having subjects complete the attitude questionnaires in the presence of a mirror (assumed to induce private self-awareness), a camera that was focused on them (assumed to induce public self-awareness), or neither. In another study (Experiment 3), the Self-Consciousness Scale (Fenigstein *et al.*, 1975) was used to divide subjects into those who were high in chronic private or public self-consciousness.

As in prior studies, when self-awareness was not manipulated, subjects displayed justificatory attitude change toward the essay's topic if they had been given high but not low choice about writing the essays. Public self-attention had the effect of enhancing attitude change by subjects who were given high choice. Subjects who were given high choice and were publicly self-attentive, either because of their dispositions or the situational induction, displayed the greatest attitude change toward their essay topics, thus justifying the conduct. Those given no choice displayed no attitude change. [Wicklund and Duval (1971, Experiment 2), similarly found that the presence of a TV camera increased attitude change.] In contrast, private self-attention, either dispositional or situational, wiped out attitude change toward the topic irrespective of initial choice. Instead, privately self-attentive subjects employed an alternative means of justifying the conduct. In both studies, subjects who had been given high choice and were privately self-attentive rated their *essays* as being *less strongly opposed* to student control than subjects in other conditions. Judges' ratings of the essays, however, revealed no basis in fact for such a contention. Thus, privately self-attentive subjects who confronted high responsibility in the forced-compliance predicament justified their conduct by describing it in a way that minimized its discrepancy from personal standards.

These results suggest that public self-attention is a necessary condition for the occurrence of attitude change following counterattitudinal behavior. Public self-attention focuses people on how their conduct will look to immediate audiences (e.g., the experimenter), evoking concerns with maintaining a desirable identity before those others. To justify untoward conduct for which they appear responsible, they shift their attitudes toward the topic of the counterattitudinal essays, thereby maintaining a desirable public identity. The similarity of the responses of subjects in the "control" condition, who did not receive a specific manipulation of self-attention, and the public self-attention condition suggests that the average participant normally experiences a reasonably high degree of public self-attention in the forced-compliance paradigm.

People who are privately self-attentive, in contrast, still justify their conduct but in a way that does not sacrifice their preexisting personal beliefs: They merely shift their descriptions of the conduct itself in a way that makes it appear less discrepant from their prior attitudes. Scheier and Carver (1980) suggested that prior attitudes were more salient for these subjects, prompting them to focus on alternative justificatory techniques. Phrased differently, privately self-attentive people seem to focus more on their own views and inclinations when constructing explanations of their conduct, whereas publicly self-attentive people seem to focus more on what they believe to be the views, inclinations, and information held by immediate others. The former appear to maintain identities that will satisfy themselves (and perhaps imagined significant others who might be evoked during the self-evaluation process), whereas the latter appear more oriented toward maintaining identitites before the specific others with whom they are presently interacting.

Scheier and Carver (1980) also raise the possibility that prior conflicting results on the effects of increasing the salience of subjects' initial attitudes in counterattitudinal behavior situations (e.g., Ross & Shulman, 1973; Snyder & Ebbesen, 1972; Wixon & Laird, 1976) can be integrated and explained by considering confoundings that may have occurred between such manipulations and the type of self-attention that should have been induced in each study. Their analysis appears to be quite viable, although space does not permit a more detailed examination.

## 2. *Identity Images*

The specific types of identity images (schemata) that people attempt to maintain should have an effect on justificatory attitude change following counterattitudinal behavior. People whose actions do not violate personal image prototypes and standards but do violate the standards of specific others with whom they are interacting (e.g., a member of a street gang who regards stealing as an acceptable way of life, but who must account to the police following an accusation of theft) may construct one explanation for the immediate audience but not privately believe it. Conversely, people whose actions violate personal image prototypes and standards but do not violate the standards of specific others (e.g., a military commander who won the battle and pleased his superiors, but did not win as decisively as his high personal standards demanded) should construct an account for themselves even if never called on to do so by others. Unfortunately, virtually no research has specifically addressed this issue. A few studies have examined the effects of global self-esteem on attitude change following counterattitudinal behavior (e.g., Cooper & Duncan, 1971), but these studies do not address the relationship between the conduct and the standards required by specific identity images.

Bem and Funder (1978, Experiment 3) did examine a closely related question. They proposed that the likelihood that people will behave in a particular way in a particular situation will depend on the match-up or similarity between their personal characteristics and the schema or template that describes the type of person who would engage in that behavior in that situation. They had expert judges construct idealized templates of the types of people who should demonstrate attitude change in the forced-compliance situation according to the predictions of dissonance theory, self-perception theory, and "self-presentation" theory. To illustrate, people who are alert to inconsistencies and find inconsistencies in their beliefs and attitudes to be aversive partially composed the template for dissonance theory; people who are insensitive to inner states and who believe their behavior reflects their attitudes partially composed the template for self-perception theory; people who are helpful, cooperative, and likely to conform to norms composed the template for self-presentation. Subjects who wrote counterattitudinal essays under conditions of high choice were rated by their friends on a series of Q-sort items that typified each theoretical approach. These ratings of the subjects' characteristics, which may partially reflect the identity images that they desire to project to others, were then analyzed to yield scores on each of the three templates; these scores were then correlated with the amount of attitude change they exhibited in the forced-compliance situation.

It was found that subjects' characteristics on the self-presentation template correlated most highly with attitude change scores ($r = + .53, p < .01$), whereas characteristics on the dissonance template displayed a nonsignificant negative correlation with attitude change ($r = - .25$); characteristics on the self-perception template fell intermediate ($r = + .32, p < .10$). Interestingly, the component of the self-perception template that did "best" in explaining the variance (though it was still nonsignificant) was a rating of being influenced by persuasion, which itself may reflect an approval-oriented approach to interactions.

These results indicate that people who display the greatest attitude change in the forced-compliance setting are characterized as being cooperative, helpful, and norm-oriented (similar in some ways to the state that is associated with public self-attention). Of course, the results do not unequivocally demonstrate that either dissonance theory or self-perception theory are in error, since (a) a few people may have behaved in accord with the predictions of each of these approaches, but in the overall sample their numbers were fewer, and (b) people who fit the characteristics of the dissonance template may also have been those who are chronically high in private self-consciousness, which should minimize attitude change toward the topic even though alternative, unmeasured accounts may have been employed (Scheier & Carver, 1980). The results do, however, provide additional convergent support for the notion that attitude change toward the topic of counterattitudinal behavior is strongly associated with the desire to maintain an identity that would be approved by immediate others.

E.  NEGATIVE AFFECT AND ATTITUDE CHANGE

Many of the recent studies of attitude change following counterattitudinal behavior have focused on the role of arousal as a mediating mechanism (e.g.,

Cooper, Zanna, & Taves, 1978; Fazio, Zanna, & Cooper, 1977; Higgins, Rhodewalt, & Zanna, 1979; Kiesler & Pallak, 1976). These studies take as their starting point the hypothesis that in searching for an explanation for physiological arousal, people may misattribute their feelings to causes other than the actual ones (Schachter & Singer, 1962). "When subjects experience discomfort, they may seek explanations for it, and the explanations they prefer are those that do not reflect negatively on themselves" (Fries & Frey, 1980, p. 405). If arousal, unpleasant arousal in particular, is a motivating factor for attitude change (as dissonance theory might be interpreted to suggest), then people might be made to misattribute these feelings to causes other than their conduct, such as to a "pill" they have taken during the experiment. The misattribution then would reduce or eliminate attitude change following counterattitudinal behavior. The data are consistent with these ideas.

From the perspective of identity analysis, such results are reasonable. People who appear to be responsible for conduct that violates standards should experience negative affect and anxiety (e.g., embarrassment, self-dissatisfaction). These tension states may play a role in signaling or intensifying perceptions of identity difficulties.

## IV.  Payments and Predicaments

### A.  THE ENIGMA

What happens if people are paid to engage in counterattitudinal behavior? That question, and the many answers it has generated, reflects the oldest controversy in the area and has produced a liberal mixture of puzzlement and frustration. Briefly, the enigma resulted from the confrontation between predictions derived from two intuitively appealing explanations of why payments should affect attitude change. Dissonance theory (Festinger, 1957) generated the prediction that an inverse relationship should occur between payments offered to induce counterattitudinal behavior and attitude change. Smaller payments provide less "justification" for counterattitudinal acts and should lead to greater dissonance; this, in turn, should produce greater attitude change. In contrast, incentive and reinforcement approaches (e.g., Elms, 1967; Rosenberg, 1965) generated the prediction that a direct relationship should occur. Larger payments should act as both incentives for superior counterattitudinal performance and reinforcements for that performance, producing greater attitude change.

After initial empirical clashes in which the advocates of each position obtained results consistent with their predictions, numerous studies found both the inverse and direct relationship under different conditions of the same experiment (e.g., Calder *et al.*, 1973; Carlsmith, Collins, & Helmreich, 1966; Holmes & Strickland, 1970; Linder, Cooper, & Jones, 1967). The immediate conclusion was that both approaches were correct, but only under certain conditions. The frustration continued, however, as the search for the specific boundary conditions of each approach proved obscure. Dissonance theory eventually settled on a responsibility-for-negative-consequences formulation that shifted the focus of the theory (see Collins & Hoyt, 1972; Greenwald & Ronis, 1978); it still could not deal with the direct relationship, though, and the interest in the effects of payments dwindled. Incentive/reinforcement approaches were not as fortunate. Despite occasional findings of a direct relationship, it is still not clear when it should occur, and results often lend no support to hypothesized mediating mechanisms even when the direct relationship is obtained. The approach retreated from the area. [See Aronson (1966), Calder *et al.* (1973), Collins & Hoyt (1972), and Elms (1967) for reviews.]

## B. THE SOCIAL MEANING OF PAYMENT

An identity analysis takes a different conceptual starting point. Instead of asking how payments affect cognitive inconsistencies or simple reinforcement, the questions become, "What are the implications of payments for the identities people desire to claim?" and "How might payments reflect on conduct that violates standards?" Payments can have social meanings, and these should not be regarded merely as artifacts that interfere with basic psychological principles.

Money is not just money. Aside from its symbolic value (e.g., for status), the manner in which it is obtained can have a profound effect on the identity of the individual who acquires it (e.g., an honest laborer vs a pimp). People have even been known to refuse "dirty money" from others who have acquired it in illegitimate ways.

Researchers have suggested numerous interpretations of payments made in forced-compliance situations, including: (a) an incentive for performance, (b) a reward for achievement, (c) a cue suggesting the experimenter's perceptions of the worth, enjoyableness, or ethicality of the task subjects must perform, (d) a cue about how many other people would comply with the experimenter's request, (e) a cue to personal responsibility for the conduct, (f) a cue about how much one is expected to conform to the experimenter's wishes and opinions, and (g) a possible bribe for illicit behavior (e.g., Collins & Hoyt, 1972; Insko *et al.*, 1975; Kelley, 1967; Rosenberg, 1965; Steiner, 1970; Tedeschi & Rosenfeld, 1981). While not wanting to minimize the subtle and potentially important implications of these differences, we shall concentrate on two major, and ultimately related, dimensions that appear to provide integration to the area: the effects of payments on (a) the appearance of responsibility for the conduct, and (b) concerns about possible illegitimate aspects of the payments in relation to conduct and identity (e.g., the payments could be a bribe to perform a morally questionable act).

The interpretation of payment that has received the most general support is that it can affect responsibility (e.g., Calder *et al.*, 1973; Collins & Hoyt, 1972; Insko *et al.*, 1975; Kelley, 1967; Steiner, 1970). High decision freedom at the time of the act combined with no or minimal payment has been presumed to maximize the actor's apparent responsibility for the conduct. If the conduct violates standards, personally desirable explanations should be constructed. Thus, we should expect that smaller payments often generate more justificatory attitude change than larger ones (when "often" occurs will be elaborated shortly).

In contrast, consider cases where payments take on connotations of illegitimacy. Illegitimacy exists when payments involve a contingency, or are of a magnitude or nature, that makes them appear inappropriate given the relevant standards (e.g., rules, norms, laws, identity-images). For example, the payment may be seen as an inducement to elicit conduct that violates standards; if it is accepted, the recipient appears to have been bribed or bought to do something morally wrong, unpleasant, stupid, and so on. Or, the payer (e.g., experimenter) may appear to be primarily interested in something other than simply having a "cover task" performed, raising questions in the recipient's mind about how it will look to take payment in these suspect circumstances, for example, does he or she appear willing to do anything for payments?

If payments take on aspects of illegitimacy, people should become concerned with not appearing to be the type who can be "bought." The greater the illegitimacy of the payment, the greater the threat to the recipient's identity. Explanations of the conduct should be proffered that attempt to discount the appearance of illegitimacy; to the extent that the conduct also violates other standards (e.g., harms others), the explanations should incorporate those aspects as well. One means of doing both, though not the only one, is to express a more favorable attitude toward the topic of the conduct.

To illustrate, take the case of subjects who are offered a large amount of money to perform a counterattitudinal speech that will have undesired consequences, and the payment appears to be illegitimate. Before considering why attitude change in the direction of the speech is appropriate under these conditions, it will be worthwhile to comment on a prevailing view of what should occur. Rosenberg (1965) suggested that subjects who do not want to appear to be bribed would do so by refusing to alter their existing attitudes, thereby expressing their strong opposition to the speech topic. If salient audiences clearly knew that subjects vigorously opposed the topic prior to the payment, then as Rosenberg suggests, any subsequent shift in attitudes that occurred might be attributed to the payment and give the appearance that the payment influenced their attitudes.

However, expressing strong opposition to the speech topic would be counterproductive given the procedures that are employed in virtually all forced-compliance studies. Such studies usually include precautions to insure that subjects believe their prior attitudes are unknown or only very generally known by the experimenter and others in the situation. If salient audiences are unaware of subjects' prior attitudes, subsequently expressing attitudes that strongly oppose the behavior would demonstrate precisely what subjects should want to avoid. They would appear to have vehemently opposed the conduct all along and therefore must have performed it solely to get the money. In other words, they would appear to have been bribed to do something condemnable. A more effective account would be to express a less negative, more moderate attitude toward the topic. Subjects then have explained the conduct in a way that suggests (a) they did not strongly oppose the behavior, and therefore may not have performed it just to get the money, and (b) the consequences of their actions are more acceptable.

When illegitimacy is salient, payment magnitude may be directly, rather than inversely, related to personal responsibility. Kelley (1967) suggested that "volition is high if the strength of illegitimate forces is high and you comply" (p. 218). A large payment to perform to questionable act thus should confer high responsibility on the recipient (e.g., the image of a "hit man" choosing to murder for personal profit). This suggests that in situations where payments are viewed as legitimate, smaller payments generate greater responsibility on the part of recipients than do larger ones. In situations where payments seem illegitimate, however, the reverse is true. One implication is that a curvilinear relationship should exist between payment magnitude and responsibility. Payments that are flagrantly oversufficient may be likely to generate suspicions about the payer's ulterior motives, and thus raise the specter of illegitimacy. Thus, responsibility should be maximal when payments are either very small and insufficient or very large and oversufficient (illegitimate). When payments are sufficient (the intermediate range), responsibility is lower and can be more readily shifted to the situation (e.g., the experimenter). Indeed, Shaw (1976) found such a curvilinear relationship between payment size and perceived responsibility. If illegitimate forces are modified in a given situation, it should have the effect of shifting such a curve. For example, if illegitimacy cues are increased in a situation, a small payment that may otherwise have been seen as insufficient (generating high responsibility) and a large payment that may otherwise have seemed sufficient (generating low responsibility), should then appear to be sufficient (low responsibility) and oversufficient (illegitimate, high responsibility), respectively.

These arguments allow us to reemerge at our earlier conclusion: Explanations of conduct are most needed and will tend to be more personally desirable when people appear to be responsible for violating standards for conduct. When payments are considered, this translates into justificatory attitude change being most likely to occur when (a) illegitimate forces are salient and payments are of a larger magnitude, and (b) illegitimate forces are not salient and payments are of smaller magnitudes.[10]

## C.  PRIOR RESEARCH ON PAYMENTS FOR COUNTERATTITUDINAL BEHAVIORS

The preceding analysis is consistent with the major studies in the forced-compliance area. The most frequent finding is that of an inverse relationship between payment magnitude and attitude change. When people are given high choice or an explicit statement that they are responsible for the conduct, *and* they produce foreseeable negative consequences, attitude change is found to be inversely related to payment magnitude (see Calder *et al.,* 1973; Collins & Hoyt, 1972). Such results should be expected if illegitimate aspects of the payments are not salient and the largest amount of money does not appear to be oversufficient; these assumptions appear, at least on a post hoc basis, to be reasonable given the procedures used in these studies.

When the direct relationship is obtained, it typically seems that some element in the situation enhanced the salience of the illegitimate aspects of payment. One means of doing so is to hold the task constant and vary payments across a wide range from very small (insufficient, high responsibility) to very large (oversufficient, illegitimate, high responsibility). Gerard, Conolley, and Wilhelmy (1974) reported a series of experiments that varied payments across such a wide range. Subjects were given the payments to perform tasks that were "unpleasant experiences" (e.g., tasting bitter solutions). Gerard *et al.* obtained a curvilinear relationship: Small, insufficient payments or large, oversufficient payments produced the greatest attitude change toward the tasks; sufficient payments generated no attitude change.[11]

An alternative technique for influencing the appearance of illegitimacy is to hold payment at two levels while varying situational cues that make illegitimacy more or less salient. One important factor that has been shown to affect the appearance of illegitimacy is the amount of decision freedom provided by experi-

---

[10]Kelman and Baron (1974) present a functional approach to cognitive consistency that does not attach direct motivational significance to inconsistency. They distinguish between "moral dissonance" situations, which they predict will generate a direct relationship between payment magnitude and attitude change, and "hedonic dissonance" situations, which they predict will generate an inverse relationship. However, most of the situations that have obtained the inverse relationship appear to fit their definition of moral dissonance, since they involve the violation of a moral precept about doing harm to others. The present focus on moral evaluation in the context of the illegitimacy of payment avoids this difficulty. Schlenker *et al.* (1980) further discuss similarities and differences between the approaches.

[11]Gerard *et al.* (1974) suggest an alternative interpretation of these findings: Dissonance is presumed to be increased as payments decrease from sufficient to insufficient, whereas reinforcement effects increase as payments increase from sufficient to oversufficient.

menters. Kaufmann (1971) found that observers of a counterattitudinal behavior situation perceived monetary payments to be more of a bribe when participants were given low rather than high choice to refuse participation. At first glance, such a result seems paradoxical, yet it might make sense from a moralistic point of view. Since subjects cannot be "forced" by experimenters to behave against their wills, the failure to mention the option of declining participation may highlight the implication that the experimenter seems to be "buying" the behavior. When greater decision freedom is provided along with payment, the payment retreats further into the background and becomes only one of many factors that might affect participation.

If this reasoning is correct and low choice makes the illegitimate aspects of the payment more salient, we should expect the direct relationship to be more frequently obtained under conditions of low decision freedom. Indeed, this is the case (e.g., Calder *et al.*, 1973; Linder *et al.*, 1967; Rosenberg, 1965; Sherman, 1970). For example, Calder *et al.* (1973) had subjects deceive another participant (a confederate) under conditions of high or low negative consequences for the other. They found that when subjects were given high choice and negative consequences occurred, an inverse relationship was obtained between payment size and justificatory attitude change. But when subjects were given low choice and negative consequences occurred, a direct relationship was obtained.

The direct relationship can still be obtained under conditions of high choice, but additional cues of illegitimacy must then be more salient. For example, Janis and Gilmore (1965) found that subjects who were paid the inordinately large amount of $20 merely to write brief counterattitudinal essays were suspicious of the payment and also tended ($p < .10$) to change their attitudes more than subjects paid only $1. This pattern is consistent with the present reasoning but goes against the effects of suspicion hypothesized by Rosenberg (1965), who argued that suspicions should decrease attitude change. (For those who recall the classic Festinger and Carlsmith [1959] $1 and $20 study that obtained an inverse relationship between payment magnitude and attitude change, their payment was not just to persuade the confederate, but to remain on call in the future for similar duty. Thus, the $20 payment in their study should have appeared more legitimate and sufficient given the nature of the task [also see Aronson, 1966].)

One of the most straightforward and intriguing manipulations of illegitimacy was performed by Nuttin (1975, Experiment 9). Subjects were run through the study by an experimenter who was an assistant of their psychology class instructor and had access to their course records. After noticing from their records that they had done rather poorly on an important recent psychology exam, she gave them the choice of either the usual payment for participation or some highly illegitimate exam "rescue" points; she would add points to their grade sheet without the instructor's knowledge, and cautioned subjects not to tell because she might be fired. Interestingly, all subjects accepted the points. Compared to subjects who wrote counterattitudinal essays but were not offered the blatant payoff, those who were showed dramatic attitude change effects.

An experiment by Elms and Janis (1965) is widely cited as providing the clearest support in the literature for an incentive approach and against a dissonance one. In it, subjects were paid a large or small amount to write essays advocating the sending of American college students to universities in the Soviet Union for their entire college education. It was explained that the Soviet government endorsed the plan enthusiastically, but the American government was reluctant to support it. In addition, the request to write the essay came from either a "favorable sponsor"—an interviewer hired by the U.S. State Department—or an "unfavorable sponsor"—an interviewer hired by the Soviet embassy. It was found that subjects changed their attitudes toward the essay only when paid the large amount by the favorable sponsor; no change was obtained in either payment condition when the sponsor was unfavorable. [Dissonance theory supposedly should have predicted greatest attitude change when subjects were paid the small amount by the unfavorable sponsor.] These results appear to be quite consistent with the present analysis. It seems reasonable to suggest that subjects in the favorable sponsor condition were being evaluated by someone who should induce high moral evaluation and concern about illegitimacy: The interviewer was presented as an extension of the government's position that the plan was "suspect." These subjects should have been especially concerned that they might appear to have been "bought" by the large payment to do something they and the interviewer might regard as reprehensible; hence, justificatory attitude change occurred. In contrast, the unfavorable sponsor was hardly in a position to create high moral evaluation: He both agreed with the position of the essay and was himself hired (bought) by the Soviet embassy. Concern about illegitimacy, at least vis-à-vis the salient interviewer-audience, should be lower, though perhaps not to the point where the inverse relationship appears.

It is worth noting that a payment may not have to be introduced prior to the conduct in order to make it appear relevant to illegitimacy. Just as the consequences of conduct are often "retrospectively" foreseeable even if they were not salient at the time of the act (Goethals et al., 1979), and the appearance of responsibility can be further modified through audience feedback after the act (Riess & Schlenker, 1977), payments given after the conduct still might affect concerns about identity. For example, payments may sometimes be retrospectively foreseeable. An experimenter might say, after the conduct has been performed, something to the effect of, "Oh, I forgot to mention it earlier, but you will, of course, be paid from research funds." Subjects then might think they should have realized they would be paid; the experimenter seemed to take it for granted, and perhaps most subjects would have known it. In addition, some payments offered after the fact may have the effect of improperly discharging obligations or indicating that the payer does not view the relationship or conduct in the same way as did the actor (e.g., people who do good deeds and then receive a large reward often explain that, of course, they did not expect such compensation and didn't do it for compensation; or, a person might awake and be chagrined to find a $50 bill left behind by the previous night's companion). Thus, payments given after the conduct has occurred may still affect the necessity for explanations of the conduct and the appearance of illegitimacy.

### D.  MANIPULATING ILLEGITIMACY

#### 1.  Increasing Moral Evaluation

Reinterpretations of existing studies have value only up to the point of generating and providing a basis for hypotheses. The hypotheses then must be tested. Schlenker, Forsyth, Leary, and Miller (1980) conducted three experiments to test the hypotheses about the effects of payment and illegitimacy on attitude change. The basic procedure was similar in all three. Briefly, subjects wrote speeches, which were videotaped, arguing against the use of seat belts in automotive vehicles. The tapes supposedly would be used in a persuasion study conducted in junior high schools, and it was said to be expected that the tapes made by college students like themselves would be effective; thus, foreseeable negative consequences existed. Low decision freedom has already been linked to a direct relationship between payment size and attitude change, so using a low-choice procedure would not provide the cleanest test of the hypotheses. Therefore, subjects in all three studies were given high choice by emphasizing they could choose to write an essay either for or against the use of seat belts. The experimenter asked, however, if they would choose the anti-seat-belt speech in order to facilitate following a prearranged pattern, but reiterated that the choice was theirs. The experimenter also noted that they would be paid either $.50 or $2.50 in addition to their regular experimental credit.

After the videotaping was finished, the experimenter stated that the session was completed, paid subjects, and signed their credit slips. He or she then noted that some observers in an adjoining room had asked if subjects would be willing to spend a few minutes before leaving to assist them with their work. The existence and rationale for these observers had been explained earlier in the session. They were supposedly from speech and communications, had been developing some new scales for coding and analyzing live speeches, and when they heard about the study had requested permission to observe and practice their techniques. It was stressed that they were not part of the study, but would be watching and listening from behind a one-way mirror. Although no such people were actually present, this cover story provided a means of introducing some of the manipulations and obtaining attitude measures.

Experiment 1 manipulated the salience of illegitimacy pressures by varying the supposed purpose of the observers' techniques. After the videotaping and in the context of explaining why the observers had requested subjects to fill out a brief questionnaire, subjects in a high-moral-evaluation condition were told that the observers were interested in developing measures that related a speaker's behaviors to his or her moral and ethical values. In a low-moral-evaluation condition, subjects were merely told that the observers were interested in developing a measure that related a speaker's behaviors to his or her attitudes toward the topic. Thus, Experiment 1 was a 2 (small or large payment) ×2 (low or high moral evaluation) factorial design with an offset control condition that involved attitude assessment only.

To test the hypothesis that people would regard the behavior as most morally condemnable when moral evaluation was high and subjects were paid the large amount, subjects in an additional group each read a detailed description of the behavior of a hypothetical subject, named Pat, in one of the four major cells of the design. As predicted, Pat's conduct was viewed as least moral when the large amount was paid under conditions of high moral evaluation; they felt Pat's behavior was less ethically acceptable and believed that both the speech raters and Pat would regard it as least moral under these conditions. They also rated the money that was paid to Pat as less earned, deserved, and honest in that condition. (A manipulation check also revealed that moral evaluation was greater in the high than low moral evaluation condition.)

Subjects' attitudes were measured on two sets of items: (a) agreement–disagreement with a statement saying seat belts can be dangerous and should not be worn, and (b) evaluative ratings of the use of seat belts on a series of bipolar adjective scales (e.g., good–bad). Since both produced similar patterns, only the former will be highlighted here. As shown in Table II, the predicted interaction between payment magnitude and moral evaluation occurred ($p < .02$). As hypothesized, when moral evaluation was low, an inverse relationship was obtained between payment size and attitude change ($p < .05$), and the small payment condition differed significantly from the control group

TABLE II
Attitudes toward Seat Belts: Experiment 1

| Condition | Condition[a] | |
|---|---|---|
| | High moral evaluation | Low moral evaluation |
| Small Payment | 3.6 | 5.8 |
| Large Payment | 5.2 | 3.5 |
| Control | | 3.4 |

[a]Higher scores indicate greater opposition to seat belts (i.e., more attitude change), on a 13-point scale.

($p < .05$). Also, although a direct relationship appeared to emerge under conditions of high moral evaluation, it failed to reach acceptable levels of statistical significance, and the $2.50 condition did not differ from the control group.

The results provide partial support for the hypotheses, showing the inverse relationship when illegitimacy is not salient, but merely suggesting the direct relationship when it is salient. One possible reason for the failure to find a stronger direct relationship may have been that subjects attempted to use alternative ways of making the payments seem legitimate. If the large payment, especially in the high-moral-evaluation condition, was made to appear more legitimate, there would have been less reason to employ justificatory attitude change. Indeed, several measures suggested subjects did just that. Unlike the uninvolved observers, who disparaged the large payment when moral evaluation was salient, the experimental subjects did not admit high moral evaluation, rated themselves as having agreed to do the speech almost totally to accommodate the experimenter and not to get the money, and rated the large payment as being offered primarily to get them to do a good job on the speech, not to induce them to make the speech. Subjects in the high- as compared to low-moral-evaluation condition also indicated they agreed to do the speech less for the money and rated the money as less of a bribe. In short, subjects attempted to legitimize the payment directly—and this was especially true in the high-moral-evaluation condition—thereby constructing explanations of their conduct that purified their motives.

### 2.  Inducement Salience

Experiment 2 blocked these alternative explanations. Most forced-compliance studies, including Experiment 1, leave the contingency between payment and behavior ambiguous, such that while it implies an inducement to agree, subjects can readily interpret it as an incentive for doing a good job. Indeed, this interpretive flexibility may be one of the reasons why the direct relationship has not been more prevalent in the literature. Experiment 2 made the contingency explicit, telling subjects that the payment was an inducement (contingent on agreeing to do the speech) or an incentive (for doing a good job on the speech). The inducement instructions should heighten subjects' concerns about illegitimacy, so a direct relationship between payment size and attitude change should occur in this condition. As in Experiment 1, the attitude questionnaires were completed for the ''speech observers,'' but no specific information was given about exactly what the observers' techniques were assessing. Thus, Experiment 2 was a 2 (small or large payment) $\times 2$ (inducement or incentive) factorial design with an offset control group.

Once again, an additional group of subjects read scenarios depicting the major conditions of the experiment, and their reactions provided support for the hypotheses about moral condemnation. The hypothetical subject portrayed in the scenarios was evaluated as least moral after receiving a large payment in the inducement condition.

Attitude change by the experimental subjects was affected by the interaction between contingency and payment size. As shown in Table III, a direct relationship occurred between payment size and attitude change in the inducement condition ($p < .02$), and the large-payment-inducement subjects were the only ones to display significant attitude change compared to the control group ($p < .05$). Subjects in the incentive condition did not moderate their attitudes. They already had a legitimate reason for the payment, so bribery should not have been salient. Also, since the payment was publicly described by the experimenter as unrelated to their motives for the act, it may have had no differential effect on feelings of responsibility, with both payments falling in the sufficient range.

Incentive theory would seem to have predicted a direct relationship between payment size and attitude change in the performance condition. Indeed, subjects who were paid $2.50 in the performance condition said they did a superior job on their speeches as compared to other subjects, just as incentive theory suggests they should. Yet, the direct relationship occurred in the agreement condition, where no differences in reports of performance quality were obtained. It is difficult to reconcile these results with the incentive position.

### 3. Accusations of Bribery

Experiment 3 took the most direct route to manipulate illegitimacy. After completing the speeches, subjects were provided with a copy of the speech observer's supposed ratings of them. The form indicated that the speeches were rated as slightly above average, but the key information was a handwritten comment on the bottom that noted payment was received by the subject and ended with either an accusation of bribery ("Bribe?!?") or the suggestion of legitimacy ("legitimate compensation; good idea to pay subjects"). In addition, instead of having written scenarios of the situation evaluated, subject-observers were yoked to the actor-subjects and watched and listened to the proceedings from behind a one-way mirror. Finally, to assess the extent to which actor-subjects' accounts of their conduct are influenced by the salience of immediate audiences who have observed their behavior, half of the actors were led to

TABLE III
ATTITUDES TOWARD SEAT BELTS: EXPERIMENT 2

| Condition | Condition[a] | | |
|---|---|---|---|
| | Inducement | Incentive | |
| Small Payment | 3.4 | 4.0 | |
| Large Payment | 6.6 | 4.4 | |
| Control | | | 3.6 |

[a]Higher scores indicate greater opposition to seat belts (i.e., more attitude change), on a 13-point scale.

believe that their attitude questionnaires were being collected for the speech observers (high self-presentational concern). The remaining actors were led to believe that the questionnaires were part of a psychology department survey to assess the reactions of participants to studies conducted under its auspices; it was completed on another floor of the building for a secretary, and subjects were told it would not be seen by the experimenter or anyone who might be directly associated with the research (low self-presentational concern). Thus, the experiment was a 2 (actor or observer) $\times 2$ (small or large payment) $\times 2$ (bribe or legitimate comment) $\times$ 2 (low or high self-presentational concern) factorial design with an offset control group.

A four-way interaction of these variables was obtained on subjects' attitudes ($p < .02$), and the three-way interaction of the manipulated variables was significant for the actor-subjects ($p < .04$). As shown in Table IV, the predicted direct relationship between payment magnitude and attitude change occurred for actors who were accused of bribery and whose self-presentational concerns were high ($p < .05$). In fact, the large-payment-bribe high self-presentational concern condition was the *only* actor condition to differ significantly from the attitude-measurement-only control group ($p < .05$). Although self-perception theory (Bem, 1972) suggests that observers should track the actors' responses when asked what they think the actors' attitudes are, the observers did not come close. Observers in virtually all conditions believed that the actors were in much greater agreement with their anti-seat-belt speeches than the actors actually were. The speech behavior appeared to engulf the field (Heider, 1958), a tendency that was probably enhanced by the high decision freedom that was provided the actors.

TABLE IV
ATTITUDES TOWARD SEAT BELTS: EXPERIMENT 3

| | Condition[a] | | | |
| | High self-presentational concern | | Low self-presentational concern | |
| Condition | Bribe | Legitimate | Bribe | Legitimate |
|---|---|---|---|---|
| Actor | | | | |
| Small payment | 3.6 | 4.3 | 5.5 | 4.2 |
| Large payment | 6.5 | 4.6 | 3.9 | 5.6 |
| Observer | | | | |
| Small payment | 8.2 | 9.4 | 5.1 | 8.5 |
| Large payment | 8.9 | 9.1 | 9.1 | 8.4 |
| Control | | | | 4.4 |

[a]Higher scores indicate greater opposition to seat belts (i.e., more attitude change), on a 13-point scale.

Furthermore, the only significant difference between observer conditions that was obtained did not match the actors' responses.

Although it had been expected that an inverse relationship would be obtained for the actors in the legitimate comment condition, no such effect was significant. In retrospect, this should not have been a surprise. The actors' involvement in the situation and possible concern about how their actions were viewed by the speech observers may have prompted them to be somewhat sensitized to the illegitimacy issue by the mention of the payment, even in the context of the legitimate comment. Indeed, several actors anecdotally reported during the debriefing that if the speech raters had felt the payment was really legitimate, they would not have mentioned anything at all about it, and wondered if the observers were being sarcastic. While the bribery-legitimacy manipulation was successful overall (as revealed by the manipulation check), its effects were more pronounced for the observers than the actors, and the actors rated the legitimate note as implying they were less moral than did the observers ($p < .04$). Thus, with neither legitimacy nor bribery clearly established for actors by the legitimate comment, these competing pressures may have cancelled out with the result being a combination of confusion and sufficiency for both payment magnitudes and no attitude change.

Actor-subjects again appeared motivated to make the larger payments appear more legitimate. Role by payment magnitude interactions ($ps < .05$) showed that actors who received the large payment, in comparison with their observers, said they did the speech more for the experimenter, less for the money, and described the money as less of a bribe ($ps < .05$). Strong support also was found for Kelley's (1967) hypothesis that large payments accepted when illegitimate forces are salient permit high choice to be ascribed to the actor. An interaction of payment by bribery emphasis ($p < .02$) revealed a direct relationship between payment size and the amount of choice ascribed to actors in the bribery condition ($Ms = 5.5$ and $7.2$ for the small and large payment conditions; 18-point scale). But when the legitimate comment was made, an inverse relationship appeared ($Ms = 7.6$ and $5.9$ for the small and large payment conditions).

In sum, the three experiments provided support for our reinterpretation of the effects of payments on attitude change in the forced-compliance situation. As predicted, the "elusive" direct relationship occurred when illegitimate forces were salient, which was accomplished by making an accusation of bribery, making the payment an explicit inducement to agree, or raising concerns about moral evaluation by an immediate audience (the latter effect was not significant, though). Furthermore, moral condemnation by observers was greatest when subjects were paid the large amount, especially under conditions of illegitimacy, and attributions of choice were directly related to payment size when illegitimacy was salient. These results converge to support the identity predictions of when the direct relationship should occur and why. In contrast, the inverse relationship occurred when illegitimacy was minimized in the low moral evaluation condition of Experiment 1. Although we also had hoped to obtain it under the legitimate comment condition of Experiment 3, it is retrospectively understandable why it did not occur there. In combination with the existing literature (e.g., Calder *et al.*, 1973; Collins & Hoyt, 1972), our hypotheses about the inverse relationship appear to have received support as well.

### E. SELF-PRESENTATION AND "GENUINE ATTITUDE CHANGE"

The three experiments by Schlenker *et al.* (1980) clearly indicated that interpersonal concerns can be quite salient to subjects who are placed in the typical forced-compliance predicament. Among other findings, the data from Experiment 3 indicated that significant attitude change occurred only when self-presentational concerns were high, that is, when subjects believed that their questionnaires would be viewed by an audience who knew about their behaviors. When self-presentational concerns were low, no significant effects emerged for actor-subjects. [As shown in Table IV, a slight inverse relationship was suggested when self-presentational concerns were low and bribery was emphasized, but it fell far short of significance ($p > .15$), as did the opposite trend when legitimacy was emphasized ($p > .20$). It is difficult to place much credence in the reliability of these "trends," but it should be noted that they are consistent with Rosenberg's (1965) analysis.] Although it had been anticipated that attitude change might be less under the private than public condition, it was not necessarily anticipated that it would be wiped out. As proposed earlier, people should construct accounts of their conduct for themselves as well as for immediate audiences, even though the amount of bias and the type of account might differ privately and publicly.

Might these results be interpreted as indicating that subjects do not privately change their attitudes following counterattitudinal behavior? Tedeschi and Rosenfeld (1981) proposed that "attitude change" in the forced-compliance setting is an uninternalized, feigned public account designed solely to mend a "spoiled identity" in front of the experimenter. One of the major bases for this conclusion was a study by Gaes, Kalle, and Tedeschi (1978), who found that attitude change was eliminated when subjects were provided with *complete* anonymity or had their attitudes assessed by a bogus pipeline device that supposedly could detect lies. These provocative findings appear to suggest again the importance of concerns about one's public identity as a mediator of attitude change following counterattitudinal behavior. However, it may be premature to conclude that the appearance of attitude change is merely a public illusion.

The procedures used to affect self-presentational concerns also may influence subjects' focus of attention. As such, the procedures may influence the form of the account that is employed (e.g., private self-attention should increase the use of accounts that do not involve contradicting salient prior beliefs, whereas public self-attention may facilitate attitude change), and whether an account of any sort occurs (e.g., the absence of self-attention should eliminate self-assessment and the construction of explanations for conduct). Scheier and Carver (1980) suggested that the bogus pipeline instructions may induce a state of private self-awareness; this would increase the salience of subjects' prior attitudes relevant to the domain of questioning and prompt concerns about how they appear to themselves. Interestingly, Gaes *et al.* (1978) obtained subjects' ratings of themselves and the experimenter in addition to the measures of attitudes. Subjects in the bogus pipeline condition, who did not demonstrate attitude change, rated themselves as more constrained, legitimate, and benevolent, and the experimenter as less constrained and more independent, than subjects in a paper-and-pencil assessment condition who did display attitude change. Gaes *et al.* suggested that subjects in the bogus pipeline condition meant they were constrained by not being able to manipulate the experimenter through a public justification. However, these subjects may have meant that they felt constrained and obligated to perform the behavior; such ratings would provide a reasonable excuse for their conduct and allow them to feel legitimate and benevolent. Similar questions can be raised about manipulations of total anonymity. If attitude change and other accounts are eliminated, is it because subjects do not have to "lie" or because they were not self-attentive (either publicly or privately)? The absence of self-attention should produce a deindividuated state under which self-assessment and the explanation of one's conduct should not occur.

A further complicating factor arises in that people's private and public accounts may sometimes differ. People sometimes tell lies in order to escape from public predicaments. In other words, their public statements may fall in their private latitudes of rejection on the issue (cf. Sherif & Hovland, 1961), and would be privately recognized as lies. This should be most likely to occur when the conduct has important public implications, people are motivated to impress an immediate audience, and they believe that their personal explanations would not permit them to escape from punishment and maintain the identities they desire (e.g., they might not have an acceptable account or believe that the audience is less likely to accept their private account than a convincing lie). On other occasions, public pressures may cause people to stretch their public statements to the limits of private acceptability. In other words, their public statements may fall in the outer regions of their latitudes of acceptance or even in their latitudes of neutrality on the issue (cf. Sherif & Hovland, 1961). A public statement that falls in people's latitudes of acceptance may represent only a temporary shift in position, one that might not constitute an enduring alteration of prior beliefs (cf. Hass, 1981). In contrast, one might speculate that a public statement that falls in the latitude of neutrality would produce a genuine shift in private beliefs that would endure over time. On some issues, publicly moderating one's attitudes enough to justify a negative counterattitudinal act may still involve endorsing an extreme position in the latitude of rejection; on other issues, it may not. As noted earlier, people's personal (private) explanations of their conduct must "fit the facts" as they see them. If a public account does not do so, it should not be privately believed.

The issue of "genuine attitude change" cannot be resolved here, and the existing data base simply does not permit firm conclusions. Until recently, researchers have not paid much attention to the possible self-presentational concerns of subjects in the forced-compliance situation, and the existing data is silent on this key point. Identity analysis indicates that one should not assume that attitude change in the forced-compliance situation is always "real," or for that matter, always a feigned public impression management tactic.

## F.  IDENTITY ANALYSIS AND DISSONANCE THEORY

Dissonance theory has evolved over the years to the point where its current version bears only a superficial resemblance to the original. The theory is now "focused on cognitive changes occurring in the service of ego defense, or self-esteem maintenance, rather than in the interest of preserving psychological consistency" (Greenwald & Ronis, 1978, p. 55). At the same time, dissonance theory is in the unique position of having the best of all possible worlds. One still sees "dissonance theory" (the original, consistency version) referenced to explain results that are consistent with it but irrelevant to the new version, and "dissonance theory" (the new, ego version) referenced to dispel the implications of data that are inconsistent with the old version. Between the two, there is little they cannot explain, at least in post hoc fashion. The theory should not be allowed to have it both ways. Social psychologists must decide what dissonance theory is and says or else the entire concept is vacuous.

Unlike the original version of dissonance theory, the identity-analytic theory that is presented here does not attach any direct motivational significance to cognitive inconsistency per se. However, the responsibility-for-negative-consequences-that-threaten-the-self version of dissonance theory can be viewed as a special case of the more general identity-analytic theory. It is doubtful that in areas where they both apply they could be empirically differentiated. This seems true despite the fact that the new version of dissonance theory still traces motivation back to cognitive inconsistencies, albeit ones that are self-threatening. In contrast, the identity-analytic approach takes the more direct route to self/identity issues by focusing on the social character and functions of explanations of events. Because of these conceptual differences, it is possible to generate an array of hypotheses from the identity-analytic approach that do not seem obvious, at least on an a priori basis, from the new dissonance theory. For example, results indicating that subjects will demonstrate more attitude change under low- than high-choice conditions irrespective of whether the conduct is attitude inconsistent (Schlenker & Schlenker, 1975) or consistent (Schlenker & Goldman, 1982), so long as it produces important identity-supporting positive consequences, do not seem obvious from either version of dissonance theory. In fact, dissonance theory would have to be modified again to add a proposition about self-esteem enhancement to go with its proposition about self-esteem protection. At that point, dissonance theory literally becomes a self/identity theory.

## V. Summary

The social character and functions of explanations of conduct provide the basis for understanding when and why people's attributions and self-presentations often appear personally biased. The explanations people employ to construe their own conduct can have effects that reverberate across their personal and public identities. Typical day-to-day events are usually interpreted and responded to automatically, without conscious assessment. However, greater attention to and assessment of events is required under certain conditions, culminating in the construction of explanations. It was proposed that explanations of conduct are proffered, to oneself and/or others, when behaviors appear to (a) violate standards in ways that threaten one's identity, or (b) meet commendable standards, but ambiguity exists about the relevance of the event for one's identity. Personally desirable explanations of conduct result, representing personally beneficial but believable interpretations of the event. Explanations that attempt to reconcile violations with relevant standards are termed *accounts,* and include *justifications,* which characterize the event in a personally beneficial, less negative manner, and *excuses,* which minimize personal responsibility. In a complementary fashion, explanations that attempt to provide credit for events that meet commendable standards are termed *acclamations,* and include *enhancements,* which characterize the event in a personally beneficial, more positive manner, and *entitlements,* which maximize personal responsibility. This identity-analytic theory of the nature of explanations integrates a wide range of phenomena under a single rubric.

The theory can be applied to understanding attitude change following counterattitudinal behavior. The recent responsibility-for-negative-consequences formulation of dissonance theory can be viewed as a special case of the more general identity analysis. People whose conduct produces negative consequences have typically violated personal and/or public standards for conduct and threatened their identities. When their responsibility for the conduct is low, they are exonerated by the excuse provided by salient evidence (e.g., the experimenter's low-choice instructions). When personal responsibility is high, however, they must go beyond the salient evidence and construct their own accounts of the conduct. One such account, though not the only one, is to change their attitudes about the topic/object of the conduct, thereby reconciling their conduct with the relevant standards through a justification. A review of the literature examined the effects of the nature of the consequences, the reactions of audiences to the conduct, self-attention, identity images, and payments on attitude change and alternative accounts. The importance of concerns about one's identity as a mediator of accounts is repeatedly suggested. The theory also provides an integration of much of the literature on the effects of payments on attitude change following counterattitudinal behaviors. The identity analysis suggests the conditions under which both an inverse and direct relationship should be obtained between payment magnitude and attitude change, and the predictions have received empirical support. In addition, the theory predicts an inverse relationship between apparent responsibility and acclamations for conduct that produces important identity-supporting positive consequences, irrespective of whether the conduct is attitude consistent or inconsistent. The relevant hypotheses have been supported in this area as well. Finally, it should be recognized that people's public and private explanations of their conduct may sometimes differ. Although the methodological problems inherent in distinguishing between public and private explanations are considerable, the issue should not be ignored.

## ACKNOWLEDGMENTS

Thanks are extended to Patricia Schlenker, whose comments and assistance were invaluable.

## REFERENCES

Abelson, R. P. Script processing in attitude formation and decision making. In J. S. Carroll & J. W. Payne (Eds.), *Cognition and social behavior*. Hillsdale, New Jersey: Erlbaum, 1976.

Abelson, R. P., Aronson, E., McGuire, W. J., Newcomb, T. M., Rosenberg, M. J., & Tannenbaum, P. H. (Eds.), *Theories of cognitive consistency: A sourcebook*. Chicago, Illinois: Rand McNally, 1968.

Alexander, C. N., Jr., & Rudd, J. Situated identities and response variables. In J. T. Tedeschi (Ed.), *Impression management theory and social psychological research*. New York: Academic Press, 1981.

Arkin, R. M., Gabrenya, W. K., Jr., Appelman, A. S., & Cochrance, S. T. Self-presentation, self-monitoring, and the self-serving bias in causal attribution. *Personality and Social Psychology Bulletin*, 1979, **5**, 73–76.

Aronson, E. The psychology of insufficient justification: An analysis of some conflicting data. In S. Feldman (Ed.), *Cognitive consistency*. New York: Academic Press, 1966.

Aronson, E. Dissonance theory: Progress and problems. In R. Abelson *et al.* (Eds.), *Theories of cognitive consistency: A sourcebook*. Chicago, Illinois: Rand McNally, 1968.

Austin, J. L. *Philosophical papers* (2nd ed.). New York and London: Oxford University Press, 1970.

Backman, C. W. Explorations of psycho-ethics: The warranting of judgments. In R. Harré (Ed.), *Life sentences: Aspects of the social role of language*. New York: Wiley, 1976.

Baer, R., Hinkle, S., Smith, K., & Fenton, M. Reactance as a function of actual versus projected autonomy. *Journal of Personality and Social Psychology*, 1980, **38**, 416–422.

Baumeister, R. F., & Jones, E. E. When self-presentation is constrained by the target's knowledge: Consistency and compensation. *Journal of Personality and Social Psychology*, 1978, **36**, 608–618.

Bem, D. J. Self-perception theory. In L. Berkowitz (Ed.), *Advances in experimental social psychology* (Vol. 6). New York: Academic Press, 1972.

Bem, D. J., & Funder, D. C. Predicting more of the people more of the time: Assessing the personality of situations. *Psychological Review*, 1978, **85**, 485–501.

Bradley, G. W. Self-serving biases in the attribution process: A reexamination of the fact or fiction question. *Journal of Personality and Social Psychology*, 1978, **36**, 56–71.

Bramel, D. Dissonance, expectation, and the self. In R. P. Abelson *et al.* (Eds), *Theories of cognitive consistency: A sourcebook*. Chicago, Illinois: Rand McNally, 1968.

Braver, S. L., Linder, D. E., Corwin, T. T., & Cialdini, R. B. Some conditions that affect admissions of attitude change. *Journal of Experimental Social Psychology*, 1977, **13**, 565–576.

Brock, T. C., & Buss, A. H. Dissonance, aggression, and evaluation of pain. *Journal of Abnormal and Social Psychology*, 1962, **65**, 197–202.

Burke, K. *A grammar of motives*. Berkeley: University of California Press, 1969.

Buss, A. H. *Self-consciousness and social anxiety*. San Francisco, California: Freeman, 1980.

Calder, B. J., Ross, J., & Insko, C. A. Attitude change and attitude attribution: Effects of incentive, choice, and consequences. *Journal of Personality and Social Psychology*, 1973, **25**, 84–99.

Cantor, N., & Mischel, W. Traits as prototypes: Effects on recognition memory. *Journal of Personality and Social Psychology*, 1977, **35**, 38–48.

Cantor, N., & Mischel, W. Protypicality and personality: Effects on free recall and personality impressions. *Journal of Research in Personality*, 1979, **13**, 187–205.

Carlsmith, J. M., Collins, B. E., & Helmreich, R. L. Studies in forced compliance: I. The effect of pressure for compliance on attitude change produced by face-to-face role playing and anonymous essay writing. *Journal of Personality and Social Psychology*, 1966, **4**, 1–13.

Carson, R. C. *Interaction concepts of personality*. Chicago, Illinois: Aldine, 1969.

Carver, C. S. A cybernetic model of self-attention processes. *Journal of Personality and Social Psychology*, 1979, **37**, 1251–1281.

Carver, C. S., & Scheier, M. F. Self-consciousness and reactance. *Journal of Research in Personality*, 1981, **15**, 16–29.

Carver, C. S., & Scheier, M. F. A control-theory approach to behavior. In P. Trower (Ed.), *Cognitive perspectives in social skills training*. Oxford: Pergamon, 1982.

Child, I. L. Personality in culture. In E. F. Borgatta & W. W. Lambert (Eds.), *Handbook of personality theory and research*. Chicago, Illinois: Rand McNally, 1968.

Cialdini, R. B., Petty, R. E., & Cacioppo, J. T. Attitude and attitude change. In M. R. Rosenzweig & L. W. Porter (Eds.), *Annual review of psychology* (Vol. 32). Palo Alto, California: Annual Reviews, 1981.

Collins, B. E., & Hoyt, M. F. Personality responsibility-for-consequences: An integration and extension of the "forced compliance" literature. *Journal of Experimental Social Psychology*, 1972, **8**, 558–593.

Cooley, C. H. *Human nature and the social order* (Rev. ed.). New York: Scribner 1922. (Originally published, 1902.)

Cooper, J., & Duncan, B. L. Cognitive dissonance as a function of self-esteem and logical inconsistency. *Journal of Personality*, 1971, **39**, 289–302.

Cooper, J., & Goethals, G. R. Unforeseen events and the elimination of cognitive dissonance. *Journal of Personality and Social Psychology*, 1974, **29**, 441–445.

Cooper, J., & Worchel, S. Role of undesired consequences in arousing cognitive dissonance. *Journal of Personality and Social Psychology*, 1970, **16**, 199–206.

Cooper, J., Zanna, M. P., & Goethals, G. R. Mistreatment of an esteemed other as a consequence affecting dissonance reduction. *Journal of Experimental Social Psychology*, 1974, **10**, 224–233.

Cooper, J., Zanna, M. P., & Taves, P. A. Arousal as a necessary condition for attitude change following induced compliance. *Journal of Personality and Social Psychology*, 1978, **36**, 1101–1106.

D'Arcy, E. *Human acts*. London and New York: Oxford University Press, 1963.

Davis, K. E., & Jones, E. E. Changes in interpersonal perception as a means of reducing cognitive dissonance. *Journal of Abnormal and Social Psychology*, 1960, **61**, 402–410.

Diener, E. Deindividuation: The absence of self-awareness and self-regulation in group members. In P. B. Paulus (Ed.), *The psychology of group influence*. Hillsdale, New Jersey: Erlbaum, 1980.

Diener, E., & Srull, T. K. Self-awareness, psychological perspective, and self-reinforcement in relation to personal and social standards. *Journal of Personality and Social Psychology*, 1979, **37**, 413–423.

Duval, S., & Wicklund, R. A. *A theory of objective self-awareness*. New York: Academic Press, 1972.

Einstein, A., & Infeld, L. The evolution of physics. In R. M. Hutchins & M. J. Adler (Eds.), *Gateway to the great books*. Chicago, Illinois: Encyclopaedia Britannica, 1963.

Elms, A. C. Role playing, incentive, and dissonance. *Psychological Bulletin*, 1967, **68**, 132–148.

Elms, A. C., & Janis, I. L. Counter-norm attitudes induced by consonant versus dissonant conditions of role-playing. *Journal of Experimental Research in Personality*, 1965, **1**, 50–60.

Epstein, S. The self-concept revisited: Or a theory of a theory. *American Psychologist*, 1973, **28**, 404–416.

Erikson, E. E. *Childhood and society* (2nd ed.). New York: Norton, 1963.

Fazio, R. H., Zanna, M. P., & Cooper, J. Dissonance and self-perception: An integrative view of each theory's proper domain of application. *Journal of Personality and Social Psychology*, 1977, **13**, 464–479.

Federoff, N. A., & Harvey, J. H. Focus of attention, self-esteem, and the attribution of causality. *Journal of Research in Personality*, 1976, **10**, 336–345.

Fenigstein, A. Self-consciousness, self-attention, and social interaction. *Journal of Personality and Social Psychology*, 1979, **37**, 75–86.

Fenigstein, A., Scheier, M. F., & Buss, A. H. Public and private self-consciousness: Assessment and theory. *Journal of Consulting and Clinical Psychology*, 1975, **43**, 522–527.

Festinger, L. *A theory of cognitive dissonance*. Evanston, Illinois: Row, Peterson, 1957.

Festinger, L., & Carlsmith, J. M. Cognitive consequences of forced compliance. *Journal of Abnormal and Social Psychology*, 1959, **58**, 203–210.

Fincham, F. D., & Jaspars, J. M. Attribution of responsibility: From man the scientist to man as lawyer. In L. Berkowitz (Ed.), *Advances in experimental social psychology* (Vol. 13). New York: Academic Press, 1980.

Foote, N. N. Identification as the basis for a theory of motivation. *American Sociological Review*, 1951, **16**, 14–21.

Fries, A., & Frey, D. Misattribution of arousal and the effects of self-threatening information. *Journal of Experimental Social Psychology*, 1980, **16**, 405–416.

Froming, W. J., & Carver, C. S. Divergent influences of private and public self-consciousness in a compliance paradigm. *Journal of Research in Personality*, 1981, **15**, 159–171.

Gaes, G. G., Kalle, R. J., & Tedeschi, J. T. Impression management in the forced compliance situation. Two studies using the bogus pipeline. *Journal of Experimental Social Psychology*, 1978, **14**, 493–510.

Gerard, H. B., Conolley, E. S., & Wilhelmy, R. A. Compliance, justification, and cognitive change. In L. Berkowitz (Ed.), *Advances in experimental social psychology* (Vol. 7). New York: Academic Press, 1974.

Goethals, G. R., & Cooper, J. When dissonance is reduced: The timing of self-justificatory attitude change. *Journal of Personality and Social Psychology,* 1975, **32,** 361–367.

Goethals, G. R., Cooper, J., & Naficy, A. Role of foreseen, foreseeable, and unforeseeable behavioral consequences in the arousal of cognitive dissonance. *Journal of Personality and Social Psychology,* 1979, **37,** 1179–1185.

Goffman, E. *The presentation of self in everyday life.* Garden City, New York: Doubleday, 1959.

Goffman, E. *Relations in public.* New York: Basic Books, 1971.

Grabitz-Gniech, G. Some restrictive conditions for the occurrence of psychological reactance. *Journal of Personality and Social Psychology,* 1971, **19,** 188–196.

Greenwald, A. G. The totalitarian ego: Fabrication and revision of personal history. *American Psychologist,* 1980, **35,** 603–618.

Greenwald, A. G., & Ronis, D. L. Twenty years of cognitive dissonance: Case study of the evolution of a theory. *Psychological Review,* 1978, **85,** 53–57.

Hamilton, V. L. Intuitive psychologist or intuitive lawyer? Alternative models of the attribution process. *Journal of Personality and Social Psychology,* 1980, **39,** 767–772.

Harré, R. The ethogenic approach: Theory and practice. In L. Berkowitz (Ed.), *Advances in experimental social psychology* (Vol. 10). New York: Academic Press, 1977.

Hart, H. L. A. *Punishment and responsibility.* London and New York: Oxford University Press, 1968.

Harvey, J. H., Town, J. P., & Yarkin, K. L. How fundamental is "the fundamental attribution error"? *Journal of Personality and Social Psychology,* 1981, **40,** 346–349.

Hass, R. G. Presentational strategies and the social expression of attitudes: Impression management within limits. In J. T. Tedeschi (Ed.), *Impression management theory and social psychological research.* New York: Academic Press, 1981.

Heider, F. *The psychology of interpersonal relations.* New York: Wiley, 1958.

Hewitt, J. P., & Stokes, R. Disclaimers. *American Sociological Review,* 1975, **40,** 1–11.

Higgins, E. T., Rhodewalt, F., & Zanna, M. P. Dissonance motivation: Its nature, persistence, and reinstatement. *Journal of Experimental Social Psychology,* 1979, **15,** 16–34.

Hogan, R., & Cheek, J. Identity, authenticity, and maturity. In T. R. Sarbin & K. E. Scheibe (Eds.), *Studies in social identity.* New York: Praeger, 1982.

Holmes, J. G., & Strickland, L. H. Choice freedom and confirmation of incentive expectancy as determinants of attitude change. *Journal of Personality and Social Psychology,* 1970, **14,** 39–45.

Hoyt, M. F., Henley, M. D., & Collins, B. E. Studies in forced compliance: The confluence of choice and consequences on attitude change. *Journal of Personality and Social Psychology,* 1972, **22,** 1–7.

Hull, J. G., & Levy, A. S. The organizational functions of the self: An alternative to the Duval and Wicklund model of self awareness. *Journal of Personality and Social Psychology,* 1979, **37,** 756–768.

Insko, C. A., Worchel, S., Folger, R., & Kutkus, A. A balance theory interpretation of dissonance. *Psychological Review,* 1975, **82,** 169–183.

James, W. *The principles of psychology.* Chicago, Illinois: Encyclopaedia Britannica, 1952. (Originally published, 1890.)

Janis, I. L., & Gilmore, J. B. The influence of incentive conditions on the success of role-playing in modifying attitudes. *Journal of Personality and Social Psychology,* 1965, **1,** 17–27.

Jellison, J. M. Reconsidering the attitude concept: A behavioristic self-presentation formulation. In J. T. Tedeschi (Ed.), *Impression management theory and social psychological research.* New York: Academic Press, 1981.

Jones, E. E., & Pittman, T. S. Toward a general theory of strategic self-presentation. In J. Suls (Ed.), *Psychological perspectives on the self* (Vol. 1). Hillsdale, New Jersey: Erlbaum, 1982.

Jones, E. E., Worchel, S., Goethals, G. R., & Grumet, J. F. Prior expectancy and behavioral extremity as determinants of attitude attribution. *Journal of Experimental Social Psychology,* 1971, **7,** 59–80.

Jones, E. E., & Wortman, C. *Ingratiation: An attributional approach.* Morristown, New Jersey: General Learning Press, 1973.

Judd, C. M., & Kulik, J. A. Schematic effects of social attitudes on information processing and recall. *Journal of Personality and Social Psychology,* 1980, **38,** 569–578.

Kaufmann, D. R. Incentive to perform counterattitudinal acts: Bribe or gold star? *Journal of Personality and Social Psychology,* 1971, **19,** 82–91.

Kelley, H. H. Attribution theory in social psychology. In D. Levine (Ed.), *Nebraska symposium on motivation* (Vol. 15). Lincoln, Nebraska: University of Nebraska Press, 1967.

Kelly, G. A. *The psychology of personal constructs* (2 vols.). New York: Norton, 1955.

Kelman, H. C., & Baron, R. M. Moral and hedonic dissonance: A functional analysis of the relationship between discrepant action and attitude change. In S. Himmelfarb & A. H. Eagly (Eds.), *Readings in attitude change.* New York: Wiley, 1974.

Kiesler, C. A., & Pallak, M. S. Arousal properties of dissonance manipulations. *Psychological Bulletin,* 1976, **83,** 1014–1025.

Kuiper, N. A., & Rogers, T. B. Encoding of personal information: Self-other differences. *Journal of Personality and Social Psychology,* 1979, **37,** 499–514.

Langer, E. J. Rethinking the role of thought in social interaction. In J. H. Harvey, W. Ickes, & R. F. Kidd (Eds.), *New directions in attribution research* (Vol. 2). Hillsdale, New Jersey: Erlbaum, 1978.

Leary, M. R., & Schlenker, B. R. The social psychology of shyness: A self-presentational model. In J. T. Tedeschi (Ed.), *Impression management theory and social psychological research.* New York: Academic Press, 1981.

Leavy, P. *Situational and dispositional antecedents of shyness.* Honor's thesis. University of Florida, 1980.

Linder, D. E., Cooper, J., & Jones, E. E. Decision freedom as a determinant of the role of incentive magnitude in attitude change. *Journal of Personality and Social Psychology,* 1967, **6,** 245–254.

Lindesmith, A. R., & Strauss, A. L. *Social psychology* (rev. ed.). New York: Holt, 1956.

Lord, C. G. Schemas and images as memory aids: Two modes of processing social information. *Journal of Personality and Social Psychology,* 1980, **38,** 257–269.

McGuire, W. J. The nature of attitudes and attitude change. In G. Lindzey & E. Aronson (Eds.), *The handbook of social psychology* (Vol. 3). Reading, Massachusetts: Addison-Wesley, 1969.

Markus, H. Self-schemata and processing information about the self. *Journal of Personality and Social Psychology,* 1977, **35,** 63–78.

Mead, G. H. *Mind, self, and society.* Chicago, Illinois: University of Chicago Press, 1934.

Meddin, J. Chimpanzees, symbols and the reflective self. *Social Psychology Quarterly,* 1979, **42,** 99–109.

Mills, C. W. Situated actions and vocabularies of motives. *American Sociological Review,* 1940, **5,** 904–913.

Modigliani, A. Embarrassment, facework, and eye contact: Testing a theory of embarrassment. *Journal of Personality and Social Psychology,* 1971, **17,** 15–24.

Mynatt, C., & Sherman, S. J. Responsibility attribution in groups and individuals: A direct test of the diffusion of responsibility hypothesis. *Journal of Personality and Social Psychology,* 1975, **32,** 1111–1118.

Neisser, U. *Cognition and reality.* San Francisco, California: Freeman, 1976.

Nel, E., Helmreich, R., & Aronson, E. Opinion change in the advocate as a function of the persuasibility of his audience: A clarification of the meaning of dissonance. *Journal of Personality and Social Psychology,* 1969, **12,** 117–124.

Nuttin, J. M., Jr. *The illusion of attitude change: Toward a response contagion theory of persuasion.* New York: Academic Press, 1975.

Pallak, M. S., Sogin, S. R., & Van Zante, A. Bad decisions: Effect of volition, locus of causality, and negative consequences of attitude change. *Journal of Personality and Social Psychology,* 1974, **30,** 217–227.

Pepitone, A. Some conceptual and empirical problems of consistency models. In S. Feldman (Ed.), *Cognitive consistency.* New York: Academic Press, 1966.

Peters, R. S. *The concept of motivation.* Boston, Massachusetts: Routledge & Kegan Paul, 1960.

Riess, M., Rosenfeld, P., Melburg, V., & Tedeschi, J. T. Self-serving attributions: Biased private perceptions and distorted public descriptions. *Journal of Personality and Social Psychology,* 1981, **41,** 224–231.

Riess, M., & Schlenker, B. R. Attitude change and responsibility avoidance as modes of dilemma resolution in forced compliance settings. *Journal of Personality and Social Psychology,* 1977, **35, 21**–30.

Rosenberg, M. J. When dissonance fails: On eliminating evaluation apprehension from attitude measurement. *Journal of Personality and Social Psychology,* 1965, **1,** 28–42.

Ross, M., & Shulman, R. F. Increasing the salience of initial attitudes: Dissonance versus self-perception theory. *Journal of Personality and Social Psychology,* 1973, **28,** 138–144.

Schachter, S., & Singer, J. E. Cognitive, social, and physiological determinants of emotional state. *Psychological Review,* 1962, **69,** 379–399.

Scheier, M. F. Effects of public and private self-consciousness on the public expression of personal beliefs. *Journal of Personality and Social Psychology,* 1980, **39,** 514–521.

Scheier, M. F., & Carver, C. S. Private and public self-attention, resistance to change, and dissonance reduction. *Journal of Personality and Social Psychology,* 1980, **39,** 390–405.

Scheier, M. F., & Carver, C. S. Private and public aspects of self. In L. Wheeler (Ed.), *Review of Personality and Social Psychology* (Vol. 2). Beverly Hills, California: Sage, 1981.

Schlenker, B. R. Self image maintenance and enhancement: Attitude change following counterattitudinal advocacy. *Proceedings of the 81st Annual Convention of the American Psychological Association,* 1973, **8,** 271–272.

Schlenker, B. R. Self-presentation: Managing the impression of consistency when reality interferes with self-enhancement. *Journal of Personality and Social Psychology,* 1975, **32,** 1030–1037.

Schlenker, B. R. Attitudes as actions: Social identity theory and consumer research. In K. Hunt (Ed.), *Advances in Consumer Research* (Vol. 5). Chicago, Illinois: Association for Consumer Research, 1978.

Schlenker, B. R. *Impression management: The self-concept, social identity, and interpersonal relations.* Monterey, California: Brooks/Cole, 1980.

Schlenker, B. R. *Self-presentation: A conceptualization and decision model.* Paper presented at the 89th annual meeting of the American Psychological Association, Los Angeles, 1981.

Schlenker, B. R., Forsyth, D. R., Leary, M. R., & Miller, R. S. Self-presentational analysis of the effects of incentives on attitude change following counterattitudinal behavior. *Journal of Personality and Social Psychology,* 1980, **39,** 553–557.

Schlenker, B. R., & Goldman, H. J. Attitude change as a self-presentation tactic following attitude-consistent behavior: Effects of choice and role. *Social Psychology Quarterly,* 1982, **45,** 92–99.

Schlenker, B. R., Hallam, J. R., & McCown, N. E. Motives and social evaluation: Actor-observer differences in the delineation of motives for a beneficial act. *Journal of Experimental Social Psychology,* in press.

Schlenker, B. R., & Leary, M. R. Social anxiety and self-presentation: A conceptualization and model. *Psychological Bulletin,* 1982, in press. (a)

Schlenker, B. R., & Leary, M. R. Audience's reactions to self-enhancing, self-denigrating, and accurate self-presentations. *Journal of Experimental Social Psychology,* 1982, **18,** 89–104. (b)

Schlenker, B. R., & Riess, M. Self-presentations of attitudes following commitment to proattitudinal behavior. *Human Communication Research,* 1979, **5**, 325–334.

Schlenker, B. R., & Schlenker, P. A. Reactions following counterattitudinal behavior which produces positive consequences. *Journal of Personality and Social Psychology,* 1975, **31**, 962–971.

Scott, M. B., & Lyman, S. M. Accounts. *American Sociological Review,* 1968, **33**, 46–62.

Secord, P. F. Consistency theory and self-referent behavior. In R. P. Abelson *et al.* (Eds.), *Theories of cognitive consistency: A sourcebook.* Chicago, Illinois: Rand McNally, 1968.

Shaw, M. E. Personal communication, 1976.

Shaw, M. E., & Sulzer, J. L. An empirical test of Heider's levels in attribution of responsibility. *Journal of Abnormal and Social Psychology,* 1964, **69**, 39–46.

Sherif, M., & Hovland, C. I. *Social judgment.* New Haven, Connecticut: Yale University Press, 1961.

Sherman, S. J. Effects of choice and incentive on attitude change in discrepant behavior situation. *Journal of Personality and Social Psychology,* 1970, **15**, 245–252.

Sicoly, F., & Ross, M. Facilitation of ego-biased attributions by means of self-serving observer feedback. *Journal of Personality and Social Psychology,* 1977, **35**, 734–741.

Snyder, M., & Ebbesen, E. B. Dissonance awareness: A test of dissonance theory versus self-perception theory. *Journal of Experimental Social Psychology,* 1972, **8**, 502–517.

Snyder, C. R., & Smith, T. W. Symptoms as self-handicapping strategies: The virtues of old wine in a new bottle. In G. Weary & H. L. Mirels (Eds.), *Integrations of clinical and social psychology.* London and New York: Oxford University Press, 1982.

Snyder, C. R., Stucky, R. J., & Higgins, R. L. *Excuses: The masquerade solution.* New York: Wiley, in press.

Snyder, M. L., Stephan, W. G., & Rosenfield, D. Attributional egotism. In J. H. Harvey, W. Ickes, & R. F. Kidd (Eds.), *New directions in attribution research* (Vol. 2). Hillsdale, New Jersey: Erlbaum, 1978.

Sogin, S. R., & Pallak, M. S. Bad decisions, responsibility, and attitude change: Effects of volition, foreseeability, and locus of causality of negative consequences. *Journal of Personality and Social Psychology,* 1976, **33**, 300–306.

Steiner, I. D. Perceived freedom. In L. Berkowitz (Ed.), *Advances in experimental social psychology* (Vol. 5). New York: Academic Press, 1970.

Sullivan, H. S. *Conceptions of modern psychiatry.* New York: Norton, 1953.

Swann, W. B., Jr., & Read, S. J. Self-verification processes: How we sustain our self-conceptions. *Journal of Experimental Social Psychology,* 1981, **17**, 351–372.

Taylor, S. E., & Crocker, J. Schematic bases of social information processing. In E. T. Higgins, P. Herman, & M. P. Zanna (Eds.), *Social cognition: The Ontario symposium on personality and social psychology.* Hillsdale, New Jersey: Erlbaum, 1980.

Tedeschi, J. T. (Ed.). *Impression management theory and social psychological research.* New York: Academic Press, 1981.

Tedeschi, J. T., & Lindskold, S. *Social psychology.* New York: Wiley, 1976.

Tedeschi, J. T., & Riordan, C. A. Impression management and prosocial behavior following transgression. In J. T. Tedeschi (Ed.), *Impression management theory and social psychological research.* New York: Academic Press, 1981.

Tedeschi, J. T., & Rosenfeld, P. Impression management theory and the forced compliance situation. In J. T. Tedeschi (Ed.), *Impression management theory and social psychological research.* New York: Academic Press, 1981.

Tesser, A. Self-generated attitude change. In L. Berkowitz (Ed.), *Advances in experimental social psychology* (Vol. 11). New York: Academic Press, 1978.

Tetlock, P. E. Explaining teacher explanations of pupil performance: A self-presentation interpretation. *Social Psychology Quarterly,* 1980, **43**, 283–290.

Turner, R. H. The self-conception in social interaction. In C. Gordon & K. J. Gergen (Eds.), *The self in social interaction.* New York: Wiley, 1968.

Verhaeghe, H. Mistreating other persons through simple discrepant role playing: Dissonance arousal or response contagion. *Journal of Personality and Social Psychology,* 1976, **34,** 125–137.

Weary, G. Examination of affect and egotism as mediators of bias in causal attributions. *Journal of Personality and Social Psychology,* 1980, **38,** 348–357.

Weary, G., & Arkin, R. M. Attributional self-presentation and the regulation of self-evaluation. In J. H. Harvey, W. C. Ickes, & R. F. Kidd (Eds.), *New directions in attribution research* (Vol. 3). Hillsdale, New Jersey: Erlbaum, 1981.

Wicklund, R. A., & Brehm, J. W. *Perspectives on cognitive dissonance.* Hillsdale, New Jersey: Erlbaum, 1976.

Wicklund, R. A., & Duval, S. Opinion change and performance facilitation as a result of objective self-awareness. *Journal of Experimental Social Psychology,* 1971, **7,** 319–342.

Wixon, D. R., & Laird, J. D. Awareness and attitude change in the forced-compliance paradigm: The importance of when. *Journal of Personality and Social Psychology,* 1976, **34,** 376–384.

Wyer, R. S., Jr. The acquisition and use of social knowledge: Basic postulates and representative research. *Personality and Social Psychology Bulletin,* 1980, **6,** 558–573.

# AVERSIVE CONDITIONS AS STIMULI TO AGGRESSION

## Leonard Berkowitz

DEPARTMENT OF PSYCHOLOGY
UNIVERSITY OF WISCONSIN—MADISON
MADISON, WISCONSIN

## I.  Introduction

It is generally agreed that frustrations often increase the likelihood of aggression. What is less clear, however, is just why this should be. Surprisingly little systematic attention has been given to the question of what psychological processes are involved in the relationship between frustration and aggression, and those writers who have confronted this problem have offered quite different answers.

ADVANCES IN EXPERIMENTAL SOCIAL
PSYCHOLOGY, VOL. 15

A few authorities have looked at the frustration–aggression connection from an evolutionary perspective. As a notable example, in his pioneering examination of the natural history of aggression, John Paul Scott (1958) suggested that a thwarted animal frequently displays aggression because its attack is adaptive in some way: "aggression could be extremely useful as an adaptation to social frustration, simply by chasing away the frustrating individual" (p. 9). It might be, then, that the animals in a broad variety of species are biologically disposed to attack the source of their frustration when they are prevented from reaching an anticipated goal; these attacks have enhanced the survival of the species in the evolutionary past.

By contrast, most American psychologists, especially those trained in social psychology and/or learning theory, are inclined to minimize or even deny the role of such genetic dispositions. For them, the individual's interpretations and previously acquired habits are a necessary link in any connection between frustration and aggression. Let us briefly consider some of the major ideas regarding the possible effects of frustration. I shall first review the position taken by cognitively oriented social psychologists and then shall advance my own conception based on general behavior theorizing. After this, I shall discuss the effects of aversive conditions on aggression, beginning with animal research and then turning to investigations with humans.

## II.  Emotional Labeling and Attributions

### A.  COGNITIONS AS ALL-IMPORTANT

According to the now-dominant notions in contemporary social psychology, the individual has to think of himself as having a particular emotional feeling if he is to show emotional behavior consistent with that feeling. Thus, if someone has just been blocked in his attempt to reach a goal, the prevailing theoretical conception in American social psychology, greatly influenced by Schachter's (1964) cognitive theory of emotion, tells us the individual has to view himself as angry if he is to react with a violent outburst in which he tries to hurt the one who had thwarted him. According to Schachter, the bodily (including neural) responses to a provocation do not in themselves provide specific stimulation to a given form of behavior or even to the qualitative feelings that are experienced. The outside event presumably generates only a general arousal. How the person feels about this occurrence and what he does about it are supposedly dependent upon his interpretation of his internal sensations. He will strike out at the source of his arousal only if he labels his sensations as "anger" but will feel "fear" and may run away if he thinks he is afraid. The specific experience and the concomitant behavior are presumably shaped by the label the person attaches to his feelings.

## 1. Attributions

Attribution theory has built on and extended this formulation. It maintains that the label given to the sensations is greatly influenced by the perceived cause of the event. The thwarted individual is most likely to regard himself as angry and then attack his frustrater if he believes this person had deliberately prevented him from achieving the goal. On the other hand, if he thinks this other person had only accidentally impeded his goal striving, he is theoretically less apt to see himself as angry and thus might not exhibit any aggressive reaction at all.

Experimental evidence indicates that cognitions about the cause of the arousal can indeed affect the subsequent aggression (Rule & Nesdale, 1976). As just one example, Zillmann has employed a version of Schachter's theory in his research on the consequences of physical exertion. He suggested that the individual will tend to attribute whatever excitation he feels to salient events in his environment. The young men in one of his experiments (Zillmann, Katcher, & Milavsky, 1972) were first either provoked or not provoked by their partners and then were required to work on either strenuous or easy physical tasks. Shortly afterward, when they had opportunities to punish their partners, they gave them the most intense shocks if they have been previously angered by them and had afterward engaged in strenuous activities. These subjects had presumably interpreted their relatively strong exercise-induced arousal as anger and then attacked their tormentors in accordance with this belief.

In yet another variation of this general theme, Rule, Ferguson, and Nesdale (1979) have more recently argued that external cues associated with arousal affect the aggressive response by influencing the person's attributions regarding the source of his arousal and the label he applies to his feelings. So, if someone is insulted and then exposed to arousing white noise, as in an experiment by Donnerstein and Wilson (1976), he might well attribute the noise-generated arousal to the insult he suffered. The insult is more salient to him; it commands his attention, and as a result, he interprets the added arousal created by the noise as intense anger.

Bandura (1973) has accepted this general line of thought in his social-learning theory of aggression. In common with these cognitive theorists, he contends that a frustration or any other aversive treatment only produces a general state of emotional arousal, and that situational cues determine how this arousal will be interpreted. More than his social-psychological compatriots, however, he also believes it is important to consider the individual's prior learning. What response he makes to the frustration is also dependent "on the types of responses the person has learned for coping with stress" (p. 53).

## B.  IS THE ANGRY LABEL NECESSARY FOR ANGRY AGGRESSION?

### 1.  Some Problems

In my own view, the aggressor's interpretation of his feelings and his beliefs regarding the cause of his arousal can influence the strength of his attacks upon the available target, but are not necessary to produce emotional aggression. There are several reasons for questioning the notion that our cognitions are all-important in shaping specific emotions out of an undifferentiated arousal state (Berkowitz, 1982; Leventhal, 1974, 1980).

For one thing, as Rule *et al.* (1979) acknowledged, some of the studies cited in support of the cognitive analysis are really equivocal in various ways. These investigations, such as the experiment by Zillmann *et al.* (1972) and a conceptually similar one by Konecni (1975), typically do not have any direct evidence that the provoked and then physiologically aroused subjects had actually misattributed their strong arousal to the provocation and thus regarded themselves as very angry. There is a much simpler alternative to the attribution account: The general arousal produced by the exercise or the white noise could have "energized" the internal aggressive reactions evoked by the prior insult. It is not that this insult had caused them to mislabel their internal arousal. Rather, the provocation had elicited aggressive responses inside the subjects which were then strengthened by the arousing manipulation.

A growing body of research findings also poses important difficulties for Schachter's analysis. Some of these studies contradict Schachter's contention that the provoking incident elicits only an undifferentiated arousal state which is then shaped by the person's cognitions. Ax (1953) and others have reported that the experiences of fear and anger are not accompanied by the same physiological patterns, while Izard (1977), Tomkins (1962, 1963), and others have shown that fairly specific expressive reactions, especially in the face, are associated with particular affective states. Taken together, these findings suggest that there is a closer connection between specific emotional feelings and bodily reactions than the cognitive-attribution notions typically suppose. Feedback from these bodily reactions could dispose the individual to experience particular affects.

Perhaps more compelling are the Marshall and Zimbardo (1979) and Maslach (1979) failures to replicate Schachter's initial results. In the former study, the emotional experiences reported by epinephrine-aroused subjects were not influenced by a peer's actions, whereas the hypnotically aroused subjects in the second experiment had negative feelings whether they were exposed to an angry or euphoric confederate. The induced arousal state apparently is not as easily molded by external events as the Schachter theory holds, and furthermore, people may have unpleasant feelings whenever they are inexplicably aroused independently of the behavior of the others around them.

Then too, the Schachterian position essentially holds that the angry aggression displayed by sentient humans is fundamentally different from what Moyer (1976) has termed irritable aggression in other animal species. Why should we deny the basic continuity of life processes in the higher animals? Other species, and even very young human children, show anger or fear in reaction to some emotional event, and they attack or try to get away from the emotional object. It seems too much to assume that these differentiated responses in animals and young children are necessarily the product of their interpretation of their internal sensations. Rather than making these cognitions all-important, I hold that they can facilitate or interfere with the development and display of specific emotional feelings and actions but are not entirely necessary for these reactions to occur.

### 2. An Alternative for Some Cases

The alternative explanation I offered just before, on the other hand, is certainly not restricted to humans. Basically in keeping with what Spence has called general behavior theory, this notion says that the aggressive responses stimulated by some event can be intensified by an irrelevant drive, as long as the situation does not also evoke reactions that are incompatible with aggression. There are indications, for example, that sexual arousal can strengthen the aggressive reactions evoked by an earlier provocation (Donnerstein, Donnerstein, & Evans, 1975; Zillmann, Hoyt, & Day, 1974). We can also see essentially the same phenomenon in an experiment not involving anger arousal. According to Geen and O'Neal (1969), moderate noise intensified the aggressive reactions that had been previously evoked by a violent movie. This increment was not instrumental to the attainment of external benefits; it occurred relatively involuntarily, and there is also no reason to think the subjects had regarded themselves as angry. Some event (the movie in this instance) had elicited aggressive responses which the irrelevant arousal (created by the noise) then strengthened. A conceptually similar process might take place at times when people are insulted, as in some of the attribution experiments mentioned previously. Here too, aggressive reactions were stimulated (by the provocation) and the arousal intensified these reactions—without the necessary intervention of labeled feelings.

## III. The Present Theory: Aversive Events as Stimuli to Aggression

### A. AVERSIVE EVENTS AS THE SOURCE OF EMOTIONAL AGGRESSION

In my view (Berkowitz, 1969, 1978), frustrations create an instigation to aggression because they are aversive. This idea is not totally new by any means. Researchers (e.g., Amsel, 1962; Azrin, Hutchinson, & McLaughlin, 1965; Ferster, 1957; Ulrich, 1966) have long noted that the failure to obtain an accustomed reward has many of the properties of punishment. In general, animals attempt to avoid frustrations, undoubtedly because they are unpleasant. It is this aversiveness that produces the aggression-facilitating reactions. Those factors that determine the strength of the aggressive response to some frustration—such as the intensity of the instigation that is unexpectedly blocked and the degree of interference with the goal attainment (cf. Dollard, Doob, Miller, Mowrer, & Sears, 1939, p. 28)—have this capacity because they govern the magnitude of the aversive reaction.

We cannot say, therefore, as some psychologists have (e.g., Baron, 1977), that frustrations are relatively weak causes of aggression in comparison to personal attacks. All thwartings are not equally aversive and all personal attacks do not generate the same displeasure. We can be bitterly disappointed at times when we unexpectedly fail to reach some goal or, on the other hand, can easily brush off a mild criticism. It is not the objective nature of the aversive incident that is important, but how aversive it is thought to be.

## 1. The Anger Experience

To spell this out in more detail, I want to make use of some of the newly developed ideas in the study of emotions, especially the analyses recently advanced by Leventhal (1973, 1980) and Bower (1981). As Leventhal envisions the emotion-generating sequence, when a person encounters an emotion-exciting event, whatever it might be, he detects the occurrence, interprets it, and also exhibits expressive-motor reactions to this perception. The individual's emotional experience grows directly out of this process, Leventhal says, and does not arise (as the Schachterians hold) from any thoughtful inferences or judgments that he makes about himself on seeing the situation and observing his responses to it. Rather, the person reacts to the perceived event, and these spontaneous reactions, particularly in the facial region, presumably feed back into the central nervous system as the primary generator of the distinctive emotional feeling. A schematic or emotional memory usually also contributes to the emotional experience. Here, relatively concrete, episodic representations of earlier emotion-eliciting events in the form of schemata are integrated with the expressive reactions, thereby enriching the perceptual–emotional experience and producing the complex subtler feelings such as envy, pride, and contentment.

Research reported by Laird is in line with this analysis. In the first of his experiments (Laird, 1974), undergraduate men were asked to contract their facial muscles in a particular manner as they looked at a series of pictures so that they sometimes had an angry frown and at other times a happy smile. After each viewing the subjects rated their mood on that occasion. Those men who were unaware of the impact of their manipulated facial expressions on them reported feeling more aggressive and less elated when they were frowning than when they were smiling, but especially if they had also just seen a picture consistent with that mood. My guess is that the picture shown to the subjects had evoked a particular disposition in them, either toward aggression or toward happiness. If they were also unknowingly exhibiting a facial expression consistent with this inclination at the time, the ideas and other internal reactions elicited by their expressive-motor reactions strengthened the picture-activated feeling enough so that they now were aware of this particular mood. Interestingly, and in further support of our conjectured linkage between expressive-motor reactions and ideas and feelings, at the end of the experimental session a number of the men spontaneously remarked that their thoughts and recollections had become consistent with their expressions. One of Laird's subjects put it this way. "When my jaw was clenched and my brows down, I tried not to be angry but it just fit the position. I'm not in an angry mood, but I found my thoughts wandering to things that made me angry" (Laird, 1974, p. 480). Even if we accept the subject's statement that he was not angry at that time, he might have developed a consciously angry mood if there were suitable anger-related cues in the situation and if he had retained the angry expression somewhat longer.

All in all, there appears to be good reason to suggest that a person's anger experience stems from the combination of (a) his awareness of the reactions within him—throughout his body—evoked by the present aversive situation and (b) his schematic memory of other, similar occurrences which includes, of course, his memory of how he had felt on these occasions. From my perspective this anger experience only parallels the internal reactions creating the dispositions to aggression and to escape. Thinking of oneself as "angry" might facilitate aggression at times, for example, by increasing the likelihood that the person will define certain features of the environment as aggressive cues so that these external stimuli evoke additional aggression-facilitating reactions. Or this self-labeling might even lessen the open display of aggression, as when the person believes his anger level is inappropriate or unjustified so that he restrains himself. Nonetheless, the specific internal changes created by the aversive incident give rise to a specific disposition to aggression even without the intervention of this anger awareness (cf. Berkowitz, 1982, for a further discussion of this parallel processing). Yet even though the anger does not in itself cause the aggressive reactions, we might well want to measure the intensity of the person's anger or perhaps even his negative affect because these feelings should have a direct relationship to the strength of his instigations to flee or fight. (Of course, the strength of the overt behavior that is actually shown will also be affected by competing action tendencies and inhibitions against these behaviors, as well as by situational cues that can facilitate the particular behavior [Berkowitz, 1981].)

### 2.   Thoughts and Other Stimuli Eliciting Emotional Reactions

In discussing the role of the emotional schemata (i.e., memories), Leventhal brings in contemporary analyses of memory and information processing.

He notes that these schemata, as representations of prior emotional experiences, can be evoked by many of the same stimuli that activate the expressive motor reactions. (Here I would add that they can also be elicited by stimuli that have been associated with these expressive-motor reactions in the past.) Leventhal's conception seems to resemble Bower's (1981) network model of the relationship between mood and memory. Both theorists posit a linkage between emotional feelings and particular thoughts so that the evocation of certain images or ideas might then elicit the feelings that had been connected with these thoughts in the past. Some such tie between thoughts and feelings undoubtedly leads to the mood changes produced by the Velten (1968) mood-induction method. As the subjects read and think about the affect-laden sentences in the Velten procedure, other images and ideas are activated in their memory, and these in turn probably evoke the associated expressive-motor reactions. A particular feeling then results.

At any rate, I might also note that all of this is compatible with the suggestion I offered some years ago (Berkowitz, 1973) that words and symbols having an aggressive meaning can evoke other ideas with the same meaning and even feelings conducive to the display of aggressive behavior.

We have now come to an important matter that will be brought up again later in this article in connection with one of my recent studies of the effect of thoughts on pain-evoked aggression. The central point here is that an individual's cognitions can influence his emotional reactions without the intervention of self-applied labels to his sensations. As Leventhal argued, "A change in cognition [can bring] a change in emotion because of the cognition's affect-eliciting properties or its past association with particular emotions. This is not the same as associating a new label with a state of general arousal" (1980, p. 154). Thus, as I shall show later, a person who is inclined to be aggressive as a result of exposure to an aversive event should display a relatively high level of open aggression if the external situation somehow leads him to have aggression-related thoughts at that time. These situationally elicited ideas evoke memories and expressive-motor reactions connected with aggression, thereby strengthening the disposition to attack someone.

### 3.   Flight or Fight?

Obviously, aggression is not always the likeliest response to the aversive situation. Humans, like many other animals, are born with a readiness to flee as well as to fight when they are confronted by an aversive event. Which reaction is predominant depends upon the particular situation and the individual's learning history. The tendency to escape or avoid could be prepotent, initially at least, when the individual thinks he has little power to control the external threat, and learning can probably modify this disposition to get away, either strengthening it further or even weakening it. Nevertheless, even though he might prefer to flee, the person might lash out impulsively at the aversive stimulus, especially if he is not incapacitated, the aggression does not require prolonged and deliberate effort, and escape appears difficult (the cornered-animal pattern).

## B.   INTERPRETATIONS CAN INFLUENCE THE LIKELIHOOD OF OVERT AGGRESSION

The thwarted individual's belief about why he had been frustrated can obviously influence how upset he will be by his failure to reach his goal. If he thinks that someone had deliberately kept him from getting what he wanted, there are *two* things that bother him: (a) the failure to satisfy his desire, and (2) an unfriendly act directed toward him. Both of these components together can be more annoying than only the first component by itself (that is, the pure frustration), especially if the individual believes he has been uniquely singled out for the harsh treatment (Dyck & Rule, 1978). By the same token, to get to our second factor, those persons who are associated with an intentionally produced thwarting are apt to acquire more unpleasant stimulus characteristics than are those who happen to be connected only with a pure frustration. Beside being paired with a strongly aversive occurrence, the former may also be associated with the idea of aggression; someone had deliberately tried to hurt him, the thwarted person may think, and this could be seen as an act of aggression. People connected with the notion of aggression theoretically are better able to elicit impulsive aggressive reactions than are those who lack this association (Berkowitz, 1971, 1973).

An unpublished experiment by Berkowitz and Knurek (see Berkowitz, 1973, p. 117) indicates how associations can affect the degree of hostility felt toward innocent bystanders. In this study each male subject worked together with a fellow student for a cash prize. Some of the participants were successful in their assignment, whereas others failed because of the partner's apparent ineptitude. Each subject then went to a supposedly different experiment in which he was to evaluate two applicants for the position of dormitory counselor. By a "coincidence," one of the job candidates had the same first name as the accomplice. This name affected the thwarted person's judgment of the applicant. If the subject had been frustrated in the first phase, he attributed reliably more unfavorable qualities to the job candidate having the same name as his partner than to the other individual. No such difference existed for the participants who had succeeded on the first task. All in all, the former job applicant was associated with someone who had been responsible for an unpleasant experience, and therefore evoked a hostile reaction. He might have drawn an even stronger negative reaction if his name had connected him with someone who had intentionally blocked his path to the goal.

Two experiments, by Burnstein and Worchel (1962) and the present writer (Berkowitz, 1981), illustrate how frustrated persons' interpretations can influence the strength of their inhibitions against aggression. In the former investigation the subjects were assembled in small groups and were required to reach a solution to an assigned problem within a specified time limit. However, some groups were frustrated because one of their members (the experimenter's confederate) frequently interrupted the discussion to ask the others what had been said. In some cases this individual wore a hearing aid so it was clear that he was not being an intentional obstructionist, whereas in the other instances there did not seem to be any good reason for his constant interruptions. Burnstein and Worchel found there was no open hostility toward the ''deaf'' frustrater when the subjects had to state their opinions publicly. Nevertheless, the participants did express some resentment toward this handicapped person on a disguised indirect measure of hostility. They apparently were reluctant to say anything bad about the person who had thwarted them when they believed he had not intended to be an obstacle, but they still exhibited some resentment toward him on a measure that was relatively free of inhibitions.

Berkowitz (1981) has reported seemingly comparable results in a study also varying the social legitimacy of the barrier to the subjects' goal attainment. In this experiment, two groups of men were frustrated just before they could obtain a cash prize. In one case (the supposedly legitimate frustration) the failure was due to a mechanical breakdown, whereas in the other condition the subjects' partner had supposedly misbehaved (illegitimate frustration). Measures of the increase in the participants' heart rate, as well as their ratings of their mood, indicated that the men in both groups were equally aroused by their frustration. In this sense, both frustrated groups were equally inclined to be aggressive. But, when the subjects were asked to give their opinion of their partner, they were less hostile to him if the failure had not been his fault. It is as if they restrained the hostility they felt when they could not blame the other person, but felt freer to express their resentment when the target appeared to be the cause of their unpleasant arousal.

## IV.   Research on Pain, Aversive Stimulation, and Aggression

Having just summarized my general thesis, I shall now discuss in more detail evidence bearing directly on the notion of aversively stimulated aggression. More specifically, I shall go beyond my analysis of the frustration–aggression relationship to a consideration of the effects of other aversive conditions, particularly physical pain. My argument here is that if a frustration (the sudden removal of a desired event) can evoke aggressive reactions because of its aversiveness, other stimuli that animals (and humans) seek to escape or avoid can also elicit an instigation to aggression. Occurrences that are physically painful are a prime example of such aversive stimuli, of course, and are particularly likely to create this inclination to aggression. Let us first look at animal research on the effects of physical pain and then turn to investigations of the impact of aversive stimulation on humans.

## A. EXPERIMENTS WITH ANIMALS

The experiments by Azrin, Ulrich, Hutchinson, and their associates (e.g., Azrin, Hutchinson & Hake, 1967; Hutchinson, 1973; Ulrich, 1966; Ulrich & Azrin, 1962) have demonstrated that physical pain can be a fairly potent stimulus to aggression in a variety of animal species ranging from birds, through the subhuman primates, to humans (cf. Hutchinson, 1973). In these studies, when two animals were cooped up together in a small chamber and exposed to noxious stimuli (such as physical blows, electric shocks, loud noises, or intense heat), they frequently began to fight. Since this reaction occurred with some regularity, emerged without any prior training, and persisted even in the absence of obvious rewards, Ulrich and Azrin (1962) referred to it as reflexive. However, Johnson (1972) and Moyer (1976) have objected to this characterization, noting that the elicited behavior is not as stereotyped as most reflexes. It is also important to recognize the important role of the surrounding stimulus conditions in the pain–aggression relationship.

### 1. External Stimulus Conditions

Aggression is by no means an inevitable reaction to painful stimulation. We know, for example, that the pained animal often prefers to flee from the aversive stimulus rather than attack an available target (cf. Potegal, 1979). According to Azrin, Hutchinson, and Hake (1967), the attack tendency is apt to be stronger than the inclination to escape if the animal has not learned how to get away from the unpleasant occurrence. Electric shocks gave rise to aggression in this research only when the afflicted organism could not escape or avoid this stimulation. We can generalize this observation even further. An aversive event undoubtedly generates both escape *and* aggressive tendencies, as I mentioned earlier. Which of these instigations will dominate in overt behavior probably varies with a number of situational conditions, including the organism's ability to get away from or even eliminate the noxious occurrence. This ability, in turn, can be a function of prior learning and also the availability of escape routes. Thus, even though the pained animal may prefer to run away, he may still lash out at some target when he is unable to escape: the cornered rat phenomenon.

The characteristics of the aversive stimulation can also affect the likelihood and/or strength of the aggressive reaction. The pained animal's attack is typically stronger the more intense the unpleasant stimulation, the longer its duration, and the more frequently the aversive occurrence had been encountered in the recent past (Hutchinson, 1973; Knutson, Fordyce, & Anderson, 1980).

### 2. Target Characteristics

These last-mentioned observations are fairly obvious. What is less appreciated is the significant role played by the target. Of course, the longer the time between the end of the painful stimulation and the appearance of a suitable victim, the weaker is the level of aggression directed against that object (Hutchinson, 1973), but over and above this time interval, the target's characteristics can also affect the strength of the attack. Almost a generation ago, along with other writers, I pointed out that certain features of the provoked organism's environment can serve much like conditioned stimuli to facilitate the open appearance of aggression (Berkowitz, 1964, 1965). As a result of classical conditioning, for example, the presentation of previously neutral stimuli that had been paired with aversive stimulation can start animals fighting (Hutchinson, Renfrew & Young, 1971; Vernon & Ulrich, 1966). Also in keeping with this conditioning idea, the available target's stimulus properties can also have an important effect on the level of aggression exhibited. Investigators have shown that pained animals will often attack a surprisingly wide range of objects: conspecifics, toys, tennis balls, and even a rubber hose (Hutchinson, 1973). This does not mean, however, that all of these objects will draw the same intensity of aggression. In at least one experiment (Ulrich & Azrin, 1962), shocked rats attacked other small animals but not inanimate objects. Similarly, in another study (Knutson *et al.*, 1980) pained rats were more apt to strike at other animals that had also been shocked than at nonshocked rats, probably because the former behaved in ways that heightened their aggressive cue value.

As I have suggested elsewhere, this target specificity may be part of a very pervasive phenomenon. Roberts and Kiess (1964) observed what seem to be comparable findings in the research on the aggressive effects of electrical stimulation of the hypothalamus. On reviewing a number of studies with cats, they noted that the animals' aggressive responses "were directed toward appropriate objects in the environment" but did not appear when the animals were alone (p. 187). In the Roberts and Kiess experiment, hypothalamic stimulation caused normally nonaggressive cats to attack rats, but there was also a target specificity. When various objects were presented separately to the stimulated animals, 100% of the cats attacked either a live or dead rat, and 89% struck at a small stuffed dog, but only 33% aggressed against a hollow red rubber rat. Moreover, only 11% attacked a "rat-sized wood block covered with white terrycloth," and none of the animals struck at a "rat-sized wood block" (W. W. Roberts, personal communication). Other researchers have published similar reports. Wasman and Flynn for example (cited by Roberts & Kiess, 1964), found that the predatory attack was weaker to a dead rat than a live rat, and still weaker to a stuffed dog.

In general, Roberts concluded ''that the stimulation elicited a readiness for attack that was only performed (or perhaps 'released') when a relatively narrow range of objects was present.'' Can it be that the stimulation—whether this is electrical stimulation of the hypothalamus or a decidedly unpleasant occurrence—produces an instigation to aggression that need not be revealed in open behavior? Although they may not be necessary for the open appearance of aggression, certain environmental stimuli may facilitate the occurrence of the aggressive reactions so that the stimulation-induced aggressive instigation is translated into open attacks. Targets having particular stimulus qualities can function in just this manner. From this perspective, these targets elicit the attacks upon them. Further research is obviously required to ascertain what these aggression-enhancing stimulus qualities might be, but it is reasonable to suggest that they stem from prior associations with either aversive events or reinforced aggression.

*Prior Learning.*   The organism's learning history is obviously an important determinant of the extent to which aversive stimulation will lead to open aggression. Beside affecting the aggression-facilitating associations I have just mentioned, this prior learning can interact with the pain-produced instigation to aggression. For example, suppose two rats are given relatively mild electric shocks in the presence of a smaller mouse and that one of these rats has acquired a strong habit of mouse killing, whereas the other animal has been only an inconsistent mouse killer in the past. In the former case, the mild pain-induced instigation should combine with a strong aggressive habit, whereas in the latter instance, we have a mild instigation combining with only a weak habit. The result, of course, is that the mouse is more likely to be killed by the pained rat who had strongly learned to be a mouse killer (Baenninger & Ulm, 1969).

Learning history can be fairly complex, involving (among other things) the extent to which aggressive actions are restrained and the organism has developed the tendency to show nonaggressive reactions to the aversive stimulus. Not surprisingly, those animals who had been consistently punished for fighting in the past are not apt to exhibit open aggression when given electric shocks (Follick & Knutson, 1978). Furthermore, if animals have learned specific nonaggressive ways of terminating the unpleasant stimulation, any one aversive event is less likely to evoke overt aggression from them (Ulrich & Craine, 1964). On the other hand, the direct reinforcement of the aggressive reaction enhances the strength of aversively stimulated attacks (Hutchinson, 1973).

The animal's social interactions with others of its own kind involve a mixture of reinforcements and punishments for aggression, sometimes rewards predominating and at other times punishments. In one experiment (Hutchinson, Ulrich, & Azrin, 1965), rats who had been raised in community cages fought more on receiving electric shocks than did other rats who had been reared in social isolation. The former, socially raised animals might have found that their aggression was at least occasionally rewarded in the course of their interactions with their peers so that they acquired aggressive habits. These aggressive tendencies were then readily evoked by the painful stimulation. But interestingly, even the socially isolated rats became extremely aggressive if they had a repeated exposure to the electric shocks so that they had a prolonged history of pain-induced fighting. This latter finding convinced the investigators "that pain-elicited aggression is principally an unlearned reaction," although learning can modify the ease with which the aversive occurrence produces attacks.

The exact nature of the organism's social environment can also be important. Ader (1975) reported that rats reared in a noncompetitive environment actually displayed more aggressive behavior on being shocked than did their competitively raised counterparts. The researcher believed that the animals growing up in the competitive situation had established a stable dominance hierarchy and, as a consequence, had learned to inhibit their aggressive reactions when they were with many of their peers. Anticipating punishment from these others, the pained animals refrained from fighting with them.

### B.  WHAT IS THE GOAL OF THE ADVERSIVELY STIMULATED AGGRESSION?

Any discussion of the influence of learning on the pain–aggression relationship inevitably raises the question of what are the reinforcements for the evoked aggressive reaction. Externally provided rewards (such as food) can clearly heighten the strength of these reactions but, we might ask, do other types of reinforcements also operate because they are intrinsic to the unpleasant situation? In ordinary words, what is the goal of elicited behavior, the attainment of which will increase the probability of a further aggressive reaction?

### 1.  The Role of Negative Reinforcement

The conception of the aversively stimulated response as reflexive—and Ulrich and Azrin (1962) have referred to it as an "unconditional reflex"—implies that there are no special intrinsic reinforcements other than the opportunity to perform the response. However, a number of investivators have contended that the elicited aggression bears a closer resemblance to naturally occurring defensive behavior than to real-life appetitive attacks on an opponent (e.g., Blanchard, Blanchard & Takahashi, 1978), and several writers have therefore referred to the aversively stimulated fighting as defensive aggression (Potegal, 1979; Scott, 1971). For Potegal (1979), this view is upheld by the evidence that many pained animals prefer to escape from the situation rather than attack an available target. According to this position, then, the primary reinforcement for the aversively stimulated aggression is the lessening or termination of the painful situation. That is, the aggression is negatively reinforced. Supporting such a possibility, Knutson *et al,* (1980) submitted some of their rats to a negative reinforcement training procedure (where an attack on a conspecific germinated the shock) and found that these animals later exhibited more fighting in response to shocks than did the control rats.

## 2.   The Opportunity to Aggress as a Reinforcement

Nevertheless, however powerful this negative reinforcement might be, I suspect that the aversively stimulated aggression can also be reinforced by the mere opportunity to attack a suitable target. For one thing, we know that shock-induced aggression can occur even when this behavior is not connected to a lessening of the painful stimulation. Ulrich and Craine (1964) have reported, for example, that their rats exhibited an increase in fighting even though the shock was turned off when nonaggressive responses were performed and was continued if the animals persisted in fighting. The aggression did not pay off by ending the aversive stimulation, and a spectrum of nonaggressive actions was negatively reinforced, but still the aggressive reactions continued to occur. There were somewhat similar results in the previously cited research by Knutson *et al.* (1980). In one of their experimental conditions, the rats were given the same number of shocks that had been received by the negatively reinforced group, but for these animals aggressive responses did not lead to the cessation of the shocks. When they were tested later in a novel situation, these rats were more likely to fight on being shocked again than were a previously nonshocked control group, although they were less aggressive than their negatively reinforced counterparts. Here too, the animals had not learned that their attacks would end the painful stimulation, but they were still inclined to fight when they were in pain.

Moreover, the aggression produced by the unpleasant event is sometimes so extreme it appears to be more than defensive behavior. Thus, in a study by Baenninger and Ulm (1969), severe electric shocks stimulated mouse-killing rats to kill a nearby mouse several seconds after the shocks were terminated. These animals apparently were provoked into seeking the slaughter. The pain-induced killing in this instance surely is not just an attempt at self-defense. It is not likely that the killer rats had attacked the hapless mouse merely because they attributed their suffering to their victim.

## 3.   Attaining the Aggressive Goal

There is a related matter that I believe should also be kept in mind. For at least several species (cf. Potegal, 1979), once an animal begins fighting it often seeks to continue the combat until some kind of ''closure'' is attained. Lager-spetz (1964, cited in Berkowitz, 1965) demonstrated, as just one example, that a mouse who had been interrupted in the midst of a fight with a submissive opponent would rush across an electrically charged floor grid to get at its victim again. According to Leshner and Nock (1976), the aggression is apt to continue in these cases until the attacker achieves victory—the submission of its opponent. But whatever the specific aim of the aggression, we can suggest that the instigation to aggression will tend to persist until the goal response is performed. Aversive stimulation might activate such an instigation to aggression, at least under certain circumstances. We have indications of this in an experiment by Azrin *et al.* (1965). When the monkeys in this study were given electric shocks, they learned to pull a chain that delivered an inanimate object they could strike. Did the pain evoke an appetitive aggressive inclination so that the mere opportunity to attack an available target was reinforcing? Assuming the unpleasant stimulation did create such an instigation, the performance of the instigated action might be somewhat calming. Some very intriguing findings by Weiss and his associates (Weiss, Pohorecky, Salman, & Gruenthal, 1976) are suggestive in this regard. All of the rats in this research were given electric shocks, but in one condition the animals were shocked in pairs and were allowed to attack each other, whereas those in a comparison condition were shocked while alone so that they did not have anything to attack. The investigators reported that the fighting animals had fewer gastric lesions than did the rats who were shocked alone and thus did not have a suitable target for aggression. Furthermore, when other animals were also shocked in pairs and could strike at each other, but without making contact because of a physical barrier between them, the gastric lesions were also reduced. The diminished gastric pathology apparently was not due to the animals being shocked in pairs. Another experiment showed that rats who received shock together, but who did not engage in fighting behavior, did not have the reduction in gastric lesions. Weiss and his colleagues pointed out that the pained animals' aggression did not terminate the aversive stimulation, and they suggested that the fighting behavior in itself could have been rewarding to them.

Taken together, the results of all these studies indicate that painful stimulation generally produces an inclination to aggression as well as a striving to escape from the unpleasant occurrence. Prior learning as well as the specific nature of the surrounding situation can affect the relative strengths of these two tendencies. But despite the exceptions that are observed at times, as Moyer (1976) concluded in his review of the literature, "there can be no doubt that under certain circumstances pain can lead to an intense attack. Such behavior has been demonstrated in the monkey . . . the cat . . . the rat . . . and the gerbil" (p. 200). Given the procedures used in social-psychological research on this topic, it is interesting to note that Moyer has also observed, "The most effective stimulus for eliciting this kind of aggression is a sharp, sudden pain, as characterized by electric shock. Other types of aversive stimulation, such as cold, loud noises, and heat, are much less effective in producing aggression" (p. 201).

## V.  Research with Humans on the Effects of Aversive Stimulation

A.  RESEARCH EMPLOYING NONPAINFUL AVERSIVE CONDITIONS

For obvious reasons, most of the research with humans into the effects of aversive conditions have employed unpleasant stimuli that people ordinarily avoid but which are not physically painful. Many of these studies indicate that aversive events can heighten the individual's inclination to be aggressive.

### 1.  Odors

Two experiments show that unpleasant odors can provoke aggressive reactions. In one of these (Jones & Bogart, 1978), nonsmokers were significantly more punitive to a fellow student in a "Buss aggression machine" paradigm when cigarette smoke was blown into their room than when they worked in a normal atmosphere. This occurred, furthermore, even when the subjects had not been provoked beforehand.

Rotton, Barry, Frey, and Soler (1978) conducted a more ambitious investigation. Undergraduates had to judge a stranger of their own sex either under normal air or while exposed to a foul odor (produced either by butyric acid or ammonium sulfide). The subjects' mood was reliably affected by the polluted atmosphere. They rated themselves as feeling more "aggressive" as well as "anxious," "fatigued," and "sad" in the two odor-filled rooms than in the normal atmosphere, evidently realizing they were feeling irritable as well as generally bad. Also in accord with our expectations, the subjects were also more hostile to the stranger under the aversive conditions.

### 2.  Disgusting Scenes

Suggestive findings obtained in two experiments employing erotic movies indicate that the observation of disgustingly unpleasant scenes can also elicit aggressive tendencies (White, 1979; Zillmann, Bryant, Comisky, & Medoff, 1981). In the second of these investigations, deliberately provoked men were shown highly arousing film segments or less-arousing pictures that were either of an erotic or neutral nature. In addition, the events depicted were either pleasant to the viewers or were unpleasant and disgusting. (To make this more concrete, the low-arousing, nonerotic, and unpleasant scenes were photos of diseased and/or suffering children or adults, whereas the highly arousing, erotic, and unpleasant stimuli were brief segments of movies showing either sadomasochism or human–animal sexual intercourse.) At the end of the presentation each subject was given the opportunity to punish the person who had tormented him earlier. The researchers found that the men exposed to the combination of highly arousing and disgustingly unpleasant film scenes administered the severest punishment to their antagonist, significantly higher than that delivered by control subjects not shown any kind of material, whether the depictions were sexual or nonsexual in nature. In other words, the decidedly unpleasant stimuli had apparently elicited aggressive tendencies which were sufficiently strengthened by the film-generated excitement so that strong punishment resulted.

### 3. High Temperatures

Common experience suggests that many people become irritable under high temperatures, and a growing body of research indicates that uncomfortable heat can instigate aggression. In one of the first of the recent laboratory experiments in this area, Griffitt (1970) found that his subjects' ratings of a same-sex stranger were harsher in a hot room (effective temperature = 90.6°F) than in a cooler environment (67.5°F). Their general mood was also much less pleasant in the former case. A later experiment by Griffitt and Veitch (1971) examined the effects of population density as well as room temperature, and showed that both variables independently affected the dependent measures. Again, the subjects' mood was worse and they were more hostile to the stranger when they were hot (effective room temperature = 93.5°F) and in a crowded room (12 to 16 people in a space 7 feet × 9 feet) than when they were comfortably cool or in a large room.

The laboratory experiments on the effects of heat are paralleled by studies of the relationship between daily temperatures and the urban riots in the United States during the late 1960s. Goranson and King (cited in Berkowitz, 1980) examined the temperatures in the 17 American cities that had major riots in 1967, and found that it had not been unusually hot in these cities until the day before the outbreak of violence. Then there was a sharp rise in temperature, which reached a peak the day after the riot first exploded. As a matter of fact, 13 of the 17 riot cities had fairly cool weather in the period before the outbreaks occurred, while 15 had abnormally high temperatures during the disorders. A rapid drop in temperature following the initial violence could have contributed to the restoration of order in these cities. On comparing the 9 cities having relatively brief riots of 2 days or less with the 8 cities having a longer period of violence, the researchers noted that the hot weather had been more severe and more persistent in the longer lasting riots.

Baron and Ransberger (1978) obtained comparable results in their analysis of 102 instances of collective violence in United States cities from 1967 through 1971. The rioting throughout this period was related fairly consistently to the summer heat.

### 4. Do Aversive Experiences Have Cumulative Effects?

Some interesting findings in the research on heat effects suggest there may not be a linear relationship between the intensity of the aversive stimulation inflicted on a person and the strength of the resulting instigation to aggression. Griffitt and Veitch (1971) cited some research with mice which pointed to a curvilinear relationship between temperature and aggressive behavior. Aggressive incidents increased until the environment reached about 95°F and then declined sharply. All motor activity including assaults decreased with the higher temperatures. Baron (1977) has emphasized this curvilinear relationship in his research. His first experiment on this topic, carried out in a hot and humid South Carolina summer (Baron, 1972), had found that uncomfortably hot temperatures (92–95°F) *reduced* the intensity of the aggression the subjects exhibited in a Buss paradigm over that shown when the participants were comfortably cool. A later experiment (Baron & Bell, 1975) complicated the picture even further. Here, nonprovoked subjects were most aggressive in the same kind of paradigm when they were in a hot room (92–95°F), but people who had been insulted beforehand actually decreased the intensity of their punishment under this condition. Baron and Bell reasonably suggested that the

> subjects in the hot–angry group found the experimental situation so unpleasant and aversive that escape or minimization of present discomfort became the dominant tendency in their behavior hierarchies. As a result, they may have. . . lowered the intensity of these attacks in order to avoid any delays which might result from their use of strong shocks (e.g., protests for the victim). (p. 830)

In both cases then, the high temperatures seemed to be too much for many of the subjects either because they had already been exposed to too much heat (the South Carolina subjects) or because they were "hot under the collar," so to say, as a result of the prior insult.

Baron (1977) now suggests that there is a curvilinear relationship between the intensity of the negative affect experienced by a person and his subsequent aggressiveness. Aversive experiences that make an individual feel bad dispose him to be aggressive, but very high levels of negative affect presumably lead to decreasing aggression. In keeping with this formulation, Bell and Baron (1976) reported that subjects in the very unpleasant condition of being in a hot room after having received a negative evaluation from a confederate whose attitudes were very different from theirs were *less* aggressive to the confederate than their counterparts who either (a) were in a cooler room while dealing with the negatively evaluating, dissimilar subject, or (b) were under high temperature but faced a noninsulting confederate with similar views.

## 5. Adding Insult to Injury

Presumably because of the curvilinear relationship between the intensity of the negative affect that was experienced and the resulting strength of the aggressive inclinations, the subjects in the Bell and Baron study who had been exposed to both aversive events—the insult and the high temperature—did not display the most aggression. In this sense the negative consequences of the unpleasant occurrences did not cumulate. There are times, however, when such a cumulative effect can be seen. Consider the case of "adding insult to injury." This common notion clearly implies that a succession of aversive events "add up" to make the unfortunate victim especially unhappy. An experiment conducted by Thome and Berkowitz (unpublished) has demonstrated just such a cumulation of negative affect, and also shows the result can be a high level of aggression toward the available target.

In this investigation male and female undergraduates interacted with two other students (of the same sex as the subject) acting as the two experimenters. After each participant was given an assigned task, one of the experimenters (E-Outcome) told each person how well he or she had done, informing the subject he or she had either succeeded or failed on the assignment. Shortly afterward, the second experimenter (E-Provoke) was either deliberately rude to the subject or treated this person in a neutral fashion. For those who had performed poorly on the initial task this second experimenter's behavior literally added insult to injury. Then, at the end of the session each subject completed several questionnaires and made a rating in which he or she recommended or did not recommend hiring each of the experimenters for later research. Since an unfavorable rating could presumably hurt the two experimenters, this item was taken as our measure of hostility.

The condition means on this hiring recommendation item are reported in Table I. If we look first at the mean ratings given the second experimenter (E-Provoke), we can see that both the women and men were more hostile to this

TABLE I

MEAN HOSTILITY TOWARD EACH EXPERIMENTER BY MALE AND FEMALE SUBJECTS AS A FUNCTION OF TASK OUTCOME AND PROVOCATION[a]

| | Provoked[b,c] | | Nonprovoked[b,c] | |
|---|---|---|---|---|
| Subjects | Failed | Success | Failed | Success |
| Female | | | | |
| E-Provoke | $66.59_a$ | $82.13_b$ | $115.64_{def}$ | $138.05_{gh}$ |
| E-Outcome | $134.21_{gh}$ | $126.29_{efgh}$ | $122.43_{efg}$ | $152.36_i$ |
| Male | | | | |
| E-Provoke | $91.62_{bc}$ | $111.04_{de}$ | $128.92_{fgh}$ | $132.61_{gh}$ |
| E-Outcome | $104.72_{cd}$ | $141.92_{hi}$ | $129.71_{fgh}$ | $134.10_{gh}$ |

[a]Data from Thome and Berkowitz (unpublished).

[b]The lower the score the lower the recommendation for hiring and, therefore, the greater the expressed hostility. The ratings could range from 0 (definitely no) to 160 (definitely yes).

[c]Means having different subscripts are significantly different ($p > .05$) by Duncan Multiple Range test.

provocateur if they had been mistreated after failing on the assigned task than if they had been insulted after a successful performance; adding insult to injury increased the subjects' hostility toward the most recent tormentor. The hostile tendencies then generalized in the case of the men to affect the subjects' recommendations for the first experimenter (E-Outcome). These people gave E-Outcome the least favorable recommendation if they had just been provoked by this experimenter's partner and had previously been told by E-Outcome that they had failed. Thus, for the men at least, the hostility elicited by the second experimenter apparently spread to influence the evaluation of the earlier experimenter, the one who had been the bearer of bad tidings.

We cannot say why the women did not exhibit a similar hostility generalization. The subjects' self-reported mood ratings indicated that the strongest negative feelings were aroused by the combination of the two aversive experiences—and that there were no differences between the sexes in this regard. It could be, then, that the women were somehow more discriminating than the men so that they differentiated between the two undergraduate experimenters.

### 6. The Target's Emotional State as a Factor Affecting the Likelihood of Aggression

I have already suggested several times now that the available target's stimulus characteristics can affect the chances that the target will be attacked by those exposed to an aversive event. One of these stimulus qualities, we have seen, has to do with the target's connection with some decidedly unpleasant state of affairs. However, I shall now argue that the way in which this association operates depends upon how it is understood. Imagine yourself in distress because you are in a harsh environment, for example, a very hot room. And let us also suppose that another person is nearby who is also bothered by the heat. The other individual is associated with the aversive stimulation and may even be suffering from it. Will he serve as an aggression-facilitating target so that he is likely to draw a hostile reaction from you? Or consider this. What if you are angry with a certain person who just provoked you, and then you learn that this offensive individual has just been attacked and hurt by someone else. Let us also say that you see the offender is suffering because of the aggression toward him, and you then have an opportunity to attack the offender yourself. How will his pain affect the strength of your own aggression? In other words, we here have two cases in which you have been annoyed by an aversive occurrence and are facing someone who is in distress. Since this person's torment has a different meaning in these two instances, it might well evoke different reactions.

Many of the experiments dealing with the effect of aversive environments on attitudes toward others have employed a reinforcement analysis of the findings. Thus, Griffitt and his associates (e.g., Griffitt, 1970; Griffitt & Veitch, 1971) maintained that the available target in their studies was associated with the negative affect generated by the aversive stimulation so that this person was then disliked. However, on reviewing the published research in this area, Kenrick and Johnson (1979) noted that the published investigations have not always obtained the same results. Several experiments found that subjects exposed to unpleasant occurrences were more strongly attracted to another person rather than being more hostile to him. As an illustration, in a study by Rotton *et al.* (1978), participants who thought the target individual was exposed to the same foul odor they were smelling tended to become friendlier, and not more hostile to this person. In the experiment by Kenrick and Johnson (1979), undergraduate women individually rated either their female partner or a simulated stranger while they heard unpredictable bursts of noise that were either very loud (95 dB) or much quieter (32 dB). In comparison to the quiet condition, the aversive noise led to increased attraction for the physically present partner but decreased liking for the absent stranger. Comparable results have been obtained in research on help giving. Dovidio and Morris (1975) found that subjects who were awaiting electric shocks were most helpful to a fellow student also about to be shocked, but were least inclined to aid someone in a pleasanter condition.

For Kenrick and Johnson the important feature that determined the research outcome had to do with whether the target individual was physically present or not; aversive events, they argued, only lead to hostility toward bogus strangers and not to those who are actually nearby. A closer reading of the literature shows, however, that the Kenrick–Johnson restriction is not valid. Rotton, Frey, Barry, Milligan, and Fitzpatrick (1979) led their subjects to think they were administering electric shocks to a fellow student *whom they had just seen*. If these men were exposed to a moderately unpleasant odor at the time, they punished their peer significantly more strongly than if they were in a normal atmosphere. Similarly, high ambient heat in the Baron and Bell (1975) experiment caused subjects to deliver stronger punishment to a fellow student *whom they had met earlier*. The people in these investigations were not dealing with a simulated stranger, but they were still aggressive to this individual.

It is not the "real" or "fictional" nature of the target that seems to be important in this research but whether the other person shares the subject's unpleasant experience. In the studies reviewed by Kenrick and Johnson, the increased liking for the possible target typically arose when the participants thought that the other individual was also facing the same aversive occurrence, whereas the heightened hostility to the target came about when the subjects believed that they alone were exposed to the unpleasant event. In sum, we may be dealing here with the effect of a "common fate:" People who are threatened by the same external stressor often develop a greater liking for each other.

This common fate reaction appears to be a fairly general phenomenon. Studies of the psychology of affiliation conducted by Schachter (1959) and others have demonstrated that many persons are attracted to those who share their unhappy experience. I (Berkowitz, 1980) have hypothesized, however, that these other persons become attractive to the extent that they seem to be displaying the same reactions to the aversive circumstances and not because they are merely present. In keeping with this suggestion, Miller and Zimbardo (1966) reported that apprehensive people were not attracted to those who were said to be confronted by the same danger but who supposedly had very different personalities. The subjects in this experiment presumably thought that the other participants would exhibit a very different response to the external stressor since they had personalities different from their own. All in all, we come to like those who (we believe) display emotional reactions similar to our own when facing the same aversive occurrence. On the other side of the coin, those who do not share our reactions when confronted by the same unpleasantness should be especially bothersome to us.

What all of this indicates, then, is that the other people who are present when someone is exposed to an unpleasant event can take on additional stimulus characteristics. If they are facing the same stressor and are exhibiting the same emotional responses, they will theoretically become much more attractive so that they are not apt to evoke strong aggression. On the other hand, those who are confronted by the same threat and who display very different emotional reactions should acquire negative stimulus qualities, and thus should elicit strong aggression.

An experiment by Berkowitz and Dunand (unpublished) was designed to investigate this analysis. Half of the participants, undergraduate women, were exposed to an unpleasant treatment by being placed in an uncomfortably hot room, while the others were in a normal environment. Every subject had a partner in an adjoining cubicle who supposedly was in the same physical condition, since we were not interested in examining the effect of a common fate per se. Rather, being more concerned with the participants' response to the other person's *reactions*, we led some of the women to think their partner felt the same way they did about the room temperature, whereas the remaining subjects believed this person's reactions were different from their own. Our expectations were quite straightforward: The subjects in the aversive surroundings would presumably want their neighbor to share their feelings about the heat, and would be especially frustrated if this person had a very different reaction. Thus, the hot people should be antagonistic to a partner not bothered by the high room temperature but should be much friendlier if the partner shared their suffering. Moreover, we also expected the participants in the normal environment would be much less affected by the other individual's reactions to the room temperature.

These expectations were generally upheld. When the subjects were given an opportunity to deliver rewards and punishments to their partner, supposedly as evaluations of the partner's ideas on a series of assigned problems, they were most punitive to this person if (a) both the subject and her partner were exposed to the uncomfortable temperature, *and* (b) this other person indicated she liked the heat. In this case the subject's partner presumably thwarted her desire to have someone be just as miserable as she was when faced by the same unpleasant environment. As a result, the other woman took on negative qualities and evoked the aggressive reactions the "hot and bothered" subject was inclined to display. The partner who reported being bothered by the heat was not given a high level of rewards, however. Maybe the positive qualities she acquired by having these similar reactions were countered by the aggressive inclinations generated by the high temperature.

## B.  RESEARCH INTO THE EFFECTS OF PHYSICAL PAIN

Much of my recent research has concentrated on the effects of physical pain. The general assumption here is that pain is decidedly aversive, and therefore, should be particularly likely to elicit an instigation to aggression. We should be clear, however, that in the case of pain as with the other types of aversive events discussed earlier, it is the perceived aversiveness and not the objective occurrence that matters. A bodily wound or immersion in cold water will not give rise to aggressive inclinations unless the individual wants to avoid this stimulus at the time.

### 1.  Interpretation of the Noxious Stimulation

Virtually all authorities are agreed that the pain experience cannot be understood solely in terms of physical sensations (cf. Melzack, 1973). What the individual experiences depends upon how the sensory input is psychologically processed. According to Melzack, some of Pavlov's experiments with dogs as well as other, more recent studies with humans have clearly demonstrated that "The meaning of the [environmental] stimulus . . . modulates the sensory input before it activates brain processes that underlie perception and response" (1973, p. 30). Melzack also suggested that cognitive processes operate selectively on both sensory processing and motivational mechanisms: "there is evidence that the sensory input is localized, identified . . . evaluated in terms of past experience, and modified before it activates the . . . motivational systems" (1973, p. 102).

One possible implication of all this is that after the noxious stimulation is received, it is evaluated in some way, thus determining the degree of negative affect that is felt. As various writers have emphasized (e.g., Leventhal, Brown, Schacham, & Engquist, 1979; Wilson, Blazer, & Nashold, 1976), this negative affect is somewhat independent of the actual physical sensations. In my view, as I suggested earlier in discussing other types of aversive events, it is this negative affect that evokes the instigation to aggression.

To test this reasoning, Pauline Thome and I (unpublished study) employed a variation of a procedure that had been followed by Leventhal *et al.* (1979). In this earlier experiment the subjects had to immerse one hand in a tank of water that was either unpleasantly cold or that was much more tolerable in temperature, and they were also given preparatory information about the way they might feel. The subjects experienced greater distress if the preparatory information warned them that they might feel pain. This information evidently caused the subjects to code their water-produced sensory input as "pain," thereby leading to the greater felt distress. Going on from here, we can ask whether this pain-expectation information would also produce a relatively strong instigation to aggression.

In my experiment with Thome, the subjects, undergraduate women, were again asked to keep one hand in a tank of water, supposedly as part of an investigation of the effects of harsh environmental conditions on supervision. Two-thirds of the women were to find that the water in the tank was quite cold (7°C), whereas for the remaining subjects the water was a much more pleasant 23°C. But just before they immersed their hand in the water they were given preparatory information. One of the cold water groups and all of the people about to be exposed to the warmer temperature were warned that they might feel pain. The other cold water condition was told only of the possible tingling sensations they might experience in their hand and the word "pain" was not used. Immediately after getting this information each person was told to place her hand in the water, and she was then required to evaluate her partner's ideas on a series of problems by administering rewards and punishments to her. At the end of the 6-min-long session the subjects rated how they had experienced the water temperature and what their mood had been while their hand was in the water.

These latter ratings generally confirmed Leventhal's earlier findings: In general, the women reported having felt the greatest distress when they were exposed to the cold water *and* had expected to feel pain. These people apparently coded their physiological sensations as "pain" so that they then experienced strong distress. More pertinent to our present interests, they also indicated the greatest level of annoyance felt on an index composed of their ratings of "anger," "irritation," and "annoyance." But most important of all, this annoyance evidently was translated into open punitiveness. As Table II indicates, the people exposed to the cold water who expected pain were reliably harsher to their worker than were any of the others.

## 2. Associations with Aversive Events

Classical conditioning can operate in pain-related aggression by humans just as it can influence animal fighting. We know that the mere presentation of stimuli that had been repeatedly paired with noxious events can provoke animals into attacking each other (e.g., Hutchinson, 1973; Hutchinson *et al.*, 1971). In much the same vein, experiments by Fraczek and his associates in Poland have demonstrated that associations with aversive events can affect the intensity of

TABLE II
THE INTERACTION OF SENSATIONS AND EXPECTATIONS ON RESPONSES TO ANOTHER PERSON

|  | 7°C Pain expectation | 7°C No pain | 23°C Pain expectation |
|---|---|---|---|
| Total number of rewards[a] | 17.3 | 21.7 | 20.9 |
| Total number of punishments[b] | 3.1 | 1.3 | 1.6 |
| Total $R - P$[a] | 14.2 | 20.4 | 19.3 |
| Annoyance index[a] | 19.2 | 15.9 | 5.5 |

[a]The 7°C pain expectation group was significantly different from the combination of the two other conditions by planned comparisons.

[b]The $t$ value for the planned comparison difference between the 7°C pain expectation condition and the two other conditions was significant at the .06 level of confidence.

human aggression. Some of the university students in one of his studies (Fraczek, 1974) were taught to associate the color green with the receipt of electric shocks. Soon afterward when all of the students were asked to punish someone else, half of the people found that the apparatus they were to employ in administering the punishment was painted green, whereas for the others the "weapon" apparatus was a different color. The most punitive subjects were those whose weapon had the color-mediated connection with their earlier suffering. Carrying this line of research one step further, Ciarkowska (1979) then demonstrated that the students delivered relatively little aggression by means of the punishment apparatus if this machine was of a color that had previously been paired with a pleasant experience (the receipt of a reward).

These pain-related associations obviously need not be confined to similarities in color or other physical characteristics. I noted earlier that people who have a name-mediated connection with earlier frustraters are apt to evoke relatively strong attacks from those who are disposed to be aggressive at the time (Berkowitz & Knurek, cited in Berkowitz, 1973). In other words, a target can facilitate the aggression that is directed against it by being associated with earlier aversive events, that is, occurrences that had previously produced an instigation to aggression.

This reasoning can be extended even further. Consider those who are handicapped in a very unfortunate way or who are afflicted with some terrible disease. We might sympathize with these people, feeling sorry for the suffering they are undergoing. However, as a great many writers have noted, there is a good chance that we will also, at the same time, experience some distaste for them. In Goffman's (1963) terminology, these persons are stigmatized. They have an undesirable physical characteristic, and we may want to get away from them. Several studies have obtained evidence of this inclination to withdraw from those who are crippled or disfigured in some way (e.g., Comer & Piliavin, 1972; Kleck, Ono, & Hastorf, 1966). At least one investigation (Piliavin, Piliavin, & Rodin, 1975) has even found that there may well be a considerable reluctance to help someone who is stigmatized in this manner. Thus, we are often ambivalent to those who are handicapped or ill, feeling sorry for them and also finding them aversive (Katz, Glass, Lucido, & Farber, 1977; Wright, 1960).

We can all think of a number of reasons why these stigmatized persons are aversive to us. For one thing, we may be threatened by their affliction. All of these possibilities may be valid at one time or another. However, the analysis I have been offering raises yet another possible explanation that may not have occurred to you: We associate those who are ill or handicapped with unpleasantness, suffering, and perhaps even pain. To a considerable extent, they are aversive to us because of this association. Assuming this is the case, then, physically stigmatized people should tend to draw hostility from those who are disposed to be aggressive and whose restraints against aggression happen to be weak on that occasion.

Frodi and I (Berkowitz & Frodi, 1979) have reported two experiments with undergraduate women showing that targets with undesirable physical characteristics tend to receive relatively strong punishment. In the second of these investigations the women first watched a televised interview between the experimenter and a 10-year-old boy whom they were later to supervise. Unknown to the subjects, the interview had been videotaped earlier and the child was made up so that he was either good-looking or fairly unattractive in appearance. Furthermore, cross-cutting this variation, in half of the cases the youngster stuttered, whereas in the other instances he spoke normally.

At the close of the interview the child worked on his assigned task with the TV moniter turned off. The subject-as-supervisor was informed each time the boy made a mistake and had to punish the child by giving him a blast of noise that he would hear over his earphones. However, the subject could select the intensity of the punishment she delivered on a 10-step scale ranging from quite weak to fairly intense. It is important to note that each woman had another job to perform as she "supervised" the boy so that she was somewhat distracted at the time and was not fully aware of what she was doing.

As can be seen in Table III, our findings generally supported our expectations. Combining all 10 of the opportunities in which the subjects had to punish the youngster, the women were significantly more punitive to the unattractive-looking than to the good-looking boy. The most intense punishment of all, as we had predicted, was administered to the child who was both "funny-looking" and who had the speech impediment. This unfortunate youngster was doubly stigmatized: in appearance and with his speech handicap. Being twice afflicted, he evoked the strongest attacks upon him.

TABLE III
INTENSITY OF PUNISHMENT GIVEN TO MALE CHILD

| | Physical appearance[a,b] | |
| --- | --- | --- |
| Child's speech | Attractive | Unattractive |
| Normal | 2.31 | 3.48 |
| Stutterer | 2.63 | 4.25 |

[a]The scores refer to the mean intensity of the noise blasts given to the boy over all 10 trials. The intensities were on a 10-step scale. One-third of a sample of judges regarded level 5 on this intensity of noise punishment scale as painful, whereas most of the others thought level 7 was painful.

[b]The planned comparison testing the prediction that the unattractive-stutterer group would be most punitive and the attractive-normal speech group would be least punitive was significant ($t = 2.47$, $p = .05$). Data from Berkowitz and Frodi (1979).

### 3.  To Hit or Hurt? The Goal of Aversively Stimulated Aggression

As we have seen, a number of investigations have now demonstrated that aversive events can evoke aggressive inclinations in humans, although it is also apparent that these dispositions are not necessarily revealed in open behavior. However, this research has not shown just what is the goal of the instigation to aggression.

For some writers (e.g., Zillmann, 1979) the aversive stimulation elicits defensive aggression. The pained animal or human supposedly mistakenly attributes the unpleasant event to the salient target in the situation and then attacks this target in order to lessen his discomfort. The goal of the aggressive action, then, presumably is the lessening or termination of the aversive occurrence. I dealt with this contention earlier in the section on animal studies, and argued there that the painful stimulation does more than create a desire to escape, avoid, or terminate the unpleasant event; it also seems to evoke appetitive aggression, an instigation to attack some target. It is difficult to see how the unpleasantly treated subjects in the human experiments summarized above could have thought the person they were evaluating or punishing (depending on the study) was the source of their discomfort or that their reactions to this individual would somehow lessen their discomfort. They were hostile to an innocent bystander. There was no reason for the participants to blame the target for their suffering.

But even assuming that the aversively stimulated persons were exhibiting appetitive aggression, were their attacks necessarily intended to injure that person? Some of the animal experiments I cited earlier (e.g., Azrin et al., 1965; Weiss et al., 1976) suggested that the pained organism can be reinforced simply by the opportunity to aggress. About a generation ago, Feshbach (1964) differentiated between the urge to hit and the urge to hurt. Employing this distinction, the animals in these investigations might have been instigated to "hit" a target, and similarly, the unpleasantly treated humans might also have been instigated to attack rather than to hurt the nearby stranger.

I have suggested, however, that the aversively stimulated individual does have the goal of inflicting injury. Whatever else he might want to do—lessen his discomfort, enhance his status, and so on—he presumably also seeks to hurt someone, especially, but not only, the source of his displeasure. The previously mentioned pain cues research is relevant here. In these investigations it will be recalled, provoked subjects apparently were reinforced by signs of their tormentor's suffering so that cues associated with this suffering tended to stimulate the previously angered people to attack their provocateur more strongly than they otherwise would have done. In sum, insulted persons clearly want to hurt the one who had provoked them. But this does not necessarily mean that those who are aversively stimulated in a nonhumiliating manner will also desire to inflict injury. The pain cues findings could conceivably have been due to the insulted men's lowered self-esteem; thinking the insult had wounded their image of themselves, they may have sought to injure their tormentor in order to restore a favorable conception of themselves (Felson, 1978). What we require is evidence that aversive stimulation alone produces a desire to hurt someone.

One way to provide this evidence is to give pained people an opportunity to inflict injury and then see how this affects their aggression. Being associated with their presumed aggressive goal (to harm someone), the information that they can do injury should spur them on to heightened goal-directed activity much as hungry persons are stimulated to increased food-getting behavior by news that they have a chance to obtain a meal. Berkowitz, Cochran, and Embree (1981) conducted two experiments based on this possibility.

As is now almost standard in the present research program, each undergraduate woman in these investigations was paired with another woman, the experimenter's accomplice, and was led to believe the study had to do with the effects of harsh environmental conditions on performance in a work setting. Supposedly to simulate such adverse conditions, the real subject was asked to play the part of a work supervisor and was required to keep one hand in a tank of water while evaluating her partner's performance on an assigned task. The partner's job was to develop solutions to various business problems that would be given to her and the "supervisor" had to judge each solution by delivering rewards or punishments to the "worker." For each solution she was to administer anything ranging from five rewards (each reward was a 5-cent coin) for a very good idea to five punishments (blasts of noise) for a very bad idea. In the first of our two experiments this was done in three phases: first, a 7-min period in which the subject had her hand in the water and listened to her partner call off 10 solutions to the two problems that had been given to her. Then, after a brief intermission in which the subject's hand was out of the water, she reimmersed her hand in the tank and heard her partner call off another 10 ideas for solving two new problems. This also lasted 7 min. Finally, there was a third phase in which the subject-as-supervisor was not required to keep her hand in the water while making her judgements. Thus, there were 10 opportunities to reward or punish the partner in each of the three phases.

There were two experimental variations in both studies. For half of the subjects, the water in the tank was quite cold (6°C), whereas it was much more comfortable for the others (18°C in study 1 and 23°C in study 2). Orthogonal to this variation, before the sessions started the subjects were also given information about the supposed effects of any punishment that they delivered. Half of them were told that, on the basis of earlier studies, their punishments were likely to help their partner's performance, whereas the others were informed that punishment would probably hurt the woman's work somewhat.

Questionnaire ratings made in the brief intervals between the phases indicated quite clearly in both experiments that the women exposed to the cold water found this treatment much more unpleasant than those exposed to the warmer water. The former regarded their experience as much more unpleasant, more painful, more stressful, more aversive, and less tolerable. When rating their moods, those in the cold water condition described themselves as feeling more tense, more hurt, more irritable, more annoyed, and less relaxed than the others. None of these ratings were affected by the other experimental manipulations. It is interesting, and I believe of some importance, to note that the cold subjects were aware that they felt somewhat "irritable" and "annoyed" even though they could not really blame their discomfort on their partner. In my view, this feeling was the product of the internal reactions created by the aversive treatment and was not due to any interpretations about someone's evil intentions.

The discipline the subjects administered to their partner was affected by the two experimental variations in both experiments, as can be seen in Tables IV and V. In particular, the water temperature interacted with punishment outcome to affect the number of rewards given the partner. Although many more rewards than punishments were given over all, the lowest number of rewards was given in the group exposed to the cold water and who were informed punishment would *hurt* their partner. These particular people apparently were most inclined not to reward the other woman, presumably because they wanted to hurt her. If we consider the total number of rewards as the obverse of punishment, so that a low frequency of rewards is somewhat punitive, the subjects' pain-induced punitiveness evidently was facilitated by the information that they had an opportunity to injure the other individual.

Interestingly enough, the experimental treatments did not produce any significant effects at all when the subjects did not have their hands in the water. It

TABLE IV
BEHAVIORAL REACTIONS TO WORKER—STUDY 1[a]

| Phase | Water temperature | | | |
|---|---|---|---|---|
| | Punish helps[b] | Punish hurts[b] | Punish helps[c] | Punish hurts[c] |
| One | | | | |
| Number of rewards[d] | $19.27_{ab}^{i}$ | $16.00_a$ | $17.36_{ab}$ | $21.46_b$ |
| Number of punishments[e] | 2.64 | 4.00 | 2.46 | 2.82 |
| Number of $R$ − number of $P$[f] | $16.63_{ab}$ | $12.00_a$ | $14.90_{ab}$ | $18.64_b$ |
| Two | | | | |
| Number of rewards[d] | 14.27 | 13.36 | 15.64 | 18.64 |
| Number of punishments[g] | $5.27_b$ | $4.91_b$ | $4.00_{ab}$ | $2.00_a$ |
| Number of $R$ − number of $P$[h] | $9.00_a$ | $8.45_a$ | $11.64_{ab}$ | $16.64_b$ |

[a]Data from Berkowitz et al. (1981).

[b]Water temperature, 6°C.

[c]Water temperature, 18°C.

[d]The analysis of variance of these scores revealed only a near-significant effect [$F(1,40) = 3.75, p < .10$] for the interaction.

[e]No significant effects were obtained in the preliminary anova.

[f]Only a significant interaction was obtained ($F = 4.31, p < .05$) in the analysis of variance of these scores.

[g]Only a significant main effect for water temperature was obtained in the analysis of variance ($F - 5.07, p < .05$).

[h]The analysis of variance of these scores yielded only a significant main effect for water temperature ($F = 5.98, p < .05$).

[i]Cells having different subscripts are significantly different at less than the .05 level of confidence by Duncan Multiple Range Test.

might be that people actually have to be undergoing a painful experience at the time if they are to be instigated to aggression.

## 4. Pain Cues as Elicitors of Aggression

Other research has also demonstrated that aversively treated people are inclined to hurt someone, especially the person responsible for their suffering. I shall briefly discuss some of these studies here in order to buttress the position I have been spelling out. Basically, these studies indicate that when strongly provoked, people learn that their provocateur's pain seems to function much like the bread crumbs given a hungry man; being closely associated with the desired goal (the infliction of injury or the attainment of food), the stimulus (pain cues or the bread crumbs) elicits stronger goal-directed activity.

Laboratory experiments have yielded supporting observations for the situation in which a person had been insulted by someone else. Rule and Nesdale

TABLE V
CONDITION MEANS ON THE REWARD AND PUNISHMENT MEASURES—STUDY 2[a]

| Phase | Water temperature | | | |
| --- | --- | --- | --- | --- |
| | Punish helps[b] | Punish hurts[b] | Punish helps[c] | Punish hurts[c] |
| One | | | | |
| Number of rewards[d] | 24.8 | 18.0 | 21.1 | 25.0 |
| Number of punishments[e] | 1.2 | 1.6 | 2.2 | 0.9 |
| Number of $R$ − number of $P$[f] | 23.6 | 16.4 | 18.9 | 24.1 |
| Two | | | | |
| Number of rewards[g] | 20.1 | 16.3 | 17.2 | 24.5 |
| Number of punishments[e] | 2.0 | 1.2 | 2.3 | 1.7 |
| Number of $R$ − number of $P$[e] | 18.1 | 15.1 | 14.9 | 22.8 |

[a]Data from Berkowitz et al. (1981).

[b]Water temperature, 6°C.

[c]Water temperature, 23°C.

[d]The only significant effect was for the interaction, $F(1,36) = 4.49, p < .05$. Planned comparison $t = 3.93, p < .005$.

[e]No significant effects.

[f]The interaction term yielded the only significant effect, $F(1,36) = 4.52, p < .05$. Planned comparison $t = 3.74, p < .005$.

[g]The interaction only approached the conventional .05 significance level, $F(1.36) = 3.97, p < .10$. Planned comparison $t = 4.25, p < .005$.

(1974) demonstrated that subjects were reluctant to punish a fellow student who had *not* provoked them earlier when they were informed the punishment would harm that person. They were much more inclined to administer the harmful punishment, however, if this target individual had previously been insulting. The angry people sought to hurt the one who had provoked them. Seeking this injury, moreover, they also could have been especially gratified by information about their tormentor's suffering. Under suitable conditions such pain cues can stimulate heightened aggression. Thus, according to Baron (1977), strongly angered subjects were more punitive than they otherwise would have been on learning that their tormentor was in pain. Since the suitable injury of the tormentor is the provoked person's goal, neutral stimuli previously associated with the provocateur's suffering can acquire the capacity to evoke impulsive aggressive reactions. In an experiment by Swart and Berkowitz (1976) angered subjects displayed the strongest impulsive aggression when they encountered stimuli that had earlier been paired with information about their tormentor's injury. Yet another study, by Sebastian (1978), also highlights the rewarding nature of the provocateur's pain. The angered men in this experiment were given fictitious information about the level of pain supposedly felt by the person who had insulted them as they punished him for making errors on a learning task. These provoked people reported greater enjoyment of the session the more their victim had suffered. But beside being gratifying, the pain feedback information apparently also strengthened their proclivity to aggression. The more the subjects said they had enjoyed punishing their tormentor, the more punitive they were to another, "innocent" individual the next day in a similar set of "learning" trials. Furthermore, findings published by Feshbach, Stiles, and Bitter (1967) indicate that this rewarding pain feedback information can also reinforce nonaggressive responses as well.

Taken together, these results show that angry aggressors are motivated to hurt the person who had offended them. Their attacks in response to the provocation are not only influence attempts, nor, for that matter, are they only efforts at restoring self-esteem. Whatever other outcome may also be pursued, these aggressive reactions are at least partly oriented toward the infliction of injury. From my perspective all of this evidence indicates that a broad range of aversive experiences produce an inclination to hurt someone. I showed earlier that people exposed to painfully cold water were oriented to harm rather than help another individual even when their victim was not responsible for their pain, and now we see that deliberately provoked persons are also desirous of hurting someone, in this case at least the one who had provoked them. Whatever else it is, the provocation is aversive and this gives rise to an instigation to inflict pain.

## 5. Thoughts of Punishment as a Facilitator of Pain-Induced Aggression

In the aforementioned studies the subjects' pain-induced inclination to aggression was most strongly translated into open punitiveness when they realized they could hurt someone. The opportunity to achieve their goal, the infliction of injury, had evidently spurred them to treat their partner relatively harshly. Other situational cues can also turn people's thoughts to the possibility of doing harm so that they exhibit a high level of punitiveness when exposed to aversive stimulation. Suppose, for example, that they had been asked to justify the use of punishment in enforcing discipline and had just finished arguing in favor of punishment before they were immersed in an unpleasant situation. Ideas of punishment could be highly salient to them at that time, and these ideas might then facilitate the subsequent pain-induced aggression.

I conducted an experiment along these very lines (unpublished). The subjects, this time undergraduate men, were first asked to keep one of their hands in a tank of water while they wrote a 5-min-long essay on an assigned topic. (The ostensible purpose was to investigate the effects of environmental stimulation on imagination.) Half of the men were instructed to argue in favor of punishment as a disciplinary technique, while the others were told to write about the advantages of life in the cold, northern states as against life in the "sunbelt." At the completion of this essay each participant was placed in our standard "supervisory'' role and was required to administer rewards and punishments to a fellow student as evaluations of that person's problem solutions. As usual, there were 10 opportunities to deliver these rewards and punishments during the 6-min session.

The essay task interacted significantly with the aversiveness of the water temperature to affect the severity of the subjects' treatment of their partner ($p < .01$). By and large, as can be seen in Table VI, the men required to think of punishment while their hand was in the painfully cold water administered the greatest number of punishments to the other person, reliably more than that given in either of the two warm water groups. Other findings we cannot go into here argue against a demand characteristics interpretation of these results and also tend to contradict the possibility that the punishment essay had merely lowered the subjects' restraints against being punitive. Instead, the data suggest that it was fairly easy for the people exposed to the 6°C water to write the essay on punishment, and that they may even have enjoyed this assignment to some extent. Thoughts of punishment evidently came readily to mind for them. These thoughts, and the semantically associated ideas about aggression, may then have facilitated the aggressive reactions elicited by the aversive stimulation.

These findings are easily explained by Leventhal's perceptual-motor theory of emotions (Leventhal, 1980) or Bower's (1981) network conception of the linkage between feelings and ideas. In general, both of these formulations posit associative bonds that connect feelings, ideas, and even expressive motor reactions. External stimuli that elicit any one of these reactions therefore also tend to activate the other components of the emotional nexus. Thus, the aversively cold water had presumably done more than produce physically painful sensations; it also evoked a variety of expressive-motor reactions and ideas, some of which were linked to aggressive behavior. If the participants had been thinking about

TABLE VI

TREATMENT OF PARTNER AS A FUNCTION OF TEMPERATURE AND PRIOR ESSAY WRITTEN

|  | 6°C Water | | 23°C Water | |
|---|---|---|---|---|
|  | Punish essay | Neutral essay | Punish essay | Neutral essay |
| Number of rewards[a] | 13.0$_a$ | 24.8$_b$ | 15.2$_a$ | 15.8$_a$ |
| Number of punishments[b] | 4.4$_b$ | 2.7$_{ab}$ | 2.2$_a$ | 1.2$_a$ |
| Number of $R$ − number of $P$[a] | 8.6$_a$ | 22.1$_b$ | 13.0$_a$ | 14.6$_{ab}$ |

[a]The analyses of variance yielded significant effects ($p < .05$) for essay topic and the interaction of essay topic with water temperature.

[b]All of the effects were significant in the analysis of variance. Cells not having a common subscript are significantly different at the .05 level by Duncan Multiple Range Test.

the benefits of punishment at the time, these thoughts could have strengthened their aversively stimulated ideas and even "feed back" to intensify their negative feelings. (The last line in Table VI, reporting the findings with an index based on the subjects' ratings of their anger, irritation and annoyance, points to just such an effect: The men in the 6°C water-punishment essay condition described themselves as being the most strongly annoyed.) Then, as a consequence, these intensified negative sensations, expressive-motor reactions and pro-aggression ideas were more facilitative of overt aggression so that the men in this condition displayed the least friendliness toward their victim (in their rewards and punishments of him).

## VI.  Conclusion

What does this all add up to? As is true for all research, the various studies I have discussed in this article are susceptible to alternative explanations. Some might claim that factor A can account for study 1, factor B can explain study 2, and so on. Yet such a list of alternative hypotheses is unparsimonious and unsatisfactory. We do not get very far by searching out all of these divergent possibilities. As scientists we must synthesize as well as analyze. We have to look for unifying principles, abstract propositions that tie a variety of phenomena together, and I believe we can find this kind of integrative idea in the notion I have repeated again and again throughout this article. Simply put, a very broad variety of aversive events gives rise to two instigations: one to escape from the unpleasant occurrence and the other to strike at a suitable target (preferably, but not only, the perceived source of the unpleasantness).

Some of the studies mentioned earlier, as well as a good many other observations that might also have been cited, demonstrate that these inclinations are not produced by the objective happenings but by the way they are understood; the event has to be interpreted as aversive. This interpretation then initiates the sequence of reactions that culminates in overt behavior—the flight or fight. In accord with Leventhal's (1980) theory of emotions, I suggest that the individual has a variety of expressive-motor reactions and ideas which give rise to the emotional experience. Depending upon the exact nature of these reactions and thoughts, the person might feel angry or afraid or perhaps have other emotions. These internal responses also produce the instigation to the overt action so that the emotional experience only parallels the inclination to behave in a particular manner and is not in itself the source of this impetus (Berkowitz, 1982).

Which action tendency is dominant and thus controls the overt behavior presumably depends on a host of factors in the immediate situation and the individual's prior learning history. Thus, quite obviously, a person might be more strongly inclined to escape from the aversive event than to attack someone if his escape reactions had been strongly reinforced in the past and/or he had often been punished for exhibiting aggression and/or he thinks he can do less damage to the aversive agent than that agent can do to him. But even when the individual prefers to flee rather than to fight, he might still react aggressively if escape is not possible. In sum, the aversive incident gives rise to both flight *and* fight tendencies, and not one *or* the other.

My hunch is that the aversively stimulated disposition to aggression is often relatively weak in adult members of our society, at least within the levels of aversive stimulation that are usually encountered in daily life, perhaps because of prior learning. Whatever the exact reason, this aggressive inclination is frequently not revealed openly in anything more than a general irritability. However, appropriate situational stimuli can strengthen the instigation to aggression enough so that an overt attack is made. The object that is available as the target for any aggression can provide such stimuli, and so, people who are associated with aversive events are especially likely to be victimized by those who are disposed to be aggressive. The victims' connection with pain and suffering or other unpleasant occurrences causes them to elicit the aggressive reactions the potential aggressors are inclined to exhibit.

Other situational influences can also increase the chances that persons exposed to an aversive experience will attack someone openly, by lowering their restraints against aggression and/or strengthening their aggression-facilitating expressive-motor reactions and thoughts. Interpretations of some unpleasant encounter can produce both effects; people who think they have been made to suffer unfairly or illegitimately may be less inclined to inhibit their aggressive tendencies and, furthermore, may also assign aversive stimulus properties to their tormentors so that these individuals become even more capable of evoking the aggression-facilitating reactions in them. Situationally induced thought processes can also intensify the aggressive expressive-motor reactions and ideas elicited by aversive occurrences. Thus, if the surrounding situation somehow leads us to think of aggression at the time we are suffering, these situationally induced thoughts can evoke other pro-aggression ideas and feelings from our schematic memories, thereby strengthening the aggression-facilitating responses stimulated by the present aversive event.

There is both bad and good news in all of this. It is impossible to be completely shielded from aversive occurrences; we will inevitably feel some pain, meet with some frustration, and have some unpleasant experiences. And as a consequence, many of us will be inclined to be aggressive at that time. It is impossible to eliminate all aversively stimulated aggression. But this aggressive disposition need not be translated into open violence. We can learn to restrain our aggressive inclinations, be led not to think of others as sources of displeasure, and turn our thoughts away from aggression-promoting ideas.

## REFERENCES

Ader, R. Competitive and noncompetitive rearing and shock-elicited aggression in the rat. *Animal Learning and Behavior*, 1975, **3**, 337–339.

Amsel, A. Frustrative nonreward in partial reinforcement and discrimination learning: Some recent history and a theoretical extension. *Psychological Review*, 1962, **69**, 306–328.

Ax, A. The physiological differentiation between fear and anger in humans. *Psychosomatic Medicine*, 1953, **15**, 433–442.

Azrin, N. H., Hutchinson, R. R., & Hake, D. F. Extinction-induced aggression. *Journal of the Experimental Analysis of Behavior*, 1966, **9**, 191–204.

Azrin, N. H., Hutchinson, R. R., & McLaughlin, R. The opportunity for aggression as an operant reinforcer during aversive stimulation. *Journal of the Experimental Analysis of Behavior*, 1965, **8**, 171–180.

Baenninger, R., & Ulm, R. R. Overcoming the effects of prior punishment on interspecies aggression in the rat. *Journal of Comparative and Physiological Psychology*, 1969, **69**, 628–635.

Bandura, A. *Aggression: A social learning analysis*. New York: Prentice-Hall, 1973.

Baron, R. A. Aggression as a function of ambient temperature and prior anger arousal. *Journal of Personality and Social Psychology*, 1972, **21**, 183–189.

Baron, R. A. *Human aggression*. New York: Plenum, 1977.

Baron, R. A., & Bell, P. A. Aggression and heat: Mediating effects of prior provocation and exposure to an aggressive model. *Journal of Personality and Social Psychology*, 1975, **31**, 825–832.

Baron, R. A., & Bell, P. A. Aggression and heat: The influence of ambient temperature, negative affect, and a cooling drink on physical aggression. *Journal of Personality and Social Psychology*, 1976, **33**, 245–255.

Baron, R. A., & Ransberger, V. M. Ambient temperature and the occurrence of collective violence: The "long, hot summer" revisited. *Journal of Personality and Social Psychology*, 1978, **36**, 361–360.

Bell, P. A. & Baron, R. A. Aggression and heat: The mediating role of negative affect. *Journal of Applied Social Psychology*, 1976, **6**, 18–30.

Berkowitz, L. Aggressive cues in aggressive behavior and hostility catharsis. *Psychological Review*, 1964, **71**, 104–122.

Berkowitz, L. The concept of aggressive drive: Some additional considerations. In L. Berkowitz (Ed.), *Advances in experimental social psychology* (Vol. 2). New York: Academic Press, 1965.

Berkowitz, L. The frustration-aggression hypothesis revisited. In L. Berkowitz (Ed.), *Roots of aggression*. New York: Atherton, 1969.

Berkowitz, L. The contagion of violence: An S-R mediational analysis of some effects of observed aggression. In W. Arnold & M. Page (Eds.), *Nebraska Symposium on Motivation, 1970*. Lincoln, Nebraska: University of Nebraska Press, 1971. Pp. 95–135.

Berkowitz, L. Words and symbols as stimuli to aggressive responses. In J. F. Knutson (Ed.), *Control of aggression: Implications from basic research*. Chicago, Illinois: Aldine-Atherton, 1973.

Berkowitz, L. Whatever happened to the frustration-aggression hypothesis? *American Behavioral Scientist*, 1978, **21**, 691–708.

Berkowitz, L. *A survey of social psychology* (2nd ed.). New York: Holt, 1980.

Berkowitz, L. On the difference between internal and external reactions to legitimate and illegitimate frustrations: A demonstration. *Aggressive Behavior*, 1981, **7**, 83–96.

Berkowitz, L. The experience of anger as a parallel process in the display of impulsive, "angry" aggression. In R. G. Green & E. Donnerstein (Eds.), *Aggression: Theoretical and empirical reviews*. New York: Academic Press, 1982.

Berkowitz, L., Cochran, S., & Embree, M. Physical pain and the goal of aversively stimulated aggression. *Journal of Personality and Social Psychology*, 1981, **40**, 687–700.

Berkowitz, L., & Frodi, A. Reactions to a child's mistakes as affected by her/his looks and speech. *Social Psychology Quarterly*, 1979, **42**, 420–425.

Blanchard, R. J., Blanchard, D. C., & Takahashi, L. K. Pain and aggression in the rat. *Behavioral Biology*, 1978, **23**, 291–305.

Bower, G. H. Mood and memory. *American Psychologist*, 1981, **36**, 129–148.

Burnstein, E., & Worchel, P. Arbitrariness of frustration and its consequences for aggression in a social situation. *Journal of Personality*, 1962, **30**, 528–541.

Ciarkowska, W. Emotional meaning of stimulus and intensity of aggressive acts. In A. Fraczek (Ed.), *Studies of psychological mechanisms in aggression. Polish Academy of Sciences, Psychological Monographs*, 1979, **27**, 33–64.

Comer, R. J., & Piliavin, J. A. The effects of physical deviance upon face-to-face interaction. *Journal of Personality and Social Psychology*, 1972, **23**, 33–39.

Dollard, J., Doob, L., Miller, N., Mowrer, O., & Sears, R. *Frustration and aggression.* New Haven, Connecticut: Yale University Press, 1939.

Donnerstein, E., Donnerstein, M., & Evans, R. Erotic stimuli and aggression: Facilitation or inhibition? *Journal of Personality and Social Psychology*. 1975, **32**, 237–244.

Donnerstein, E., & Wilson, D. W. Effects of noise and perceived control on ongoing and subsequent aggressive behavior. *Journal of Personality and Social Psychology*, 1976, **34**, 774–781.

Dovidio, J. F., & Morris, W. N. Effects of stress and commonality of fate on helping behavior. *Journal of Personality and Social Psychology*, 1975, **31**, 145–149.

Dyck, R. J., & Rule, B. G. Effect on retaliation of causal attributions concerning attack. *Journal of Personality and Social Psychology*, 1978, **36**, 521–529.

Felson, R. B. Aggression as impression management. *Social Psychology*, 1978, **41**, 205–213.

Ferster, C. B. Withdrawal of positive reinforcement as punishment. *Science*, 1957, **126**, 509.

Feshbach, S. The function of aggression and the regulation of aggressive drive. *Psychological Review*, 1964, **71**, 257–272.

Feshbach, S., Stiles, W. B., & Bitter, E. The reinforcing effect of witnessing aggression. *Journal of Experimental Research in Personality*, 1967, **2**, 133–139.

Follick, M. J., & Knutson, J. F. Punishment of irritable aggression. *Aggressive Behavior*, 1978, **4**, 1–17.

Fraczek, A. Informational role of situation as a determinant of aggressive behavior. In J. de Wit & W. W. Hartup (Eds.), *Determinants and origins of aggressive behavior.* The Hague: Mouton, 1974.

Geen, R. G., & O'Neal, E. C. Activation of cue-elicited aggression by general arousal. *Journal of Personality and Social Psychology*, 1969, **11**, 289–292.

Goffman, E. *Stigma: Notes on the management of spoiled identity.* New York: Prentice-Hall, 1963.

Griffitt, W. Environmental effects on interpersonal affective behavior: Ambient effective temperature and attraction. *Journal of Personality and Social Psychology*, 1970, **15**, 240–244.

Griffitt, W., & Veitch, R. Hot and crowded: Influence of population density and temperature on interpersonal affective behavior: Ambient effective temperature and attraction. *Journal of Personality and Social Psychology*, 1971, **17**, 92–98.

Hutchinson, R. R. The environmental causes of aggression. In J. K. Cole & D. D. Jensen (Eds.), *Nebraska Symposium on Motivation*, 1972, Lincoln, Nebraska: University of Nebraska Press, 1973.

Hutchinson, R. R., Renfrew, J. W., & Young, G. A. Effects of long-term shock and associated stimuli on aggressive and manual responses. *Journal of the Experimental Analysis of Behavior*, 1971, **15**, 141–166.

Hutchinson, R. R., Ulrich, R. E., & Azrin, N. H. Effects of age and related factors on the pain-aggression reaction. *Journal of Comparative and Physiological Psychology*, 1965, **59**, 365–369.

Izard, C. E. *Human emotions*. New York: Plenum, 1977.

Johnson, R. N. *Aggression in man and animals*. Philadelphia, Pennsylvania: Saunders, 1972.

Jones, J. W., & Bogat, G. A. Air pollution and human aggression. *Psychological Reports*, 1978, **43**, 721–722.

Katz, I., Glass, D. C., Lucido, D. J., & Farber, J. Ambivalence, Guilt, and the denigration of a physically handicapped victim. *Journal of Personality*, 1977, **45**, 419–429.

Kenrick, D. T., & Johnson, G. A. Interpersonal attraction in aversive environments: A problem for the classical conditioning paradigm? *Journal of Personality and Social Psychology*, 1979, **37**, 572–579.

Kleck, R., Ono, H., & Hastorf, A. The effects of physical deviance upon face-to-face interaction. *Human Relations*, 1966, **19**, 425–436.

Knutson, J. F., Fordyce, D. J., & Anderson, D. J. Escalation of irritable aggression: Control by consequences and antecedents. *Aggressive Behavior*, 1980, **6**, 347–359.

Konecni, V. J. The mediation of aggressive behavior: Arousal level versus anger and cognitive labeling. *Journal of Personality and Social Psychology*, 1975, **32**, 706–712.

Laird, J. D. Self-attribution of emotion: The effects of expressive behavior on the quality of emotional experience. *Journal of Personality* and Social Psychology, 1974, **29**, 475–486.

Leshner, A. I., & Nock, B. L. The effects of experience on agnostic responding: An expectancy theory interpretation. *Behavioral Biology*, 1976, **17**, 561–566.

Leventhal, H. Emotions: A basic problem for social psychology. In C. Nemeth (Ed.), *Social psychology*. Chicago, Illinois: Rand McNally, 1974.

Leventhal, H. Toward a comprehensive theory of emotion. In L. Berkowitz (Ed.), *Advances in experimental social psychology* (Vol. 13). New York: Academic Press, 1980.

Leventhal, H., Brown, D., Shacham, S., & Engquist, S. The effects of preparatory information about sensations, threat of pain, and attention on cold pressor distress. *Journal of Personality and Social Psychology*, 1979, **37**, 688–714.

Marshall, G. D., & Zimbardo, P. G. Affective consequences of inadequately explained physiological arousal. *Journal of Personality and Social Psychology*, 1979, **37**, 970–985.

Maslach, C. Negative emotional biasing of unexplained arousal. *Journal of Personality and Social Psychology*, 1979, **37**, 953–969.

Melzack, R. *The puzzle of pain*. New York: Basic Books, 1973.

Miller, N., & Zimbardo, P. Motives for fear induced affiliation: Emotional comparison or interpersonal similarity? *Journal of Personality*, 1966, **34**, 481–503.

Moyer, K. E. *The psychobiology of aggression*. New York: Harper, 1976.

Piliavin, I. M., Piliavin, J. A., & Rodin, J. Costs, diffusion and the stigmatized victim. *Journal of Personality and Social Psychology*, 1975, **32**, 429–438.

Potegal, M. The reinforcing value of several types of aggressive behavior: A review. *Aggressive Behavior*, 1979, **5**, 353–373.

Roberts, W. W., & Kiess, H. O. Motivational properties of hypothalamic aggression in cats. *Journal of Comparative and Physiological Psychology*, 1964, **58**, 187–193.

Rotton, J., Barry, T., Frey, J., & Soler, E. Air pollution and interpersonal attraction. *Journal of Applied Social Psychology*, 1978, **8**, 57–71.

Rotton, J., Frey, J., Barry, T., Milligan, M., & Fitzpatrick, M. The air pollution experience and physical aggression. *Journal of Applied Social Psychology*, 1979, **9**, 397–412.

Rule, B. G., Ferguson, T. J., & Nesdale, A. R. Emotional arousal, anger, and aggression: The misattribution issue. In P. Pliner, K. R. Blankenstein, & I. M. Spigel (Eds.), *Perception of emotion in self and others*. New York: Plenum, 1979.

Rule, B. G., & Nesdale, A. Differing functions of aggression. *Journal of Personality*, 1974, **42**, 467–481.

Rule, B. G., & Nesdale, A. Emotional arousal and aggressive behavior. *Psychological Bulletin*, 1976, **83**, 851–863.

Schachter, S. *The psychology of affiliation*. Stanford, California: Stanford University Press, 1959.

Schachter, S. The interaction of cognitive and physiological determinants of emotional state. In L. Berkowitz (Ed.), *Advances in experimental social psychology* (Vol. 1). New York: Academic Press, 1964. Pp. 49–80.

Scott, J. P. Theoretical issues concerning the origin and causes of fighting. In B. E. Eleftheriou & J. P. Scott (Eds.), *The physiology of aggression and defeat*. New York: Plenum, 1971.

Sebastian, R. J. Immediate and delayed effects of victim suffering on the attacker's aggression. *Journal of Research in Personality*, 1978, **12**, 312–328.

Swart, C., & Berkowitz, L. The effects of a stimulus associated with a victim's pain on later aggression. *Journal of Personality and Social Psychology*, 1976, **33**, 623–631.

Tomkins, S. S. *Affect, imagery, consciousness, Vol. 1, The positive affects*. New York: Springer, 1962.

Tomkins, S. S. *Affect, imagery, consciousness, Vol. 2, The negative affects*. New York: Springer, 1963.

Ulrich, R. E. Pain as a cause of aggression. *American Zoologist*, 1966, **6**, 643–662.

Ulrich, R. E., & Azrin, N. H. Reflexive fighting in response to aversive stimulation. *Journal of the Experimental Analysis of Behavior*, 1962, **5**, 511–520.

Ulrich, R. E., & Craine, W. H. Persistence of shock-induced aggression. *Science*, 1964, **143**, 971–973.

Velten, E. C. A laboratory task for the induction of mood states. *Behaviour Research and Therapy*, 1968, **6**, 473–482.

Vernon, W., & Ulrich, R. E. Classical conditioning of pain-elicited aggression. *Science*, 1966, **152**, 668–669.

Weiss, J. M., Pohorecky, L. A., Salman, S., & Gruenthal, M. Attenuation of gastric lesions by psychological aspects of aggression in rats. *Journal of Comparative and Physiological Psychology*, 1976, **90**, 252–259.

White, L. A. Erotica and aggression: The influence of sexual arousal, positive affect, and negative affect on aggressive behavior. *Journal of Personality and Social Psychology*, 1979, **37**, 591–601.

Wilson, W. P., Blazer, D. G., & Nashold, B. S. Observations on pain and suffering. *Psychosomatics*, 1976, **17**, 73–76.

Wright, B. *Physical disability: A psychological approach*. New York: Harper, 1960.

Zillmann, D. *Hostility and aggression*. Hillsdale, New Jersey: Erlbaum, 1979.

Zillmann, D., Bryant, J., Comisky, P. W., & Medoff, N. J. Excitation and hedonic valence in the effect of erotica on motivated intermale aggression. *European Journal of Social Psychology*, 1981, **11**, 233–252.

Zillmann, D., Hoyt, J. L., & Day, K. D. Strength and duration of the effect of aggressive, violent and erotic communications on subsequent aggressive behavior. Communication Research, 1974, 1, 286-306.

Zillmann, D., Katcher, A.H., Milavsky, B. Excitation transfer from physical excersise to subsequent aggressive behavior. Journal of Experimental Social Psychology, 1972, 8, 247-259.

# INDEX

# CONTENTS OF OTHER VOLUMES